# MYTHS OF THE UNDERWORLD JOURNEY

Plato, Aristophanes, and the creators of the 'Orphic' gold tablets employ the traditional tale of a journey to the realm of the dead to redefine, within the mythic narrative, the boundaries of their societies. Rather than being the relics of a faded ritual tradition or the products of Orphic influence, these myths can only reveal their meanings through a close analysis of the specific ways

myth

liter

The

neith

a ref

Rado

Stud

*Maw*

*Anci*

# Myths of the Underworld Journey

## Plato, Aristophanes, and the 'Orphic' Gold Tablets

RADCLIFFE G. EDMONDS III

Bryn Mawr College

CAMBRIDGE
UNIVERSITY PRESS

iii

CAMBRIDGE UNIVERSITY PRESS
Cambridge, New York, Melbourne, Madrid, Cape Town,
Singapore, São Paulo, Delhi, Mexico City

Cambridge University Press
The Edinburgh Building, Cambridge CB2 8RU, UK

Published in the United States of America by
Cambridge University Press, New York

www.cambridge.org
Information on this title: www.cambridge.org/9781107407305

First published 2004
First paperback edition 2012

*A catalogue record for this publication is available from the British Library*

*Library of Congress Cataloguing in Publication data*
Edmonds, Radcliffe G. (Radcliffe Guest), 1970–
   Myths of the underworld journey in Plato, Aristophanes, and the 'Orphic'
gold tablets / Radcliffe G. Edmonds III.
      p. cm.
   Includes bibliographical references and index.
   ISBN 0-521-83434-1
   1. Mythology, Greek. 2. Voyages to the otherworld. 3. Dionysia.
   4. Plato. Phaedo. 5. Aristophanes. Frogs. 6. Mythology, Greek, in literature.
   7. Voyages to the otherworld in literature. I. Title.
   BL735.E36 2004
   292.1′3 – dc22                                    2003065204

ISBN 978-0-521-83434-6 Hardback
ISBN 978-1-107-40730-5 Paperback

ἔστι δὲ ἄρα ἡ πορεία οὐχ ὡς ὁ Αἰσχύλου Τήλεφος λέγει·
ἐκεῖνος μὲν γὰρ ἁπλῆν οἶμόν φησιν εἰς Ἅιδου φέρειν,
ἡ δ᾽ οὔτε ἁπλῆ οὔτε μία φαίνεταί μοι εἶναι.

So the journey is not as Aeschylus' Telephus describes it:
he says it is a simple path that leads to Hades,
but to me it seems to be neither simple nor single.

(Plato *Phaedo* 107e4–108a2)

# Contents

# Preface

Like the road to the underworld, the path of a book to publication is neither simple nor single, and I cannot begin to thank all those who have helped on the journey. This project, which grew out of my doctoral dissertation from the University of Chicago, first took shape in a reading class with Arthur Adkins on the myths of Plato, and its path was further defined in the 1997 Brauer Seminar on Myth led by Bruce Lincoln and Wendy Doniger. Along the way, many people provided invaluable help, inspiration, and insight, most notably the chair of my committee, Chris Faraone, without whose guidance I might still be writing. Special thanks must also go to my other readers, Bruce Lincoln and Martha Nussbaum, who provided sharp and insightful critiques of every stage of the dissertation and helped me to shape the overall thesis as well as the individual parts. From the beginning, James Redfield has inspired my approach to these materials and shown me ways of looking at the texts and their contexts that opened them up to my understanding. As I worked to transform the dissertation into a more coherent book, I have benefited from the advice and critiques of many people, especially Fritz Graf and Claude Calame, who gave me important suggestions on the manuscript both as a whole and in its parts. At Cambridge University Press, Beatrice Rehl has sped the project along its path with superb diligence and care.

Finally, this journey could never have been completed without the assistance of my friends and family. My parents have shared with me their love both of story-telling and of research and have encouraged me throughout this whole process. My friends and colleagues at the University of Chicago, at Creighton University, and at Bryn Mawr College have helped me work through various problems and ideas, arguing with me and correcting me, stimulating me to new thoughts and projects. Special thanks must go to Sheila Kurian and Kathryn Haines for all their efforts and assistance with everything from ideas and arguments to syntax and punctuation. Above all, my wife Susannah has helped and supported me throughout this process. Not only has she been my best friend and the first (if not the severest) critic of all my writings, but her constant love and support have made this long and difficult journey of writing a pleasurable excursion; she fills my life with light and joy.

# 1 | Introduction

## THE START OF THE JOURNEY

So the journey is not as Aeschylus' Telephus describes it: he says it is a simple path that leads to Hades, but to me it seems to be neither simple nor single. For then there would be no need of guides; since no one, surely, could lose the way anywhere, if there were only a single road. But in fact it probably has many forkings and branchings; I speak from the evidence of the rites and observances followed here. [1]

In this passage from Plato's *Phaedo*, Socrates is making a mythological and philosophical argument, arguing for the immortality of the soul by referring to traditional myths well known to his interlocutors as he prepares to tell his own myth of life after death, the *Phaedo's* fantastic vision of the many levels of the earth. But Socrates is not merely mentioning a myth well known to his audience; he is contesting it. In place of Aeschylus' myth of a journey to the underworld, Socrates proposes his own different version of the tale and unfolds the details to his interlocutors. Socrates, moreover, with the self-conscious precision characteristic of a Platonic persona, even explains his reasons for contradicting the famous Aeschylus, countering the authority of the great tragedian with his references to the evidence of the rites. I find this passage fascinating because of what it reveals about the way the Greeks handled myth – not as canonical formulations of religious dogma but as a contest of competing authorities vying to provide an explanation.

---

[1] ἔστι δὲ ἄρα ἡ πορεία οὐχ ὡς ὁ Αἰσχύλου Τήλεφος λέγει· ἐκεῖνος μὲν γὰρ ἁπλῆν οἶμόν φησιν εἰς Ἅιδου φέρειν. ἡ δ' οὔτε ἁπλῆ οὔτε μία φαίνεταί μοι εἶναι. οὐδὲ γὰρ ἂν ἡγεμόνων ἔδει· οὐ γάρ πού τις ἂν διαμάρτοι οὐδαμόσε μιᾶς ὁδοῦ οὔσης. νῦν δὲ ἔοικε σχίσεις τε καὶ τριόδους πολλὰς ἔχειν· ἀπὸ τῶν θυσιῶν τε καὶ νομίμων τῶν ἐνθάδε τεκμαιρόμενος λέγω. (*Phaedo*, 107e4–108a6; translation from Gallop 1975.)

1

This passage also reveals the enormous gaps that modern scholars face as we try to understand the Greeks and their mythic tradition. The *Telephus* to which Socrates refers without even bothering to quote is completely lost, as are the versions of the other major tragedians, and none of the evidence that survives about the story of Telephus provides any clues as to the context of the reference. Not only do modern readers lack the myth Socrates is arguing against, they do not know to what rites and customs he is referring as evidence for his own position. His reference to the guides, blithely accepted by his interlocutors, leaves us puzzled. What sort of background lies behind this mythic argument?

The questions that this passage raises are not only methodological – how are myths used? – but also historical – what kinds of stories *did* the Greeks tell about life after death? And why did these people tell these particular stories? Every human culture has stories about death and what happens after it; the experience of death intrudes into every human life, demanding explanation. The question of what happens after the moment of death fascinates humanity: at one moment there is a person, the next only a thing; where did the person go?[2] The answers to these questions are as varied as the people who ask them, but that other world where the dead are, "that undiscovered country from whose bourne no traveler returns," always presents a contrast to the here and now, the everyday world of the living. It "puzzles the will," as Hamlet says, prompting speculation and imagination about the difference between life and death. The contrast may be slight or enormous; the other world may be better or worse than the present one, but it is always different.

In any description of the other world, therefore, lurks an implicit contrast with this world; for the strange, the unfamiliar, the other can only be explained in terms that are familiar, even if only by a negation of those terms – not to be grasped by the senses but invisible, not present but far away, not now but hereafter.[3] The idea of a journey to the realm of the dead

---

[2] As Redfield notes, "The survival of the dead is in some sense a culture universal, since it is undeniable; they survive in our memories of them, in the consequences of their acts, in their judgement of us which we carry with us internalized as an ethical standard." (Redfield 1991, p. 105.)

[3] Lincoln comments on the prevalence of descriptions of paradise in terms of a negative of familiar worldly woes. "The intent of this negative definition is to emphasize the radical otherness of the Otherworld. In truth, nothing positive is said of paradise for the reason that it is so totally unlike our own mortal sphere that our very language and normal set of images are thoroughly inadequate for the task of describing it. Of the other world, all that can be said is that things there are totally *other*, completely opposed to all of this earth. The logic which supports the negative definition is thus much like that which undergirds

brings out this contrast between the worlds as the traveler moves from one realm to the other. The stories people tell about the journey to the other world, the realm of the dead, thus reveal their implicit assumptions about the world in which they, as the living, dwell. These stories act as a kind of mirror that reflects the picture of their world. This vision "through a glass darkly" comes at times through a comically distorted mirror that reflects a carnival image of the quotidian world; at other times it comes through a magic mirror in which all the evils and uglinesses of life are removed, leaving a fresh and beautiful idealized reflection. Whether a projection of desires unrealized in this world or a nightmare image of one's worst fears, the description of the realm of the dead reflects a conception of the realm of the living, locating the narrator within this world as he or she sees it.

This kind of self-definition – locating oneself and one's society in relation to the rest of the world, both natural and supernatural – not only occurs in eschatological stories of the life after death but also forms an important part of the religion of any culture. Scholars of religion in the modern era, however, operating with Christian paradigms of religion that centrally involve faith and salvation, have perhaps unduly privileged eschatology as one of the primary concerns that distinguishes a 'real' religion from the so-called 'primitive' religions that define identity in relation to the cosmos in other ways.[4] The Greek eschatological myths provide a particularly interesting object of study in this regard, of course, because they set the terms for so much of the later discourse about the afterlife in Western civilization. Not only Hellenistic and Roman societies but also later Christian empires debated the immortality of the soul and its fate after death largely in terms of images and names borrowed from Greek mythology. Scholars have been very concerned to discover the impact of these ideas on later religious concepts, but often the interest in the later ideas overshadows the reading of the Greek myths themselves. This focus on the chain of influences neglects the contexts that shaped these myths and creates distortions in the understanding of the texts themselves as well as of the way the Greeks used their myths. Read carefully in their own contexts, however, the tales of the journey to the land of the dead

---

the view of the next world as a topsy-turvy kingdom, where people walk on their hands, trees chop down woodsmen, and the like." (Lincoln 1991, p. 28.)

[4] As Smith notes, "In the hands of many scholars, both past and present, it is primarily soteriological notions which supply an evolutionary scale that ranks religions, with Protestant Christianity often serving as the implicit or explicit norm or the culmination of the exercise." (Smith 1990, p. 119.)

can not only reveal much about those who produced these myths but also bring a better understanding of their impact on the later recipients of the tradition.

The questions raised by the above passage from the *Phaedo* – what sort of stories did the Greeks tell and why did they tell these particular stories – thus provide the starting point for my research, from both the methodological and the religious historical standpoints. In this study, I explore the ways in which different authors make use of myth, the way they manipulate a common set of traditional elements in various ways to achieve different ends. To this end, I examine a set of Classical Greek texts, all of which concern a journey from the land of the living to the realm of the dead: the so-called Orphic gold tablets, Aristophanes' *Frogs*, and the eschatological myth in Plato's *Phaedo*. None of these texts is telling exactly the same story, but they all narrate some sort of journey to the other world, the realm of the dead. In Levi-Strauss's metaphor,[5] the authors of these texts are all doing *bricolage* with the same pieces of tradition, but the pieces they use and the narratives they come up with are different. Each of these texts employs elements from a pool of traditional motifs, the limited ragbag of the *bricoleur*, in a narrative of the journey to the realm of the dead; and the tale that each author produces reflects, through its image of the other world, the author's perspective on the world in which he or she is living. Not only can an exploration of the various ways in which authors use a common set of elements uncover the different agendas of these authors and provide a deeper understanding of the individual texts, but it can also shed light on the ways in which myth was used by the Greeks in the late fifth and fourth centuries BCE – not as sacred scripture, not purely as entertainment, but as a device for communication, a mode of speaking in which they could convey meaning densely through the manipulation of mythic motifs and patterns that each had its own resonance for the audience.

## DEFINITION OF MYTH

One of the first projects of any scholar discussing myth should be to provide a working definition of the term. I propose, therefore, to use my analysis of the specific authors' manipulations of myth to provide a

---

[5] cp. Levi-Strauss 1966, pp. 16–36.

model of myth as an agonistic form of cultural discourse, a traditional language for the communication of ideas from the author to his audience, in which the competing versions vie for authority.[6] To a certain extent, as Detienne has pointed out in his *Creation of Mythology*, myth is a modern construct.[7] Moreover, the category of myth is often constructed in opposition to another modern category, such as religion, history, or science, creating distinctions alien to the ancient Greeks.[8] In order to understand the ways in which the Greeks handled their myths, it is necessary to employ a definition of myth that is consonant with, rather than contradictory to, their usage. As Fritz Graf puts it, "It is still difficult to define myth satisfactorily, for all the intense scholarly attention that the problem of definition has received in the course of two and a half centuries. Many solutions have been proposed, only to be rejected. The most banal and least controversial of these may serve as a starting point: myths are traditional tales."[9] Yet even this definition contains the seeds of a number of problems. What is the tradition and what is the relation of each individual telling to the tradition? Some use the term 'myth' to refer to the tradition behind any given telling; others use it to refer to a specific telling of the tale. Many, unfortunately, use the term indiscriminately to mean both. The Greeks themselves had no term to designate all of the things that modern scholars group under the heading of myth, but they used a variety of terms to refer to their traditional tales. I use the term 'myth' to refer to a specific telling, in an attempt to remain close to its etymological sense from the Greek word, μῦθος, meaning something told. To designate the story, variously told and retold in the tradition throughout the ages, of which any given myth is a specific version, I use the term 'traditional tale'.

A traditional tale obviously requires a tradition; it is the product of a specific culture. A traditional tale derives its meaning and authority from its relation to the ideas of the culture as they are handed down from

---

[6] cp. Barthes' description of myth as a form of second-order language (Barthes 1972, pp. 109–159). See also Calame 1990, p. 48, and Calame 2000, pp. 47–50. For the competition to provide what Calame terms 'vraisemblance', cp. Calame 1996, p. 6.

[7] Detienne 1986.

[8] The ancient Greeks had their own set of categories and oppositions, but these do not coincide precisely with the modern categories. For discussion of the indigenous categories, see Calame 1996, pp. 25–44; cp. the histories of the modern constructions with regard to myth in Most 1999 and Lincoln 1999.

[9] Graf 1993b, p. 1.

generation to generation.[10] The traditional element of a myth is essential in distinguishing myth from what might be termed 'fiction', a tale invented by the teller without necessarily incorporating elements that have been passed down in the tradition. As Sourvinou-Inwood notes, myths are "not wholly 'individual' constructs independent of cultural constraints; they are shaped by the parameters created by the social realities, collective representations, and beliefs of the society that generated them. They are articulated by, and thus express, those realities and idealities."[11] In the terminology of Geertz, the Greek poetic and mythic tradition provides the *models of* and *models for* the society, models which are given authoritative status as a description of the way the cosmos is constituted and of the proper modes of behavior within it.[12] Thus, these constructs, the traditional tales, have a paradigmatic function; their elements are symbols that enunciate a model with a general application.

However, each myth, each telling of a traditional tale, presents a different variation of the model, as the teller shapes the narrative according to his perceptions of the cultural models. As Segal argues, the symbolic elements within the tradition are manipulated by the teller. "Myth comprises a system of symbols, verbal, visual, and religious. Each myth is built up of already existing symbols and forms and, like all narrative, reforms and reorganizes those symbols in its own structures."[13] This symbolic system provides a language by which the myth-teller may communicate with his audience. As a result, every myth is shaped by its context and the motivations of its narrator. As J. Z. Smith cautions, myths

---

[10] Brisson defines it as follows: "Le mythe apparaît alors comme ce discours par lequel est communiqué tout ce qu'une collectivité donneé conserve en mémoire de son passé et transmet oralement d'une génération à l'autre, que ce discours ait été élaboré par un technicien de la communication comme le poète, ou non." (Brisson 1982, p. 12.) Some connection to a tradition is part of other definitions of myth proposed, e.g., by Burkert, Edmunds, and Graf, all of which mention the importance of tradition, but do not sufficiently develop the ramifications. (Burkert 1979, pp. 1–2; Edmunds 1990, p. 15; Graf 1993b, pp. 1–9.)

[11] Sourvinou-Inwood 1991, p. 20.

[12] "Culture patterns have an intrinsic double aspect: they give meaning, that is, objective conceptual form, to social and psychological reality both by shaping themselves to it and by shaping it to themselves." (Geertz 1973, p. 93.) cp. Lincoln 1999, p. 17, "*Mythos* is an assertive discourse of power and authority that represents itself as something to be believed and obeyed." Lincoln here applies the arguments of Martin 1989.

[13] Segal 1986, p. 49.

must be understood primarily as texts in context, specific acts of communication between specified individuals, at specific points in time and space, about specifiable subjects. Kenneth Burke's definition of a proverb as a "strategy for dealing with a situation" provides an important insight when extended to these materials.[14]

The significant variations among myths arise from the intent of the teller with regard to his audience. A myth expresses the teller's perspective on the 'realities and idealities' of the world, or rather on those 'realities and idealities' that are pertinent to the specific issue around which that myth is centered. Different tellings present conflicting perspectives and messages, and these tellings compete for acceptance as authoritative by their audiences.[15] The tellings that are accepted as authoritative reshape the tradition from which later myth-tellers draw traditional elements to create their own new models.

A myth, then, is a telling of a traditional tale, in which the teller shapes the traditional material in response to his context and audience, and in which aspects of the culture's models of the world are selected or rejected by the teller in his crafting of the story according to his view of the significant tensions and issues involved with the narrative. A myth is the specific example of the general form of discourse that is often termed 'myth' (without an article), but which, to avoid undue confusion, I shall refer to by the somewhat cumbrous 'mythic discourse'. Mythic discourse is thus the mode of communication that involves the telling of particular myths. Mythic discourse, as such, is distinct from any genre - epic, tragedy, comedy, philosophical dialogue, etc. Different tellers made use of mythic discourse to relate the traditional tale of Oedipus and his family relations in myths that took the form of epic, choral lyric poetry, and tragedy. To be sure, the genre exerts certain constraints on the telling of any myth, and, in this way, the choice of genre is one of the means by which the teller shapes the traditional elements in a myth.

These traditional elements are the features of the narrative that are familiar to the audience for whom that myth is composed. Two types of elements may be distinguished: motifs and patterns of action. Traditional

---

[14] Smith 1982, p. xiii. cp. Nagy's argument about Homeric use of myth: "For the poets of ancient Greece, I shall argue, creativity is a matter of applying, to the present occasion, myths that already exist." (Nagy 1992, p. 312.)

[15] cp. Griffith 1990 on the agonistic nature of Greek poetic discourse, esp. pp. 188–189.

motifs are the people, places, and things familiar from other stories that have been passed down in the culture. These motifs may range from broad types (e.g., the hubristic tyrant, a strange and far-off land, or a magic gift that aids the hero) to specific names like Zeus or Herakles, Athens or the Isles of the Blessed, the winged sandals of Hermes or the waters of Lethe. The traditional patterns of action are familiar actions or sequences of actions that are recognizable from one story to another.[16] Traditional patterns include such actions as slaying a monster or the failed infanticide of the hero as well as the journey to the underworld or the quest to found a city.

Again, these elements range from the general to the specific. The more specific the pattern, the more focused is the set of resonances it evokes when recognized by the audience. Any audience, for example, will expect that the plague that disrupts the normal order of things in Thebes at the beginning of Sophocles' *Oedipus Rex* will be followed by a restoration of order by the end of the play. An audience, however, that is familiar with the traditional pattern of a supernatural plague being resolved by the uncovering of an offense and the expulsion of the criminal will have the resonances of this pattern in mind as they follow the tale of Oedipus's self-discovery and exile. The narrative of a myth, then, weaves together not only traditional motifs but also traditional patterns of action, plot elements and sequences that are familiar from previous stories, to shape the story and evoke recognition from the audience.

Like myth, ritual is an expression of ideas by means of traditional symbols passed down through the generations. A ritual, however, is not a narrative, not a traditional *tale*, but a sequence of performed *actions* that are familiar from the cultural tradition.[17] Like the motifs and patterns of action in the mythic narratives, the actions and the arrangements of the sequences of actions in a ritual are traditional elements that create their

---

[16] The functions or motifemes described by Propp are a selection of fairly specific patterns of action, e.g., 'the hero receives a helper' or 'the marriage of the hero'. (Propp 1990, pp. 25–65.) Scholars such as Greimas have revised Propp's specific set of 31 motifemes into a smaller set of more general patterns, e.g., a bipartite pattern of the rupture of the order followed by a restoration of order. cp. Greimas 1986, pp. 199ff., and Adam 1984 for a general overview of scholarly adaptations of Proppian structures.

[17] Calame sees myth and ritual as two types of cultural expression. "Ils sont tous deux des manifestations distinctes du même processus d'élaboration intellectuelle: construction et manipulation d'objets conceptuels par le moyen de la langue et de la narration dans un cas, travail conceptuel par l'intermédiaire du corps et des objects du monde naturel ou culturel dans l'autre." (Calame 1990, p. 29.)

effect through the familiarity the audience has with them.[18] Zuntz points out the importance of ritual's connection to this familiar tradition. "Ritual is a pattern of action redirected to serve for communication. . . . [The symbols] are not chosen arbitrarily, but are taken from a continuous tradition; they are neither independent nor self-evident, but bound to the system in which they function. Their richness of meaning coincides with the complex effects they produce in predetermined interactions."[19] The transmission from one generation to the next of the familiar elements of both myth and ritual is part of the same cultural tradition.

Although myths and rituals are different modes of communication, the spheres of myth and ritual can overlap. A ritual, for instance, may act out a narrative sequence or it may employ the recitation of a myth in the ceremony; the performance of the traditional narrative is thus a symbolic action that is itself traditional. In the same way, a myth can employ a familiar ritual in its narrative action. Perhaps the best example from the Greek myths of journeys to the realm of the dead is Homer's tale of the shade of Patroklos, who begs Achilles to perform the burial ritual for him so that he can cross the boundary river into the underworld.[20] Here the idea that Patroklos needs this burial to enter the underworld is meaningful to the audience because of its familiarity with the customary funeral rituals designed to mark the transition of the deceased from the world of the living to the world of the dead. The narrative description of a ritual sequence of actions becomes a recognizable pattern of action within a myth, one of the traditional elements from which that myth is crafted. Rituals often serve as the solution to a problem within the narrative of a myth, just as they can serve outside the narrative to prevent or forestall potential problems within the society, whether they are, for example, the problems attendant upon transition from one cultural category to another or the problems involved in the relations of mortals and gods.

---

[18] Tambiah defines ritual as follows: "Ritual is a culturally constructed system of symbolic communication. It is constituted of patterned and ordered sequences of words and acts, often expressed in multiple media, whose content and arrangement are characterized in varying degree by formality (conventionality), stereotypy (rigidity), condensation (fusion), and redundancy (repetition)." (Tambiah 1985, p. 128.)

[19] Zuntz 1971, p. 41. As Redfield puts it: "A ceremony is the enactment of a concept. Through ceremonies persons are classified and placed in categories; their analogical unity with similar persons is asserted. Persons are thus rescued from the flux of nature and purified as they are given a definite standing in the cultural pattern." (Redfield 1994, pp. 162–163.)

[20] *Iliad* XXIII.65–107.

The fact, however, that a myth and a ritual contain similar elements and even sequences of actions does not imply that the myth derives from the ritual or the ritual from the myth. The relation of ritual to myth is rarely so direct; more often both simply draw upon elements from the same pool of ideas or images, which they express and deploy in different ways.

Whereas a myth or a ritual is a particular expression created from traditional material, a traditional tale may be defined as the whole set of stories centered around a certain traditional element, be it a character like Theseus, a plot structure like slaying a monster, or even a ritual like sacrifice. All tales that involve Theseus as a central character evoke in the audience a recollection of the other stories that have been told about the hero, and the associations connected with these other tales enhance the meaning of the individual tale. Likewise, tales that feature the hero slaying a monster recall other tales with this pattern of action, so that Theseus slaying the sow of Megara evokes Herakles' slaying of the Hydra and the Nemean Lion, not to mention the Erymanthian Boar. Thus, while a myth is shaped and defined by its teller, a traditional tale is a secondary classification, defined by the audience that makes the associations among different myths, grouping various tellings together.

Often, a sequence of actions becomes associated in the tradition with a single figure as, for example, the sequence of patricide and incest is attached to Oedipus or the journey to the underworld to bring back a loved one is linked to Orpheus. Scholars often refer to such traditional tales as 'the myth of Orpheus' or 'the Oedipus story' when discussing the varied appearances of these patterns of action within the tradition. However, the pattern of action is, strictly speaking, separable from the motif of the hero who is most often associated with it. Such connections between patterns and motifs nevertheless illustrate the complex of resonances that any traditional element builds up in the course of its transmission. The name of Oedipus evokes the ideas of patricide and incest, just as the name of Theseus evokes the Minotaur, Ariadne, the labyrinth, etc. The audience of the individual telling, be it an Athenian spectator at the performance of Sophocles' Oedipus Rex or a post-Freudian scholar reading a handbook of mythology, categorizes the myth as a telling of the traditional tale of Oedipus because of the familiarity of the traditional elements (patricide, incest, Jocasta, Oedipus, etc.) that make up the story.[21]

[21] Levi-Strauss would claim that all the tellings of the traditional tale from Sophocles to Freud count as variants of the myth: "We define the myth as consisting of all of its

The teller of a myth weaves together the traditional elements, both motifs and patterns of action, to produce a tale that is meaningful to the intended audience. To the extent that this myth is remembered and accepted by the audience, it becomes part of the tradition that other myth-tellers can draw upon to produce their own stories.[22] Insofar as this myth becomes part of the tradition, the teller's perspective on 'the realities and idealities' of the world becomes authoritative and influential. The teller of a myth thus tries to shape the narrative to make it memorable and acceptable to the audience, since his version is always in competition, implicit or explicit, with alternative versions.[23] In this kind of crafting of the story, the teller makes use of the fact not only that myth is traditional but also in narrative form; it is a tale rather than a ritual or a static piece of art.

The narrative form, the *tale*, has two specific features that the teller can make use of in a myth. First of all, the narrative structure of the tale can be used to illustrate the teller's ideas. The pattern of action of a myth and the relations of the elements to one another can be used to convey meaning on a structural level beyond the meaning of the component parts. Already in the third century CE, Plotinus comments on this function of myth: "Myths, if they are really going to be myths, must divide out in time

versions; or to put it otherwise, a myth remains the same as long as it is felt as such." (Levi-Strauss 1963, p. 217.) It is important, however, to distinguish between the variants that would have had associations for the ancient audience and those that have resonance for the modern scholar. The Freudian retelling of the story of Oedipus, while indelibly part of the traditional tale for a contemporary reader, could not be considered as such by an ancient audience who could never have heard Freud's peculiar version. While Levi-Strauss's synchronic method admirably disposes of the need for a quest for the origin of the myth, it neglects the fact that the audience's chronological position determines the range of interpretations open to it.

[22] The technology of writing naturally makes a big difference in the preservation of myths. In an oral context, the audience's acceptance of the telling plays a much larger role in the preservation of the story than in a written context, where even a myth that is unacceptable to its original audience may be preserved and drawn upon by later tellers. cp. Brisson 1982, pp. 31–50, 76–80; also Havelock 1963.

[23] Sahlins discusses the dynamic nature of a cultural sign system, wherein the meanings of signs are constantly being revised by different actors in their own expressions. "The subjective risk consists in the possible revision of signs by acting subjects in their personal projects. Contradiction arises from the inevitable difference between the value of a sign in a symbolic system, i.e. its semantic relations to others signs, and its value to the people using it. In the cultural system, the sign has a conceptual value fixed by contrasts to other signs; whereas, in action the sign is determined also as an 'interest,' which is its instrumental value to the acting subject." (Sahlins 1985, pp. 149–150.)

the things they relate and separate from one another many realities which are together, but which stand apart in rank or powers."[24] The narrative form separates ideas in the chronological sequence of the story line and sets up their relations in the logical sequences of the narrative. Another attribute of mythic discourse as narrative is the power of persuasive imagery. The fantastic images in the narrative, crafted by the artist's skill, impress themselves upon the audience, creating a vivid encapsulation of the ideas the teller is trying to express. A myth is more memorable for the audience because of the imagery and the narrative logic that holds the ideas together.

A myth's connection with the tradition also has two important effects – polyvalence and authority. Mythic discourse, as a system of symbols, each of which can evoke a range of resonances for the audience familiar with the tradition, permits particularly dense communication. Aristotle remarks on the usefulness of mythic references, since one need only refer to a well-known tale to make one's point. "One need only make mention of well known things. Because of this, most people have no need of narrative, if you wish to praise Achilles, for everyone knows his deeds."[25] The use of traditional motifs, names, etc., allows a rich discourse on multiple levels as the teller exploits the associations connected with, for example, Heracles or the halls of Hades. Because mythic discourse is one of the primary forms of authoritative discourse in Greek society, one of the primary ways of articulating the models of the world and models for behavior within it, a myth is not only a rich kind of discourse but an influential one. Insofar as it includes elements that are recognizable to the audience as being part of the common cultural ground, the account seems to fit with that which is already accepted by all.[26] The authoritative status of mythic discourse thus makes it a particularly effective mode of communication.

Not only, then, does the narrative logic of the tale help to articulate the distinctions that are important to the teller, but the use of traditional

---

[24] Δεῖ δὲ τοὺς μύθους, εἴπερ τοῦτο ἔσονται, καὶ μερίζειν χρόνοις ἃ λέγουσι, καὶ διαιρεῖν ἀπ' ἀλλήλων πολλὰ τῶν ὄντων ὁμοῦ μὲν ὄντα, τάξει δὲ ἢ δυνάμεσι διεστῶτα. (*Ennead* III.5.24–27.)

[25] δεῖ δὲ τὰς μὲν γνωρίμους ἀναμιμνήσκειν· διὸ οἱ πολλοὶ οὐδὲν δέονται διηγήσεως, οἷον εἰ θέλεις Ἀχιλλέα ἐπαινεῖν (ἴσασι γὰρ παντες τὰς πράξεις). (*Rhetoric*, III.xvi.3)

[26] Again, Aristotle, in his *Rhetoric* (II.xxi.11), advocates the use of well-known proverbs and stories that are from the common tradition, "for because they are common, they seem to be correct, since everyone agrees upon them." διὰ γὰρ τό εἶναι κοιναί. ὡς ὁμολογούντων πάντων. ὀρθῶς ἔχειν δοκοῦσιν.

material helps make the point to the audience. The familiar elements in the tale – the traditional motifs and the recognizable plot elements – enhance the power of the tale to communicate with the audience. These elements all carry their own resonances, the associations built up by countless uses of these elements in myths, that permit complex ideas to be communicated compactly. The definition of a myth as a telling of a traditional tale permits us to recognize how each individual tale is carefully crafted from traditional elements and how myth as a discourse is used to communicate the teller's perspective on the world in an effective and authoritative manner.

## THE TALE OF THE JOURNEY TO THE UNDERWORLD

In this study, I employ the above definition of myth in the analysis of a set of Greek texts from roughly the same period, texts in which the myths have presented particular problems for interpretation. Each text contains a myth, an adaptation of a traditional tale. The Orphic tablets describe the journey of the deceased to the realm of the dead, providing instructions for handling the dangers of the other world. The *Frogs* tells of the journey of Dionysos to the underworld to bring back a tragic poet to save Athens. Plato's myth in the *Phaedo* also describes the journey of the deceased after death. All of these texts describe the journey of some individual to the realm of the dead, and they all seem to share a certain set of common elements in their descriptions of that realm.

Previous scholarship seems to have taken two approaches to the interpretation of these texts, grouping them either by the common set of elements or by their shared pattern of action. The former approach often involves *Quellenforschung*, a search for the common origin of all of these motifs. The search for the context that originally contained these motifs in a coherent form, however, often winds up attributing the greatest significance of the element to its origin. This approach has been largely abandoned by more recent scholars, who prefer to seek the meaning of the text in the underlying pattern of action, often connecting the sequence of actions to a similar ritual pattern. Both approaches have their merits, but each neglects important aspects of the texts. By examining the way myth is employed in the texts, rather than simply noting which elements are employed, I hope to rectify the problems inherent in the other approaches.

The first route taken by scholars in classifying these texts depends on the similarity of certain motifs in the tales. Common features of the realm of the dead that appear in a number of the myths from the Greek tradition have caused some scholars to group these tales together as the products of a common background. The myths so grouped describe a rather lively life after death, full of tortures and rewards based on ethical criteria, in contrast to the somber picture of mindless shades in the gloom that the Homeric epics present.[27] In order to explain the contrast, scholars have sought the common origin of these motifs, the specific line of transmission within the Greek mythic tradition that is responsible for the spread of these ideas.[28] So different do these stories seem from the quintessentially Greek Homeric view that even the features in Homer that resemble these tales, such as the torments of Tantalus and Sisyphus, have been explained away as later interpolations dependent on the same common source.[29] These scholars see these myths, which seem to privilege over the present life an afterlife full of colorful details in which the inhabitants suffer or celebrate according to their just deserts, as alien to Greek culture, a drop of foreign blood, as Rohde called it.[30] Accordingly, the origin of these ideas has been sought outside of Greece – in Thrace, in Egypt, in Mesopotamia, even in the Indo–European tradition. Rohde sees the Thracian invasion of Dionysos worship as ultimately responsible for this alien stream.[31] Egypt has been a popular source for the foreign origin of these ideas ever since Herodotus, who marked the unusual nature of these ideas by attributing them (along with many other things) to

[27] cp. Guthrie 1952, p. 148ff; Rohde 1925, pp. 3–4.

[28] "Everyone has noticed that there is a certain common body of doctrine, largely eschatological, to be observed in various writings of the sixth to the fourth centuries B.C. Empedocles, some of the great myths of Plato, certain passages of Pindar and the gold plates from South Italian graves are the most outstanding examples. The resemblance extends sufficiently into details to be striking. . . . Clearly none of these writers were inventing the main scheme; they were relying on a common source." (Guthrie 1950, pp. 309–310.)

[29] "It may be taken as one of the few certain results of the critical analysis of the Homeric poems that the narrative of the Descent of Odysseus to the Underworld did not form part of the original plan of the Odyssey." (Rohde 1925, p. 32) cp. also Macchioro 1928, pp. 239–249.

[30] "Ein fremder Blutstropfen im griechischen Blut," Rohde 1895, p. 27.

[31] Rohde 1925, pp. 253ff. cp., "Der Quellpunkt aller griechischen Mystik liegt in der Dionysischen Religion. Nicht von Anfang war dies ein griechischer Cult." (Rohde 1895, p. 21.) Although Rohde's theory of Dionysos as a late Thracian invader is followed by Dieterich and other scholars, recent scholarly consensus accepts the presence of Dionysos in Greek religion from its earliest appearances (including the presence of Dionysos on Mycenaean Linear B tablets). cp. Dieterich 1893.

Egypt.[32] Near Eastern parallels have been suggested by some, while others have traced certain motifs back through the Indo-European tradition.[33] However, even when specific motifs can be traced to earlier sources or different cultures, little is learned about the significance of these texts for the people who produced and used them, the authors and audience, as it were, of the individual texts. Even if ideas were borrowed or if forms were influential, the use of the similar elements and motifs in nearby cultures cannot reveal what these elements meant to the Greeks who were using them.[34]

These scholars also try to trace the transmission of these ideas from these foreign sources through the Greek tradition. Albrecht Dieterich's *Nekyia* tracks these motifs through the Greek tradition from the Homeric epics all the way to the *Apocalypse of St. Peter,* an early Christian apocryphon that describes the torments of sinners in Hell.[35] A *Quellenforschung* approach to these texts is, however, ultimately fruitless. Too many pieces of the puzzle are missing to reconstruct a concrete chain of influence, even if literary influence could ever be charted as simply as a manuscript tradition. Between Homer's *Odyssey* in the eighth century and Aristophanes' *Frogs* in the fifth, there must have been many poems, tragedies, and comedies that described the journeys to the other world of Herakles, Theseus, and other heroes, but few of these survive. This kind of search for influences quickly becomes highly hypothetical in the absence of so many of the poetic treatments of world journeys, not to mention the complete absence of all the informal tellings – the tales of heroes that children heard at their grandmother's knee or the ghost stories with which they were terrified by their parents.[36]

---

[32] cp. Hdt. II.81.

[33] cp., e.g., Ziegler's Pauly-Wissowa article, s.v. Orphische Dichtung, 1385; Clark 1979, pp. 13–36; and the first several chapters in Lincoln 1991 with related bibliography.

[34] Dieterich 1893, for example, discusses the motif of the land of the dead in the west as a representation of the setting sun symbolizing the death of the individual. Lincoln also tries to pin down a meaning for individual motifs in the Indo-European tradition, e.g., Charon is old age, the earthen walls of Hades are the grave, etc. (Lincoln 1991, pp. 62ff.; 107ff. cp., however, Lincoln's methodological critique of these earlier essays, pp. 119ff.)

[35] Dieterich 1893.

[36] Plato, for one, is certainly aware of the influence of these informal tales, when he has Socrates suggest the necessity of censoring the nurses' stories in the ideal state (*Republic,* 377c). Graf, on the contrary, claims that such informal tellings lack the 'cultural relevance' of the formal tellings. (Graf 1993b, pp. 3–6.) Whereas the authority and influence

In the absence of extant sources, many scholars, following Dieterich, are reduced to postulating a canonical, but underground, Orphic katabasis poem that provides the model for elements that are clearly well known but do not appear until late sources. This hypothesis of an Orphic tradition accounts for all the various testimonia to these motifs of a lively afterlife and for the influence in Greek culture of these non-Homeric views of the importance of the world beyond. This influence becomes especially important for those who, like Rohde and Dieterich, are tracing the course of Greek religion from Homer to Platonic philosophy and to Christian eschatology. Nietzsche's idea that Socrates (or Plato) was responsible for the transformation of the world-affirming Hellenic spirit to the world-hating ethic later dominant in Christianity seems to have profoundly influenced not only Nietzsche's friend Rohde, but generations of scholars who followed in the wake of Rohde's fundamental study of Greek eschatological beliefs.[37] The Orphic ideology postulated by Rohde and others provides a chain of transmission for these motifs, whether these ideas of the afterlife are regarded in a Nietzschean spirit as the downfall of Hellenic culture or, in the views of other scholars, as the first blossoms of the Greek's true legacy to Western Civilization: the rational philosophy of Plato and the spiritual religion of Christianity.[38]

of each individual tale are undoubtedly less, the potential for these informal tellings to preserve and transmit ideas and elements within the tradition should not be discounted.

[37] Rohde vigorously places the blame for Christian eschatology on the perversions of the Orphics and the Platonic philosophers. "From such gloomy severity, from the rigid and overpowering dogmatism that a people without imagination had constructed for itself out of religious speculations and visions won by much labour and thought, the Greeks were fortunately preserved by their own genius. Their fancy is a winged god whose nature it is to pass lightly over things - not to fall heavily to earth and there remain ponderously prostrate. Nor were they very susceptible during their best centuries to the infectious malady of a 'sick conscience'. What had they to do with pictures of an underworld of purgatory and torment in expiation of all imaginary types and degrees of sin, as in Dante's ghastly Hell? It is true that even such dark fancies of the Christian Hell are in part derived from Greek sources. But it was only the misguided fancy of particular isolated sects that could call forth such pictures as these, and recommend itself to a philosophic speculation which in its worst excesses violently contradicted all the most fundamental principles of Greek culture. The people and the religion of Greece, the mysteries which her cities organized and deemed holy, may be freely acquitted of such aberrations." (Rohde 1925, p. 242.)

[38] "The Orphic conception of the soul marks an important advance in the development of man's consciousness of selfhood. Without it Plato and Aristotle could never have developed the theory that the human spirit is divine, and that man's sensual nature can be dissociated from his real self, which it is his true function to bring to perfection." (Jaeger 1945, pp. 168-69.) Guthrie also describes the Orphic idea of the assimilation

As convenient as such an explanation might be, however, the hypothesis of an Orphic tradition has come under repeated attack because the pieces of evidence to support such a hypothesis are so few in number and so questionable in quality.[39] To account for the fact that many of the central pieces of this Orphic tradition do not appear in the evidence until very late, the Orphic tradition must be imagined as a secret tradition that preserved its integrity over the centuries with only an occasional allusion in texts that suggests its existence. Moreover, scholars such as Thomas and Graf point out that the motifs that are supposedly Orphic in fact appear in a wide variety of contexts and in close conjunction with other non-Orphic ideas, making a single chain of transmission highly unlikely.[40] Indeed, Norden, in his study of the roots of Virgil's description of the underworld, must imagine both an Orphic *katabasis* that provided the chain of transmission of the Orphic motifs and an equally lost, equally canonical Heraclean *katabasis* that supplies the remaining elements.[41] Unquestionably, various tellings of these descents, now lost to us, were influential, but that there was a single canonical but lost version of these is highly doubtful. The quest for a single point of origin seeks a simple explanation for the presence of certain influences in the Greek tradition, particularly on Plato and early Christianity, but the construction of a secret Orphic tradition to fill this place distorts the little evidence that remains and obscures rather than illuminates the nature of the texts and perspectives on the world expressed in them.

Some scholars, rather than classifying these texts as Orphic because of the presence of certain motifs, choose instead to group the texts according to the narrative pattern of action common to them, the journey to the underworld. Many of these scholars, however, seek the meaning of such myths in the origins of the pattern of action itself. For them, the tale

---

of the human soul to divinity as the bridge between religion and philosophy. (Guthrie 1952, pp. 206ff. cp. Cornford 1952, pp. 107–126; Vernant 1983, pp. 354–364. In histories of philosophy, the Pythagoreans often appear as the link between the Orphic religious tradition and real philosophy.)

[39] "Toutes les reconstructions de l'orphisme ont pour fondement un très petit nombre de témoignages sûrs et un plus grand nombre de textes dont l'exégese me paraît arbitraire." (Festugière 1936, p. 310.) The most extreme attack was mounted by Linforth 1941, whose devastating critique of the way the evidence was reconstructed has often been neglected because of the overly narrow way in which he limited what might count as evidence.

[40] Thomas 1938; Graf 1974.

[41] Norden 1995 (1927). cp. the attempts of Lloyd-Jones 1967 to reconstruct a canonical katabasis of Herakles.

grows out of a description of a ritual, and the context of the ritual provides the key to understanding the myth. These scholars explain the peculiar pattern of a person's departure from the land of the living and journey to the realm of the dead as the relic of a ritual of initiation, which entails the death of the old self and rebirth into the new mature personality. Eliade sees a universal pattern of such initiatory experiences: "Descending into Hades means to undergo 'initiatory death', the experience of which can establish a new mode of being."[42] The descent to the underworld fits into van Gennep's schema of the *rite de passage*, the three-part transition consisting of separation, liminality, and reaggregation.[43] The deceased separates himself from the world of the living, goes through a liminal period in the realm of the dead, and is finally brought back into the normal world as a new person. The old, childish self dies and the new, adult self comes into being at the end of the rite; in structuralist terms, the tale expresses the bipolar opposition of life and death, as well as the mediation between them. Whether the protagonist is the hero descending alive into Hell, the initiand experiencing initiation, or the deceased suffering death, the pattern and the meaning are taken to be the same – the replacement of the old self with the new.

The origin of this pattern is traced by some scholars to some underlying historical reality. Vladimir Propp concludes that the wondertale derives ultimately from the narration of the events of initiation rituals, which in turn correspond to the experience of the deceased at death.[44] As a good Marxist, Propp seeks the historical roots of the wondertale in a time when the sequence of events in the tale corresponds to the means of production of the tellers of the tale.[45] The assumption that a story pattern can be traced to the historical reality that gave rise to it is not confined

---

[42] Eliade 1972, p. 27. "From one point of view, we may say that all these myths and sagas have an initiatory structure; to descend into Hell alive, confront its monsters and demons, is to undergo an initiatory ordeal." (Eliade 1958, p. 62.)

[43] Van Gennep 1960.

[44] "If one envisions everything that happens to the initiate and narrates it in sequence, the result will be the compositional basis of the wondertale. If one narrates in sequence everything thought to happen to the deceased, the story will produce the same core, with the addition of some elements absent from the rites." (Propp 1984, p. 117.)

[45] "We must find in history the mode of production that gave rise to the wondertale.... The wondertale arose on the basis of precapitalist modes of production and social life, and we must discover exactly which ones.... The wondertale must be compared with the historical realities of the past, and its roots should be sought there.... We have to decipher this concept and determine just which element of the past explains the wondertale." (Propp 1984, pp. 103–104.)

to Propp. Dodds, following the research of Eliade and Meuli, explains these stories within the Greek tradition as the heritage of a shamanic tradition, possibly from the Thracian or Scythian North.[46] Thus, the specific features and narrative sequence of the journey to the underworld derive from the ecstatic ritual experiences of these shamans.[47] Dodds traces the influence of this shamanic tradition through the Orphics to Plato and his revolutionary revision of the Greek tradition.[48] In his recent work on Orphism, West subscribes to this theory of shamanic survivals transmitted through the Orphic religious current.[49]

Other scholars seek the origin of the pattern not in a concrete historical reality, but in some fundamental structure of human consciousness or way of interpreting the world.[50] The binary opposition of life and death is mediated by the journey between the realms of life and death, and the living individual overcomes death and comes to new life through this journey.[51] All these explanations, however, of the journey to the underworld

[46] Meuli 1935; Eliade 1964; Dodds 1951. Burkert traces the origin of the pattern even further back, to ritualized animal behavior patterns. (Burkert 1979, 1983, 1996.)

[47] cp. Eliade's assertion: "It is probable that a great many features of 'funerary geography,' as well as some themes of the mythology of death, are the result of the ecstatic experiences of shamans. It is equally probable that a large number of epic 'subjects' or motifs are, in the last analysis, of ecstatic origin, in the sense that they were drawn from the accounts of shamans narrating their journeys and adventures in the superhuman worlds." (Eliade 1972, p. 41.) Graf makes a similar assertion: "The ultimate source of the theme was the ritual experience of the shamanistic journey of the soul and, along with it, the ritual schema of the rite of passage: these thematic and structural echoes contributed greatly to the success of the Platonic myth." (Graf 1993b, p. 190.)

[48] "If I am right in my tentative guess about the historical antecedents of the Pythagorean movement, Plato in effect cross-fertilised the tradition of Greek rationalism with magico-religious ideas whose remoter origins belong to the northern shamanistic culture.... The crucial step lay in the identification of the detachable 'occult' self which is the carrier of guilt-feelings and potentially divine with the rational Socratic *psyche* whose virtue is a kind of knowledge. That step involved a complete reinterpretation of the shamanistic culture-pattern. Nevertheless the pattern kept its vitality, and its main features are still recognizable in Plato." (Dodds 1951, pp. 209–210.)

[49] West 1983, pp. 4–7, 144–160. West, unlike Dodds, gives little explanation of the process of reinterpretation and adaptation necessary for the transmission of the motifs and patterns.

[50] Thiercy discusses the initiation pattern he sees in Aristophanes: "L'essentiel n'est pas pour nous attribuer une origine plus ou moins précise à cette notion d'initiation chez Aristophane, mais de constater que dans toutes les religions, les littératures et les civilisations, quels qu'en soient l'époque ou le niveau, la notion d'initiation est ancrée dans l'esprit humain, d'autant plus qu'elle répond toujours à un même scénario dont seuls les noms et les détails varient." (Thiercy 1986, p. 305.)

[51] Jungian interpreters have developed this idea of personal development at great length, e.g., Campbell, Joseph, *Hero with a Thousand Faces*. cp., Knight, *Elysion*. Eliade links this pattern of death and rebirth not only to the personal experience but also to natural

stories presume that the meaning of the myth must be contained in the pattern of action, whether in its mediation of bipolar oppositions or in its repetition of ritual patterns. To be sure, structural analysis of the underlying bipolar oppositions may illuminate some of the important issues at stake in the myth, but it fails to reveal what Plato or Aristophanes was saying about those issues. Similarly, the discovery of an underlying ritual sequence or even, following Burkert, the biological, pragmatic origin of such a ritual may explain why the traditional pattern of action consists of the parts that it does, but it not explain the significance of each of the parts in the text. Above all, these approaches leave out a fundamental part of these stories: the specific characters, places, and things. In short, while interpreting the verbs, these approaches ignore the nouns. The patterns of action may indeed have meaningful resonances; that is, after all, why the author chose to tell such a story. But the specific characters and circumstances the author chooses also have important meanings. Consider the different messages that may be sent if the hero is female instead of male in a familiar fairy tale or if a comic buffoon like Dionysos of the *Frogs* instead of the heroic Herakles goes to the underworld. These aspects of a myth can change the meaning as greatly as the pattern of action. Insofar as a myth exists only in its tellings, the meaning of the myth must lie in the individual texts and vary according to the purpose of the author.[52] Only a careful comparison of the authors' uses of the traditional mythic material can provide an understanding of the meaning of the myths they tell.

### DISTINCT AND DIFFERENT WAYS

In my analysis, I regard all of the texts I am considering – the gold tablets, Aristophanes' *Frogs*, and the myth in Plato's *Phaedo* – as sharing a common traditional mythic pattern of action, the journey to the underworld. Choosing for analysis a set of mythic tellings that follow the same pattern of action provides a ground of similarity against which to make

---

vegetative cycles. "It is above all Dionysus who is characterized by his periodic epiphanies and disappearances, by his 'death' and his 'renascence', and we can still discern his relation to the rhythm of vegetation and, in general, to the eternal cycle of life, death, and rebirth. But in the historical period this fundamental connection between the cosmic rhythms and the presence, preceded and followed by the absence, of supernatural Beings was no longer apparent." (Eliade 1972, p. 27.)

[52] Note Lloyd's prescription for a meaningful comparison of myths: "not the comparison of individual motifs, or even ordered sets of them, but the analysis of what those who used this material used it *for*, how they thought about it, in particular the use they made of the various categories they had in which to think about it." (Lloyd 1999, p. 165.)

comparisons.[53] However, while the shared pattern of action provides a basis for comparison, this common ground should not be taken as the essence of each of these myths. The agenda according to which the author of the text told his story is primary, while the scholar's classification of these texts by their common pattern of action is only secondary. The pattern of action is *one* of the traditional elements that the author is manipulating in his mythic telling, but it is not necessarily the crucial element in his story. The fact that a story is about Theseus, for example, may be far more important than the fact that it is an underworld journey. Previous scholarship has largely neglected the other elements of the underworld journey myths in attempting to grasp the inner meaning of the pattern of action.

The structure of this shared pattern of action can, however, provide a framework for the analysis of the individual texts, for this traditional tale of the journey to the realm of the dead is not simply a conglomeration of *traditional* elements, but comprises a *tale*, and no story is interesting without conflict of some kind. Anomaly and crisis make interesting and tellable stories; normality and quotidian tedium do not. Only when the deceased experiences difficulty in the transition or when a living person crosses to the realm of the dead and then back again is there a story to be told. The specific nature of those difficulties creates the individual character of the story, but the obstacles that the protagonist faces are frequently drawn from traditional material, as are the solutions to those obstacles and the results that the protagonist expects. In my analysis, I focus upon the nexus of obstacle, solution, and result in these myths to observe the ways in which the author manipulates the traditional mythic elements. It should be stressed that this complex of obstacle–solution–result is not, in itself, a traditional pattern of action whose meaning or even whose set of resonances I am attempting to determine. Rather, the obstacle–solution–result complex serves as an analytic tool for breaking the narrative up into manageable pieces, carving it up at the joints of the narrative action the better to see how the teller has constructed the story.[54]

---

[53] As Smith notes, "Comparison requires the acceptance of difference as the grounds of its being interesting, and a methodical manipulation of that difference to achieve some stated cognitive end." (Smith 1987, p. 14.)

[54] cp. Plato's *Phaedrus* 265e. While Greimas' bipartite structures could likewise be considered analytic tools that divide the tale into the problem and the resolution of the problem, I find that separating the solution to the problem from the final result provides a more comprehensive understanding of the teller's manipulations of the mythic

Taking the shared pattern of action as the basis for comparison of the texts, I examine the differences among these stories of a journey to the underworld, differences that lie primarily in each teller's selection of motifs. As the *Quellenforschung* scholars have noted, these texts do indeed share, not necessarily the same few motifs, but rather a limited pool of traditional elements, none of which appear in every text, but some of which appear in each. In my analysis, I examine the different obstacles that are presented in the journey to the underworld, the solutions that these obstacles demand, and the varied results that success or failure to apply the correct solution may bring. A brief overview of this pool of elements from which the tellers of these myths are drawing may serve as an introduction to the analysis of why and with what effect the teller has selected the particular elements in a given text.

Among the most common obstacles in Greek myths of the journey to the underworld are barriers that prevent one from entering the realm of the dead, the dangers of losing one's way in the underworld, and the confrontations with the powers that reside in the underworld. Often a geographic barrier separates the world of the living from the realm of the dead. The underworld is far away, to the east or to the west, up on high or down below. While the barrier may simply be a large physical distance between the realms, bodies of water frequently appear as barriers, varying in size from the small, "running stream they dare na cross" to the vast depths of the ocean. Another kind of physical barrier is the great gates that divide the realm of Hades from the world of the living or walls that surround the kingdom of the dead.

The journey to the underworld may not be over when the traveler has crossed the borders; many myths describe the difficulties of finding one's way in the underworld and the dangers of wandering lost. The realm of the dead is often characterized by darkness and shadows that make it easy for the traveler to lose the way. Even if there is a path through this realm, the motif of the fork in the road and the multitude of paths occurs frequently, and the choice of paths is not a simple one.

The powers that hold sway in the underworld may also present an obstacle to the traveler. In some myths, a guardian bars the way in or

elements. Calame, on the other hand, has adapted Greimas' bipartite structure to great effect in his studies (Calame 1990, 1996). My tripartite analytic structure should not, however, be confused with the tripartite schema of van Gennep for understanding a rite of passage, which a number of scholars have indeed tried to apply to the myths in the gold tablets, Aristophanes' *Frogs*, and Plato's *Phaedo*.

out of the realm of the dead. Such a guardian is often monstrous, like the hellhound Kerberos, whose grotesque form displays the threat to the traveler. This guardian may, however, be instead a personage of authority in the kingdom of the dead, whose favor must be obtained to complete the journey successfully. This personage can range from a mere doorkeeper or ferryman to the ruler of the dead herself.

The solutions to these obstacles vary as much as the obstacles themselves, for the type of solution is always linked to the particular choice of obstacle. Reaching the underworld, finding one's way, and encountering the powers of the underworld all call for different kinds of solutions. To overcome the physical barriers of distance or bodies of water, some sort of magical means of crossing otherwise uncrossable distances must be supplied, be it the golden cup of the sun or simply a normal ship with a divinely aided wind. Directions from a previous traveler or some guide in the underworld are necessary to help the traveler find the way in the murky shadows of the realm of the dead. The solutions for getting past a guardian differ according to the nature of the guardian. A monstrous guardian must often be fought and conquered, whereas a doorkeeper or ferryman may be paid off or placated. If the guardian is a figure of authority in the underworld, the solution lies in winning the favor of this guardian, be it by undergoing certain ritual performances, by having lived a pure life, or by any other means of establishing a claim to preferential treatment.

The results that the tradition provides fall into positive and negative categories. If the traveler has the proper solution for the obstacle he or she faces, then the result will be positive. The journey will be complete, and the traveler will not be stranded between the worlds, unable to get past the barrier that separates the living from the dead. In some cases, mere completion of the journey is insufficient for a happy ending; the traveler who applies the correct solution finds some reward – a pleasant location in the next world, blissful activities, a happier condition of life. For those who have failed to find the proper solution, an unpleasant fate awaits. This negative result may be a bland and boring existence as a witless shade, an actively unpleasant lot such as being trampled into mud and filth, or even an ingenious set of excruciating tortures carefully tailored to the failings that led to this negative result.

The struggle involved in the journey, the necessity for the traveler to overcome the difficulties that obstruct an easy passage between one world and the next, sets up an implicit contrast between those who successfully overcome these obstacles and those who fail. These differentiations, between living and dead as well as between happy dead and unhappy dead, serve as a way of articulating the boundaries between other groups of people – the initiate and uninitiate, the just and unjust, the noble and base, the pure and impure, the heroic and cowardly, the real and unreal, the mortal and immortal. While the distinction between successful and unsuccessful travelers is built into the plot structure of the journey to the underworld, the other distinctions that are mapped onto this opposition depend upon the individual teller and the way he or she shapes the myth.

The choice of the obstacles that face the traveler and what constitutes a successful solution to these obstacles are thus determined by the distinctions that the teller is trying to draw in the myth. If the heroic virtues of courage and strength are being praised, the obstacle may very well be depicted as a ferocious monster, like Kerberos, which requires the strength and courage of a Herakles to overcome it. On the other hand, if the teller is stressing the importance of living a pure life dedicated to the service of the gods, initiation into the mysteries of a certain deity or undergoing certain kinds of purification may be the way to avert the threat of torment in the underworld and to win instead a blissful afterlife. Not only the choices of obstacle, solution, and specific results, but even the emphasis on one section over another – the elaboration of the solution rather than the result or the expansion of the possible results at the expense of describing the obstacle and solution – depends on the specific distinctions that interest the teller of the myth. This set of distinctions constitutes a descriptive model of the world, reflecting in the mirror of the other world the significant attributes of the realm of the living, as well as a prescriptive model for change in this world.

The myths of the journey to the realm of the dead, like all myths, create a narrative world that reveals the teller's models of the world and models for behavior within it; but the story pattern of the underworld journey permits the teller to lay out these models in a particularly clear way. The land of the dead is the ultimate other world, a realm in which normal conditions do not apply. The transition from the familiar everyday world to this unknown realm articulates the contrasts between this world and the other, between the living and the dead. In describing the conditions of life in the realm of death, that is, the hierarchies and distinctions between those whose journey was successful and those who failed to find the proper solutions to the obstacles that faced them, the teller can reinscribe the boundaries of the cosmos, the world order.

## THE ROUTE OF THE TEXTS

From the numerous myths in the Greek tradition that relate the tale of the journey to the underworld, I have selected three sets of texts to analyze: the collection of nearly twenty so-called Orphic gold tablets, the *Frogs* of Aristophanes, and the myth at the end of Plato's *Phaedo*. The earliest extant Orphic gold tablet was produced around the end of the fifth century BCE and the majority date from the fourth and third centuries. Aristophanes, too, wrote at the end of the fifth century, while Plato's works come from the fourth century. Not only does this chronological proximity provide a convenient bracket for distinguishing these particular texts from the large number of other similar myths, but also the examination of the use of myth in these texts from the same period provides an ideal case study in the range of ways myth could be used, from the highly self-conscious productions of Plato to the magico–religious use in the gold tablets. These texts also span the gamut of oral and literary elements. The Orphic tablets contain primarily oral poetry that happens to have been inscribed for the audience of a single deceased; Aristophanes' *Frogs* is a written text in verse designed for an oral performance in an Athenian dramatic festival; and Plato's dialogues are elaborately crafted prose texts that give a written representation of an oral narration of a myth.

Not only do these texts represent a diverse collection of myths from a limited chronological period, but all of these texts have suffered misinterpretation in the previous scholarship. The gold tablets have been categorized as the products of Orphism and interpreted in the light of hypothetically Orphic doctrines, rather than examined in their own right as mythic texts that express their own models of the world through the description of the deceased's journey in the realm of the dead. Individually analyzed, the gold tablets provide evidence of countercultural religious movements in which the individual deceased marks her separation from the mainstream of her society by means of her privileged status in the other world. The instructions on the gold tablets show how the deceased can overcome the obstacles of the underworld journey and win a blissful afterlife beyond the lot of ordinary mortals.

Aristophanes' *Frogs*, on the other hand, has been read in terms of an initiatory pattern because the tale of a descent to the underworld is thought to stem from such a ritual of initiation. Scholars have claimed that the comic hero, Dionysos, undergoes a process of initiatory maturation as he progresses through the underworld and have tried to force the episodes of his journey into such a ritual pattern, particularly one associated with the Eleusinian Mysteries. This emphasis on ritual has caused distortions of the evidence the text provides for Aristophanes' view of his world, the society of Athens on the brink of destruction in the Peloponnesian War. Instead of relating the maturation of Dionysos as the Spirit of Comedy through his symbolic death and resurrection in an initiatory journey to the underworld, Aristophanes uses his comic picture of the realm of the dead to provide a critique of Athenian society and to offer possible strategies for the city's salvation. Through his manipulations of the familiar mythic elements, Aristophanes reconfigures the boundaries of society in the underworld to produce an image of an ideal Athens to serve as a model for the city in its time of peril.

Plato's eschatological myths have always been problematic because his attacks on the poets' uses of myth have led to great confusion over his own use of myth. In modern commentaries on Plato, myth tends to be vaguely defined in opposition to dialectic argument, and then, according to the prejudice of the scholar, either the myths are dismissed as frivolous bits of childish entertainment – a sop for the masses or those unfit for serious thinking – or they are regarded as symbolic expressions of the Truth, embodiments of religious dogma, or a theology in rudimentary form.[55] As a result, these myths are either neglected or placed in a special category of Plato's religious beliefs and traced back to the Orphics or the shamans. The role of Orphic or Pythagorean sources in Plato's choice to employ myth in his dialogues has been often debated, but the debate has most often centered around the contrast between rational argument and myth.[56]

Why does Plato make use of a form of discourse whose authority he repeatedly tries to undermine? Scholars have, for the most part, failed to understand that Plato's critique and use of myth are both part of the contest for authoritative discourse that characterizes the Greek use of myth

---

[55] These are obviously the extremes, but it is by no means unusual to find the myth entirely omitted from the discussion of a Platonic dialogue, as Bostock 1986 does in his commentary on the *Phaedo*. Elias 1984 (esp. pp. 77–84) describes the spectrum of attitudes to Plato's myths, ultimately siding with those who see the myths as Plato's expressions of truths inexpressible in rational discourse.

[56] This contrast is often expressed in terms of λόγος and μῦθος. While Plato does, at times, draw a distinction between these two forms of discourse, his use of these words is far from systematic, which creates serious problems for those modern scholars who try to maintain a radical dichotomy. Zaslavsky's classification of Plato's myths simply by the presence or absence of a form of the word μῦθος shows the absurd lengths to which this dichotomy may be taken. (Zaslavsky 1981.)

in general. Plato seeks to co-opt the traditionally authoritative mythic discourse in service of his own philosophic projects.[57] The failure to understand Plato's use of myths, I would argue, weakens any understanding of the dialogues in which they are placed. Like Aristophanes and the creators of the gold tablets, Plato makes use of the underworld journey to present a model of the world, playing off the contrasts between this world and the other world. But whereas the gold tablets place the deceased on the margins of society and Aristophanes redefines the center of Athenian society, Plato makes a more complex move, separating out the philosopher from the mainstream but relocating the philosopher at the center as the ideal citizen. For such an audacious project, Plato needs not only to make use of the traditionally authoritative discourse of myth but to subvert it and subsume it under the guidance of philosophy as he defines it in his dialogues. In the myth of the *Phaedo*, Plato manipulates the tale of the underworld journey to present the life and death of the philosopher and illustrate his superior position with respect to the cosmos and the other types of people in it.

### THE ENDS OF THE ROAD

In this study, then, I analyze the use of myth in Aristophanes' *Frogs*, the Orphic gold tablets, and the *Phaedo* of Plato, exploring the ways in which each author's use of myth reflects the renegotiation of societal boundaries. These texts represent different productions of *bricolage* by authors manipulating a common set of traditional elements for a variety of ends. Aristophanes uses his myth of a journey to the other world, made comically quotidian, to talk about the problems of contemporary Athens. The Orphic tablets emphasize the *déviance* of the deceased from mainstream society in their use of the underworld journey story, while Plato uses it to argue, in a variety of ways, for the importance of practicing philosophy. While these texts share a common set of traditional mythic elements, the meaning of each differs dramatically according to the agenda of its author.

Not only does understanding the differences among these myths provide a better understanding of the individual texts, but the analysis sheds light upon the Greeks' use of their mythic tradition. These myths are

---

[57] As Brisson notes, "Si Platon s'intéresse tant au mythe, c'est qu'il veut en briser le monopole pour imposer le type de discours qu'il entend développer, c'est-à-dire le discours philosophique." (Brisson 1982, p. 110.)

neither solemn religious dogma nor entertaining childish nonsense, but rather they are competing forms of authoritative cultural discourse. Each author uses the richly evocative mythic elements to make specific points, but this use of the traditional elements validates the perspective of the world that the teller presents and lends authority to the text through the very familiarity of the elements. Each teller competes with alternative versions for the authority of the tradition; but Plato, Aristophanes, and the creators of the tablets manipulate the traditional elements with varying degrees of reflection upon the workings of mythic discourse and the impact of their tellings upon the later tradition; Plato, Aristophanes, and the gold tablets make use of myth in a way that is neither simple nor single, and an examination of their different paths illuminates the contestive process of myth-telling in Greek culture.

## 2 | Roadmaps of Déviance: The 'Orphic' Gold Tablets

### INTRODUCTION

> Pure I come from the pure, Queen of those below the earth,
> and Eukles and Eubouleus and the other immortal gods;
> For I claim that I am of your blessed race.[1]

So boasts the deceased woman of Thurii on a gold tablet buried with her, identifying not only herself, but her antecedents as worthy. This enigmatic tablet, similar to others found throughout the margins of the Greek world, from Thessaly to southern Italy and Crete, has piqued the interest of scholars ever since its discovery in 1879. Although the tablet proclaims the identity and lineage of the deceased woman with whom it was buried, the identity and lineage of the tablets themselves — what sorts of religious phenomena they represent and where they come from — remain largely mysterious. These so-called Orphic gold tablets present one of the most intriguing puzzles in the study of Greek religious beliefs. In all the graves from classical antiquity excavated by modern scholars, fewer than twenty examples have been found of these enigmatic pieces of gold foil inscribed with instructions for the deceased in the afterlife.

In contrast to gold tablets that are simply blank or contain only the name of the deceased or a dedication "To Persephone and Plouto," the nearly twenty tablets with sizable inscriptions evoke a narrative; they present a piece of the story of the deceased's journey to the underworld and her encounter with the powers there.[2] An analysis of the way in which

---

[1] ἔρχομαι ἐκ κοθαρ(ῶν) κοθαρά, χθονί(ων) βασίλεια, Εὐκλῆς Εὐβουλεύς τε καὶ ἀθάνατοι θεοὶ ἄλλοι· καὶ γὰρ ἐγὼν ὑμῶν γένος ὄλβιον εὔχομαι εἶμεν. Dates and locations for all the gold tablets considered here may be found in the appendix at the end of this chapter.

[2] cp. the Pella tablet inscribed with the lines, Φερσεφόνηι Ποσείδιππος μύστης εὐσεβής, and another that simply has the name of the deceased, Φιλοξένα. At Aigion, three tablets have

29

the myth of the underworld journey is used in these tablets can reveal much about the mysterious religious context in which these tablets were produced. Each of the tablets presents, albeit in fragmentary form, a tale of the deceased's journey to the realm of the dead. In this chapter, I analyze these narratives through the nexus of obstacle, solution, and result. I review the problems that have plagued the scholarship on the tablets, most importantly the assumption of a single Orphic background, and I suggest that the tablets and the religious phenomena they represent can be better understood as a whole if the texts are examined individually with attention to the variations of detail. Such an analysis reveals the various ways in which the tablets use the traditional pattern of the journey to the underworld to express a protest against the mainstream of polis society.

## Placing the Gold Tablets

Since the publication of the Thurii tablets by Comparetti in 1879, scholars of Greek religion and myth have argued over the meaning and significance of the tablets, most often attributing them to an Orphic religious context.[3] Although the Petelia tablet was published decades earlier in 1836, Comparetti was the first to postulate an Orphic context for it and to associate it with the newly discovered Thurii tablets.[4] After Comparetti's publications, the most influential early interpretations were those of Albrecht Dieterich, Erwin Rohde, and Gilbert Murray in Jane Harrison's *Prolegomena to Greek Religion*.[5] The collected texts of all the tablets then discovered were published by Comparetti and Olivieri, and Comparetti's Orphic interpretation was codified into the standard interpretation by the texts'

---

been found, inscribed Δεξίλαος μύστας; Φίλων μύστας; and simply, μύστης. In Macedonian Methone, a tablet was found in the mouth of the deceased, inscribed with her name, Φυλομάγα. See Dickie 1995. Guarducci 1985 mentions another tablet found in Crete, [Πλού]τωνι καὶ Φ[ερσ]οπόνει χαίρεν. Comparetti included this text in his 1910 edition, cp. n. 6. Several other graves with tablets in the mouths of the deceased have been discovered, but the tablets have only the name of the deceased. All these texts have now been collected and published in Bernabé and Jiménez 2001, pp. 279–280.

3 Comparetti 1879.

4 Comparetti 1882. The earlier publications of the Petelia tablet debated whether the tablet pertained to the Trophonios oracle at Lebedeia or was a Pythian oracle regarding the Trophonios oracle. cp. Franz 1836; Goettling 1843.

5 Dieterich 1891, 1893; Rohde 1925 (German 1st ed. vol. 2 in 1894); Gilbert, Murray *apud* Harrison 1991 (reprint of 1922 3rd ed., 1st ed. in 1903), p. 667ff.

inclusion in the collections of Kern and Diels.[6] However, Zuntz's 1971 edition and commentary on the tablets challenged many of the accepted notions about them, although his efforts to argue for a sharp dichotomy between the religious background of the texts and the Dionysiac mysteries have been fatally undermined by the discovery of the Hipponion and Pelinna tablets.[7] Despite the biases against 'Orphic superstition' which he brings to the interpretation, however, Zuntz's philologically acute reexamination of the tablet texts remains the foundation for all subsequent work on the tablets, including the recent publications of the tablet texts by Pugliese Caratelli, Riedweg, and Bernabé and Jiménez.[8]

One of the primary problems facing scholar's investigating the tablets is the lack of any contemporary literary evidence for the phenomenon. No author contemporary with the gold tablets seems to mention them, even though they range in date from the fifth century BCE to the third century CE. Clearly, these tablets are evidence for a religious tradition that had a long life but was outside of the mainstream, either marginal or so secret that no mention could be made of it. But what sort of religious tradition could have produced these tablets? The archaeological evidence provides little context, so the tablets themselves must be analyzed for clues to the issues and ideas that were important to their creators.[9]

The gold tablets bear some resemblance to the lead curse tablets, since both are some kind of metal lamella, usually folded and inscribed with a text and frequently found buried with bodies. Moreover, contrary to the assertion of Zuntz and others that the lead tablets are a later

---

[6] Comparetti 1910; Olivieri 1915; Kern 1922; Diels 1907. Until the publication of Bernabé's forthcoming new edition, Kern remains the standard reference for all evidence pertaining to Orphism, even though the parameters of what is considered Orphic have shifted since his publication. Fragments from his collection will be referred to as OF#, testimonia as OT#.

[7] Zuntz 1971.

[8] Pugliese Carratelli 1993 and 2001. Pugliese Carratelli's editions have texts, Italian translations and some commentary, but he provides no critical apparatus for the texts. The 2001 edition includes the most recents finds from Pherai and central Sicily but is missing many of the beautiful color photos from the 1993 edition. Riedweg 1998 includes all these texts with a critical apparatus, grouping the texts according to Zuntz's classification. The new edition of Bernabé and Jiménez 2001 includes texts with critical apparatus and a translation into Spanish of all of the tablets. This edition also contains extensive commentary on each of the tablets, but it is marred, in my opinion, by the authors' reliance on the 'Zagreus myth' as the central dogma of Orphism to which most of the details of the tablet texts should be referred.

[9] Bottini 1992 brings together the archaeological reports on the findings of the tablets, esp. pp. 27–62, 125–135.

phenomenon, a degeneration into superstition, the earliest lead tablets date from the fifth century BCE, approximately the same period as the gold lamellae.[10] Nevertheless, the Orphic gold tablets differ from both the lead curse defixiones and other lamellae of gold and silver because they contain a narrative, a mythic tale of the deceased's journey after death, and these narratives provide clues to the meaning and function of the tablets that the other tablets cannot provide.[11] The texts on the Orphic tablets depict the journey of the deceased to the underworld, providing details of the concepts of the afterlife for which these tablets were preparing the deceased. Although the earliest of these tablets can be dated to the fifth century BCE, they seem to come from an older tradition since even the oldest examples show errors in the copying of the texts, omissions, and confusions in the meter of what must have originally been hexameter poetry. The tablets therefore seem to be part of a tradition that quite possibly stems from an oral source.[12] The varying ways in which the familiar story of the underworld journey is told in these tablets reveal the concerns of those who shaped the story.

Many scholars have looked to earlier parallels in other cultures to shed light on these Greek gold tablets. Zuntz, for example, compares the themes and mythic motifs found in the gold tablets with certain spells found in the Egyptian Books of the Dead.[13] Kotansky also draws attention to the

[10] "The bright and imperishable metal no doubt was chosen to symbolize the perpetuity of life, just as its opposite, the dark and heavy lead, was used to promote destruction and death. It does not, in fact, seem unreasonable to assume that the 'Orphic' lamellae were consciously devised as a positive counterpart to the traditional *defixiones*. This new departure implies a new attitude to death and after-life." (Zuntz 1971, pp. 285–286.) Kotansky, however, notes, "Many scholars insist that in both cases we can see an earthly (re)application of protective incantations designed (originally) for the afterlife, either as a result of a conscious and outright 'theft' of the religious material or as the result of a long period of degeneration of the 'pure' religion whence it came. Unfortunately our earliest examples of these allegedly secondary creations are often contemporaneous with the earliest evidence for the alleged religious 'prototypes.' (Kotansky 1991, p. 122.)

[11] The narrative text, this myth of an underworld journey, does not mean that these tablets were not used as amulets in the way that other lamellae were used, but these texts provide an unusual opportunity to examine the set of beliefs that underlie the construction of these amulets.

[12] cp. Janko 1984, esp. pp. 90–91; 97–98, on the oral transmission of the tablet texts. Zuntz 1971, pp. 339–343.

[13] Zuntz 1971, pp. 370–376. cp. Merkelbach 1999. Tom Dousa has provided a more informed examination of the parallels and divergences between the gold tablets and the Egyptian material in an unpublished paper presented at a conference on the gold tablets at the

mostly uninscribed gold and silver tablets found in ornate amulet cases in Sardinia and other Punic sites.[14] The cultures that produced these artifacts were certainly in contact with Greek culture, and the exchange of ideas between cultures is not only possible but probable. A search for specific origins, however, not only would prove fruitless because of the lack of evidence about direct contacts but also would reveal very little about the significance of these texts for the people who produced and used them. Even if ideas were borrowed or if forms were influential, the fact, for example, that the deceased requests water in the Egyptian Books of the Dead does not explain the deceased's request for water from the lake of Memory in some of the gold tablets. Instead, a comparative analysis of the use of mythic elements in the tablets themselves reveals the issues and ideas most important to those who produced the texts (the authors) and those who chose to be buried with them (the audience). Those who produced and used the tablets (except for the latest tablet, A5), remain entirely anonymous, giving neither their own names nor that of the community from which they came. These texts, however, like all texts, were produced in a context – by someone for someone.

Unfortunately, the question of author and audience is extremely vexed by the enormous gaps in the evidence. The primary audience for the tablet is obviously the deceased herself,[15] since the tablet contains instructions for her after death. The religious community, in its funeral ritual, provides the text, shaping its form according to the ideas considered most important. Insofar as the deceased is a member of the group, she is herself involved in the authorship of the text that is given to her, and perhaps not only to her but to group members before and after her. Furthermore, insofar as the group is applying to all its members the ideas of the text it puts in the graves of its members, the group is itself the audience of the text. The complete lack of evidence about such a community, however, precludes any firm conclusions being drawn about it. The group responsible

Chicago Humanities Institute in December 1997. Zuntz 1971 also looks at Mesopotamian parallels, pp. 387–392.

[14] Kotansky 1991, p. 114, nn. 55–58.

[15] Rather than use the clumsy he/she, the confusing alternation of masculine and feminine forms, or the traditional masculine pronoun as a non-gender-specific term to signify either a male or female deceased, I will use the feminine form when referring to the audience in the tablets in general to highlight the fact that a majority of the deceased appear to be female (see further below). In cases in which I am specifically referring to a tablet with a male deceased, I will, however, use the masculine form.

for the production of any particular tablet might have come from the most aristocratic elite or the most oppressed poor and could have ranged in size from a well-organized and sizable sect to a charismatic Orpheotelest with a single follower.[16] Throughout this analysis, therefore, I consider the one member of the group for whom there is evidence – the deceased. Since the deceased represents the group, the conclusions from my analysis about the deceased should apply also to whatever kind of community of which the deceased was a part.

By making the deceased the protagonist of the narrative, the community defines itself through its representative, the deceased. The narrative of the journey to the other world thus serves as a means of self-definition for the members of the group in that it sets forth the special qualifications and privileges that set them apart from others. In contrast to an ordinary grave marker, which is designed for public viewing, the tablets are meant to be seen only by the deceased and those who buried her. Whereas a grave monument serves, Sourvinou-Inwood notes, as an "articulation of the deceased's social persona and preservation of his memory through the grave monument," the tablet instead articulates the deceased's identity not in public, socio-political terms, but through the appeal to standards meaningful to the deceased personally.[17] The narrative of these texts always results in the deceased's achieving a favorable afterlife because of the kind of person she is. The traditional mythic elements are manipulated to describe how she is privileged, different from the ordinary folk who do not know, for example, to claim that they are of the race of the gods or to choose the spring of Memory. The mythic elements in the tablet texts are undoubtedly drawn from other tellings of the traditional tale of the underworld journey, but each tablet produces different meanings and significances for these elements by the way they are deployed in the texts.

### The Approach: Obstacle–Solution–Result

The texts all contain instructions for the deceased after death: "Do not even go near this spring" or "Tell Persephone that Bacchios himself has

---

[16] cp. Burkert's descriptions of the possible compositions of such religious movements in Burkert 1982 *passim*. Guthrie 1952 (p. 148ff.) presumes the Orphic movement originated with the lower social classes, whereas Musti 1984 (p. 75) argues that such groups must have begun among the aristocracy and filtered down the social scale.

[17] Sourvinou-Inwood 1995, p. 180; cp. her analysis of the ways in which the grave marker appeals to the standards of the community, pp. 170–180.

freed you." The very fact that the deceased needs these instructions implies a narrative of the deceased's journey to the underworld and the confrontation of the deceased with some sort of difficulty or obstacle in this journey. Clearly, the purpose of these tablets is to provide a solution to whatever difficulty or obstacle is envisioned for the person after death. The deceased is buried with the gold tablet because it was believed, by the deceased or those who buried her, that the solution provided by the tablet would allow her to obtain a desirable result in her journey after death. My analysis of these tablets will consider these three crucial aspects of the texts of the tablets: the obstacle that the deceased faces, the solution provided by the tablet, and the result that the deceased hopes to obtain. The analysis of these three aspects reveals the ways in which those who created and used these tablets conceived of themselves and their relation to the world around them, resulting in an understanding of the religious contexts that produced the tablets that a mere *Quellenforschung* could not uncover.

In my analysis of the gold tablets, I examine two different complexes of obstacle–solution–result that form the crux of the text. The first complex seems common to all the tablets: the confrontation with the powers of the underworld. I follow Zuntz's division of the tablets into A and B series, based on textual similarities, with the addition of the tablets from Pelinna (the P tablets) and the tablet from Pherai, all of which were discovered after Zuntz's edition.[18] The A and P tablets all have confrontation with Persephone as the obstacle, whereas the B tablets have nameless guardians, but the basic type of obstacle is nevertheless the same. The solution to this obstacle in each case is a proclamation of identity by the deceased, and the result of the successful solution is some favorable status in the other world; but the specifics of the obstacle, solution, and result differ from tablet to tablet. The longer B texts (B1, B2, B10, B11), however, present another obstacle to resolve before the deceased can confront the powers of the underworld. The first task on these tablets is for the deceased to find her way in the underworld to the correct spring where the guardians wait. The solution provided by the tablets is to persist until reaching the second spring, with the result that the deceased obtains a drink from the water of Memory. The obstacles, solutions, and results described in the gold tablets all derive from traditional elements of the underworld

[18] Riedweg 1998 makes a similar classification, but Pugliese Caratelli 1993 and 2001, Colli 1977, Kern 1922, Janko 1984, and Bernabé and Jiménez 2001 all use different sets of sigla. See the appendix at end of the chapter for a chart of the tablets and sigla.

journey tale, but the tablets represent different works of *bricolage* with these mythic elements.

Similarity is, of course, essential for comparison, and the similarities among the texts of the gold tablets have caused them to be grouped as a single phenomenon, the Orphic gold tablets, just as the similarity in the pattern of action among the gold tablet texts and various other texts have caused them all to be grouped as underworld journeys. However, the fact of similarity itself provides little information about the individual tablets and the beliefs of those who produced and used them. The differences among the tablets provide the most information about the significant issues in the tablets. Since the texts show signs of oral transmission, the act of inscribing of the tablets was not simply a matter of copying, more or less perfectly, from a single set form.[19] Rather, the verses on the tablets were reformulated each time they were inscribed, according to how much was remembered and what was felt to be most important to fit onto the tiny gold leaf. The analysis of the differences among the gold tablets reveals the issues about which the producers of the tablets were most concerned. While the narratives in the tablets all use traditional mythic elements to envision some sort of obstacle, pose some sort of solution, and forecast some sort of result, the different obstacles, solutions, and results that are described in the tablets reveal the different conceptions about the afterlife, the different agendas and eschatological hopes.

Previous scholars have generally presumed that the religious beliefs underlying the tablets were uniform.[20] Their concern has been more to define the single background of these tablets in contrast to other types of Greek religious practice than to analyze the specific ideas that the individual tablets express. However, this assumption of a single background causes scholars to miss important nuances in the beliefs underlying the tablets and produces a false picture of the contexts that produced them. The problem is not just that a single background has been assumed, but that a *certain* single background has been assumed. As noted above, the similarity of the form of the tablets and the use of common motifs have caused scholars to lump all the tablets into a single group, usually termed

---

[19] cp. Janko 1984 and Zuntz 1971, note 12 above.

[20] Zuntz 1971 points to some differences between the specific tablets, as does Graf 1993a, see further below. Pugliese Carratelli draws a distinction between the tablets that mention Mnemosyne and those that do not (Pugliese Carratelli 1993, pp. 11ff., cp. 2001, pp. 23ff.)

'the Orphic gold tablets'. The label 'Orphic' for these tablets implies that a certain kind of context has been presumed – Orphic gold tablets must come from some Orphic context, must have been produced by some group of Orphics, or must exhibit characteristics of Orphism. The interpretation of the tablets is thus linked to the definition of Orphism, one of the most controversial and difficult problems in the study of Greek religion.

## Orphic Controversies

I shall have to traverse ground which has been churned to deep and slippery mud by the heavy feet of contending scholars; ground, also, where those in a hurry are liable to trip over the partially decayed remains of dead theories that have not yet been decently interred. We shall be wise, then, to move slowly, and to pick our steps rather carefully among the litter.[21]

Dodds' warning is no less apt for the scholar of today than it was nearly half a century ago. The very definition of Orphism remains contested, and the debates over the religious beliefs associated with it are far from settled. I will briefly review the history of modern scholarship on Orphism, noting the important controversies that have defined the debate. While the earlier scholarship tried to define Orphism as a religious movement, using models based more or less implicitly upon a Christian (and specifically Protestant) model, more recent specialists in the field have produced definitions of Orphism and related religious movements that better account for the evidence without indulging in reconstructions that owe more to Christian theological speculations than to evidence of ancient Greek religious practice.

The history of modern Orphic scholarship begins with Lobeck's *Aglaophamus* (1829), in which he assembled many of the testimonia regarding Orpheus and the poems and rituals associated with him. This study criticized the reverence for the divine wisdom of Orpheus that went back to the neoplatonic commentaries.[22] After *Aglaophamus*, a variety of scholars explored Orphism as the remnant of the primitive religious customs of the Greeks, but the discovery of the Thurii gold tablets in 1879 marked the real turning point for the scholarly notions of Orphism.

---

[21] Dodds 1951, p. 136.

[22] As Burkert comments, "Lobeck's book marks the waning of metaphysical interest, the triumph of historicism combined with rationalism; there are no sublime secrets left, but only primitive tales and customs." (Burkert 1977, p. 1.)

Comparetti saw the tablets as evidence for an Orphic religion centered on salvation from the Original Sin that burdens mankind as the result of the Titans' murder of Dionysos Zagreus. This interpretation, which was without precedent in the scholarship, quickly became the foundation for debates regarding the nature of Orphism.[23] The influence of Orphism on the pre-Constantinian early Christian church was an important issue in these debates. Of special concern was whether Orphism was more akin to the pure and spiritual (i.e., Protestant) early Church or whether Orphism was part of the pagan ritual complex adopted by the later (Catholic) Church.[24] Some saw Orphism in terms of an organized religion very like Christianity, with doctrines and scriptures and congregations. This was viewed either as a religious development within Greece that foreshadowed the spirituality of Christianity or as an invasion from outside, a "drop of foreign blood" as Rohde called it, into the world of Homeric Greek religion.[25] This picture of an Orphic church, however, was called into question by Wilamowitz and his successors, such as Linforth and Zuntz.[26] Linforth indeed limits the definition of Orphism to only those texts bearing the name of Orpheus himself, thus ruling out the gold tablets along with a good many other documents and practices that had been considered Orphic. While Linforth's skepticism represents the extreme, the Judaeo–Christian model of an Orphic church has rightly been discarded by scholars.[27]

As the controversy over the definition of Orphism has become more complex, scholars have also attempted to place the gold tablets in relation to religious currents similar to Orphism but somewhat more securely

---

[23] I have discussed Comparetti's innovation and the place of the Zagreus myth in the scholarship of the late nineteenth and early twentieth centuries in my "Tearing Apart the Zagreus Myth: A Few Disparaging Remarks on Orphism and Original Sin." (Edmonds 1999.)

[24] cp. Smith 1990 for the impact of Protestant anti-Catholic polemic in the history of the study of mystery religions and the early Church.

[25] Rohde 1895, p. 27.

[26] von Wilamowitz-Moellendorff 1932, pp. 182–207; Linforth 1941; Zuntz 1971. cp. Burkert's comments, "It is easy to dwell on the motives that have dominated the scholarly controversies about Orphism: on the one side the craving for a more spiritual, quasi-Christian religion with a 'church' and a saviour god; on the other, the irritated reaction of the 'pure' Hellenists against this 'drop of foreign blood'." (Burkert 1982, p. 2.)

[27] As Dodds puts it, "I cannot help suspecting that 'the historic Orphic Church,' as it appears, e.g., in Toynbee's *Study of History*, V. 84ff., will one day be quoted as a classic example of the kind of historical mirage which arises when men unknowingly project their own preoccupations into the distant past." (Dodds 1951, p. 170, n. 88.)

attested: Pythagoreanism, Dionysism, and the Eleusinian Mysteries. Since the Eleusinian Mysteries are the best known example of a mystery religion in ancient Greece, some scholars have attempted to explain features of the obscure gold tablets by postulating influence from the more famous cult. Picard and Boyancé suggest that the wide diffusion of the tablets must be due to the influence of a long-standing, organized mystery cult such as that at Eleusis.[28] While contact between the Eleusinian Mysteries and the religious groups that created the tablets is entirely plausible, not all mystery cults in the Greek world owed their ideas to Eleusis. Other scholars, indeed, deny that the individualistic religion of the tablets (and Orphism) ever had anything to do with the state-sponsored cult at Eleusis.[29]

The issue of the connection between the gold tablets and Dionysiac religion has also been hotly debated. Orphism was seen by Rohde as an offshoot of Dionysiac religion, while Harrison saw the Orphism of the tablets as a Puritanic protest against the ecstatic and sensuous Dionysiac rituals.[30] Nilsson, among other scholars, even sees Orpheus as a kind of martyr to a new and purer religion.[31] Here again the implicit models of Christianity can be found, in however moderate a form: Harrison's championing in a Nietzschean spirit the deeply felt Dionysiac rituals, with their primitive power, against the puritanical Orphic religion is as full of world resentment as Nietzsche's idea of Christianity. Nilsson, from the opposite perspective, compares Orpheus to the Christian martyrs and thus, implicitly, Orpheus's religion of asceticism to the pure and spiritual Christian church that replaced the old pagan superstitions.

The same sort of division occurs when the ideas in the tablets are compared with Pythagoreanism. Zuntz contrasts the pure asceticism of

---

[28] "La seule explication possible de la diffusion des tablettes dites orphiques, [c'est] celle de leur origine éleusinienne." Boyancé's response, p. 130, in Picard 1961, pp. 127–30. Picard himself says, "Il s'agit de talismans d'initiation, propres à régler le voyage et le comportement après la mort dans le monde infernal, pour les initiés seulement d'une religion officielle, durablement armée en ses affirmations doctrinales et ses interdits, pendant de nombreux siècles." cp. Bernabé and Jiménez 2001, pp. 234–242, who use the same reasoning to label the tablets 'Orphic'.

[29] Rohde sees Eleusis and its eschatology as fundamentally different from the ideas of immortality deriving from Dionysiac cult and Orphism. The former derives from the traditional worship of the ancestral dead, while the latter is a later idea stemming from ecstatic practices. (Rohde 1925, passim, esp. pp. 217–235.)

[30] "The grace [the Orphic] sought was not physical intoxication but spiritual ecstasy, the means he adopted not drunkenness but abstinence and rites of purification." (Harrison 1991, p. 476.)

[31] cp. Nilsson 1935.

Pythagoreanism that he finds in the tablets with the superstition and savagery of Orphic and Dionysiac religion. Zuntz constantly denigrates the possibility of any influence of Orphic or Dionysiac ideas on the tablets because he sees the tablets as a survival of a strain of primitive Mediterranean goddess religion that found an exalted expression in the philosophy of Pythagoras. He contrasts the religious spirit of the tablets to the magical curses and other inscriptions found on similar lead tablets and on papyri.[32]

This contrast between magic and religion is one of the ways in which the contrast between good religion (spiritual, pure, and Protestant) and bad religion (emotional, savage, and Catholic) is frequently drawn.[33] Modern scholars such as Kotansky and Kingsley have argued against such a dichotomy in interpreting the tablets. As Kotansky notes, "The language of prayer in magic texts indicates normative religious sentiments and values and vitiates the supposed antithetical dichotomy between 'magic' and 'religion' still expressed or tacitly assumed by scholars still unduly influenced by the antiquated anthropological views of Sir James Frazer."[34] As Dodds predicted, the "partially decayed remains of dead theories that have not yet been decently interred" continue to obstruct the interpretations of the gold tablets and the contexts from which they come.

### Replacing 'Orphism'

Recent scholars have sought to define Orphism in ways that take into account all the various pieces of evidence without forcing them into

---

[32] "Viewed against this background the Gold Leaves retain their primary religious character, even though the clarity and profundity of the original conception appears now to be dimmed by a penumbra of superstition." (Zuntz 1971, p. 354.)

[33] Zuntz even makes the comparison to Catholicism explicit. In discussing the proliferation of the tablets as a later degeneration of their true religious spirit, he remarks: "One cannot but conclude that these lamellae were articles of a local mass-production; objects of a beadle's trade like the picture of the Madonna and of saints sold at Roman Catholic churches. This fact is significant enough, for it implies that they came to be appreciated as material objects rather than as carriers of the words engraved upon them." (Zuntz 1971, p. 353.) Other scholars are less blatant; cp., e.g., Guthrie 1952, p. 172, or Harrison 1991, p. 584.

[34] Kotansky 1991, p. 122. cp. Kingsley 1995, pp. 312–313. One should note that Rohde argued against this dichotomy over a hundred years ago, "To attribute the practical side of Orphism to a late degeneration of the once purely speculative character of sect (as many have done) is a very arbitrary proceeding and quite unjustifiable on historical grounds.... The Orphic sect from the very beginning derived its strength from its *telestic* and *kathartic* practices." (Rohde 1925, n. 14, p. 351.)

a model based on Christian preconceptions of what a religion should be. As West comments in the introduction to his treatment of the Orphic poems, "It is a fallacy to suppose that all 'Orphic' poems and rituals are related to each other or that they are to be interpreted as different manifestations of a single religious movement.... There was no doctrinal criterion for ascription to Orpheus, and no copyright restriction. It was a device for conferring antiquity and authority upon a text that stood in need of them."[35] In these definitions, Orphism thus appears as one example of a type of countercultural religious movement that sets itself in opposition to the mainstream religion in ancient Greece.

Defining countercultural religion in the context of a religious system like the ancient Greek, which had no real orthodoxy as it is understood in the Judaeo-Christian tradition, is admittedly problematic. As Sourvinou-Inwood has argued, however, the primary religious system of Greek culture in the Classical period must be understood in relation to the primary form of social organization, the polis.[36] The mainstream religion of the Greek polis in the Classical period was part of what J. Z. Smith has termed a 'locative' world view. "At the center of these religions were complex systems governing the interrelationships between gods and men, individuals and the state, living men and their ancestors. The entire cosmos was conceived as a vast network of relationships, each component of which, whether divine or human, must know its place and fulfill its appointed role."[37] The religious expressions of polis religion, including myths and rituals, provide models of these relationships, rearticulating the order on every level from the personal to the community to the entire cosmos.[38]

---

[35] West 1983, p. 3. cp. Burkert's comments about the practitioners of Orphic rituals: "Thus we should not expect consistency of beliefs or even dogmas; each individual would select, adopt, and discard according to the exigencies of his career." (Burkert 1982, p. 10.)

[36] "The Greek polis articulated religion and was itself articulated by it; religion became the polis' central ideology, structuring, and giving meaning to, all the elements that made up the identity of the polis, its past, its physical landscape, the relationship between its constituent parts. Ritual reinforces group solidarity, and this process is of fundamental importance in establishing and perpetuating civic and cultural, as well as religious, identities." (Sourvinou-Inwood 1987, pp. 304–305.)

[37] Smith 1974, p. 750.

[38] As Sourvinou-Inwood puts it: "Greek religion is, above all, a way of articulating the world, of structuring chaos and making it intelligible; it is a model articulating a cosmic order guaranteed by a divine order which also (in complex ways) grounds human order, perceived to be incarnated above all in the properly ordered and pious polis, and providing certain rules and prescriptions of behaviour, especially towards the divine through cult, but also towards the human world." (Sourvinou-Inwood 1987, pp. 301–302.)

The proper maintenance of these relationships comprised the primary religious activities in the Greek polis.

The standard Greek rituals of sacrifice provide perhaps the best example of this locative religious phenomenon.[39] In the sacrifice, humans depict their relations with the gods, giving them offerings consisting of the inedible parts of the sacrificial animal. These offerings are burned and rise to the heavens as smoke, the scent of which is pleasing to the gods. The edible parts are carefully apportioned according to the ritual standing of the various people participating in the sacrifice. The unequal division of the sacrificial animal between gods and man illustrates the fundamental separation between these two types of entities, while the unity of the sacrificing group of humans is asserted by their sharing of the meat.[40] At the same time, the distinctions in social status among the community are reaffirmed through the distribution of the various parts of the animal. In the ritual, everyone is categorized, placed into an appropriate spot in the hierarchical order, ranging from the most honored deities to the lowest, most marginal person in the human social order.[41]

This locative order of Greek polis religion is by no means entirely static since not only does every myth or ritual permit some subtle shiftings of the order but the system has some built-in opportunities for the reformation of the order. Rites of passage such as initiations, weddings, and funerals are all designed to mark the transfer of an individual in the society from one category to another.[42] Certain festivals, moreover, often those

[39] Rituals of sacrifice in Greek religion have been the subject of many excellent studies, of which Bowie 1995 provides a nice overview. He cites the regulations regarding sacrificial portions in Leges Sacrae 60.7–17 as an example of the hierarchically organized distribution of portions.

[40] Hesiod tells the myth of the foundation of sacrifice as an explanation of this fundamental separation of men and gods, the start of the unequal relations wherein humans must honor the superior gods who nevertheless make life difficult for mankind. Hesiod, W&D 45–105 and Theogony 535–616; cp. the analyses by Vernant 1990, pp. 183–201, and Detienne and Vernant 1989, pp. 21–86.

[41] "A ceremony is the enactment of a concept. Through ceremonies persons are classified and placed in categories; their analogical unity with similar persons is asserted. Persons are thus rescued from the flux of nature and purified as they are given a definite standing in the cultural pattern." (Redfield 1994, pp. 162–163.)

[42] "Culture is a moral order. To each role belong determinate claims and obligations. We do not merely understand social structure; we rely on it. It is legitimate . . . The 'chromaticism' of initiations is therefore appropriately monstrous; the initiation evokes a kind of moral terror. The rules are being changed. At the same time, the community demonstrates by its power to control these monsters that it is above the rules – or more accurately, that

associated with Dionysos but also including the Kronia and Thesmophoria, mark a temporary suspension of the normal order that reinforces the normal order upon its restoration but also creates the opportunity for a renegotiation of that order during its suspension.[43]

While some, especially those whose place in this locative order is central and privileged, have an interest in affirming this order that supports their lives, others, including those who are relegated to the margins, may find the normal order oppressive and seek some way of escape from its strictures. Such people set themselves up against the normal order of the culture, transgressing the boundaries by their unusual behavior. As Detienne has pointed out, such abnormal ways of living may be hyper-cultural as well as subcultural: the excessive purity of the Pythagoreans is as much a protest against the normal order as the bestial behavior of the Cynics.[44] The religious lunatic fringe, as it were, consists of those who take otherwise acceptable religious practices to an excess. Hippolytus's complete refusal of sexual relations and singleminded devotion to a single deity provokes his father's condemnation, while the neurotic practices of Theophrastus's deisidaimonic man, who must have several purifications each day and is endlessly looking for omens and oracles, brings him the scorn of mainstream society. Note, however, that *déviance* is relative; not every person who resisted the normal order went to such extremes. Theophrastus's caricature shows that the degree of *déviance* might be fairly small and that many who made use of these extraordinary religious options could nevertheless remain for the most part within traditional, normative Greek social and religious practices.[45]

Since the current order that governs their society is unsatisfactory to them, these marginal, countercultural figures appeal to a different standard to evaluate themselves and their society, one centered not on the existing pattern but on an ideal pattern located elsewhere in space or time. Most familiar perhaps is the idea of a golden age, a primordial time in which the defining features of the contemporary world are not

---

the rules include rules for changing the rules. They form a moral meta-order." (Redfield 1990, p. 122.)

[43] Sabbatucci 1979, p. 51, on the role of Dionysos. cp. Versnel 1986 on the Kronia (pp. 121–152).

[44] Detienne 1979, pp. 53–95, Detienne and Vernant 1989, pp. 1–21. cp. Vernant 1990, pp. 143–182.

[45] Contra Detienne, who portrays Orphic renunciation as absolute and total rejection of normal civic life. cp., e.g., Detienne 2003, pp. 155–156.

present – no separation between men and gods or men and animals, no need to work, no bloodshed or sickness or death, etc.[46] Alternatively, this ideal may be elsewhere, not in time but in space – in the other world of the dead, beyond the western horizon, on the other side of the moon, etc. To live one's life according to the pattern of this utopian ideal instead of the normal, quotidian order is an attempt to escape from the strictures imposed by ordinary life.

Plato refers to this kind of lifelong protest as the 'Orphic life', βίος Ὀρφικός. This Orphic life replicates the way of life described in the traditional tales of the golden age: "Men abstained from flesh on the grounds that it was impious to eat it or to stain the altars of the gods with blood. It was a kind of Orphic life, as it is called, that was led by those of our kind who were alive at that time, taking freely of all things that had no life, but abstaining from all that had life."[47] The Orphic life is a rejection of the ordinary way of living governed by the customs and hierarchies of the polis society in favor of living in accordance with the ideal of the golden age, free from violence and bloodshed.

The life of the Pythagorean seems to be conducted along similar lines. The Pythagoreans engage on a daily basis in the prohibitions, offerings, and practices appropriate to special ceremonies.[48] Such a mode of life is conducted in opposition to the normal way of living, marking the Pythagoreans as countercultural, even marginal members of the society. As Burkert notes, the fragments of Attic comedy attest to the contempt lavished upon these strange folk by the other members of society.[49]

---

[46] The canonical formulation is in Hesiod's description of the life of the golden race, W&D 109ff.

[47] σαρκῶν δ' ἀπείχοντο ὡς οὐχ ὅσιον ὂν ἐσθίειν οὐδὲ τοὺς τῶν θεῶν βωμοὺς αἵματι μιαίνειν, ἀλλὰ Ὀρφικοί τινες λεγόμενοι βίοι ἐγίγνοντο ἡμῶν τοῖς τότε. ἀψύχων μὲν ἐχόμενοι πάντων, ἐμψύχων δὲ τοὐναντίον πάντων ἀπεχόμενοι. Laws 782c; cp. Aristophanes' Frogs 1032, where Orpheus is listed among the culture heroes as the one who taught men to abstain from bloodshed.

[48] As Burkert describes it: "The Pythagoreans were left with their acusmata applying no longer to festivals but to normal life, which, as a consequence, seemed to others abnormal. Prohibitions like those of beans, heart, certain fishes, and baths are now absolute and must be observed at all times; and the Pythagorean always wears white clothing. He lives every day of his life as though he were preparing for initiation at Eleusis, for incubation at Asclepius' temple, or for the journey to Trophonius. He follows not the cult rules of a certain holy site, but those of a βίος which he has personally and consciously chosen." (Burkert 1972, p. 190.)

[49] Diogenes Laertius (8.37ff.) and Athenaeus (4.160ff.) cite a number of these fragments from no longer extant comedies: Antiphanes Corycus fr.135 = Ath. 4.161a, Mnemata fr.

While all of these movements can be seen as religious currents presenting an alternative to the standard religious cult practice of the Greek city-state, understanding the interrelation of these various countercultural religious movements remains problematic due to the dearth of evidence. The most useful model is that proposed by Burkert, in which he depicts Orphism, the Eleusinian Mysteries, Pythagoreanism, and Dionysiac cult as interlocking circles of a Venn diagram. "One has to think of the interrelations not so much as those of tied-up parcels but as those of superimposed circles with some areas shared, some not."[50] Burkert points out that Dionysos is a god, Orpheus a mythical singer and founder of rites, Pythagoras a historical figure who founded a religious sect, and Eleusis a place in which certain rituals were performed. Pythagoreans could celebrate rituals to Dionysos created by Orpheus at Eleusis; no one element need exclude another.

Detienne describes these movements as *chemins de déviance* from mainstream Greek religious practice:

Orphisme, dionysisme et pythagorisme ne sont plus des tentatives isolées mais les pièces d'une même système, c'est-à-dire les différentes formes de refus ou de protestation contre un ordre politico–religieux. Ils cessent de nous apparaître commes des objets exotiques. Leur marginalité, au lieu de les renvoyer à une origine étrangère, en fit un lieu privilégié pour mesurer les distances, les ruptures, les déviations, pour repérer les rejets et les refus.[51]

Different religious groups had different forms of protest against the mainstream socio-political and religious order. The task for the interpreter of the gold tablets is thus to analyze what form of *déviance* is represented in the tablets, rather than to try to squeeze the tablets into a preconceived parcel such as Pythagoreanism or Orphism. Such a task, however, is extraordinarily difficult due to the fragmentary and difficult nature of the small amount of available evidence. Henrichs provides the

---

160 = Ath. 4.161a, Neotis fr, 168 = Ath. 4.108ef, fr. 226 = Ath 2.60d; Mnesimachos Alcmaeon fr.1 = D.L 8.37; Alexis *Pythagorizousa* frr. 196–7 = Ath. 4.161cd, fr. 198 = Ath. 3.122f, fr. 199 = Gell. 4.11.8, Tarentini fr. 219 = Ath. 11.463de, frr. 220–1 = Ath. 4.161bc, fr. 222 = Ath. 4.134ab; Aristophon *Pythagoristes* fr. 9 = Ath. 4.161e, fr. 10 = Ath. 6.238cd, frr. 12–3 = D.L. 8.38; Kratinos *Pythagorizousa* fr. 6 = D.L. 8.37, Tarentini fr. 7 = D.L. 8.38. cp. also Aristophanes' portrait of Socrates in the *clouds*.

[50] Burkert 1977, p. 7.

[51] Detienne 1975, p. 53. Detienne unfortunately still regards Orphism as a monolithic movement with a well-defined *chemin* of its own, in contrast to the views of Burkert and others, who see variation within Orphism as well.

best metaphor, "Trying to reconstruct a coherent body of Orphic lore, beliefs and behavior for the archaic, classical, or Hellenistic period is like doing a sophisticated and large-scale jigsaw puzzle with an incomplete set that lacks most pieces and has no picture on its front cover."[52] In most cases, however, rather than using the tablets as pieces by which we may get a better idea of what that whole front cover picture might actually be, scholars have tried to clear up the ambiguities in the tablets with reference to a front cover picture reconstructed more from their ideas of what it ought to look like than from the evidence available.

The mythic narratives on the gold tablets provide important evidence for understanding the varieties of ancient Greek religion, particularly those forms that set themselves apart from the mainstream religious practices of the polis. Those who are buried with the gold tablets are using the traditional language of myth to make claims that distinguish them from the ordinary run of mortals. The journey to the underworld that is depicted on the tablets shows the various ways in which the users of the tablets claim difference: the obstacles they envision, the solutions they devise, and the results they expect all indicate the religious ideas of the communities that produced the tablets. The analysis of the specific ways the tablets narrate the underworld journey provides pieces of the puzzle for scholars to reconstruct a picture of all the different *chemins de déviance* that these communities employ to differentiate themselves from the socio-political world in which they live.

## FINDING THE PATH IN THE UNDERWORLD

ἀλλ' ὁπόταμ ψυχὴ προλίπηι φάος Ἀελίοιο...

But when the soul has left the light of the sun...

With this introduction, the anomalous tablet A4 presents a fragmentary description of the journey of the soul after death. The choice of his path through the underworld must present an obstacle or difficulty of some kind, for the deceased is told to remain on guard, πεφυλαγμένον εὖ μάλα

---

[52] Henrichs, comments in Burkert 1977, p. 21. cp. Festugière in his review of Guthrie's reconstruction of Orphic doctrines, "Toutes les reconstructions de l'orphisme ont pour fondement un très petit nombre de témoignages sûrs et un plus grand nombre de textes dont l'exégese me paraît arbitraire. En ce cas, c'est affaire de prudence et de goût. On peut ressentir plus ou moins d'inclination pour le jeu des hypothèses." (Festugière 1936, p. 310.)

πάντα, but the danger he faces is not made explicit. In some of the other gold tablets too, the soul faces an obstacle before she can confront the powers of the underworld, finding her way in the dark underworld. In the long versions of the B tablets (B1, B2, B10, B11), the first obstacle the deceased faces is finding her way in the shadowy underworld to the correct spring where she may obtain a drink to relieve her parching thirst. Before the thirsty soul can ever proclaim her identity to the guardians at the waters of Memory, she must find the correct spring from which to drink.

The shadowy darkness of the unfamiliar underworld presents an obstacle to the thirsty soul seeking to assuage its thirst. All the B tablets describe what the deceased sees as the soul wanders in the underworld: a white cypress tree and a spring nearby. In the shorter B tablets from Crete and Thessaly, the deceased has already found the desired spring and the tree that marks it. The longer tablets, however, explicitly make the obstacle facing the deceased a choice between two springs, whereas only one spring is mentioned in the short tablets. The long tablets thus combine the traditional mythic element of seeking desired water in the underworld with the element of the choice between two paths.

The mythic motif of the thirsty soul appears to be a universal human idea, perhaps arising from the fact that dying persons often become very thirsty before they die. The idea is found in the myths of cultures throughout the world, not merely in desert climates such as Egypt, so no direct Egyptian pedigree need be postulated to explain its appearance in these Greek tablets.[53] In the tablets, moreover, the motif of the thirsty dead appears with a specifically Greek wordplay in tablets B10 and B11. The souls of the dead, ψυχαὶ, quench their thirst by cooling themselves, ψύχονται, at the springs of the underworld.[54] In the *Odyssey*, too, the dead are thirsty, crowding around to drink the blood spilled by Odysseus (xi.36–7), an image that perhaps reflects the practice of pouring libations for the dead on their graves.[55]

---

[53] cp., Deonna 1939.

[54] Aeschylus uses the same pun: "to chill my soul with a two-pronged goad," ἀμφήκει κέντρῳ ψύχειν ψυχὰν ἐμάν. *Prometheus Bound*, 693. cp. Cratylus 399d. Prontera 1978 sees in this pun a connection between the refreshment of the soul and its reanimation. cp. in Homer, *Odyssey* IV, 567 where Zephyr is said to ἀναψύχειν the souls in Elysium. Eustathius and other scholiasts comment on the senses of refreshment and reanimation.

[55] cp., e.g., Garland 1985, pp. 113ff. Aristophanes makes it a necessity for the dead to drink in the underworld, καταβάντας εὐθέως πίνειν ἔδει. διὰ ταῦτα γάρ τοι καὶ καλοῦνται μακάροι,

To be sure, the Egyptian parallels that are often cited are striking. The Egyptian Books of the Dead contain spells in which the deceased requests water from underworld powers.[56] The scenario in the Books of the Dead is very similar to that of the tablets: the deceased is faced with some potent underworld figure whom he must supplicate to obtain the drink that will assuage his thirst. The Books of the Dead, like the gold tablets, serve as a guide book for the deceased, giving him the necessary information to surmount the obstacles that face him in the afterlife. The funerary inscriptions from Hellenized Egypt in which Osiris is requested to give cooling water to the deceased, δοίη σοι ὁ Ὄσιρις τὸ ψυχρὸν ὕδωρ, seem to follow this tradition of the Book of the Dead, although undoubtedly with Greek influences.[57] The identification of Dionysos with Osiris, made already by Herodotus (II, 42), perhaps points to a Dionysiac connection in these later Egyptian testimonies, but the influence clearly worked both ways.

The origin of the motif, however, even could it be traced with any degree of certainty, does not explain its function within the tablets themselves. δίψηι δ᾽ εἰμι αὔη καὶ ἀπόλλυμαι, "I am parched with thirst and I perish," says the deceased. The idea of a thirsty soul in torment from eternal thirst reminds one of myths of the punishment of Tantalus (cp. *Odyssey*, xi.582–592), but how can the deceased claim to perish further? Clearly, the drink has an importance for the soul journeying to the other world that goes beyond the mere relief from the feeling of thirst. The result of successfully overcoming the obstacle through the deceased's knowledge of the second spring and persistence in face of her thirst is the chance for a draught from the waters of Memory.

---

although he is perhaps humorously alluding to compulsory drinking at symposia. Fr. 504, 8 Kassel-Austin (Poetae Comicae Graecae). Velasco-Lopez finds it impossible to believe that the μακάροι dead could be drinking anything but wine, "puisqu'il en fait la cause de l'expression μακάροι attribuée aux défunts, il serait difficile de la comprendre s'ils buvaient de l'eau." (Velasco-Lopez 1992, p. 213.)

[56] Most recently discussed in Merkelbach 1999. cp. Zuntz 1971, pp. 370–376. Zuntz, however notes the differences: "In the Greek, the essential point lies in the presence of guardians, possibly hostile, and their propitiation by that avowal of descent from Heaven and Earth which is the very heart of these texts. The Egyptian has nothing like it; on the contrary: the dead man, on reaching the spring, is at once and most readily refreshed; not only with water but also with fruit and frankincense." (Zuntz 1971, p. 372.) Tom Dousa provides a more comprehensive comparison in his unpublished paper, further pointing out that, while Egyptian texts do contain both a tree and a pool of water before the first millenium BCE, the texts from later periods closer in time to the tablets emphasize the tree but omit the water, unlike the tablets, whose focus is on the water rather than the tree.

[57] cp., e.g., I.G. xiv. 1488, 1075, 1782.

## Obstacle: Finding the Way to the Right Spring

The deceased has reached the shadowy underworld, and the darkness of Hades covers her, σκότος ἀμφικαλύψας (B1.14, cp. B11.3). In the Hipponion and Entella tablets, the guardians ask why the deceased has come to the dark shadow of Hades, Ἀΐδος σκότος ὀρφνήεντος.[58] The tablet provides instructions to navigate through this darkness to find the spring from which the deceased must drink. The first signpost, as it were, is the λευκὰ κυπάρισσος, which marks the way for the deceased. Zuntz and Guarducci both read the λευκὰ κυπάρισσος as meaning the glowing white or, perhaps, phosphorescent cypress tree, rather than simply white cypress.[59] Guarducci sees the tree as a marker that provides a welcome relief from the fearsome darkness of the underworld, a sign that gives hope of salvation from the all-encompassing darkness of death.[60]

However, this cypress does not always mark the correct spring in the tablets. The cypress marks the correct spring only in the shorter versions of the B tablets, where there is no choice of springs. In the longer versions, by contrast, the cypress marks the wrong spring, the spring which the deceased will first encounter but which she must carefully avoid. In the long versions, the deceased has an explicit choice between two springs at which she may quench her thirst. The location of these springs, however, varies from tablet to tablet. In B1, the first spring is on the left, ἐπ᾽ ἀριστερὰ, while the second, ἑτέραν, is presumably on the right. In B2, however, the

---

[58] B10.9, B11.11. The uncertain reading of ΟΡΟΕΕΝΤΟΣ in B10 seems confirmed by the parallel in B11; cp. Riedweg 1998, Pugliese Carratelli 2001, p. 47, and Bernabé and Jiménez 2001, p. 260. Whatever the exact meaning and whatever the original word intended, the sense of dark and destructive is clear.

[59] Zuntz 1971, p. 373, and Guarducci 1974, pp. 19-20, apparently independent of one another. Giangrande proposes that it means simply fresh green cypress, "l'aggettivo λευκός, in greco, è spesso usato *de plantis* per designare il colore verde chiaro (materiale in Kühn-Fleischer, *Index Hippocraticus* V, s.v. λευκός (ἐλαίη, ποίη, κίσσος, etc.) . . . L'albero detto λευκὰ κυπάρισσος al verso 3 della lamina di Hipponion è, dunque, un cipreso giovane, dal colore verde chiaro, non ancora divenuto verde scuro." (Giangrande 1993, p. 238.) While the word, λευκός, may at times mean fresh green, it is uncertain whether it would have been interpreted as such in this context, since the meaning of white and glowing not only is the primary sense but also fits quite well in the context of the shadows of Hades.

[60] "λευκὴ κυπάρισσος come dell'albero lucente che provvidamente interrompe l'oscurità del monde ultraterrano, indicando alle anime la via della salvezza." (Guarducci 1974, p. 19.) "L'orrore delle tenebre, istintivo per i viventi che ancora godono la luce del sole, può tuttavia temperarsi volta nella speranza - suggerita soprattutto dalle dottrine misteriche - di trovare oltre la morte una qualsiasi luce, più o meno viva, che consenta alle anime un'esistenza se non lieta per lo meno serena." (p. 20.)

first spring is ἐνδέξια, on the right, and the second spring is farther along the road, πρόσσω. The same seems to be true for B10, in which the first spring is ἐπὶ δεξιὰ and the second is πρόσθεν. B11 seems to have the same structure as B10, although the lacunae prevent absolute certainty of anything but that the first spring is on the right, [ἐν]δεξιὰ or [ἐπὶ] δεξιὰ. In all cases, however, the first spring is by the cypress and should be avoided, and the second spring is the correct one.

Many scholars have been bothered by the fact that in B2, B10, and B11, the bad spring is on the right and the good apparently on the left, since the right side is generally associated with the good and the left with the bad. The Pythagorean table of opposites, preserved by Aristotle, links the right with good, straight, male, and light, while the left is linked with bad, crooked, female, and darkness.[61] According to this set of hierarchies, then, the right spring should be the right one, not the left.[62]

### Solution: The Second Spring, from the Lake of Mnemosyne

This problem, I believe, stems from seeing only one dichotomy at work in the B tablets, that of right and left. In the anomalous A4, this is indeed the operative dichotomy; the highly corrupt lines, δεξιὸν †ΕΣΟΙΑΣΔΕΕΤ† ⟨ἱέ⟩ναι, and δεξιὰν ὁδοπόρ⟨ει⟩, most likely refer to the choice of paths at a crossroads, at which the deceased must take the positive, right-hand way. However, although B2, B10, and B11 mention the first spring as being on the right, they do not characterize the second spring as on the left, but as farther along. In these tablets the operative dichotomy is first and second or near and far, rather than right and left. While Zuntz argues, "B2 thus indicates one straight path and not that 'parting of the ways' which B1 at least implies,"[63] I would argue that a crossroads is still envisaged here. The first spring is not actually close at hand to the road, for the deceased is warned not to come anywhere near it, but to pass on, ταύτας τᾶς κράνας μηδὲ σχεδὸν ἐγγύθεν ἔλθῃς. The image seems to be

---

[61] Aristotle, *Met.* 986a22. cp. Burkert 1972, pp. 51ff.

[62] As Smith notes, no dichotomy is simply neutral; the choice is always valorized. "For there is a specious symmetry to language of the dual – the implication of equality, balance, and reciprocity. And yet, this is clearly not the case. *Up* and *down, front* and *back, right* and *left*, are almost never dualities of equivalence; they are hierarchically ranked in relations of superordination and subordination, with radically different valences." (Smith 1987, p. 41.)

[63] Zuntz 1971, p. 369, writing before B10 and B11 had been discovered.

of a side road leading off to the spring, with the main road continuing past. The significance of this arrangement of mythic motifs seems to be that the deceased should not stop and turn aside to quench her thirst at the first possible opportunity, but that, by persevering and waiting until the second spring, the deceased will earn the reward. Most souls do not have the fortitude or the knowledge to continue past the first spring, since they feel they are dying of thirst, δίψαι δ' ἧμι αὖος καὶ ἀπόλλυμαι. As B10 and B11 have it, these ordinary souls cool themselves at the spring by the cypress, κατερχόμεναι ψυχαὶ νεκύων ψύχονται. The soul of the deceased, who has been initiated and instructed how to act by the gold tablet, can conquer the lure of the first spring and wait until she reaches the second.

This valuation of the later spring, the one farther along, perhaps implies an ascetic context. The conquest of desires, which in the earthly life serves to mark the separation of the initiate from the body and from worldly concerns, is projected into the afterlife, where the *askesis* practiced in life serves to help the deceased obtain a drink of the water of Memory. Such practices were characteristic of the Pythagoreans and other countercultural religious groups. These people extended the ritual prohibitions that for the ordinary person applied only in special circumstances to a lifelong practice that kept them in a condition of extraordinary purity. Even if the deviance from mainstream practice was not lifelong or complete, the extent of unusual practices marks the protest against the mainstream.[64]

Plato's myth in the *Republic* offers a parallel to the obstacle facing the deceased in the longer B tablets. In the final myth of Er, only those who have practiced philosophy are prepared to make the correct choice in the lottery of souls. Those who have lived good lives without the *askesis* run the risk of heedlessly making a poor choice. Moreover, when all the souls must drink from the water Ameles, those who restrain their thirst after the journey through the parching plain of Lethe do not drink more than is necessary of the waters that make the soul forget everything.[65] Plato is here clearly playing with the same elements from the mythic tradition that are found in the long B tablets – magic water, memory and life, a choice dependent upon previous experiences – but, although the pieces

---

[64] cp. Burkert's 1972 discussion of the differing extents to which some Pythagoreans (*acusmati* vs. *mathematici*) took the taboos set down by Pythagoras (pp. 192–201). See also note 48 above.

[65] *Rep.* 618c–619e, 621a. Plato characteristically transforms the solutions offered by other religious contexts into philosophy as the ultimate solution.

are the same, the arrangement is different. Instead of restraining one's thirst to limit how much one drink of the waters of forgetfulness, the deceased in the B tablets is restraining her thirst so that she can drink freely from the waters of Memory.

### Result: Memory

The correct spring flows from the Lake of Mnemosyne in the long versions of the B tablets, and it is a drink of this that the deceased so earnestly desires. But what is the actual result of drinking the water of Memory? The tablets themselves provide no answer, but a number of different possibilities are suggested by the Greek mythic tradition. It seems safe to assume that the first, rejected spring in the longer B tablets has a function contrary to that of the second spring, which flows with the water of Memory. It may not be titled the Fountain of Lethe, as it is at the Lebedeia Trophonius oracle described by Pausanias, but it must, like the River Ameles in Plato, serve to make the thirsty souls of the dead forget.[66] The deceased on the tablets seeks instead the water of Mnemosyne, trying to achieve memory rather than oblivion.

Mnemosyne, the personification of memory, has a variety of significances in the Greek tradition. Mother of the Muses, she represents the way in which epic heroes attain their immortality through the preservation of their deeds in epic song. The epic heroes remain alive in the memories of the poets and their audiences long after their mortal remains have crumbled into dust.[67] In the epic tradition, Memory offers the possibility of immortality through κλέος, a means of transcending death and the mortal condition.

---

[66] cp. Pausanias IX.39.8, and see pp. 106–108 below.

[67] Vernant explains the function of memory thus: "By eliminating the barrier that separates the present from the past it throws a bridge between the world of the living and that beyond to which everything that leaves the light of day must return. It brings about an 'evocation' of the past comparable to that effected for the dead by Homer's ritual of the ἔκκλησις. This is a summons, for one brief moment, of one of the dead from the underworld to the land of the living and into the light of day. It is also comparable to the journey which is mimed out in certain consultations of oracles: the descent of a living person into the underworld for the purpose of finding out – and seeing – what he wants to know. The privilege that Mnemosune confers upon the bard is the possibility of contacting the other world, of entering and returning from it freely. The past is seen as a dimension of the beyond." (Vernant 1983, p. 80.)

The deceased, however, does not hope that by drinking the water of Mnemosyne that she will live on in the memories of those still living.[68] The tablet, unlike a conventional grave marker, is not a public display that preserves the deceased in the community's memory.[69] Rather, the power of Mnemosyne to rescue the heroes from oblivion is called upon to provide salvation for the individual in the world of the dead by her own recollection of herself. Those of the dead who do not drink of Memory but drink of Forgetfulness instead might wander witless and confused, knowing nothing of their past or future, like the shades in the *Odyssey* nekyia before they drink the blood. The draught of the waters of Memory permits the deceased to remember her true origins and identity.[70] This type of memory provides a kind of immortality very different from the κλέος ἄφθιτον of the hero who is honored by his city, his clan, and his family; this focus, through memory, on the individual identity apart from the different lives places value on the self that exists outside of the mortal world, on an immortal part whose proper place lies outside the hierarchies and boundaries of the earthly, political, material world. In one sense, it is the body that is devalued in comparison to the soul; in another sense, it is the present time that is devalued in comparison to the time when the individual is in the proper place, in the community of the immortals. Memory serves to recall the individual from the mortal world and the normal order back to the world of the immortals.[71] The idea, moreover, that memory provides not the immortal glory of epic but a personal immortality through the recollection of the self may appeal to those, such

---

[68] Epic κλέος, in any case, offered less consolation to women than to the male heroes, since their immortal glory is usually described as a connection to a husband (or divine lover), father, or son.

[69] cp. Sourvinou-Inwood: "Thus, a person's posthumous memory is focused on, and activated or reinforced by, the grave monument. The idea is that the deceased's memory will survive within the community, and the grave monument will keep it alive longer by activating it and serving as a focus for it." (Sourvinou-Inwood 1995, p. 139.)

[70] As Pugliese Carratelli puts it, "Probabile, ancora, che nella facoltà mnemonica sia stato riconosciuto un segno del persistere della individualità: perché è nella memoria, cioè nella consapevolezza delle sue proprio esperienze, della responsibilità delle sue azione e delle conseguenze ch'esse comportano oltre la morte, che l'anima acquista la coscienza della sua identità." (Pugliese Carratelli 1983, p. 75.)

[71] As Vernant puts it, "Thus the central place given to memory in eschatological myths indicates an attitude of refusal with regard to temporal existence. Memory is exalted because it is the power that makes it possible for men to escape time and return to the divine state." (Vernant 1983, p. 88.)

as women and nonaristocratic men, who are unlikely to be immortalized by epic κλέος.

This function of memory in preserving the identity of the individual is especially important in the context of a belief in reincarnation. Memory enables the individual to recall the events of previous lives, to avoid the errors committed in those lives, and to understand the hardships of the present life as penalties for those previous misdeeds. The Pythagoreans, who believed in metempsychosis, stressed the importance of memory even in the mortal life. Pythagoras instructed his followers to train their memories by practicing the recollection of their daily activities so that, as a result of their training in this life, they might be able to recall this life when they had moved on to the next one. Of Pythagoras himself it was said that he could recall a whole series of lives, including a life as Euphorbus, a warrior slain by Menelaus in the Trojan War. Empedokles claimed to recall a series of incarnations, not only human but animal and vegetable as well.[72]

The function of memory in the reincarnation process obviously differs depending on what sort of reincarnation is envisioned, but the prominent role played by Mnemosyne in these texts suggests that some doctrine of metempsychosis underlies the religious beliefs of the tablets.[73] The references in the long version of the B tablets to the sacred road and the company of heroes or initiates give no clear indication whether the deceased wants the draught of Memory to preserve her memories for her next incarnation or whether the draught of Memory is envisaged as a final and total recall of the true identity, as a result of which the deceased need never again be reborn. Especially since the belief in metempsychosis seems to have been limited to a few contexts, a Pythagorean or Empedoklean background for the longer versions of the tablets remains a strong possibility.[74] Three of the four long versions of the B tablets were found in the regions where Pythagoras and Empedokles had the most influence. The exact provenances of B1 and B11 are admittedly uncertain, but the region around Petelia in southern Italy and the regions of central Sicily are likely locations for such a movement. The case of B2 from Pharsalos is more difficult to explain because the context of the burial of the deceased

---

[72] Empedokles, fr. 117; on Pythagoras's incarnations, see Rohde 1925, pp. 598–601, Appendix X on the Previous Lives of Pythagoras. cp. Burkert 1972, pp. 137–141.

[73] For a discussion of types of reincarnation and their ramifications, see below, pp. 95–96.

[74] cp. Pugliese Carratelli 2001, pp. 51–57, and Pugliese Carratelli 1983.

with tablet B2, unfortunately, provides no useful evidence on this score, but it is by no means impossible that a Pythagorean exile or Empedoklean teacher could have found an audience in a religious community in Thessaly.

## Conclusion

This obstacle complex in the longer B tablets thus provides some information about the religious context in which these tablets were produced. Although the instructions to take the right-hand path in A4 provide little beyond a statement of the familiar valuation of right over left, the choice of the later spring and its identification as the water of Memory in B1, B2, B10, and B11 suggest a religious context in which ascetic practices and perhaps a belief in reincarnation were significant. The details of the result are never spelled out in any of the tablets; indeed, only B1 and B10 (and perhaps B11) include a single line stating that the guardians will in fact give the water to the deceased who has found the correct spring. The emphasis on the solution – the knowledge that there is a second spring and the self-control to avoid slaking one's thirst at the the first – over the result again suggests that, for the creators of the tablet, the nature of the person is more important than the details of the reward for that nature. The deceased's knowledge and self-control are superior qualities that distinguish her both in this world and the next, and this identification that marks her as different from the ordinary is the primary concern in the long B tablets, just as the identification that provides the solution to the confrontation with the powers of the underworld is the most important thing in all of the gold tablets.

## CONFRONTATION WITH THE POWERS OF THE UNDERWORLD

### Obstacle: Confrontation with the Powers of the Underworld

The central narrative feature of all the gold tablets that contain texts that evoke the tale of a journey to the underworld is the description of the deceased's encounter with the powers in the realm to which she has come after death.[75] However, the scenario of this confrontation differs

---

[75] The exception is the anomalous A4, whose highly corrupt text provides little material for narrative analysis. The central complex of obstacle–solution–result seems to be the

significantly between the tablets of the B series and those of the A and P series. To obtain favorable treatment in the underworld, the deceased must face Persephone and other deities of the underworld in the tablets from Pelinna, Thurii, and Rome. In the B tablets, by contrast, nameless guardians question the deceased as she approach the waters of Memory, parched with thirst.

*Audience with Persephone in the A and P Tablets*

The mythic element chosen for the obstacle in the A and P tablets is envisioned as the confrontation with a deity of the underworld who must be greeted as a ruler rather than with a monster who must be battled or with some inanimate barrier, such as water or gates, that must be crossed. The deceased arrives as a suppliant to a presumably favorable ruler, not as a prisoner coming to judgement, as in tales told by Pindar and Plato, where the past deeds of the deceased are weighed by special judges who lay down sentences of appropriate punishment or reward.[76] Instead, like Orpheus before Persephone or like Odysseus coming as a suppliant to Arete in Phaeacia, the deceased must win the favor of the ruler of the realm in which she finds herself.[77] That the obstacle is depicted in such a way calls for a certain kind of solution by the deceased, a status claim appropriate to the relation of a suppliant to a ruler.

Whom then does the deceased confront and what are the significances of the figures encountered? Although clearly the most important, Persephone is not the only deity involved in the scenes described on the tablets.

---

choice of paths (as discussed above), but some confrontation with Persephone may be implied by the proclamation, paralleled in A1, that the deceased will become a god.

[76] The first references to the actual process of judgement come in Pindar's *Second Olympian*, where the "wicked souls straightway pay the penalty and some judge beneath the earth judges the crimes committed in this realm of Zeus, having delivered the strict account in accord with the harsh order of things." αὐτίκ’ ἀπάλαμνοι φρένες ποινὰς ἔτεισαν. τὰ δ’ ἐν τᾷδε Διὸς ἀρχᾷ ἀλιτρὰ κατὰ γᾶς δικάζει τις ἐχθρᾷ λόγον φράσαις ἀνάγκᾳ. Pindar, O.II.57–60. Although the judge is unspecified in Pindar, Aeschylus makes Hades the judge of mortals when they come to his realm. μέγας γὰρ Ἅιδης ἐστὶν εὔθυνος βροτῶν ἔνερθε χθονός, "Hades calls men to reckoning there under the ground." *Eumenides* 273–274. In the *Suppliants*, this judge is referred to as κἀκεῖ δικάζει τἀμπλακήμαθ’, ὡς λόγος, Ζεὺς ἄλλος ἐν καμοῦσιν ὑστάτας δίκας, "another Zeus among the dead [who] works out their final punishment." (*Suppliants* 230–231, Lattimore translations.) Although facing the judges plays a small part in the soul's journey to the underworld in the *Phaedo* (107d–114d) and the *Republic* (614b–621d), Plato elaborates the description of judges in the *Gorgias* myth (523a–527a).

[77] Orpheus – Eur. Alcestis 357–62, Moschos Lament for Bion 3.123–4; Odysseus comes as a suppliant to Arete, Od. vii.146–152, cp. 53–77.

The A tablets mention not only Phersephoneia as χθονίων βασίλεια, but also Eukles and Eubouleus, along with other unnamed divine figures.[78] The Pelinna tablets mention both Persephone and Bacchios, and the Pherai tablet seems also to be referring to Persephone in the name of Brimo, while Dionysos seems to be the referent of the sacred symbolon, ἀνδρικεπαιδόθυρσου.[79] In this section I explore the specific aspects and prominence of the Persephone whom the deceased confronts, and I address the question of the role and presence or absence of Dionysos and Hades. The relative prominence of the different deities in the Thurii and Pelinna tablets signals the different ideas about the way the underworld is governed and points to different solutions for obtaining the favor of the rulers. While in the Thurii tablets the deceased needs to claim a special lineage, in the Pelinna tablets Dionysos trumps the authority of Persephone.

While all of these tablets refer to Persephone, it is worth considering under what aspects this divinity is being invoked. In the myths of Eleusis, Persephone is best known in her aspect of Kore, the virgin daughter of Demeter carried off by Hades. The tablets, however, seem to be invoking Persephone not as the hapless victim but as the powerful queen of the realm of the dead, who has the power to determine the fate of each mortal's soul. The focus on this aspect seems in keeping with what is known of the role of Persephone in the myths and cults of southern Italy, especially in the cultural sphere of Epizephyrian Locri. In this southern Italian region, Persephone appears as a figure of independent power, the ruler of the underworld and the patroness of marriage and children.[80] While

---

[78] While A1 and A5 do not explicitly name the underworld queen as Persephone, as A2 and A3 do, there can be no doubt that Persephone is the reference.

[79] This symbolon remains incomprehensible, but the elements male, child, and *thyrsos* seem to be present. The *thyrsos* points to Dionysos, especially since male and child would not apply to maenads or satyrs, the other creatures associated with the *thyrsos*. Brimo is an epithet that seems to be used of Persephone, Hekate, or even Demeter but refers in each case to the Queen of the Dead as *kourotrophos*.

[80] As Sourvinou-Inwood notes, "Persephone's personality at Locri includes some of the aspects which characterize her Panhellenic personality, but without the close association with Demeter. Moreover, it contains some other functions not associated with her elsewhere: she presided over the world of women, with special reference to the protection of marriage and the rearing of children, that is of those female activities that were most important for the life of the polis." (Sourvinou-Inwood 1991, pp. 145–188, p. 180.) cp. Price, who sees the *pinakes* with Persephone and an infant in a basket as dedications by mothers for Persephone's protection of their children. (Price 1978, p. 172.) cp. Musti on the relations between the Panhellenic aspects of Persephone to her personae at Eleusis and in Magna Graecia. "Abbiamo insomma nell' insieme 1) *un complesso di credenze sull'oltretomba;*

there was undoubtedly variation among the cults in different locales, Persephone at Thurii would certainly have shared features with the conception of Persephone in the region in general. For example, while the return of Persephone is a crucial element of the Eleusinian myth of Demeter and Persephone, in southern Italy the story seems to have been told differently, with Persephone accepting her new role as queen of the underworld and refusing to return to her mother.[81] The aspect of Persephone as queen of the dead was particularly important in southern Italy, then; and this importance seems reflected in the fact that the Thurii tablets (A1–3) refer to her not only by her name, Φερσεφόνεια, as the Pelinna tablets do, but also by the titles χθονίων βασίλεια and δεσποίνα. Even when referring to her by name, the Thurii tablets emphasize her divinity and majesty when the deceased comes as a suppliant to ἁγνὴν Φερσεφόνειαν.[82]

Another role that has been suggested for Persephone in these texts is that of the mother of Dionysos.[83] Certainly Persephone seems to stand in some sort of close relation to Dionysos, particularly to Dionysos as Bacchios in the Pelinna tablets, but the relation is not necessarily that of mother to child.[84] In any case, no filial relation need be assumed to

---

2) *aspetti di religiosità agraria; 3) motivi ierogamici*, tutti presenti in questa 'massa' di nozioni e rappresentazione religiose; questa 'massa' assume tuttavia un'assialità diversa nei diversi luoghi, per ciò che attiene al contenuto ed alla funzione stessa dell'espressione religiosa. Ad Eleusi prevalgono in definitiva gli aspetti della religiosità agraria, accanto ad esigenze di purificazione individuale attinenti a speranze ultraterrene (1–2); a Locri prevale Persefone (ce l'ha ribadito, da un lato, ed anche approfondito, dall'altro, Torelli nella sua relazione al convegno 1976 su Locri) e l'aspetto della ierogamia, fortemente simbolico dell'istituto storico e sociale del matrimonio local (1–3); nei testi orfici prevale la prospettiva dell'oltretomba (1)." (Musti 1984, pp. 71–72.)

[81] Zuntz refers to the clay *pinakes* found in the temple area to Persephone at Locri that depict Persephone enthroned in the underworld, receiving a variety of divine visitors, and notes that not only is Demeter never present, but that the Locrian Persephone seems never to have returned to the world of the living, remaining instead as Queen of the Dead. (Zuntz 1971, p. 400.) In the *Georgics*, Vergil has Persephone refuse to follow her mother back to the world of the living, *nec repetita sequi curet Proserpina matrem.* (*Georgics* I.39.) Harrison and Obbink 1986 cite other texts in which Persephone refuses to return, although they imagine that she was eventually compelled to return.

[82] By contrast, Segal remarks of the Pelinna tablets: "We should note that our tablets, unlike the Eleusinian texts, emphasize the 'release' rather than the initiate's visual experience, and they give Persephone no particular emphasis…This feature of the Pelinna texts seems to be in keeping with their emphasis on the experience of the initiate rather than the awe and power of the chthonic divinities or the landscape of Hades." (Segal 1990, p. 416.)

[83] cp. e.g., Graf 1993a, p. 244; Bernabé and Jiménez 2001, pp. 66, 97, 144, etc.

[84] Persephone is certainly not imagined as Dionysos's mother in Aristophanes' *Frogs*. As Moulinier reminds us, "Les documents que nous rappelons ici ne nous permettent pas

understand the role of Persephone in these tablets; her importance stems straightforwardly from her position as queen of Hades, rather than her status as the daughter of Demeter or mother of Dionysos.[85]

However, Persephone is not merely the consort to the king of the underworld. Rather she appears as the supreme power in the realm of the dead, the figure to whom the deceased must appeal to complete successfully the journey to the underworld. Her husband, Hades, is not even mentioned in the Pelinna tablets, while the Thurii tablets contain a only a passing reference to Eukles, who seems to be the equivalent of Hades, the consort of Persephone in the underworld, the male ruler of the dead.[86] Eukles, however, seems to play no important role in the deceased's journey; he is merely saluted, along with Eubouleus and all the other gods to whom the deceased must give honor.

Eubouleus, despite Zuntz's vehement protests, is likely to be an epithet of Dionysos, since Plutarch refers to Eubouleus as an ancient name for Dionysos (*Quaest. Conv.* vii.9, 714c). Zuntz, concerned to keep any hint of Bacchic or Orphic superstition out of his pure Pythagorean tablets, vigorously asserts that Eubouleus is merely an epithet of a chthonic god and argues that Eubouleus as Dionysos is the result of late syncretism.[87]

d'admettre que le thème du Dionysos, fils de Perséphone, ait été orphique dès l'époque classique." (Moulinier 1955, p. 64, n. 5.) The first reference to Dionysos as the child of Persephone rather than of Semele comes in a fragment of Callimachus (Fr. 171) preserved in the Etymologicum Magnum. While the genealogy may go back much earlier than Callimachus, it may also be a later invention designed to explain the relation between Persephone and Dionysos as a chthonic power. West argues that the Derveni papyrus would have told of the birth of Dionysos from Persephone if more of the scroll had survived, because the papyrus breaks off at the point at which Zeus commits incest with Demeter, a union which undoubtedly will produce Persephone. West argues that symmetry requires that this episode be followed by Zeus' incest with Persephone to produce Dionysos. (West 1983, p. 94.) While this is certainly possible, other endings to the Derveni genealogies are equally plausible, and I would prefer to see some evidence that the symmetry West postulates was important to the author of the genealogies.

[85] The same is true of the Toledo vase that depicts Dionysos shaking hands with Hades with Persephone looking on. (See cover illustration) Johnston and McNiven 1996 have argued that this scene illustrates the power of Dionysos in the underworld, but their inference that the scene provides evidence for the filial relation of Dionysos and Persephone does not necessarily follow from their argument.

[86] Hesychius's definition of Εὐκλῆς as ὁ Ἅιδης would seem to support this, but perhaps the tablets are referring to Εὔκολος, whom Hesychius defines as Ἑρμῆς παρὰ Μεταποντίοντοις. In any case, the tablets seem to be referring to the chthonic deity known from an Oscan tablet from Agnone as Euklúi paterí, whom Zuntz notes is equivalent to the later Dis Pater, Lord of the Dead (Zuntz 1971, p. 310).

[87] Zuntz 1971, p. 311. Eubouleus is identified with Dionysos in Orphic Hymns 29.8; 30.6; 52.4 as well as in Macrobius *Saturnalia* i.18.12 (= OF 237). Eubouleus is identified with

The identification of Eubouleus with an aspect of Dionysos such as the Bacchios Lusios who appears on the Pelinna tablets is perhaps not absolutely certain, but the identification of Eubouleus as Dionysos should be seriously entertained, since the evidence for Bacchios on the Pelinna tablets and *bacchoi* on the Hipponion tablet has disproven Zuntz's attempt to show a wide separation between the Bacchic mysteries and the gold tablets in general.

In the Pelinna tablets, moreover, we have clear evidence for the figure of Dionysos Lusios under the name of Bacchios. Damascius, in his commentary on Plato's *Phaedo*, quotes Orpheus on the nature of this aspect of Dionysos: "Dionysos is responsible for release and because of this the god is called 'Deliverer'. And Orpheus says: 'People send perfect hecatombs in all seasons throughout the year and perform rites, seeking release from unlawful ancestors. But you, having power over them, you will release whomever you wish from harsh suffering and boundless frenzy'."[88] While controversy has raged over the precise interpretation of this passage,[89] it is nevertheless clear that mortals make sacrifices to Dionysos Lusios so that he will give them relief, λύσις, from the troubles in store for them as punishment for past crimes. In the Pelinna tablets, the deceased must tell Persephone that Bacchios has released him: εἰπεῖν Φερσεφόναι σ' ὅτι Βά⟨κ⟩χιος αὐτὸς ἔλυσε (P1 and P2.2).[90] The Pelinna Bacchios who looses the deceased is most probably the Dionysos Lusios of whom Damascius speaks. While Persephone may be the deity responsible for determining the lot of the dead as they enter her realm, her authority has been trumped by the action of Bacchios, from whom the initiate claims an exemption from the judgement of Persephone.

Adonis in Orphic Hymn 56.3 and as Pluto in 18.2. cp., Rohde 1925, pp. 220, 159, and 185, n. 19.

[88] Damascius, *In Plat. Phaedon*. Β ιά = OF 232 ὁ Διόνυσος λύσεώς ἐστιν αἴτιος· διὸ καὶ Λυσεὺς ὁ θεός, καὶ ὁ Ὀρφεύς φησιν· ἄνθρωποι δὲ τελησέσσας ἑκατόμβας πέμπουσιν πάσηισι ἐν ὥραις ἀμφιέτηισιν ὄργια τ' ἐκτελέσουσι, λύσιν προγόνων ἀθεμίστων μαίομενοι· σὺ δὲ τοῖσιν ἔχων κράτος, οὕς κ' ἐθέλησθα, λύσεις ἔκ τε πόνων χαλεπῶν καὶ ἀπείρονος οἴστρου. This commentary has also been attributed to Olympiodorus, but Westerink argues against Norvin for the attribution to Damascius. (Westerink 1977, pp. 15–17.)

[89] cp. Tannery 1899 vs. Reinach 1899; Guthrie 1952; Linforth 1941; and others. See further below.

[90] In the Pherai tablet, the *symbolon*, ἀνδρικεπαιδόθυρσου, seems to contain the characteristic *thyrsos* of Dionysos, perhaps indicating a similar role for Dionysos in intervening with Persephone, called here by the name of Brimo. For Dionysos as Bacchios and Lusios, see the discussion in Casadio 1999, pp. 122–143.

In the Thurii tablets, therefore, Persephone is the key figure; she alone must be addressed with titles of majesty and holiness as the powerful kourotrophic ruler of the dead and supplicated to provide the deceased with a favorable result in her underworld journey. Eubouleus is merely mentioned along with Eukles and others as one the deceased must greet. In the Pelinna texts, by contrast, while Persephone still rules the world of the dead, Bacchios has the power to intervene on behalf of the deceased and affect the judgement of Persephone. The difference in the relative prominence of Persephone and Dionysos on the tablets in the first series reflects the differing natures of the religious groups that served as the context for the production of these texts. The Pelinna tablets undoubtedly come from some type of Dionysiac religious group that honors Persephone as ruler of the dead. Dionysos Bacchios, however, is seen as the figure who can provide salvation and freedom. This focus on Dionysos as Lusios reveals the preoccupations with bondage and escape that must have been central to the religious group that produced the tablets. A similar situation seems to underlie the Pherai tablet, although the symbolon ἀνδρικεπαιδόθυρσου does not give the same kind of prominence to Dionysos. The differences in the way the confrontation with Persephone is described in the tablets set up the differences among the solutions.

*The Thirsty Soul and the Guardians of the Spring in the B Tablets*

In the B series of tablets, the deceased, seeking a drink from the Lake of Memory, must get past the guardians, φύλακες, who stand near the spring. In response to their questions, the deceased must proclaim her identity as a child of Earth and starry Heaven and beg the guardians for a drink. This complex of the thirsty soul faced with the guardians asking for a password of identity appears in all the B tablets, even though many of them do not specify the result of the successful bypassing of the guardians. In the short versions, the presence of these guardians is implied by the questions asked of the deceased, but they are mentioned explicitly in the longer versions. Even in the long versions, however, they are only referred to as φύλακες, their names and natures remain unspecified. They are not chthonic powers who may be propitiated by name, not Persephone or Hades, the rulers of the dead.[91] Their place is indeed in the halls of Hades, Ἀΐδαο δόμους,

---

[91] Lloyd-Jones 1975 suggests that B10.13 be read ἐλεοῦσιν ὑποχθόνιοι βασιλεῖ(ς), referring to the guardians as the rulers of the underworld. Janko reluctantly agrees: "While Lloyd-Jones' interpretation is exposed to West's objection that the guards are not likely to

as the long versions (B1, B2, B10) specify in various constructions, but the mention of Hades seems only to specify the location and not to imply the presence of the deity. Whereas in the A series Persephone is clearly the most significant deity, in the B series she has no presence at all and her consort, whose rulership over the realm of the dead is implied by his possession of the halls, does not seem to play any role in the reception of the dead soul.[92] The same may be said of Bacchos, who plays an important role on the Pelinna tablets, but who is entirely absent from the whole B series. The Hipponion tablet, B10, does mention βάκχοι in its final verse, which implies some kind of Dionysiac context for the tablet.[93] Nevertheless, although the deceased from Hipponion may have participated in Bacchic initiations before death and may look forward to the company of her fellow initiates after death, Dionysos has no direct role in freeing the deceased from the trials of the journey to the other world as he has in the Pelinna tablets. Even if it is supposed that Dionysiac initiation rituals provide the deceased with the correct statement to obtain her drink, it is not the mention of those rites that allows the deceased to get past the guardians.

These nameless guardians present a contrast to other underworld guardian figures in the mythic tradition. Not only are they not named

be kings, nor the kings so casually introduced, no superior alternative is apparent at present." (Janko 1984, p. 96.) The reading of this particular line is extremely vexed, and none of the proposed interpretations is at all satisfactory. Neither the guardians nor the deceased can be identified with the king of the underworld, but the suggestion of Pugliese Carratelli 1975, ἐλεοῦσιν ὑπὸ χθονίωι βασιλῆι, that the guardians pity the deceased by the will of the king of the underworld, as Zuntz (1978, pp. 144–145) points out, hardly works grammatically. Ultimately, I would suggest that the guardians must be the subject of the plural verb, be it ἐλεοῦσιν, ἐρέουσιν (Bernabé and Jiménez 2001, p. 75), or ⟨τ⟩ελέουσι, as West (1975, p. 233) would have it. The ὑποχθόνιοι βασιλει, singular or plural, masculine or feminine, relates to the guardians and the deceased in some way, now lost in the corruptions of the text.

[92] Pugliese Carratelli and Guarducci argue that the use of Hades' name in this context implies that he, rather than Persephone as in the A tablets, is the sovereign in the realm of the dead. cp. Guarducci 1974, p. 27; Foti and Pugliese Carratelli 1974, p. 124. While this may be true, it does not imply his actual presence nor give him any active role in the text. Moreover, the fact that Ἀΐδαο δόμους is a standard epic way for describing the underworld should make one hesitate to lay too much stress on the mention of Hades rather than Persephone.

[93] A great deal of scholarly excitement arose over the mention of βάκχοι in B10, because Zuntz's argument against any kind of Dionysiac context for the gold tablets could finally be decisively disproven. The best summation of the controversy is probably in Cole 1980. However, too much should not be made of this reference, especially since its contrast with the active presence of Dionysos Bacchios in the Pelinna tablets points out the varying importance that Dionysos can have in these religious contexts.

authority figures, but they are also not monstrous beasts. They do not serve as an obstacle to the journeying soul through their ferocious and horrifying appearance, like Empousa (whose very name signals her impeding role) or the gorgon Odysseus fears in Homer's Nekyia.[94] The monstrous figure of Kerberos, the three-headed watchdog of Hades who appears regularly in the Apulian vase underworld scenes, has no place here.[95] The deceased does not need the strength of Herakles to drag the monster away from the gates of Hades. One might expect some creature like the sphinx, guarding the spring as the Theban sphinx guarded the entrance to Thebes, asking all comers about their identity. The sphinx, which is often found in funerary iconography, could perhaps be described, like these guardians, as having sharp wits, φρένες πευκαλίμαι. The guardians in the tablets, however, pose no riddles requiring the brilliance of an Oedipus, but simply ask the identity and purpose of the deceased in a straightforward manner.

In the short version tablets, the guardians are merely implied by the fact that the questions are asked; they are, in effect, the personification of the twofold question: who are you, where are you from? Verdelis interprets this latter question genealogically, as equivalent to τίνος υἱὸς εἶ; and, indeed, this makes the most sense given the answer of the deceased.[96] In B2 and B10, however, the question is not 'who?' but 'why?', ὅ τι χρέος εἰσαφικάνιες, or ὅτ⟨τ⟩ι δὲ ἐξερέεις Ἀΐδος σκότος, even though the answer is the same formula as in the shorter versions. Nevertheless, all three questions represent the same kind of challenge to the deceased – 'what right have you to be here?' These anonymous watchmen are simply sentries asking for the proper password. No heroic strength or courage or cleverness is required to get past them, only the knowledge of the proper response.

*Conclusion*

In each of these tablets, then, the deceased must confront the powers of the underworld, but the precise nature of the powers encountered differs among the A, P, and B tablets. These differences reflect different religious contexts for these tablets, since the deities emphasized in each indicate the importance of the deities to the creators of the text. In the context underlying the A tablets, for example, Persephone is supreme, whereas Bacchios is the crucial figure in the P tablets. In the B tablets, by contrast, no personal encounter with the rulers of the underworld is

---

[94] Empousa, Aristophanes, *Frogs*, 289–304; Gorgon, *Odyssey*, xi.633–635.
[95] For the range of appearances, literary and visual, of Kerberos, see LIMC s.v. Kerberos.
[96] Verdelis 1953–1954, p. 60.

envisioned; the deceased instead is confronted by anonymous and feature-less guardians, which suggests that the personality of Persephone (dread or kourotrophic) and the salvific function of Dionysos were not as central to the group. Despite all these differences of emphasis, however, all the texts share the same basic kind of obstacle – the formal confrontation with the powers of the underworld. In none of these encounters is there a threat of violence or danger as from the dreadful Kerberos who con-fronts Herakles or the Gorgon's head feared by Odysseus. The solutions presented in these texts for a successful bypassing of this obstacle corre-spond to the nature of these encounters. The deceased peacefully presents herself to the powers of the underworld; heroic *bie* and *metis* are not required.

## Solution: Statement of Identity

The gold tablets depict the confrontation of the deceased with the powers of the underworld when the deceased enters the realm of the dead. Faced with this obstacle, what must the deceased do to ensure that the con-frontation has a positive outcome? Challenged as if by a sentry's 'Halt, who goes there?', the deceased must proclaim her identity in order to pass. The identity that the deceased proclaims in these tablets is composed of a variety of elements, each of which is worth examining in detail. The way in which the deceased defines herself is central to the way in which the texts manipulate the traditional tale of the underworld journey to separate the deceased from the mainstream of society. Each element provides some information about the nature of the *chemin de déviance* chosen by the cre-ator of the tablet. I turn first to the implicit statement of feminine gender made by the deceased in the tablets, an aspect that is still for the most part neglected by scholars. Next, I examine the claims to ritual purity and divine lineage, self-identifications that set the deceased in opposition to the ordinary ways of defining identity. The A tablets contain the claims of both ritual purity and divine lineage. The P tablets, however, claim only special ritual status, whereas the B tablets concentrate wholly on the claim to divine lineage. Although these claims of identity have most often been interpreted in terms of the single supposed Orphic doctrine of Origin Sin from the murder of Dionysos Zagreus and the creation of men from the ashes of his Titanic murderers (a modern fabrication dating from 1879), the differences between these strategies indicate not a single and simple background for all the gold tablets but rather a variety of religious contexts.[97] In different ways, the self-identifications in these tablets all define the deceased in opposition to the mainstream of the polis community, rejecting the ordinary measures of status and position within the polis for standards based on a special connection with the gods.

*Gender Issues*

The feminine gender of the deceased in these tablets is a matter of some dispute. While the Pelinna tablets were indisputably found in the grave of a woman (complete with a statue of a maenad) and the deceased at Hipponion was identified as female, the gender of the deceased was not noted by the excavators of the earlier tablets. In some cases, the texts of the tablets themselves can provide indications of the gender of the deceased. The B tablets from Crete, with one exception, seem to be for males, since the deceased proclaims: "I am the son (υἱός) of Earth and Starry Heaven." By contrast, B6 reads ΓΥΗΤΗΡ in line 4, most likely for θυγάτηρ, instead of the υἱός of the other texts. These differences imply that the deceased in B3, B4, B5, B7, and B8 are probably male, while the deceased in B6 seems to be proclaiming herself female, despite using the masculine form αὖος in the first line. The use of the feminine form, αὔη, in line 8 of tablet B1, by contrast, suggests that the deceased might have been female. The masculine forms in B2 and B11 do not rule out the possibility that the παῖς in the tablet is a daughter, like the Hipponion woman of B10. Although the later Roman tablet A5 bears the name of a woman, Caecilia Secundina, the genders of the deceased in the Thurii tablets of the A series have been questioned.[98] Tablets A1–3 open with the line, ἔρχομαι ἐκ καθαρῶν καθαρά, pure I come from the pure, just as the Caecilia Secundina tablet A5 does. However, some scholars have argued that the feminine gender of καθαρά does not indicate that the deceased is herself female.[99] Rohde and others, citing masculine forms

---

[97] See Edmonds 1999.

[98] The Pelinna material is described in Tsantsanoglou and Parássoglou 1987. For the Thurii graves, see Comparetti 1879. The Hipponion discovery is detailed in Foti and Pugliese Carratelli 1974. The material is also summarized in Bottini 1992.

[99] Murray, on metrical grounds, puts a comma between καθαρῶν and καθαρά, making the feminine adjective apply to the Queen of the Underworld rather than the deceased, thus permitting the reader to presume a masculine gender for the deceased. Zuntz comments that this reading "reduces the noble and profound original to a platitudinous ditty and can serve, if anything, to show how much harm can be done by a misplaced comma." (Murray in Harrison 1991, p. 667, Zuntz 1971, p. 306.) Zuntz cites a barrage of parallels to prove that the two words must go together to describe the deceased as not only

used in the texts, assume the male gender of the deceased and interpret the feminine gender as referring not to the gender of the deceased but the feminine gender of the word ψυχή.[100] However, it is far less unusual for a female to be referred to by the linguistically unmarked masculine form than for a male to use the marked feminine form for self-reference, even if the word ψυχή is grammatically feminine.[101] The possibility, therefore, that the deceased are female in the Thurii tablets and the B tablets from Petelia, Pharsalia, Hipponion, and Entella (B1, B2, B10, B11) should be taken seriously. More recent scholars, especially since the discovery of the Pelinna and Hipponion tablets in the graves of women, have favored the idea that these tablets were written for women.[102]

The fact that so many of these tablets may have been found in the graves of women raises the question as to whether the religious circles from which these tablets came were exclusive to women or were particularly appealing to women marginalized in a male-dominated society. In the case of the gold tablets, it could be argued that the eschatological benefits promised by the religious groups that created the tablets appealed to women who were excluded from the benefits of the worldly society available to men. Women, who did not have the positive ideal of a glorious death in battle and everlasting fame that were held up in polis ideology as a counterbalance to the fear of death, may have sought reassurance in ways that the adult citizen males were less apt to need.[103] Admittedly,

---

pure personally but from pure lineage: Soph *Phil.* 324, 874; Arist. *Frogs* 731; Soph. *Ant.* 471; Eur. *Rhes.* 185, 388; Theognis 185; Andokides *de Myst.* 109. (Zuntz 1971, p. 307.) Kotansky 1994 suggests that καθαρά could conceivably be taken to refer secondarily to Persephone in addition to the deceased, poetically linking the two by the qualification of purity.

[100] "The feminine...refers probably to the ψυχή and not to the sex of the dead person as though a woman were speaking in all three cases. Moreover, in No. 1, 9 [A1.8], Persephone speaks as though to a man, ὄλβιε καὶ μακαριστέ, θεὸς δ'ἔσηι ἀντὶ βροτοῖο." (Rohde 1925, p. 447 n. 50.)

[101] Note the use of masculine forms in the Pelinna and Hipponion tablets, which demonstrates that the unmarked masculine was in fact used to refer to women. The Hipponion woman even calls herself the son (υἱός) of Earth and starry Heaven.

[102] As Graf comments, "Indeed I should think it likelier that the feminine ending points to the real person and not simply to the soul (in Greek, the feminine word *psukhe*), in view of the fact that in nearly all the other texts, the dead indicate their sexual identity." Graf 1993, p. 255. cp. Kotansky 1994, p. 109: "What we should conclude from this is that καθαρά in older models of the 'A' group, just like the καθαρά of the Caecilia Secundina text, perhaps signals texts designed or specifically written for *women* devotees."

[103] Sourvinou-Inwood has pointed out that, on the Athenian white-ground lekythoi representing scenes of a deceased greeting Charon in his ferryboat, adult males are never

the small number of tablets found makes any generalization suspect, but the marking of the gender of the deceased in the tablets is, at the least, highly suggestive. Lewis notes that 'peripheral' cults have a special appeal for women in male-dominated societies and cites numerous parallels that suggest that women may have found, in the sort of cults that produced the gold tablets, a relief from the strictures of the mainstream Greek society.[104] But what sort of religious cult might this be?

In the case of the Pelinna tablets, the prominence of Bacchios and the statue of the maenad found in the tomb point to a context of Dionysiac mysteries in which women took part, perhaps even to the exclusion of men.[105] Ritual maenadism has been attested in various periods for such places as Delphi and Miletus, and the woman of the Pelinna grave may have been a part of an organized group of women who performed maenadic rituals at certain festivals.[106] While such a scenario is more likely than a symposiastic organization like the Athenian Iobacchoi, which seems to have been mostly male, the Pelinna woman may have been part of a Dionysiac association that was not part of a civic cult, as the ritual maenad groups or the Iobacchoi were, but rather part of a countercultural association or 'peripheral cult' that marked a permanent protest against the mainstream society. An example of such a group would be those buried in the cemetery at Cumae, which an inscription says was limited to those who were initiated in the bacchic rites. οὐ θέμις ἐν τοῦθα κεῖσθαι ἰ μὲ τὸν

represented, and women or, less frequently, children make up the great majority of the examples. She argues that the figure of Charon in these vases was designed as a reassuring and comforting figure meant to help alleviate the anxieties about death. She also points out that the adult citizen males could project their anxieties about death onto the marginal groups. "The symbolism associated with Charon, which reflected attitudes inappropriate for the male adult, drifted toward the 'marginal' categories women, children, and adolescents (including the marginal ephebes), who became the vehicle for the articulation of these perceptions into images in which, in fact everyone, including men, and certainly the male artists who created them, could also see the prefiguration of death in terms of a reassuring image." (Sourvinou-Inwood 1995, p. 345.)

[104] Lewis 1971, esp. pp. 27-33. Kraemer 1980 applies Lewis's terms to Greek Dionysiac religion.

[105] Men were part of the religious context of the B tablets, of course, given the formula of the 'son' of Earth and starry Heaven that appears not only on the Cretan tablets but also on the tablet of the Hipponion woman. The fact that one of the Cretan tablets alters the formula to mark herself as a daughter of Earth and starry Heaven suggests that, at least in that community, gender was a significant issue.

[106] Henrichs 1978 points out that the evidence for ritual maenadism reveals something more like a regulated civic group than the raving, primitive ecstatics imagined by Harrison and others.

βεβαχχευμένον. As Turcan points out, the form of βεβαχχευμένον indicates that the initiate was not merely βάκχος during the limited period of a Dionysiac ritual, but that a permanent status was envisaged.[107] The Dionysos cult in the polis provides a controlled and temporary disruption of the normal order, but to prolong this disruption throughout one's life in a mystic religious group is to register a protest against the normal, civic order.[108]

Dionysiac cults are not the only *chemins de déviance* open; a Pythagorean context also presents itself as a likely candidate. Southern Italy was the stronghold of the Pythagorean movement, and as Burkert notes, the Pythagoreans were well known for "the equal status of women side by side with men. The fact that there were female as well as male Pythagoreans is often stressed in the sources."[109] Just as one who is βεβαχχευμένος extends the special ritual status of Dionysiac worship beyond the ordinary worship to his whole life, so too the Pythagoreans engage on a daily basis in the prohibitions, offerings, and practices appropriate to special ceremonies.[110] Such a mode of life is conducted in opposition to the normal way of living, marking the Pythagoreans as countercultural, even marginal members of the society.[111]

---

[107] "Il se fait βεβαχχευμένος grâce à la constance d'une vie ascétique, et non pas simplement *bacchos* dans l'exaltation éphémere de l'orgie." (Turcan 1986, p. 237.)

[108] cp. Sabbatucci 1979 on the role of Dionysos cult in the polis to reaffirm the order by a temporary suspension of it. "Pertanto tutte le manifestazioni cultuali che sotto il segno di Dioniso realizzavano una *temporanea* rottura dell'ordine, vanno correttamente interpretate, almeno fino allo scoperta del contrario (il che può avvenire di volta in volta, caso per caso, e non mediante uin giudizio di carattere generale) come espedienti rituali per rinnovare, reintegrare, rafforzare l'ordine stesso, e non come tentavi di distruggere l'ordine vigente." (Sabbatucci 1979, p. 51.) This function of Dionysos as the bringer of temporary disorder may, of course, be expanded by the mystical movements into a permanent disruption of the normal order.

[109] Burkert 1982, p. 17.

[110] cp., Burkert 1972, p. 190.

[111] While an 'Orphic' community has yet to be satisfactorily identified (or even defined), an 'Orphic' context for a group comprised largely of women should also not be ruled out on the grounds that the figure of Orpheus is in some places associated with misogyny or male homosexuality. The association of Orpheus with the rites at Eleusis should be sufficient to prove that rituals attributed to Orpheus need not exclude women, even if some of the stories about Orpheus emphasized the aspects of his character that dealt with the initiation of men. See Graf 1986 and Bremmer 1991. Detienne 1979 (p. 216 n. 138), Detienne 2003 (p. 164), and Guthrie 1952 (pp. 143, 61), e.g., extrapolate the exclusion of women from all Orphic movements from their exclusion in some Orphic contexts.

The tablets, of course, merely represent an expression of such a protest against ordinary life; how the individual enacted this *déviance* might have differed radically from the βίος Ὀρφικός. Such a protest as the tablets express need not be as dramatic as that of the Pythagoreans or the Euripidean Hippolytus or chorus of Cretans, involving a significantly different lifestyle and an aggressive clash of values with polis society.[112] Nevertheless, the claims to ritual purity and divine lineage, discussed below, suggest that the women who were buried with the gold tablets identified themselves as standing apart from the mainstream, however that *déviance* may have been manifested in their lives.

*Ritual Purity*

The primary importance accorded to the claim of ritual purity in the A and P tablets supports the idea that these tablets come from countercultural religious contexts and indicates the type of *déviance* by which the creators of the tablets defined themselves. This claim to special status, however, is articulated in different ways in the tablets. In addition to a basic claim to purity, some tablets specifically claim that the deceased no longer needs to atone for any misdeeds, either because she has already paid the penalty or because she has been freed by Dionysos.

While the A tablets all seem implicitly to affirm the identity of the deceased as a female, the first explicit statement of identity in the Timpone Piccolo tablets from Thurii and the parallel tablet found in Rome centuries later is a declaration of the purity of the deceased, "Pure I come from the pure" (ἔρχομαι ἐκ καθαρῶν καθαρά). Not only has the deceased herself attained purity, but she comes from a lineage that is also pure. The concern with purity was characteristic of the religious movements that arose as a counterculture to the mainstream polis life and religion. Purification rituals that had formerly been performed only in abnormal moments of crisis became a normal practice for those who defined their

---

[112] Euripides *Hippolytus* 950ff.; Euripides *Cretans* fr. 472 = Porphyry *De Abst.* 4.56 ἁγνὸν δὲ βίον τείνων ἐξ οὗ Διὸς Ἰδαίου μύστης γενόμην, καὶ νυκτιπόλου Ζαγρέως βροντὰς τούς ὠμοφάγους δαίτας τελέσας μητρί τ᾽ ὀρείῳ δᾷδας ἀνασχὼν καὶ κουρήτων βάκχος ἐκλήθην ὁσιωθείς. πάλλευκα δ᾽ ἔχων εἵματα φεύγω γένεσίν τε βροτῶν καὶ νεκροθήκης οὐ χριμπτόμενος τήν τ᾽ ἐμψύχων βρῶσιν ἐδεστῶν πεφύλαγμαι. "Pure has my life been since the day when I became an initiate of Idaean Zeus and herdsman of night-wandering Zagreus, and having accomplished the raw feasts and held torches aloft to the Mountain Mother, yea torches of the Kuretes, was raised to the holy estate and called Bakchos. Having all-white garments, I flee the birth of mortals and, not nearing the place of corpses, I guard myself against the eating of ensouled flesh."

lives outside the normal order of the society.[113] The claim to superior status by these marginal groups on the grounds of the purity of their life served to compensate for their unsatisfactory status within the social order.

The claim, then, to come from the pure, ἐκ καθαρῶν, seems most likely to refer not to the actual parentage of the deceased but to her ritual predecessors; i.e., rather than claiming that she was born of parents who are also pure, the deceased is claiming that she has been made pure by those who are themselves pure. The ritual genealogy thus replaces the polis-centered family lines as the efficacy of the purification becomes more important for determining one's place in the cosmos than the ordinary distinctions of gender, family, clan, or polis. This replacement need not imply a full-fledged religious community or sect.[114] Itinerant specialists in purification are a well-attested phenomenon, and some of them perhaps gathered small groups on whom they imposed a certain regulation of life.[115] However, the fact that the mention of a group of the pure appears in three roughly contemporary graves from the same locale in Thurii does suggest the presence of some more or less organized group with a purificatory agenda.

*The Payment of the Penalty*

In tablets A2 and A3, but not in A1, the deceased further claims to have paid the penalty for unjust deeds, ποινὰν δ' ἀνταπέτεισ' ἔργων ἕνεκ' οὔτι δικαίων. This claim, with its implication that the deceased need no longer

[113] Burkert 1982 has shown the distinction between the craftsmen who were brought in as specialists in time of crisis and the members of the religious sect, who routinized the practices of the specialists in their protests against the normal order. cp., Sabbatucci 1979, p. 68: "La catarsi orfica potrebbe non voler risolvere una crisi occasionale, ma risolvere piuttosto la crisi esistenziale; non purificare da una follia episodica, ma purificare dal vivere profano, inteso come una lunga follia, eccetera eccetera...Onde la catarsi diventerebbe propriamente una iniziazione alla nuova vita, l'*orphikos bios*."

[114] cp. Burkert's definition of a sect, "A sect is a minority protest group with (1) an alternative lifestyle, (2) an organization providing (2.1) regular group meetings and (2.2) some sort of communal or co-operative property, and (3) a high level of spiritual integration, agreement on beliefs and practices, (3.1) based on authority, be it a charismatic leader or a sacred scripture with special interpretation, (3.2) making the distinction of 'we' versus 'they' the primary reference system, and (3.3) taking action on apostates. The historian will add (4.1) the perspective of diachronic stability...and (4.2) local mobility." (Burkert 1982, p. 3.) Burkert argues that this definition applies fairly well to the evidence for the early Pythagoreans.

[115] cp. Burkert 1982, pp. 10–11. cp. also Plato, *Republic* 364e–365a.

worry about the penalties that others might still need to pay, resembles the statement in the Pelinna tablets that the deceased has been freed by Bacchios and the Pherai tablet that declares, ἄποινος γὰρ ὁ μύστης. These unjust deeds for which the penalty is no longer needed may either be those of the deceased herself or those committed by some ancestor, as Plato's discussion of purificatory rituals for unjust deeds in the *Republic* shows. "For beggar priests and prophets go to the doors of the rich and persuade them that they have the power from the gods to perform sacrifices and spells. If they or one of their ancestors has done something unjust, they have the power to heal it with pleasurable things and festivals."[116]

The idea of a descendant paying for the crime of his ancestor has a long tradition in Greek mythology. Solon assures the wicked that even if they do not pay for their crimes in their lifetime, their descendants will pay (ἀναίτιοι ἔργα τίνουσιν ἢ παῖδες τούτων ἢ γένος ἐξοπίσω). While the affliction of an entire family line for such crimes as murder and perjury goes back to Homer and Hesiod, the tales of the punishment of an entire family as retribution for the murder of a family member, incest, or cannibalism become a favorite subject in tragedy.[117] Nor is the family curse, from which each member must pay for the misdeed of an ancestor, confined to tragedy; this mythical idea was employed in practical politics as well. The prominent Athenian noble family of the Alcmaeonids, which boasted such members as Cleisthenes and Pericles, contended constantly with their political enemies about the stain that the murder of Cylon had left upon their family.[118]

Along with the idea of paying for an ancestor's crimes naturally comes the idea of somehow evading the penalty. Herodotus's myth of the fall of Croesus is fascinating in this regard: Croesus is doomed to fall, despite his many sacrifices to Apollo, because his ancestor Gyges murdered King Candaules and took his throne and his wife. When Croesus rebukes

---

[116] ἀγύρται δὲ καὶ μάντεις ἐπὶ πλουσίων θύρας ἰόντες πείθουσιν ὡς ἔστι παρὰ σφίσι δύναμις ἐκ θεῶν προζομένη θυσίας τε καὶ ἐπῳδαῖς, εἴτε τι ἀδίκημά του γέγονεν αὐτοῦ ἢ προγόνων, ἀκεῖσθαι μεθ᾽ ἡδονῶν τε καὶ ἑορτῶν. (*Republic* 364bc, cp. 364e–5a, 366ab.)

[117] Solon fr. 1.31, cp. esp. 25–35. Hereditary punishment of perjury – *Il.* 4.160–2, cf. 3.300ff; Hesiod *W&D* 282–5. For affliction of whole families *Il.* 6.200–5; *Od.* 20.66–78; cp. *Od.* 11.436. In tragedy – Aeschylus: *Sept.* 653–5, 699–701, 720–91; *Ag.* 1090–7, 1186–97, 1309, 1338–42, 1460, 1468–88, 1497–1512, 1565–76, 1600–2; Sophocles: *El.* 504–15, *Ant.* 583–603, OC 367–70, 964–5, 1299; Euripides: *El.* 699–746, 1306ff, *IT* 186–202, 987f., *Or.* 811–18, 985–1012, 1546–8, *Phoen.* 379–82, 867–88, 1556–9, 1592–4, 1611. See further Parker 1983, pp. 191–206.

[118] cp. Hdt. V.70–72; Thucydides I. 126–127.

Apollo for ingratitude, Apollo informs him that his sacrifices were not ignored, but rather they procured for him a three-year delay of the inevitable
downfall.[119] The Orpheotelests described in Plato's *Republic* seem to have
promised more complete results from the sacrifices they advised, and in
the *Phaedrus*, Plato mentions Dionysiac purifications as bringing relief to
those suffering under the burdens of the crimes of their ancestors.[120]

Plato's Orpheotelests and the practices of Theophrastus's superstitious man indicate that individuals and whole cities tried to relieve their
anxieties about the misdeeds of their forebears.[121] However, Plato's discussion also shows that these ancestors are unlikely to be the Titans as
universal ancestors of mankind, for every mortal has ancestors who were
less than perfectly just.[122] Although Graf argues that the ancestors from
whose penalty Bacchios releases the deceased must be the Titans, the
Pelinna tablets' statement, εἰπεῖν Φερσεφόναισ' ὅτι Β⟨άκ⟩χιος αὐτὸς ἔλυσε,
need not be explained by the Zagreus anthropogony.[123] Dionysos appears
in a number of contexts as the deity who suspends the normal constraints,
who bursts the bonds that regulate the order of the cosmos, providing

---

[119] Hdt. I.90–91.

[120] *Republic* 364e–365a; *Phaedrus* 254de, 265b. Damascius refers to the role of Dionysos
Lusios and his rites in freeing an individual from the penalty of crimes committed by
ancestors (OF 232). See note 88 above.

[121] Plato, *Rep.* 364e–365a; Theophrastus, *Char.* xvi.12. Empedokles, with his doctrine of
reincarnations, combines the idea of paying for one's own crime with that of paying for
the crimes of an ancestor by making the predecessor for whose crimes the individual is
paying a previous incarnation. The doctrine of reincarnation neatly solves the theodicy
problems that arise from an innocent descendant paying for an ancestor's crimes.

[122] As Bianchi comments, "Il n'est pas nécessaire, pour expliquer cette conception, de
recourir à un péché particulier (mais, en tout cas, de quelque manière, préhumain
et 'antécédent'), tel que le démembrement de Dionysos par les Titans, le rapt de
Perséphone, le crime de Kronos, ou même la faute de Prométhée." (Bianchi 1966,
p. 120.)

[123] "But these ancestors," Graf claims, "are not just ordinary deceased, since Dionysus has
power over them: the only ancestors of humans who are closely connected with Dionysus
are the Titans, who killed the god - though it is somewhat unclear what power Dionysus
has over them." Graf 1993a, p. 244. Graf's hesitation betrays the flaw in his argument.
Dionysos's role as Lusios in fact makes little sense within the context of the Zagreus
myth; it is rather an aspect of his character that derives from other portions of the Bacchic
mythology. The one possible explanation, that it is the Dionysiac bits within each mortal
that provide the release, depends heavily on just that portion of the story that appears
only in Olympiodorus and is most likely to be his own idiosyncratic contribution in
service of his argument against suicide. See Edmonds 1999 for further argument. cp.
Brisson 1992 and 1995 on the neoplatonic and alchemical allegory involved, and West
1983, p. 165.

relief for those constricted or burdened by the normal order.[124] Dionysos's power as Lusios depends not on any special relation to the Titans as the criminals (or to the humans with a divine tidbit of Dionysos in them), but on his general function as the loosener, a trait illustrated even by the effects of wine, the most widespread symbol for the god. His role in freeing his special initiates, in this life or the next, from the penalties due for the crimes of ancestors is simply an extension of this essential aspect to eschatology.[125]

The use of this mythic element in the tablets, then, would have evoked a wide range of traditional stories of individuals paying the penalty not only for their own crimes but also for those of their ancestors. However, the deceased from Timpone Piccolo who claim to have paid the penalty, like the woman from Pelinna, are confident that proper atonement has been made and that they now may be at one with the gods with whom they claim kinship.

### Struck by Lightning

In all the Timpone Piccolo tablets, A1, A2, and A3, the deceased also makes the claim to have been struck by lightning.[126] This claim admits of more interpretations than simply that of the Titans, although they are undoubtedly some of the more famous victims of Zeus's thunderbolt. Zuntz and Rohde took it completely literally and claimed that the corpses in Timpone Piccolo were of people who had actually been killed by

---

[124] For the role of Dionysos within polis-cult as the one who provides the necessary temporary relief from the normal order, cp. Sabbatucci 1979, p. 51. Also cp. Versnel 1990, pp. 139, 166, Casadio 1987, pp. 199ff., and Casadio 1999, pp. 122–143, on the functions of Dionysos Lusios.

[125] The Apulian vase in Toledo that depicts Dionysos greeting Pluto in the underworld (see cover illustration) seems to symbolize Dionysos's power to save his worshippers in the realm of the dead (see Johnston and McNiven 1996).

[126] The reference to the thunderbolt appears in slightly different forms in these tablets. A1 says that fate *and* the lightning bolt have overpowered the deceased, ἀλλά με μοῖρ' ἐδάμασσε... καὶ ἀστεροβλῆτα κεραυνῶι, while A2 and A3 phrase it as *either* fate *or* the lightning bolt, εἴτε με μοῖρ' ἐδάμασσ' εἴτε ἀστεροπῆτι κεραυνῶ(ν). As Zuntz notes, the form of A1 has numerous Homeric parallels for the idea of Moira and a specific deity being credited with someone's destruction, and he explains ἀστεροβλῆτα/ἀστεροπῆτα as an epithet of Zeus as the hurler of the thunderbolt, rather than a description of the bolt itself. He sees the change between A1 and A2 and A3 as due to simple corruption, dismissing Rohde's suggestion that the verse was changed to apply to someone who was not actually killed by lightning. (Zuntz 1971, pp. 314–316. cp. Rohde 1925, n. 54, p. 448.)

lightning.[127] As Graf notes, "It is impossible to prove or disprove this 're-alistic' explanation," but whether or not the deceased were *actually* killed by lightning, the *claim* to have been struck by lightning has a number of interesting mythic resonances.[128] The Titans were by no means the only ones to have felt Zeus's lightning bolt. Apart from other monstrous enemies of Zeus, like Typhon, a number of heroes were struck by lightning in a variety of myths.[129] In some versions, Herakles' apotheosis upon the pyre at Oeta was accomplished by Zeus's thunderbolt, and Semele and Asclepius, for example, were also struck by lightning before their final apotheosis or heroization.[130]

These examples are particularly interesting because each of these heroes could better serve as the mythic reference for the statement of identity in the gold tablets than the Titans. Each of them was originally a mortal but divinely descended or connected; each committed unjust deeds; and each was heroized after being hit by the lightning of Zeus. For Herakles, the lightning strike was strictly part of the apotheosis or heroization process rather than punishment for his misdeeds; but for both Asclepius and Semele, the lightning bolt directly served as the punishment for the unjust deeds, with the apotheosis or heroization following. Although Kingsley indeed suggests that Herakles was *the* figure to whom the deceased was assimilated, as Seaford and other have argued with regard to the Titans, I would rather argue that Herakles, Semele, Asclepius, and others served more as analogies for the individual rather than as a specific model.[131] The

---

127 "It is perfectly natural to assume that this tumulus, the Timpone Piccolo, was erected over the grave of a person killed by lightning and thereby sanctified – and that two others who, later, found their death in the same way were buried in this most appropriate place." (Zuntz 1971, p. 316.) Rohde 1925 speculates that perhaps only the deceased with tablet A1 was actually killed by lightning, and that A2 and A3 were altered to give an alternative to fate and the lightning bolt for those who had died a natural death. (n. 54, p. 448.)

128 Graf 1993a, p. 253.

129 As Rohde states in his appendix on the "Consecration of Persons Struck by Lightning," "In many legends death by *lightning* makes the victim holy and raises him to godlike (everlasting) life." (Rohde 1925, pp. 581–582.)

130 Herakles: D.S. 4.38.4–5. Semele: Pind. O. ii.27; D.S. 5.52.2; Charax ap. Anon. *de Incred.* xvi, p. 325.5ff West; Arist. 1, p. 47 Dind.; Philostr., *Imag.* i.14; Nonnus, *Dion.* viii.409ff. Asclepius: Hesiod fr. 109 Rz.; Lucian *DD.* 13. Also cp. figures such as Erechtheus, Kapaneus, and Amphiaraus. The sacralizing effect of lightning may been seen from later testimonies in the reverence for the lightning-struck tombs of Lycurgus and Euripides in Plut. *Lyc.* 31 and Pliny's report that the thunderbolting of the statues of Olympic victor Euthymos indicated his heroic status (*N.H.* vii.152).

131 "The geographical spread of the evidence – and in particular its concentration at Thurii, one of the greatest centres for the cult of Heracles in southern Italy – leaves little doubt

use of the mythic element of the lightning strike conjured up the tales about these heroes and conferred some of the authority of these tales to the deceased's account of herself, as well as transferring some of the prestige of these figures to the deceased. The deceased did not necessarily see herself as another Semele or even another Herakles, but rather these figures served as the mythic precedents. The traditional tales of all of these heroes share the common elements of the hero undergoing the same process of heroization, a purification through the fire of the lightning bolt, which simultaneously stripped him of his mortal impurities and translated him to the realm of the immortals.

*Divine Lineage*

The claims to special purification are not the only kind of self-definition used as a solution in the gold tablets; the claims to divine lineage in the A and B tablets also permit the deceased to succeed in their encounters with the powers of the underworld. In tablets A1–3, the deceased claims to Persephone and the other deities that she is a member of their own lineage, whereas, in the B series of tablets, the deceased announces to the guardians: Γῆς παῖς εἰμι καὶ Οὐρανοῦ ἀστερόεντος, I am the child of Earth and starry Heaven. These statements seem to be the key statement of identity for the deceased to complete successfully her journey into the land of the dead.

The self-definition in the A tablets takes the form of a general declaration of the deceased's divine lineage, καὶ γὰρ ἐγὼν ὑμῶν γένος ὄλβιον εὔχομαι εἶναι. As Depew notes of εὔχομαι: "The verb denotes an interactive process of guiding another in assessing one's status and thus one's due. The purpose is not to 'boast' or 'declare' something about one's past, but to make a claim on someone in the present, whether in terms of an actual request or of recognition and acknowledgement of status."[132] The connective, καὶ γὰρ, further indicates that it is because of this kinship with the powers whom she is addressing that the deceased may make the claim

that this initiatory heroization schema was more or less consciously modeled on the figure of Heracles." (Kingsley 1995, p. 257, n. 21.) cp. Seaford 1986, esp. pp. 4–9, for the Titans as a model.

[132] Depew, drawing on the research of Adkins and Muellner, describes the epic uses of the verb. "When Homeric heroes εὔχονται, what they are doing is asserting their identity and their value in the society they inhabit, and by means of this assertion creating a context in which the claim they are making on another member of that society will be appropriate and compelling." (Depew 1997, p. 232. cp., Adkins 1969; Muellner 1976.)

to purity and ask Persephone for special treatment in her realm. The late tablet A5, although it has the same statement of purity, is missing this line, although some scholars have seen in the words, Διὸς τέκος ἀγλαά, an equivalent claim, interpreting this statement to mean that Caecilia Secundina is claiming to be the child of Zeus.[133]

The claim of a mortal to be ὑμῶν γένος ὄλβιον, when addressing Persephone, is unlikely to be a reference to a myth of human descent from the Titans, but rather it indicates that the deceased considers herself to be a part of the community of the gods. As mainstream a poet as Hesiod says he will tell how the gods and man came from the same origin, ὡς ὁμόθεν γεγάασι θεοὶ θνητοί τ' ἄνθρωποι, and closer to these tablets in time and space, Pindar begins the Sixth Nemean Ode by affirming the same idea.[134] Moreover, in addition to this idea of a general connection between the divine and human families, numerous individual families told myths in which they laid claim to specific divine ancestors. By claiming to be of the γένος of the gods, the deceased is employing this familiar mythic element, not to support the prestige of an aristocratic family in the competitions within the locative order of the polis, but to make a claim that transcends the clan politics of her contemporary world. Her claim to be treated as a member of the divine family recalls instead the ideal of the time before the separation of mortals and immortals. "For there once were common feasts and councils of immortal gods and mortal men together."[135] Hesiod's description of the unity of men and gods, which ended with the divisive sacrifice at Mekone, is only the most obvious of the numerous myths of an idealized primeval communion of men and gods. The appeal to this primordial unity of gods and mortals signals a rejection of the contemporary world in favor of a return to the golden age of purity and divine communion.

The declaration of the deceased in the B tablets, "I am the child of Earth and starry Heaven," is perhaps one of the best known features of

---

[133] However, Διὸς τέκος ἀγλαά could equally be referring to Persephone, child of Zeus. West and Kotansky prefer to read the line, Διὸς τέκος, ἀλλὰ δέχεσθε..., eliminating the feminine adjective and making the child of Zeus refer to Eubouleus as Dionysos. (Kotansky 1994, p. 111. See West's suggestion in West 1975, p. 231.)

[134] *Works and Days*, 108. Pindar Nem VI.1-2 ἓν ἀνδρῶν, ἓν θεῶν γένος· ἐκ μιᾶς δὲ πνέομεν ματρὸς ἀμφότεροι.

[135] ξυναὶ γὰρ τότε δαῖτες ἔσαν, ξυνοὶ δὲ θόωκοι ἀθανάτοισι θεοῖσι καταθνητοῖς τ' ἀνθρώποις. *Eoiae*, fr.1.6-7 Merkelbach-West; *Theog.* 535ff. cp. also the feasting of Tantalus and Ixion with the gods for other tales of the disruption of primordial unity. At W&D 120, Hesiod's golden race live blissful lives, "dear to the blessed gods," before the split with the gods: φίλοι μακάρεσσι θεοῖσιν.

the gold tablets. This formula of self-identification serves as the password for the deceased to bypass the guardians and obtain the crucial drink of the water of Memory. Unfortunately, just as Comparetti immediately associated the line, ποινὰν δ' ἀνταπέτεισ' ἔργων ἕνεκ' οὔτι δικαίων, in A2 and A3 with the murder of Zagreus by the Titans, so too he linked Γῆς παῖς εἰμι καὶ Οὐρανοῦ ἀστερόεντος, to his story of the supposed Orphic doctrine of original sin.[136] This self-identification, however, does not identify the deceased as a Titan, but like the claim in the Thurii tablets of being of the race of the gods, the formula connects the deceased with the divine community, evoking the primordial paradise when the gods and humans lived together in bliss.

Admittedly, the Titans are children of Earth and starry Heaven, but they are far from the only descendants of Earth and Heaven in the Greek mythic tradition. The phrase, Γῆς καὶ Οὐρανοῦ ἀστερόεντος, or a close substitute, is used a number of times in Hesiod, but never of the Titans alone. Rather it refers to the entire ἀθανάτων ἱερὸν γένος αἰὲν ἐόντων, the holy race of ever-living immortals.[137] The claim, Γῆς παῖς εἰμι καὶ Οὐρανοῦ ἀστερόεντος, is no more specific than the claim, ἐγὼν ὑμῶν γένος ὄλβιον εὔχομαι εῖμεν, found in the A tablets. Since Ge and Ouranos are primordial forces, the first parents of the immortal beings, from them come all the immortals, not just the Titans.

A papyrus fragment that makes Triptolemos the son of Ge and Ouranos may throw an interesting light upon the meaning of Γῆς παῖς εἰμι καὶ Οὐρανοῦ ἀστερόεντος in the gold tablets.[138] This parentage for

---

[136] "The Titanic origin of the soul is here explicitly confirmed; it is well known that the Titans were the sons of Uranos and Gaea." (Comparetti 1882, p. 116.) Before Comparetti, the only discovered tablet of the B series, B1 from Petelia, was thought to be associated with the Trophonius oracle, and Mnemosyne, not the deceased, was thought to be the child of Earth and starry Heaven, as indeed she is in Hesiod (*Theog.* 135). cp. Goettling 1843, p. 8. Since Comparetti's time, however, the increase in the number of tablets that make no reference to lightning or paying a penalty (12 new tablets) seems to indicate that the death by lightning is a unique feature of the context that produced the tablets of Timpone Piccolo, rather than a feature of the doctrine underlying all the tablets but simply abbreviated out of B1, which happened to have an explicit identification of the Titans in the reference to the child of Earth and starry Heaven. A1, A2, and A3 are the only tablets that make any reference to lightning, and only A2 and A3 mention a punishment for unjust deeds.

[137] Hesiod, *Theogony*, 105-106. cp. 45, 154, 421.

[138] The papyrus contains genealogies for a number of heroes connected with mysteries and the afterlife: Rhadamanthys, Musaios, Eumolpos, Trophonios, and Triptolemos. Henrichs argues that the papyrus should provoke reconsideration of the neglected manuscript readings of Apollodorus's *Library* I.5.2, which give Ge and Ouranos as the parents of Triptolemos according to Pherekydes, instead of Ge and Okeanos. (Henrichs

Triptolemos, the first to be initiated into Demeter's mysteries at Eleusis, may reflect a doctrine that used the race of Earth and starry Heaven to refer to those specially privileged in the mysteries. It is certainly not inconceivable that the myth of Triptolemos as the son of Earth and Heaven was told outside the Eleusinian Mysteries and that the makers of the gold tablets used this idea to characterize the specially privileged. Alternatively, of course, the idea of an initiate as a child of Earth and Heaven, as a member of the race of the immortals, could have made its way from the circles that produced the gold tablets and into the Eleusinian sphere.

Such a mythic motif of being the child of Earth and Heaven would be appealing to the religious communities that produced the gold tablets. The deceased employs this mythic motif in a claim of descent that supplants the ties of the human, mundane, and civic *genos* with those of a divine, otherworldly, and primordial *genos*. Ge and Ouranos represent the primordial forces of the cosmos; to claim descent from them is not merely to lay claim to divine descent, but to link oneself to the primordial order, the ideal order from which the present mundane world has degenerated.[139] Just as the idea of feasting with the gods and the practice of vegetarianism represent a desire to return to the ideal life in which mortals and immortals were not separated, so also to claim to be a child of the cosmogonic forces of Earth and Heaven represents a claim to be a part of that ideal life rather than a part of the normal, mundane order. Sabbatucci describes the claim to be part of the divine *genos* that descends from Earth and Heaven as a way of rejecting the political hierarchy that depends on human families. "Il fatto che il defunto si proclami 'figlio di Urano e di Gaia', se non stabilisce la realtà storica contestuale di una identificazione del 'genetico' col 'mondano', è probativa soltanto della rinuncia da parte del defunto al *genos* determinato dai suoi genitori reali."[140] The deceased

---

1986, p. 250 and nn. 30–31.) cp. Pausanias 1.14.3, who rather dubiously cites Musaios for a parentage of Ge and Okeanos, which as Henrichs (n. 31) remarks is an unparalleled pair within extant Orphic genealogies, while Ge and Ouranos are as common a pair in Orphic sources as in other genealogical traditions.

[139] Burkert argues: "Colui che si chiama 'figlio del cielo e della terra' si rappresenta non nella sua dualità, ma nella sua unità originaria. Matrimonio tra il cielo e la terra esisteva soltanto in tempi primordiali, prima delle separazioni e dei limiti del nostro mondo. Il morto iniziato ha una posizione primordiale e cosmica." (Burkert 1975, p. 89.)

[140] Sabbatucci 1975, pp. 44–45. As Sabbatucci explains the mystic's point of view, the human condition is unreal in comparison with the reality represented by the divine condition because the life of a human is ephemeral, while that of a god is eternal. The *genos*, however, represents a human reality that transcends the brief mortal lifespan and

in the tablet has rejected her identity as a part of one of the lineages that define the places of all the ordinary people in the human world. Instead, she has chosen to identify herself as part of a divine order that transcends the vicissitudes of mortal life. The deceased's claim to be a child of Earth and starry Heaven, then, is not a claim to be a Titan, the heir to the blood guilt of the murder of Zagreus, but rather a claim to have become part of the race of immortals, to be one with the original cosmogonic order.

Three of the eleven B tablets have an addition to this primary statement of identity.[141] B1 and B9 add the qualification, αὐτὰρ ἐμοὶ γένος οὐράνιον, "but my lineage is celestial." B2 has a statement that seems to convey the same idea, Ἀστέριος ὄνομα, "Starry is my name." As Zuntz notes, "The second verse is a later addition, quite incompatible with the first; an addition made when it was felt that descent from Heaven was the essential qualification for bliss in the other world."[142] While the original claim to be the child of both Earth and Heaven implies not dualism but primeval unity, the modification, beginning with the strongly adversative αὐτὰρ, seems to point to a more dualistic outlook that privileges the starry sky of Heaven over the material world of the Earth.

This change might be connected with an alternate set of myths that locates the gods in the sky, in the celestial spheres, instead of in particular places within the world such as Olympus. The Pythagorean saying, of uncertain date, that the Isles of the Blessed are the sun and the moon would also seem to reflect such a change.[143] No chronological point can be fixed for such a change; indeed, the tablets, B1, B2, and B9, which have the extra verse, are among the earliest of the tablets found. They are certainly older than the Cretan tablets, all of which lack the extra verse. Two of the tablets come from the northern parts of Greece, B2 from

provides a permanent framework within which the individual can define herself for the entirety of her life. If, however, one rejects this framework and the hierarchies into which it is tied, the divine *genos* and the ideal world of the gods provide a substitute framework within which the individual can define herself.

[141] B11 contains a line which might also have this addition, αὐτὰρ ἐ[μοὶ γένος οὐράνιον, reconstructed for the first line in the second column of text. While this is possible, the verse does not follow the primary Γῆς παῖς εἰμὶ καὶ Οὐρανοῦ ἀστερόεντος, as it does in the three other parallels. Especially since B11 appears to contain verses unknown from the other tablets, the reconstruction of this verse from so few characters and so far from its normal place seems highly doubtful.

[142] Zuntz 1971, p. 366.

[143] Preserved in Iamblichus's *Vita Pythagori*, 82, probably drawing on Aristotle's lost work on the Pythagoreans. cp. Burkert 1972, pp. 363ff.

Pharsalos and B9 from somewhere in Thessaly, so the difference could conceivably be local, but no real evidence supports such an idea. Such a cosmology would differ markedly from the chthonian underworld of the Thurii and Pelinna tablets, which address the χθονίων βασίλεια or promise celebrations beneath the earth, ὑπὸ γῆν.[144]

The change in the B tablets could also be connected with a rejection of the political identity centered on myths of autochthony. Sabbatucci points out that the political ideology of democracy at Athens sought to replace the aristocratic definition by clan lineage with a definition of the citizen as part of a people who are all descended from the soil of their territory, rather than from competing clans.[145] The citizens of the polis are rooted to the earth from which their ancestors, the founders of the polis, came, and the political order also is fixed in place. The assertion that one is not a child of the Earth like the citizens whose claim to authority in the polis stems from that descent may be a way once again of rejecting the hierarchies of civil society and laying claim to an order beyond the bounds of the polis.

*Statements of Identity as Solution*

The statements of identity that the deceased makes in her confrontation with powers of the underworld help her obtain a favorable resolution to the potential problems she faces in her underworld journey. The varying statements of identity on the different tablets need not be interpreted as all referring to a single myth; rather, the variations reflect the different solutions conceived for handling the same difficulty facing the deceased: how to obtain a favorable end to the journey of death. This favorable result is granted because of the identity of the deceased, whose special status entitles her to proceed past the obstacle posed by the meeting with the powers of the underworld.

The proclamations of identity found in these tablets – the claim to divine lineage or specifically to be the child of Earth and starry Heaven, the claim to have been struck by lightning, and the claim to have paid the penalty for unjust deeds or to have been released by Bacchios – are still

---

[144] As Bernabé and Jiménez 2001 point out, p. 167, the afterlife in the tablets is firmly in the underworld, rather than in the heavens.

[145] Sabbatucci 1975, p. 45. While this suggestion is feasible for places like Athens, such a use of autochthony is less probable for colonies in Italy or other places on the margins of the Greek world.

interpreted by many scholars in simple terms of the Zagreus myth and Titanic anthropogony. I have argued elsewhere that this myth and the doctrine of Orphic orginal sin derived from it are in fact the inventions of Comparetti and other late nineteenth century scholars who, beginning with Comparetti's explanation of the Thurii tablets in 1879, constructed a central doctrine for Orphism on the model of familiar Christian theology.[146] All of these claims in the tablets, however, identify the deceased as an extraordinary person, who is not only ritually pure but who stands in a special relation with the gods, a relation that entitles her to status and treatment in the afterlife far beyond that of her position in the mundane world of the living. The composers of the gold tablets employ the language of myth, drawing on a variety of mythical elements familiar from the tradition to communicate the important facets of the deceased's identity. The resonance of each of these elements is lost if they are all read as referring to a single myth, a myth not told until more than two millennia after the tablets were composed.

The A tablets proclaim that the deceased is pure and of the race of the gods. Both of these claims indicate a rejection of the normal standards and measures of status. Rather than defining her identity by her genetic ancestors and their place in the socio-political hierarchy, the deceased defines herself in terms of a lineage of the ritually purified and in terms of a link with the gods. This concern with genealogy and identity, both in the claims to ritual purity and to divine lineage, shows the mode of protest adopted by the creators of these A tablets, a rejection of the socio-political hierarchy of the polis centered around the aristocratic families.

The statement of identity, the password which the deceased in the B tablets gives to the guardians of the spring, permits the deceased to bypass the obstacle presented by the guardians and obtain the drink she so desires. The deceased's credentials as a child of Earth and starry Heaven suffice for the guardians to permit her to drink from the fountain, the access to which they guard. This statement differentiates the deceased from the ordinary run of souls who come to quench their thirst in the underworld, who lack or fail to realize their connection with Earth and Heaven. The deceased proclaims her place in the divine lineage from the cosmogonic forces of Earth and Heaven, replacing her identification within the civic order through her human genealogy and asserting her

[146] See Edmonds 1999.

participation in the divine order through the traditional language of myth i.e., discourse.

The Pelinna tablets do not show this same concern with genealogy; their mode of *déviance* is different. The Pelinna deceased draws the contrast between herself as freed and others who have not been freed by Bacchios; ritual action has provided her credentials. Against the bounds and constraints of the normal order, which bind the uninitiate, the Pelinna deceased has a remedy, the assistance of Dionysos. So too, the purifications undertaken by the deceased in A1, A2, A3, and A5 qualify her for special treatment by Persephone. The efficacy of the purification becomes more important for determining one's place in the cosmos than the ordinary distinctions of gender, family, clan, or polis. The claim to superior status by these marginal groups, on the grounds of the purity of their life, served to compensate for their dissatisfaction with their status within the social order.[147]

### Result: Eschatological Hopes

The differences among the tablets in the presentation of identity correspond with the differences in the eschatological hopes. In A2 and A3, the deceased portrays herself as a suppliant, ἱκέτης, beseeching the favor of the great Queen of the Underworld. In A1, however, and in the Pelinna tablets, the deceased, although she declares her identity as the key to favorable treatment by Persephone, more confidently proclaims her reward in the afterlife.[148] The results that the deceased expect from successfully getting past the powers of the underworld differ in the tablets, not only between the different types of tablets, the Pelinna tablets and the B and

---

[147] Such dissatisfaction need not be that of lower class or disenfranchised members of a society; indeed, it seems more likely, considering the historical parallels, to imagine that the resentful are members of the elite who are losing in competition with their peers. As J. Z. Smith notes in his discussion of magic, *ressentiment* of any kind triggers the language of alterity, whether it be accusations of witchcraft or claims to arcane power. "Any form of *ressentiment*, for real or imagined reasons..., *may* trigger a language of alienating displacement of which the accusation of magic is *just one possibility* in any given culture's rich vocabulary of alterity." (Smith 1995, p. 19.)

[148] As Graf comments, "Il faut souligner les différences entre P et A, dans la phraséologie aussi bien que dans la mise en scène. A2 et A3 parlent de la ποινή active, P de la libération passive par le dieu; ... Ce qui est plus important, c'est que l'eschatologie de A1-3 est différente." (Graf 1991, p. 96.)

A series, but even between the tablets found in Timpone Piccolo: A1, A2, and A3.

Since eschatology has long been one of the favored typologies for historians of religion, scholars have compared the eschatology revealed in the tablets to label them as Orphic and Bacchic, Egyptian and Pythagorean, or even Eleusinian. The texts, however, are frustratingly vague about the eschatological rewards imagined for the deceased, offering only a few hints and allusions to mythic motifs to illuminate the result the deceased expects from the successful journey to the underworld. From Dietrich to West to the most recent study by Merkelbach, scholars have sought to construct a stemmata of influence that limits the use of these mythic elements to certain contexts, like errors passed down in a manuscript tradition, rather than accept them as options within a larger tradition that could be employed in a wide variety of contexts within Greek culture.[149] It is the use of the motifs, not their mere presence, that provides understanding of the particular contexts that produced these texts, and the very uncertainty of the eschatological vision in the tablets is indicative of the emphasis in the tablets on the solution rather than on the result of the encounter, on self-definition rather than on eschatology.

The afterlife represents the beginning of a new existence, whether this transformation is described in terms of a birth or a change of location. The Pelinna tablets offer, as the result of being freed by Bacchios, a blessed existence in a new life after death. Death merely leads to a new birth; the woman has died and been born on the same day, νῦν ἔθανες καὶ νῦν ἐγένου, τρισόλβιε, ἄματι τῶιδε. Thrice-blessed, the deceased has entered a new life after her death from her old life. It is impossible, in this context, not to think of the bone tablets from Olbia, inscribed with the words life-death-life: βίος-θάνατος-βίος.[150] Both the Pelinna and the Olbia tablets seem to imply that death is not the end of the mortal progression, but that beyond death, a new life awaits, one which the Pelinna deceased, at least, expects to be better, for she is now τρισόλβιος. The new life may be only one of many new lives in a series of reincarnations or the final life after death for the blessed initiate. The tablets, however, present different visions of this new life, ranging from the celebration of rites and festivals to the ultimate transformation, apotheosis.

---

[149] Dieterich 1893; West 1983; Merkelbach 1999.
[150] See West 1982 and 1983, p. 17. cp. Plato *Meno* 81b; Eur. frg. 638.

*The Symposium of the Blest*

The new existence for the deceased, as described in the Pelinna tablets, seems to be a version of one traditional picture of an afterlife existence, the symposium of the blessed. Plato refers mockingly to the συμπόσιον τῶν ὁσίων as the promise of eternal drunkenness that is held out by certain mysteries, but the image of the deceased in a symposium setting is well known in funeral iconography.[151] The line in the Pelinna tablets, οἶνον ἔχεις εὐδ⟨α⟩ίμονα τιμήν, "You have wine as a happy honor,"[152] clearly refers to the familiar mythic element of the symposium of the blest. Although the precise meaning of the final line of P1, κἀπ⟨ι⟩μενεῖ σ᾽ ὑπὸ γῆν τέλεα ἅσ⟨σ⟩απερ ὄλβιοι ἄλλοι, is unclear, the implication is that the deceased will participate in rituals, τέλεα, in the underworld, along with all the others who are blessed, ὄλβιοι. So too, in the *Frogs* of Aristophanes (85ff.), Eleusinian initiates celebrate and feast in the underworld, although this shared image does not imply that the Pelinna tablets betray any specifically Eleusinian influence. Rather the idea of such a symposium recalls the feasting together of men and gods that was a feature of the period before the rupture of men and gods, the time of primeval purity.[153] For the deceased in her new life, there is constant festival, like the life of the golden race in Hesiod, who "with legs and arms ever made merry together in festivals, far removed from all evils."[154]

While they lack the specific references to wine and festivals, some of the Thurii tablets reveal a similar picture of the new life for the deceased. In A2 and A3, the deceased begs Persephone to send her to the seats of the blessed, ἕδρας ἐς εὐαγέων. This seems to imply a separate place in which those who have been favored by Persephone may go, apart from the place to which those who have been unsuccessful in their meeting with Persephone must go. It is clear from the situation that the deceased expects to obtain a better result than those who lack her special credentials. The ordinary people may have to lie in the filth, εἰς πηλόν, as Plato puts it, or

---

[151] Plato, *Rep.* 363cd, cp. Graf 1974, pp. 98–103; for the *Totenmahl* reliefs, see Garland 1985, pp. 70ff.

[152] The original editors of the tablet suggest that the line might be read, οἶνον ἔχεις εὐδ⟨α⟩ίμον ἄτιμον, meaning that the deceased would have as much wine as she wanted free of price, ἄτιμον, which is a bit of a stretch. (Tsantsanoglou and Parássoglou 1987, p. 14.)

[153] cp. Hesiod, *Eoiae*, fr.1.6–7 Merkelbach-West.

[154] αἰεὶ δὲ πόδας καὶ χεῖρας ὁμοῖοι τερπόντ᾽ ἐν θαλίῃσι κακῶν ἔκτοσθεν ἁπάντων. (Hesiod, *W&D* 114–115.)

perhaps merely flit as senseless shades, νεκροὶ ἀφραδέες, in the Homeric phrase, but the deceased may expect to go to the special place where the favored of the gods, the blessed, go.[155] The fact that the deceased is of the γένος ὄλβιον of Persephone and the other powers whom she addresses, along with the fact that she has paid the penalty for unjust deeds, apparently permits the deceased to hope that she may reach this destination at the end of her journey to the land of the dead, as the thrice righteous in Pindar reach the Blessed Isles.[156]

These tablets, however, give no further details about the seats of the blessed to help the interpreter determine the mythic referent. It is tempting, given the prominence of lightning in these particular tablets, to speculate that the seats of the blessed here may be the Elysian Plain, known from *Odyssey* (4.563) as the destination of the hero, Menelaus, who found favor with the gods. Burkert has pointed out the connections made in antiquity between the Ἠλύσιον πεδίον and the term for a field struck by lightning, ἐνηλύσιον πεδίον. Hesychius, for example, defines ἠλύσιον: Elysion – a land or plain that has been struck by lightning. Such places are not to be walked upon, and are called 'enelysia'.[157] There is, of course, no evidence to prove that the seats of the blessed in these tablets were ever thought of as the Elysian Plain of Homer, rather than being conceived along the model of the Isles of the Blessed found in Hesiod and Pindar.[158] Nevertheless, the possibility that Elysium is the mythic referent is certainly suggested by the deceased's claim to having been struck by lightning.

Most of the B tablets provide no description of the outcome of a successful encounter with the guardians. B1 and B10 alone (and possibly B11) state that, after hearing the deceased's statement of identity, the guardians will give her water.[159] These two tablets, however, also describe

---

[155] Plato, *Republic*, 363d6; Homer, *Odyssey*, xi, 475–476.

[156] Pindar, *Ol.* ii. 61–67, cp. fr. 129 and Hesiod, *W&D*, 170–173.

[157] κεκεραυνωμένον χωρίον ἢ πεδίον· τὰ δὲ τοιαῦτά εἰσιν ἄβατα, καλεῖται δὲ καὶ ἐνηλύσια. See Burkert 1961. Puhvel 1969, however, argues that the association with lightning is a late etymologizing upon a word that originally meant 'meadowy field.' cp. also Gelinne 1988, pp. 227–229.

[158] cp., "If we make bold to ask which place this was thought to be, one naturally thinks first of the 'meadows of Persephone' of A4, v.6. . . . One may alternatively equate the εὐαγέων ἕδραι with the place of the ἥρωες of the Petelia tablet; the station described by Pindar, *Ol.* ii. 61–7 and, one may think, in fr. 129." (Zuntz 1971, p. 318.)

[159] cp. καὐτ[ο]ί (σοι) δώσουσι πιεῖν θείης ἀπ[ὸ κρή]νης (B1.10) and καὶ δή τοι δώσουσι πιεῖν τᾶς Μναμοσύνης [ἀπὸ λίμνας (B10.14). B11 has a place that could contain such a line,

a further result for the deceased, placing the deceased in the company of other privileged dead, apparently apart from the general masses.

Because B1 had to be trimmed before it could be stuffed into the amulet case in which it was discovered at Petelia, the lines describing the fate of the deceased suffer from lacunae in crucial places. B1 seems to promise that the deceased will do something among the heroes, καὶ τότ᾿ ἔπειτα [ ] ἡρώεσσιν ἀνάξει[ς. According to the reading of ἀνάξει[ς currently favored by scholars, the deceased will not only join the community of the heroes favored by the gods, but she will be a leader among them, taking ἀνάξει[ς from ἀνάσσω. Earlier editors, however, read ἀνάξει[ς as the future of ἀνάγω, which can mean to lead back (especially from the dead) or to conduct or celebrate festivals or rituals.[160] On this reading, the Petelia deceased will, like the Pelinna woman, continue to celebrate the mystic rites after death, but now among the heroes, the privileged dead.[161] The race of heroes in Hesiod are the ἡμίθεοι, who lead an ideal and idyllic existence in the Isles of the Blessed. Their life in the Isles of the Blessed approximates the golden age existence of the primordial times, for the earth still produces food abundantly and they are ruled by Kronos, the king who represents the primeval order.[162] To reign among the heroes, taking ἀνάξει[ς from ἀνάσσω, would also imply an existence in the Isles of the Blessed for the deceased, but it is unclear what sort of privilege ἀνάξεις might imply. Although Odysseus in the *Odyssey* (xi.485) tells Achilles that he is mighty among the dead, μέγα κρατέεις, Kronos or Hades are generally depicted as the rulers of the dead.[163]

according to Frel's reconstruction, but the reconstructions are far from certain. Bernabé and Jiménez (2001) read σὺ πιών in B10.15, which would be the only description of the deceased actually consuming the water.

[160] cp. Cougny 1890.

[161] The term, ἥρως, here has a parallel only in the recently discovered B11, which mentions ἥρως in the second line. Unfortunately, this line appears to have no parallel among all the other tablets, and it is impossible to tell who or what is being described as a hero.

[162] Hesiod, *Works & Days*, 156–173. cp. Versnel's treatment of the rule of Kronos (Versnel 1986, pp. 121–152), cp. also Versnel 1990.

[163] Achilles' response (488–91), that he would rather be a portionless slave in life than to rule (ἀνάσσειν) over the dead, should not be taken to imply that Achilles *does* rule over the dead, since his claim is a characteristic impossible wish, illustrating the wretched condition to which even the greatest of mortal heroes is reduced in Homer's vision of the afterlife. Bernabé and Jiménez take it very loosely to mean simply being freed from others' control. "Si bien, dado que es un reinado compartido con un grupo ('reinarás con los demás héroes', L3,11), suponemos que no se quiere decir otra cosa sino que el alma se ha liberado de cualquier sometimiento." (Bernabé & Jiménez 2001, p. 230.)

Some scholars read line B10.13 as ἐλεοῦσιν ὑποχθονίωι βασιλῆι, imply-ing a similar rulership for the deceased, now made a king (or, given the gender of the deceased, a queen?) of the underworld.[164] Zuntz, Gallavotti, and Janko object to this reading, however, on the grounds that the verb must take an accusative, not dative, object, and no really satisfactory read-ing of this line has yet been proposed. Moreover, the deceased is explicitly promised another result, to walk along the sacred road in the company of the other μύσται καὶ βάκχοι. This line seems to place the deceased among a company of privileged initiates, like the deceased of B1 in company with the heroes, perhaps in the Isles of the Blessed. Again, the deceased may be performing rituals like the ὑπὸ γῆν τέλεα mentioned in P1 or the mystic festivals of the Eleusinian initiates in Aristophanes' *Frogs*.[165] Among the parts of the Eleusinian festival that seem to continue in the underworld is the procession along the Sacred Way (*Frogs*, 397–403). The πολλὴν ὁδὸν of this chorus seems akin to the ἱερὰν ὁδὸν in B10. 15–16. The Hipponion tablet may not actually be referring to the Eleusinian procession along the Sacred Way from Athens to Eleusis, but it is, at the very least, using the same imagery of initiates processing along the sacred way that is familiar from the Eleusinian mysteries.

Pindar uses a similar image in his Second Olympian Ode (68–80), in which he describes how those who have lived three pure lives go along the road of Zeus, Διὸς ὁδὸν, to the Blessed Isles, where, with the heroes of epic, they are ruled by Kronos. Pindar here seems to use ideas expressed in each of the tablets B1 and B10, in that those who are specially qualified journey together along the sacred road, as in B10, and arrive at the Blessed Isles among the heroes, as in B1. However, while Pindar speaks of those who have kept their souls from unjust deeds, B10 speaks specifically of initiates, μύσται καὶ βάκχοι, implying that some rites of initiation make the journey to this destination possible.[166] Neither B1 nor B10 describes

---

[164] Merkelbach 1974, p. 9. None of the commentators who read the line as identifying the deceased with the ruler of the underworld takes into account the issue of the deceased's gender. See above note 91.

[165] See further below, ch. 3, pp. 138–141.

[166] Burkert (1975, pp. 90–91) points out that the double description, μύσται καὶ βάκχοι, does not designate two groups, one of initiates and one of Bacchic revelers, but rather gives an intensified description of one group of initiates who are truly Bacchoi, i.e. who really have experienced the ecstatic rites. cp. the saying, which Olympiodorus calls Orphic, found in Plato's *Phaedo* 69c, ναρθηκοφόροι μὲν πολλοί, βάκχοι δέ τε παῦροι, which makes the same distinction between those who perform the rites and those who have truly experienced the initiation. (cp. OF 5.)

the final destination of the initiates who traverse the sacred way, but something like Pindar's description of the Blessed Isles ruled by Kronos makes the most sense as a final destination for the deceased, given the parallels.[167]

This result gets short shrift in the B tablets in comparison with the focus on the description of the obstacle and the solution to it. The lot of the deceased in the company of other privileged dead is only briefly alluded to in these two tablets, and none of the shorter versions of the B tablets have any mention of the result that the deceased hopes to gain from the guardians. Nevertheless, these tablets, like A2, A3, and the P tablets, seem to indicate that the deceased can expect an afterlife in the company of other privileged dead, perhaps continuing the sacred festival celebrations these people shared when alive.

*Rebirth*

The imagery of a new birth into a new life is developed in a few of the gold tablets. Tablet A1 gives indications that death was regarded as the birth into a new life guided by Persephone Kourotrophos, the infant-nourishing goddess who rules the realm of the dead. Moreover, the enigmatic imagery of the animal falling into milk in this tablet and the Pelinna tablets may also symbolize the infancy of the deceased's new life after death. This rebirth may even signify the tranformation from mortal life to divine status.

The deceased in A1 makes the enigmatic claim, δεσποίνας δ' ὑπὸ κόλπον ἔδυν χθονίας βασίλειας, "I have passed beneath the bosom of the Mistress, Queen of the Underworld." Scholars have put forth widely varying interpretations of this line, but the image suggests Persephone plays a kourotrophic role. Farnell insists that it is nothing more than a metaphor for burial; to enter into the bosom of the earth is simply to be inhumed. Harrison prefers to see it as signifying a ritual rebirth or adoption, parallel to what Hesychius says of the δευτερόποτμος, who was born again in the rites of the Semnae by being led διὰ γυναικείου κόλπου, or to Diodorus

---

[167] Gigante suggests that on the analogy to this Pindar passage, the ὑποχθονίος βασιλεύς be interpreted as Kronos, who rules over the final destination of the initiate. (Gigante, comments in Romanelli 1975, pp. 177–178.) However, this suggestion does not clarify the difficulties in B10.13 of the exact role of the ὑποχθονίος βασιλεύς in giving a drink to the initiate, nor is it particularly appropriate for Kronos to be located in the halls of Hades beneath the earth. If Kronos were to appear, it should be *after* the journey along the sacred road from the place of the springs to the Blessed Isles, if indeed such a destination was part of the vision of the tablet.

Siculus's myth of Hera's ritual adoption of Herakles by having him crawl beneath her robes.[168] Zuntz, on the other hand, sees it simply as an image of an infant seeking comfort from a loving mother and cites Homeric parallels for such an image.[169] Burkert argues that the most convincing parallel comes at the end of Plato's myth of Er in the *Republic*, where those about to be reborn into mortal life pass beneath the throne of Anagke in what Burkert terms "la cerimonia del sorteggio," modeled on Eleusinian rites.[170] The common factor in all the explanations seems to be the relation between the deceased as an infant to a maternal Persephone. Even the scene in the Platonic myth is clearly symbolic of birth. Nor is Farnell's burial metaphor incompatible with the image of a maternal Persephone enfolding the deceased.

While the idea of Demeter's maiden daughter Kore as a maternal nurturer may seem strange to those accustomed only to Persephone's aspects at Eleusis, the kourotrophic aspect of Persephone, Queen of the Underworld, was highly important in southern Italy. Hadzisteliou-Price cites the type of figurine found in various locations about southern Italy of Persephone holding a tiny figure at her breast as a visual representation of this concept of Persephone caring for the deceased. "The large class of terracotta figurines or relief portraying a woman with a female or male, winged or wingless tiny ker or eidolon on her breast or arm should be connected with the Locrian Persephone as *Kourotrophos* of the Orphic initiates."[171]

---

[168] Farnell 1921, p. 378; Harrison 1991, p. 593. Hesychius s.v. δευτερόποτμος; Diod. Sic. IV.39.

[169] *Il.*8.271; 6.467; 6.136; 18.398; *Od.* 4.435; *Hom. Hymn Dem.* 187. cp. Zuntz's criticism of Harrison. "Who would think, in these analogous instances, of 'rites of adoption' and 'sacred marriage'? Or acquiesce in Jane Harrison's vague and lachrymose pseudo-poetry, 'I have sunk beneath the bosom of Despoine'? Ships may 'sink beneath' the surface of the sea, but Persephone's ward 'rushes' or 'dives', trustfully for safety to his goddess, as Teucer to his big brother or a child to its mother or nurse." (Zuntz 1971, p. 319.)

[170] Burkert 1975, p. 97. cp. Plato, *Rep*, 620ef. Burkert rejects any parallel with Hellenistic rites that scandalized some of the early Church fathers, "Né l'allusion oscena τῶν ὑπὸ κόλπον τι nella descrizione dei misteri adulterati dei Alessandro di Abonouteichos né il simbolo ὑπὸ τὸν παστὸν ὑπέδυν dei misteri di Attis." (Burkert 1975, p. 97.) cp. Luc. *Alex.* 39; Clem. *Protr.* 2.15.3; Schol. Plat. Gorgias 497c; Firm. *err.* 18.1; Posidippus in Pap. Lond. 60.

[171] Price 1978, p. 175. cp. also Hadzisteliou-Price 1969, pp. 51-55, pls. 29, 30. The fact that some of the figures at Persephone's breast grasp a tiny crown recalls the line in A1, ἱμερτοῦ δ'ἐπέβαν στεφάνου ποσὶ καρπαλίμοισι, "I have sped on fleet feet to the desirable crown."

Persephone's role as *Kourotrophos* raises another possible implication of the line, δεσποίνας δ' ὑπὸ κόλπον ἔδυν χθονίας βασίλειας, particularly, perhaps, when taken in conjunction with the final line of the tablet, "A kid I fell into milk," ἔριφος ἐς γάλ' ἔπετον. Kingsley argues that these images should be taken as referring to the deceased going to suckle at the breasts of Persephone. "The individual in question makes straight for the breasts of Persephone, queen of the underworld, just like an infant to the breast of its nurse or mother. Ultimately, only prejudice and preconception can justify failing to see in this and the other statements on the gold plates the use of a consistent, coherent, and starkly simple imagery: a new birth, making straight for the maternal breast, rushing for milk."[172] Suckled like a newborn infant, the deceased is, in effect, transformed into or adopted as the child of Persephone. This interpretation gains credence with the parallel of the adoption of Herakles by Hera, which is sometimes depicted, especially in Etruscan and south Italian art, as a ritual suckling.[173] Not only does the ritual suckling signify Herakles' adoption by his stepmother, Hera, but the adoption into the family of the goddess itself signifies Herakles' apotheosis. Just as with the motif of lightning as a mode of apotheosis, we may have here a motif used in the story of the apotheosis of Herakles used to describe the fate of the deceased in the tablets. As with the lightning, this mythic reference need not imply Herakles as an explicit model, but rather that the traditional mythic motif of being suckled by a goddess signified the process of apotheosis, particularly in southern Italy, and that the story of Herakles was one of the most prominent appearances of this idea in the mythic tradition. δεσποίνας δ' ὑπὸ κόλπον ἔδυν χθονίας

---

[172] Kingsley 1995, pp. 267–268. The prejudice and preconception to which he refers is, of course, that of Zuntz, who reacted with outrage to the suggestion of Dieterich, "lepidissime sane dicitur et haedulum nunc domum rediisse ad matris lactea ubera et Dionysi ministrum et mystam, nunc et ipsum deum, qui ὑπὸ κόλπον ἔδυ Φερσεφονείας, adiisse ad beatae vitae prata lactea."(Dieterich 1891, p. 37.) Despite his own suggestion that the imagery is that of an infant and mother, Zuntz rejects Dieterich's suggestion, most probably because Dieterich included the identification of the deceased with Dionysos as a kid, an 'Orphic' idea intolerable to Zuntz's interpretation of the tablets as purely Pythagorean. "The speaker is standing before the chthonian Goddess. Is he, the *renatus*, rushing to suck the milk of immortality from her *lactea ubera*? This idea, though quite proper with Egyptian devotees of Isis, makes him shudder who has the slightest notion of Persephone, the goddess of the dead." (Zuntz 1971, p. 324.)

[173] cp. Renard 1964. cp. Pausanias ix.25. 2; Diod Sic. iv.9.6–7. Jourdain-Annequin notes that this scene has been "accepté par les historiens comme le symbole de l'adoption d' Héraclès par la déesse...le symbole de la 'renaissance' du héros, renaissance à un monde différent: celui des dieux auxquel il accède grâce à cette Mère divine." (Jourdain-Annequin 1989, p. 400.)

βασίλειας may signify, in the language of myth, the process by which the deceased, newly born into a different life, is adopted as Persephone's own and transformed from mortal to immortal, θεὸς δ' ἔσηι ἀντὶ βροτοῖο.

The image of Persephone as a nursing *kourotrophos* for the deceased, however, may or may not have anything to do with the enigmatic formula that appears at the end of A1 and, with variations, in the Pelinna tablets: A kid I fell into milk, ἔριφος ἐς γάλ' ἔπετον. Kingsley insists that the milk in this line must be linked with the bosom of Persephone.[174] The milk does seem to indicate a rebirth process,[175] but this does not explain the kid or the bull and ram found in parallel expressions in the Pelinna tablets: ταῦρος εἰς γάλ(α) ἔθορες. αἶψα εἰς γ⟨ά⟩λα ἔθορες. κριὸς εἰς γάλα ἔπεσ⟨ες⟩. Ever since the Thurii tablets were discovered, scholars have been looking for explanations of this bizarre formula, some of which can now be discarded with little regret. The Pelinna tablets have made clear, at least, that no explanation that rests upon the unique significance of the goat kid will suffice, so the popular parallel of the Old Testament prohibition against boiling a kid in its mother's milk may finally be decently interred.[176] Ultimately, one must conclude with Guthrie, "Ancient sources provide no parallels which will throw a direct light on this, and the opinions of scholars make rather amusing reading."[177]

*Apotheosis*

As the parallel with Herakles suggests, one possible result of such a rebirth is the transition from the mortal to the immortal state. In tablets A1

---

[174] "From the sequence of the statements here it is quite clear that this imagery of a young goat rushing for milk is itself meant to be understood as referring to the process of immortalization." (Kingsley 1995, p. 264.)

[175] cp. Salustius, *On the Gods* 4, of feeding new initiates with milk, like newborn babies in Attis rituals, and Aelian, *Varia Historia*, 8.8, of the phrase, 'being in milk' as beginning a new existence.

[176] While Graf rejects the possibility that the formulae represent grades of initiation like the *hippoi* in Athenian Iobacchoi LSCG no. 51, remarking that, "it is impossible to belong to three grades at the same time" (Graf 1993a, p. 245), the three formulae could perhaps represent a succession of initiations. cp. the suggestions of Dieterich in his dissertation, written nearly one hundred years before the discovery of the Pelinna tablets: "se iam antea donavisse commemorat τάς τε βοῦς καὶ τοὺς βουκόλους. Quid igitur? suntne αἱ βόες verae boes an potius eaedem ac βασσάραι? memineris, quaeso, Dianae ministras vocatas esse ἄρκτους, Bacchi et τράγους, postea mystas Mithrae, cui saepe ut solis deo leoninam attribuant faciem, λέοντας et λεαίνας, nec inutile est comparare apud Ephesios eos adulescentes qui festo Neptuni die potum ministrarent ταύρους esse adpellatos." (Dieterich 1891, p. 5.)

[177] Guthrie 1952, p. 178.

and the anomalous A4, the deceased, in addition to plunging as a kid into milk, becomes a god. ὄλβιε καὶ μακαριστέ, θεὸς δ'ἔσηι ἀντὶ βροτοῖο, "happy and blessed one, you will be a god instead of a mortal." The late example, A5, promises apotheosis for the deceased: Καικιλία Σεκουνδεῖνα, νόμωι ἴθι δία γεγῶσα, although the meaning of νόμωι is unclear.[178] Indeed, the meaning of the whole verse is somewhat unclear. "Caecilia Secundina, come, having become a goddess by the custom." What does it mean for a mortal to become a god? The mythic tradition contains many stories of such mortals as Herakles, Semele, and Asclepius, who were translated from a mortal condition to godhead, stories that go back at least as far as the reference to Herakles on Olympus in the Odyssey Nekyia (xi.602-604). Some mortals, by fantastic deeds (not necessarily good deeds), might be elevated to heroic or divine status, breaking the barrier that separated men from the gods.[179] However, stories also abound of the punishment of those who dared to attempt to violate the fundamental division between man and god. Figures such as Tantalus are condemned to exemplary punishment for having tried to make themselves immortal without the gods' consent. Several different types of explanations have been given of this transformation, which seems to violate the most fundamental dichotomy of Greek religion, the distinction between mortal and immortal. One type of explanation focuses on the immortality of the soul, arguing that the transformation from mortal to god is a representation of the permanent and divine nature of the individual soul. Either the soul is an immortal entity being punished for some misdeed by mortal incarnation, from which it is now emerging, or the human soul is a potentially divine being that seeks to realize its own divine nature.[180]

Seaford links the notion of the individual soul as a god to the idea, found in Hesiod, of the exile of a god who has broken his oath or committed some other transgression, as Prometheus or the other Titans did. "Mystic

---

[178] Harrison 1991, p. 586, explained it as due to the corruption of the ritual through institutionalization. "It is the usual priestly confusion. The Soul is divine – that no Orphic priest dare deny – yet this divine soul needs the 'due ritual', or 'the law' to make sure of its divinity."

[179] cp. the stories of Demophoon and Achilles, who almost are made immortal by the care of their divine mothers (or nurses). Hom. Hymn Dem. 260; Apollodorus Bib. 1.5.1; 3.13.6. cp. Odysseus's offer from Kalypso (Od. IV.116-144) and the fate of Tithonos in Hom. Hymn Aph. (218-238) for another kind of failed immortalization.

[180] See Seaford 1986 for a discussion of the way such an idea could develop as an exegesis of the Hesiodic tradition. cp. the essays collected pp. 159-207 of Bianchi 1978, esp. Bianchi 1966.

discontent with the suffering of mankind in the present order of the world adapts the tradition not only by imagining the suffering deities to be mankind but also by creating the prospect of release."[181] The soul of the individual is depicted in myth as a higher being, condemned for past crimes to suffer in exile in mortality. This type of belief seems to underlie Empedokles' famous statement, ἐγὼ δ' ὑμῖν θεὸς ἄμβροτος οὐκέτι θνητός, I stand before you an immortal god, no longer a mortal.[182] It is mystic in the sense of Sabbatucci or utopian in the terminology of J. Z. Smith, in that it offers the hope of salvation *from* the world rather than *in* it.[183] The exiled deity's true home is not in the mortal world in which his mortal self is suffering, but in a divine world of bliss to which he can return when his penance is over.

However, this idea of mortality as punishment for an erring god who will soon return to his divine status is not the only explanation of the change from mortal to god. In his explanation of how the gods and men came from one source, ὡς ὁμόθεν γεγάασι θεοὶ θνητοί τ' ἄνθρωποι, Hesiod tells of the golden race of men who lived a perfect existence and became δαίμονες after death, τοὶ μὲν δαίμονες ἁγνοὶ ἐπιχθόνιοι καλέονται.[184] Detienne, in his study of the meanings of the word δαίμων among the Pythagoreans, shows how this passage in Hesiod was interpreted to mean that the golden race achieved the status of δαίμων because of their virtuous and pure behavior, and that the Pythagoreans associated living a virtuous and pure life with a return to this age of the golden race and the possibility of achieving the status of δαίμων.[185] Detienne distinguishes the idea of transformation into a δαίμων through purifications from the claim of already being a divine being.[186] Every individual, therefore, was

---

[181] Seaford 1986, p. 7. cp. Hesiod, *Theog.* 793–806 on exile beneath the river Styx.

[182] DK 112.4; cp. DK 115.

[183] Smith 1978, p. 101; cp. Sabbatucci 1979, pp. 32–33.

[184] Hesiod, *Works and Days*, 108, 122.

[185] "Toutes ces indications vont dans la même direction: *retrouver l'âge d'or* ou *devenir démon* sont des expression synonymes. Et nous avons vu ailleurs que revêtir la qualité d'un héros des Iles des Bienheureux avait encore la même signification dans la pensée religieuse des Pythagoriciens." (Detienne 1963, p. 115.) The idea that virtuous behavior makes one like the golden race and thus like the δαίμονες appears in the etymologizing of δαίμων in Plato's *Cratylus* 397d–398c and in Plutarch's *De Genio Soc.* 593a ff., both of which explicitly refer to the Hesiod passage. It is, of course, impossible to prove that this particular exegesis goes back before Plato, but Detienne cites a variety of evidence to suggest the plausibility of an earlier Pythagorean tradition.

[186] "On peut être δαίμων de son vivant comme Pythagore ou Empédocle, mais aussi on peut *réaliser* son δαίμων. Dans certaine pensée religieuse, c'est un mode d'existence ou

*potentially* a divine being, if he could so purify his soul in this life that he would be able to realize the δαίμων.[187]

Indeed, as the example of Empedokles shows, these latter two explanations for the origin of the concept of apotheosis are not necessarily mutually exclusive. Both assume the divine and immortal nature of the individual, and both recognize the importance of some sort of purification during mortal life to achieve the divine state. The former view, however, focuses on the previous crime and need for penance, while the latter focuses on the transformation after death. Both interpretations derive, at least to some extent, from the exegesis of a part of the mainstream tradition embodied in Hesiod. This kind of manipulation of mythic elements from an existing tradition better explains the concept of apotheosis in the tablets and also provides a background for the lines in A2 and A3 in which the deceased claims to have paid the penalty, although these two tablets have no claim of apotheosis for the deceased.

The idea of the mortal body as a prison, in which the soul suffers for past misdeeds, attributed in Plato's *Phaedo* to the 'mysteries' and in the *Cratylus* to οἱ ἀμφὶ Ὀρφέα, is used by Plato to argue that the immortal soul undergoes a series of reincarnations.[188] Such an idea of the body as a prison for the soul does not, however, necessarily imply the Platonic idea of a cycle of reincarnations; it could as easily refer to the idea of a divine being punished by a single incarnation for some misdeed. In tablets A2 and A3, though, nothing indicates that the deceased expects her sojourn in the seats of the blessed to be only temporary, a brief holiday before a return to mortal life and further expiation. While the claim in the tablets to have paid the penalty, ποινὰν δ' ἀνταπέτεισ' ἔργων ἕνεκ οὔτι δικαίων,

---

plutôt la finalité d'une μελέτη ou ἄσκησις. Toutefois, le plus souvent, c'est la conclusion d'une longue vie de vertu, et elle coïncide avec la mort." (Detienne 1963, p. 99.)

[187] Detienne 1963 discusses this in terms of the transition from *having* a good δαίμων, i.e. being εὐδαίμων, and *being* a good δαίμων. Although this argument is couched entirely in terms of becoming a δαίμων, rather than a θεός, it is important to recognize that the distinction was not always drawn between the two. Significantly, Empedokles, who refers to himself as a θεός, uses the term δαίμων to refer to the divine entities, such as himself, who have entered mortality to pay penance (fr. 115).

[188] *Phaedo* 62b = OF 7, *Cratylus* 400c = OF 8. Casadio defines reincarnation or metempsychosis: "Per metempsicosi si intende univocamente il passaggio (definito convenzionalmente migrazione o trasmigrazione) di un'anima da un corpo a un altro: passaggio che dà luogo a uno sequenza o fusso o ruota (in greco *kyklos*, in sanscrito *samsara*, in ebraico *gilgul*) di nascita e di morte." (Casadio 1991, p. 121.)

does appear similar to the Platonic expression that the soul is kept safe in a prison so that it can pay the penalty, neither necessarily implies a cycle of reincarnations rather than a single life of punishment.[189]

It is essential, however, to distinguish within the mythic tradition three different ideas of rebirth, which form a logical, if not necessarily chronological evolution. Most basic is the idea, expressed in the Olbia bone tablets, of life followed by death followed by rebirth into a new and unending life in an other world. More complicated is the idea that, after death, one is reborn again into a life in this world. This process of transmigration or metempsychosis need not have an end; the individual may be endlessly reborn as different creatures, according to chance or according to some ethically determined schema. In this cycle of transmigration, the lives in the mortal world may alternate with periods spent in the other world, such as Hades or the Isles of the Blessed. Finally, there is the idea that this process of metempsychosis might terminate at some point, that the individual might be able to avoid rebirth. This escape might imply a final nonexistence, like the Hindu Nirvana, or perhaps a permanent blissful state in an other world.

The type of rebirth imagined in a text will naturally depend on the agenda of its creator. If salvation from the world is the primary concern, then the prospect of an immortal life and escape from any further rebirth in the mortal world will be held out, either after only a single mortal life or at the end of the current one. If, on the other hand, the concern is with theodicy, the emphasis will lie on the inescapability of justice. If each incarnation is seen as a period of punishment, the individual may escape the cycle only when he has done penance in full. In the simplest pattern, a single mortal life is seen as sufficient punishment, but, as Casadio points out, the cycle of reincarnations is envisaged because one mortal lifetime often seems insufficient for complete expiation.[190] Thus, the idea that the soul lives again after death does not imply metempsychosis, and metempsychosis does not necessarily imply the possibility of an end to the transmigrations. Depending on the agenda of the teller, the story

---

[189] cp., Plato, *Cratylus*, 400c – δίκην διδούσης τῆς ψυχῆς, ὧν δὴ ἕνεκα δίδωσιν, τοῦτον δὲ περίβολον ἔχειν, ἵνα "σώιζηται," δεσμωτηρίου εἰκόνα.

[190] "Se il corpo è per l'anima uno strumento di *timoria* e *kolasis*, una sola *ensomatosis* certament e non basta per garantire l'espiazione dei molti peccati di cui l'anima ha subito il giogo." (Casadio 1991, p. 126.)

of life after death could be told so as to include any one of these three possibilities: rebirth into a new life, a cycle of rebirths, and an escape from the cycle of rebirths.

In A1, the deceased claims, κύκλου δ' ἐξέπταν βαρυπενθέος ἀργαλέοιο, I have flown out of the circle of wearying heavy grief. This circle has most often been interpreted as a cycle of rebirths undergone by the soul in the process of metempsychosis, but it may also be seen as a term for the burdens of a single lifetime.[191] Aristotle uses the phrase, κύκλος τὰ ἀνθρώπινα πράγματα, to refer to human life rather than to transmigration.[192] On this interpretation, the deceased has escaped from the toils and trammels of mortal life and looks forward to a blissful and apparently endless afterlife. In either case, the line represents a rejection of the importance of earthly life in comparison to the afterlife, whether that earthly life is envisaged as occurring once only or multiple times before the individual can escape from it.

On the other interpretation, however, the deceased in A1 is claiming that she has escaped from the necessity of being reborn, that she is free from the sorrows of repeated incarnation. The κύκλος mentioned would then be similar to the κύκλος ἀνάγκης that Diogenes Laertius attributed to Pythagoras as the cause of rebirths.[193]

Zuntz, however, points out, "There is no hint in these simple words of any involved or abstruse theological speculation; certainly nothing 'Orphic'; nor even, as far as this poem goes, is there an explicit statement of a belief in reincarnation."[194] Nevertheless, because he believes firmly in a Pythagorean context for the tablets and because metempsychosis is well attested for Pythagoras, he concludes that metempsychosis must be implied.[195] But a specifically Pythagorean context for these tablets is far

---

[191] Casadio has no doubts, "Che nella laminetta più lunga e meglio conservata delle tre proveniente dal 'Timpone piccolo' sia fatto espresso accenno al dogma della metempsicosi nessuno l'ha mai dubito." (Casadio 1991, p. 135.)

[192] Aristotle (Phys. iv. 14, 223b24; Prob. xvii. 3, 916a28). cp. Herodotus I 107.2, simply meaning the affairs of human life in its cyclical patterns.

[193] D.L. VIII.14, cp. Empedokles Ἀνάγκης χρῆμα, fr. 115DK.

[194] Zuntz 1971, p. 318.

[195] "That Pythagoras taught the doctrine of metempsychosis is generally regarded, and rightly, as the one most certain fact in the history of early Pythagoreanism." (Burkert 1972, p. 120.) cp. Xenophanes 21b7 = Diog. Laert. 8.36; Aristotle De anima 407b20, 414a22. Zuntz's argument is not terribly convincing: "The word 'wheel' is, in any case, a metaphor. One easily understands that it was applied, as a descriptive *predicate*, to human life with its changes and suffering, but its use as a *synonym* for life presupposes

from certain, Zuntz's protests notwithstanding. To use the Pythagorean background as a reason to interpret the κύκλος as implying metempsychosis, and then to use the doctrine of metempsychosis in the tablets to argue for a Pythagorean context, is somewhat, dare I say it, circular reasoning.

Moreover, even if Pythagorean metempsychosis does underlie the text, there is no evidence to prove that Pythagorean metempsychosis included the possibility of escape from rebirth. Indeed, the evidence seems to indicate the contrary. Pythagoras stressed the importance of memory to recall one's previous lives as a means to obtaining a better life next time, not as a way to cease the process of being born. In the story of the Pythagorean Lysis recounted by Plutarch, Lysis's friends were concerned that he be buried with proper Pythagorean rites, not lest he be born again if he lacked the proper rites, but so that his soul could be free to go on to its next rebirth. They were reassured that his soul, already judged, had gone off to another birth, having been allotted another daimon.[196] Even in Plato, who is adapting the Pythagorean idea of metempsychosis to his philosophical ends, the idea of an escape from incarnation is by no means certain. The myth of Er in the *Republic*, in fact, shows that even those who lived well must choose a new life to be born into after they have had a respite from mortal existence. Even the philosophers can only hope, at best, to make an educated choice of their next life.[197] Even later in this tradition, Augustine makes a point that Porphyry believed the soul could escape the cycle of reincarnations, which seems to suggest that other Platonists denied an end to the cycle.[198] The fact that these later authors do

more than the consciousness of life's instability; it has, in addition, a terminological ring which implies some particular doctrine." (Zuntz 1971, p. 321.) He may very well be correct, but one could wish for more evidence than a 'terminological ring' to the word.

[196] τὴν δὲ ψυχήν, ἤδη κεκριμένην, ἀφεῖσθαι πρὸς ἄλλην γένεσιν ἄλλῳ δαίμονι συλλαχοῦσαν. Plutarch, *de Gen Socr.* 585ef.

[197] Plato, *Rep.* 614de, 617d–620d. In fact, the only ones who can escape being reborn are the extraordinarily wicked, like Ardiaeus, who remain forever in torment. Admittedly, the possibility of a final escape is conceivable in the *Phaedrus* myth, but even there it is uncertain. Socrates' description of the soul chariot ascending with the gods to the plain of Truth at 248c suggests that, if one has good control of the soul chariot and if one is not tangled up in the crush with someone else whose control is less good, one can retain the wings of the soul and keep from reincarnation. However, every revolution of the heavens brings the same chance that, this time around, the soul chariot may not get a sufficient view of Truth.

[198] *Civ. Dei* 10.30; 13.19; 22.27; contrast Servius 6.745, who claims that sooner or later all souls fall back into incarnation. The neoplatonists Simplicius and Proclus, in discussing

not assume the possibility of escape does not, of course, prove that such a possibility was not present in the Pythagorean conception of metempsychosis, but it should warn us against presuming that such a possibility was necessarily an actuality. Empedokles may have asserted that he could escape the cycle of incarnation and regain his status as a god, but such may not have been the case for all.

If the κύκλος should refer to a cycle of reincarnations, however, the verse in A1 would seem to signify the escape of the deceased from this cycle. Zuntz interprets the differences between tablet A1 and tablets A2 and A3 as signifying that the deceased in A1 expects to escape from the cycle of incarnations, while the other two merely desire from Persephone a respite in a favorable location before they resume their wearying, deeply grievous cycle of incarnations.[199] He notes the contrast between the fate of the deceased in A1, who gains apotheosis, and those of A2 and A3, who go as suppliants after paying the penalty for unjust deeds. "This reciprocity is not due to chance. He who becomes a god has no injustice to amend; he that has to make amends does not become a god. . . . Behind these differences there lies more than a variety of temperament, sanguine or modest; so systematic a set of alternatives reflects a systematic conception of the after-life."[200] However, the differences could equally be explained by a variation in the conception of the afterlife, in which the focus on the idea of the ultimate divinity of the individual is replaced by a concern with punishment for personal or ancestral crimes in A2 and A3. Within the system of A2 and A3, the best a purified, initiated, and properly buried person can hope for is to be among the blessed, rather than having to undergo further purification and penance in the afterlife. In A1 (and A4),

---

the cycle of births, κύκλος γενέσεως, attribute to Orpheus a prayer in the rites of Dionysos and Kore for relief from the cycle of evils, ἧς καὶ οἱ παρ' Ὀρφεῖ τῷ Διονύσῳ καὶ τῇ Κόρῃ τελούμενοι τυχεῖν εὔχονται· "Κύκλου τ' αὖ λῆξαι καὶ ἀναπνεῦσαι κακότητος." The idea that the soul may escape from this grievous cycle of births does seem to be envisaged in these Neoplatonic interpretations. Proclus in Plat. *Tim.* 42cd, v.330 = OF229, cp. OF230 = Simplicius, In Arist *de Caelo* ii.1. Rohde conjectures that the original verse must have been, Κύκλου τε λῆξαι καὶ ἀναπνεῦσαι κακότητος. (Rohde 1925, n. 48, p. 357.)

199 "In that one timpone, then, there was buried one who felt that he had completed the series of incarnations (and so, too, felt he who was laid to rest, with our tablet A4, in the neighboring Timpone Grande); the other two, though equally sure of their pure life, hoped for an interval of bliss but expected (after a 'long year' if we may here interpolate notions known from Hesiod and Pindar, Empedokles and Plato) to return to a life on earth." (Zuntz 1971, pp. 336-337.)

200 Zuntz 1971, p. 336.

however, the purified deceased need not think of penance, but rather she may, because of her preparations in her mortal life, expect to realize her own divinity. Purification and divinization need be neither two tracks within a single systematic conception nor two successive stages of a single evolving eschatology, in which divinization ousts purification as the final goal (or vice versa), but rather they represent two different options available to those imagining the afterlife. The two sets of tablets (A1, A4 and A2, A3) thus employ different mythic elements to convey these two different concepts of the afterlife.

*Conclusion*

In all of these tablets, then, the result expected by the deceased from her encounter with the powers of the underworld must be pieced together from indications that are far from clear. The short B texts give no details of the result at all, while other tablets describe the results in brief and cryptic references. The picture that emerges from an analysis of these clues is of a happy life of celebrations, either as a hero or initiate with the other fortunate dead or as a god among the gods. The image of an afterlife different from the gloomy vision of the Homeric epics is one reason that the tablets have been categorized as Orphic, but all of these eschatological motifs, from the differentiation between the happy and unhappy to apotheosis, appear in a variety of other contexts in the mythic tradition, starting with Homer and Hesiod themselves. The details of the results in the tablets are insufficient to use the eschatology implied in these texts to pinpoint any particular religious context, be it Pythagorean (because of the hints of reincarnation) or Eleusinian or Orphic. The very uncertainty of the eschatological vision in the tablets is indicative of the emphasis in the tablets on the solution rather than the result of the encounter. This focus on the solution stands in contrast to other tellings of the journey to the underworld. Particularly in a medium, gold leaf, in which every extra word included takes up space that is literally valuable, the choice to expand upon one section rather than another is significant. The structure and elaboration of the narratives themselves can convey information about the context of production, and the focus in all the tablets is not upon the obstacle the deceased faces or the result she obtains, but rather upon the solution by which she overcomes the obstacle.

Some texts that tell of a journey to the underworld elaborate the result, the heavenly pleasures or hellish torments that the traveler experiences.

While, for example, a fragment of Pindar and portions of the Platonic and Plutarchan myths of the journey to the other world describe the delights awaiting the worthy, more often the gruesome tortures in store for all the wicked dominate narratives that describe the life in the afterlife.[201] In any case, such an emphasis on the result signals the cosmological or theological interests of the creator of the text, who wants to illustrate the nature of the cosmos and the powers that rule it by this juxtaposition of a description of the other world with the familiar world of the audience of the text.

Other texts focus on the obstacle, how horrific or mighty it is and how great the power or effort needed to overcome it. Description of the obstacle creates suspense in the plot of the story, building the narrative tension to be released by the hero's successful solution. With each gruesome detail about Kerberos, the question arises, will even Herakles be able to handle the beast? And then, when he does wrestle the beast down, his heroic status is even more greatly magnified. Such a telling sets the ground for a solution that involves heroic, clever, or courageous action on the part of the protagonist, an effort or activity commensurate with the magnitude of the obstacle.

By contrast, a tale that puts little emphasis on the obstacle creates no suspense about the outcome of the protagonist's confrontation with the obstacle. The conclusion to the narrative is foregone; the only point of interest is in the precise details of the solution that brought it about. The narrative evoked in the tablets focuses upon the declaration of identity, whether that self-definition is the "pure I come from the pure" of the A tablets or the "I am the child of Earth and starry Heaven" of the B series. The guardians in the B tablets are nameless and featureless, and even Persephone in the A tablets is invoked with a minimum of epithets, in contrast to other hymns and prayers. In the shorter B tablets, the

---

[201] In a fragment of a Dirge, Pindar describes the blissful afterlife of those in the Isles, including their recreations. Pindar fr. 130; cp. Pindar *Olympian* II. 71-77. Plato's *Phaedo* (on which more below, ch. IV) describes the heavenly realm for pure spirits (111b1-c1). Some few of the souls headed for realms above go beyond the surface of the earth into indescribable realms of purity and dwell there entirely freed from bodies. (114c2-6.) This realm, like the realm above the heavens in the *Phaedrus*, is so far beyond mortal experience that "of that place beyond the heavens none of our earthly poets has sung, and none shall sing worthily." Τὸν δὲ ὑπερουράνιον τόπον οὔτε τις ὕμνησέ πω τῶν τῇδε ποιητὴς οὔτε ποτὲ ὑμνήσει κατ' ἀξίαν. (*Phaedrus* 247c2-3.) By contrast, the impure must suffer in rivers of fire and mud (Phaedo 111d4-e2, cp. 112e-113c). Plutarch's imagery is even more vivid, e.g., *de Sera Num.* 563d ff. and *de Genio Soc.* 590b ff.

obstacle is indicated only by the questions: "Who are you? Where are you from?" No suspense arises because the whole point of the narrative is that the deceased will have no trouble overcoming the obstacle. She need do nothing beyond proclaiming her identity; she is defined by her own statements, not by her actions within the plot.

Because this definition of identity is a self-definition, it highlights all the more clearly what the deceased considers important in life: not aristocratic lineage but divine lineage, not heroic action but ritual purity. The deceased need not boast of her achievements in the competitive excellences, the *aretai* by which the hero might win *kleos aphthiton*, immortal glory, in overcoming dreadful obstacles.[202] She relies instead on the virtues of justice and purity to link her to immortality; these are the qualities which distinguish her from others. Moreover, it is the contrast itself, not the results of that contrast, that occupy her attention. Whereas Plato refers to those who contrast their own afterlife of everlasting drunkenness with those who will lie wretchedly in the filth,[203] the tablets make such an eschatological vision secondary to the essential contrast of identity; what will happen in the afterlife is less important than who they are. The qualities of the deceased – ritual purity, divine lineage – are, after all, truly important, more important than the marks of status that might normally be recorded in a grave – family name, profession, etc. Of course, all these ways of defining oneself are meaningful not only after death but during life as well, so the claim to superiority is just as valid in this life as in the next, even if the exceptional qualities are not given the recognition and reward by mainstream society that they deserve.

---

[202] cp. Adkins 1960 on the shift of values from competitive to cooperative exellences. In the mythic tradition, the first people to receive a blissful afterlife were those who had achieved mighty deeds. The heroes, of Hesiod's semi-divine fourth race, go to the Isles of the Blessed as a result of their valiant deeds in the battles of epic (*W&D* 167ff.). While Hesiod speaks in general terms, later authors named specific heroes, such as Achilles and Diomedes or even Harmodios the assassin of Pisistratid Hipparchos, as worthy of an afterlife on the Blessed Isles (cp. Ibycus 291 = Simonides 558, Pindar *Nem.* 10.7, Carm. Conv. 894 = Diehl 10 = Lattimore 1). See further below, ch. IV, pp. 198–200.

[203] In the *Republic*, Adeimantus refers to this symposium of the blessed, συμπόσιον τῶν ὁσίων, as the promise of eternal drunkenness held out by Musaeus and his son, "where, reclined on couches and crowned with wreaths, they entertain the time henceforth with wine, as if the fairest meed of virtue were an everlasting drunk." εἰς Ἅιδου γὰρ ἀγαγόντες τῷ λόγῳ καὶ κατακλίναντες καὶ συμπόσιον τῶν ὁσίων κατασκευάσαντες ἐστεφανωμένους ποιοῦσιν τὸν ἅπαντα χρόνον ἤδη διάγειν μεθύοντας, ἡγησάμενοι κάλλιστον ἀρετῆς μισθὸν μέθην αἰώνιον. (Plato, *Rep.* 363c4–d2.)

## CONCLUSIONS

"Who are you?" ask the unnamed guardians, as the deceased begs for the water of Memory. "Where are you from?" Ever since the discovery of the gold lamellae in the nineteenth century, scholars have asked much the same questions about the tablets themselves: Who are the people who chose to have these enigmatic scraps of gold foil buried with them in their graves? Where do these texts come from? How can we reconstruct the religious context of these mysterious texts?

### 'Orphic' Sources

Rather than looking to the complexities revealed by the way the tablets tell the tale of the journey to the underworld, scholars have often tried to answer these questions by trying to identify the 'original' source of the verses on the tablets. These verses have clearly gone through a process of transmission, probably oral transmission, over a long period of time. Someone, however, must have composed a set of verses that served as a starting point for the transmission. Scholars have suggested a number of possibilities for the 'original' of the tablets, ranging from oracle responses, such as might come from a *katabasis* ritual like that at Lebedeia, to lost epic poems. The favorite candidates have been Orphic poems, particularly those ascribed to Pythagoreans.[204] However, none of the fragments attributed to Orphic or pseudo-Orphic poems provide any clear parallel to the texts of the gold tablets, and the attribution to one source or another seems largely dependent upon the preconceptions of the attributing scholar.

Orpheus would, of course, be a good choice for a pseudonym for whoever actually composed the verses on the tablets; his own underworld experiences and his associations with the rites of Dionysos and Persephone would make him a reasonable choice. Whether the verses on the tablets

---

[204] Zuntz prefers the *Hieros Logos* ascribed to Pythagoras rather than the *Katabasis* ascribed to the Pythagorean Kerkops, although he admits that the "sensitive and poetical imagery has no counterpart among the dry admonitions surviving from the *Logos*." (Zuntz 1971, p. 341.) *Katabasis* 15 DK, cp. 19 DK = Sotion *apud* Diog. Laert. viii.7.14 for the attribution of a hexameter *Hieros Logos* to Pythagoras. Riedweg and Bernabé and Jiménez also imagine the source of the tablet verses to be some unspecified Orphic *hieros logos*, but do not attempt to specify a particular text mentioned in extant sources (Riedweg 1998, pp. 377, 389; Riedweg 2003; Bernabé and Jiménez 2001, pp. 249–251).

are thought to come from a poem in which Orpheus describes what the deceased may expect in the underworld or from a ritual founded by Orpheus, the attribution to Orpheus would lend authority to their vision of the afterlife. Because he was considered older than Homer or Hesiod, Orpheus's authority supplants that of the most mainstream poets, giving sanction to the ideas of the countercultural groups.[205] An association with Orpheus, however, indicated no specific doctrine or eschatology; rather, it was a way for the ancient Greeks to label the extraordinary in the religious tradition, from the prestigious Eleusinian Mysteries to innovative cosmologies to the itinerant charlatans who took advantage of the superstitious.[206] Whether or not the people who produced the gold tablets claimed any authority from Orpheus, the tablets themselves may have been seen as 'Orphic' in such terms, since they are the kind of material that might very well have been attributed to Orpheus.[207]

Such a label must be used with caution in modern scholarship, however, since the word 'Orphic', like the word 'magic,' has suffered much abuse in the past century, being used to evoke a particular set of doctrines of original sin and redemption that have little to do with ancient Greek religion and a great deal to do with the debates over the origins of Christian doctrine among historians of religion.[208] With cautionary quotes, however, the term 'Orphic' may be used to indicate the nature of religious cults such as those that produced the gold tablets, groups to whom the difference between themselves and the common herd was of primary importance, who emphasized their ritual purity and special divine connections over other qualifications more valued by the mainstream

---

[205] Herodotos's expression of skepticism on this point (II.53) indicates the prevalence of the idea that Orpheus and Musaeus were the predecessors of Homer and Hesiod. Contrast Hippias DK 86 B6, Aristophanes *Frogs* 1032ff., Plato *Apology* 41a, Gorgias DK 82 B25, Damastes *FGrH* 5 F11a, Pherecydes 3 F167, Hellanicus 4 F5.

[206] I develop this argument further in my paper, "Pure from the pure and the sheep from the goats: 'Orphism', 'Magic', and the (re)constructions of ancient Greek religion." (Presented at APA 2002 Annual Meeting in Philadelphia) cp. West 1983, p. 3, "It is a fallacy to suppose that all 'Orphic' poems and rituals are related to each other or that they are to be interpreted as different manifestations of a single religious movement. . . . There was no doctrinal criterion for ascription to Orpheus, and no copyright restriction. It was a device for conferring antiquity and authority upon a text that stood in need of them."

[207] cp., e.g., the initiates in the fragment from Euripides *Cretans* (fr. 472 = Porphyry *De Abst.* 4.56), who never associate themselves with Orpheus, but who make a similar set of claims about themselves.

[208] As I argue in Edmonds 1999, cp. Smith 1990.

society. These 'Orphics,' then, whatever they may have called themselves – *hoi katharoi*, the pure, or *Asterioi*, the children of Earth and starry Heaven – left traces in the narratives evoked by the gold tablets of what their most important religious ideas were.

### The Ritual Approach

Recent scholars, puzzled by the fragmentary form of the narrative in the tablets, have sought the origins of the texts in ritual, trying to reconstruct a lost ritual context that might have produced such peculiar texts. The deposit of the gold tablets in the tomb with the corpse of the deceased was naturally only one part of the funeral rituals that were performed for the deceased by the religious community of which she was a part, whether that community was simply her family or some special religious sect. These funeral rituals, although they were different in different times and places, all had the function of preparing the deceased for the journey to the other world, to the realm of the dead. The fact that the creation and placement of the gold tablet must have been a part of the funeral ritual of the community to which the deceased belonged raises the question of the relation of the mythic elements in the tablet texts to ritual practices. Graf has examined the tablets from a ritual perspective, concluding that a funerary context is more likely than an initiatory one, and recent studies by Riedweg and Calame have examined the texts of the tablets from a semiotic or narratological perspective, trying to identify the ritual contexts in which the words might have been uttered.[209]

Some of the lines, particularly in the A and P tablets, do seem to imply some sort of ritual practice. It is hard to imagine that Bacchios's freeing of the deceased was *not* marked by some ritual, and the claims to come pure from the pure, ἔρχομαι ἐκ καθαρῶν καθαρά, in the Thurii tablets seem to imply some ceremony of purification that qualifies the deceased for her new state. There is, however, little evidence to suggest which kinds out of the many types of purificatory rituals known from Greek religion are implied here. Harrison imagines a ritual for practically every line in A1, with each step of the deceased's transition from mortal to immortal acted out with elaborate rituals of entering and departing the Circle, a ritual

---

[209] Graf 1991, 1993a. cp. Calame 1995 and Riedweg 1998.

adoption, and a baptism in milk.[210] Zuntz, on the other hand, imagines the texts as coming from some sort of "Pythagorean *Missa pro Defunctis*," a sacred text read simply at the graveside. Both of these recreations seem to have more to do with the religious background and inclinations of the scholar than with evidence of parallel rituals or texts. While the fact that all of these tablets have been found only in graves certainly supports a funerary context, the motifs of death and new life and the *makarismoi* would also be appropriate for an initiation that the deceased underwent before death, especially if the rite of passage was a trial run, as it were, of the process of dying and descent to the underworld.[211]

The goods in the Pelinna grave perhaps suggest a pre-death initiation. The maenad statue may indicate that the deceased was a member of a Bacchic group, possibly a member who had undergone special initiatory rituals to mark her status. The gold tablet, which proclaims that she has died and is born, may repeat ritual formulae used in the initiation rituals of her Bacchic group. The prose formulae of the animals in milk could be interpreted as *symbola*, which could have been used in either the initiation or funeral rituals to mark the new status of the participant.[212]

While the Thurii graves provide less evidence to support a ritual context for the use of the tablets, both funeral and initiation rituals are again possibilities. However, the initiatory ritual need not be the ritual of initiation into an organized sect; the religious specialists whom Burkert terms 'craftsmen' also had initiations that marked the initiate's transformation of state, from impure to pure and perhaps even from mortal to immortal. Plato's *agurtai* performed *teletai*, initiations, to cleanse the initiand from the taint of previous unjust deeds, and the chorus of Euripides' Cretans proclaim that they have been made holy and are now *mystai* and *bacchoi*.

---

[210] Harrison 1991, pp. 588–599.

[211] cp. Plutarch, fr. 178, on the parallel experiences of initiation and death. Not all initiations, it should be pointed out, make use of the imagery of death and rebirth (cp. Barry and Schlegel 1979), but such imagery was certainly apt for the purpose.

[212] Graf, however, reasonably suggests funeral ritual as the most likely context for the Pelinna tablets. "The sequence of assertion of death and new life, then the libations [of wine and milk], and finally the *makarismos* over the grave all fit slightly better in to the context of a funeral [than an initiation]." Graf 1993a, pp. 249–250. Riedweg assigns lines 3–5 to an initiation ritual, lines 1 and 6 to a funeral rite, and lines 2 and 7 to a description of the journey to the underworld. (Riedweg 1998, p. 375.) While his division perhaps puts each of the lines in its most appropriate context, it does not explain why the collection of lines should have been inscribed on the tablet and placed in the grave.

Kingsley suggests the Mithras Liturgy from the Great Paris Magical Papyrus as a parallel for a ritual in which the performer uses the ritual to achieve immortality as the result of a confrontation with a deity.[213] The Thurii tablets, especially A1 and A4, could certainly come from a context in which the texts were used in a ritual to confer immortality upon the performer before her physical death. Zuntz's protests that such 'magical' uses could only come as the result of corruption and degeneration of the originally pure religious impulse are baseless, but equally baseless are any attempts to prove that the texts had a purely this-worldly and 'magical' function rather than an eschatological one.[214]

The context of a rite of passage remains a possible interpretation of the B series of texts as well. The questions of the guardians, articulated in the short versions, might also be imagined as ritual formularies, performed at the ceremony marking the initiate's new status. The proclamation of identity, "I am the child of Earth and starry Heaven", may represent the initiate's proper response to these questions, illustrating her new awareness of her connection with the primordial and cosmogonic forces of Earth and Heaven. While some sort of ritual 'libretto' is unlikely, the tablets may preserve the key phrases and ideas from a ritual of initiation into a religious group, perhaps even a Pythagorean one.

Initiation into a group is not the only *rite de passage* that is a possible context for the B tablets; the initiate may have experienced a ritual descent into the underworld as a preparation for the descent after death or as a special means of obtaining sacred wisdom. The motif of the waters of Lethe and Mnemosyne in the long tablets may have had some ritual function similar to the one they had at the oracle of Trophonius in Lebedeia, with which, indeed, the Petelia tablet B1 was associated before the discovery of the Thurii tablets. Pausanias gives an account of this oracle, where

---

213 "The immortalization envisaged both in the Thessaly plates and in the gold plates from Italy is a *ritual* immortalization . . . there can be little room for doubt that the theme of mystical union with the divine arose, in the first instance, out of magical and ritual practice." (Kingsley 1995, p. 313.) cp. also Scarpi 1987.

214 Indeed, the religious sincerity of the tablets and the extent to which the deceased believed in the literal truth of the ideas cannot be ascertained. Those, like Zuntz, who pronounce on the purity of the religious feeling do little more than reveal their own prejudices and assumptions. The tablets provide an expression of religious self-definition that locates the deceased in relation to the world of mortals and immortals, and this expression can be evaluated in terms of the model of the world that it depicts, not in terms of the sincerity of the expression itself or the extent to which the ideas expressed in the tablets corresponded to actual religious behavior.

the questioner undergoes a ritual descent to the underworld to consult the oracular hero. After the questioner has completed the preparatory ritual purifications, the officiating priests take him to two fountains near to one another, from which he drinks before he begins his katabasis.[215] Here, as in the tablets, are two fountains, one of which is of Memory. Unlike the tablets, however, the oracle of Trophonius requires the one journeying to the Underworld to drink from *both* springs. The effect of the spring of Memory is to make the descender remember his experience in the underworld, while the spring of Forgetfulness makes him forget all that has happened to him beforehand.[216] Certainly, the function of the springs differs in the ritual of the Trophonius oracle from that in the tablets, but the katabasis in each case is serving a different purpose for a different person. The deceased buried with a gold tablet is not a living person seeking to bring back information or revelation from the land of the dead to the land of the living, but she is instead concerned with her existence after death. This memory cannot be, as it is in the Trophonius oracle, memory of the revelation received during the journey, but rather it must be the memory of the deceased's mortal life and of the journey to and in the other world. Nevertheless, the usage of these mythic motifs in the tablets could be imagined in a ritual ceremony in which the water of Memory was used to symbolize the initiate's training in memory or

---

[215] κάτεισι δὲ οὕτω.... ὑπὸ τῶν ἱερέων οὐκ αὐτίκα ἐπὶ τὸ μαντεῖον, ἐπὶ δὲ ὕδατος πηγὰς ἄγεται· αἱ δὲ ἐγγύτατά εἰσιν ἀλλήλων. ἐνταῦθα δὴ χρὴ πιεῖν αὐτὸν Λήθης τε ὕδωρ καλού-μενον, ἵνα λήθη γένηται οἱ πάντων ἃ τέως ἐφρόντιζε, καὶ ἐπὶ τῷδε ἄλλο αὖθις ὕδωρ πίνειν Μνημοσύνης· ἀπὸ τούτου τε μνημονεύει τὰ ὀφθέντα οἱ καταβάντι.... τὸν δὲ ἀναβάντα παρὰ τοῦ Τροφωνίου παραλαβόντες αὖθις οἱ ἱερεῖς καθίζουσιν ἐπὶ θρόνον Μνημοσύνης μὲν καλούμενον, κεῖται δὲ οὐ πόρρω τοῦ ἀδύτου, καθεσθέντα δὲ ἐνταῦθα ἀνερωτῶσιν ὁπόσα εἶδέ τε καὶ ἐπύθετο· (IX.39.8), "The procedure of the descent is this.... He is taken by the priests, not at once to the oracle, but to fountains of water very near to each other. Here he must drink water called the water of Forgetfulness, that he may forget all that he has been thinking of hitherto, and afterwards he drinks of an-other water, the water of Memory, which causes him to remember what he sees after his descent.... After his ascent from Trophonius the inquirer is again taken in hand by the priests, who set him upon a chair called the chair of Memory, which stands not far from the shrine, and they ask of him, when seated there, all he has seen or learned."

[216] Zuntz waxes sarcastic about what he sees as a perversion of the concept found in the tablets, "How lucky that the waters had so specific an effect!... This is not myth, but allegory materialized and exploited; a device by smart priests aiming to refurbish the waning lustre of their patrimony." (Zuntz 1971, p. 379.) Zuntz here fails to appreciate that the same traditional elements that appear in myths may be employed, for different purposes and in different forms, within a ritual.

understanding of the cycle of reincarnations and the things she must do in this life to remedy or atone for in past lives.

All these ritual hypotheses, however, must remain almost entirely speculative in the absence of evidence beyond the texts of the tablets themselves. It remains entirely possible, of course, that these texts belong to no funeral or initiatory ritual at all, but are simply transcriptions from poetic tellings of myths that had eschatological significance for the deceased and the religious community from which she came. A journey to the underworld is a passage from one location to another, but that does not necessarily mean that the narrative represents a rite of passage, much less an initiation ritual. Pausanias' text illustrates the difference between the description of a ritual and the recounting of a narrative. While any tale of a journey could be divided up according to van Gennep's schema of separation, liminality, and reaggregation, his analytic tool for making sense of rituals of passage is not necessarily the best suited for understanding a narrative.[217] The traditional elements employed may be the same, but the structure of a narrative is different from that of a ritual. To be sure, a ritual can include the recitation of a narrative, but it is unnecessary to imagine a ritual context in which a narrative is being performed and then to analyze the hypothetical ritual. To glean the information about the context that is embedded within the structure of the narrative (even if that narrative should actually happen to have been recounted during a ritual), a narrative analysis is most useful.

## Conclusion

Through such a narrative analysis, the gold tablets provide evidence for the various *chemins de déviance* pursued by the different religious contexts that produced the tablets. Whether these modes of protest were simply ideological or whether the ideas corresponded as well to special practices or rituals, the tablets use the narrative of the soul's journey to the underworld to depict the deceased's separation from mainstream society and her membership in an exclusive group of privileged souls who were destined for greater things than the common herd. It is, of course, impossible to know to what extent the tablets express the personal beliefs

---

[217] Van Gennep 1960.

of the people with whom they were buried. To some extent, the tablets themselves served as 'magical' objects whose potency as protection after death depended not on the deceased's familiarity with the message of the texts but on the tradition of power that was associated with them. The fact that the Pelinna woman had two almost identical tablets buried with her shows that the object themselves had traditional power. The distinction, however, between magical power and religious belief should not be drawn too sharply. Much of the absolute separation made, for example, by Zuntz between the use of the tablets as magical amulets and as expressions of religious belief, stems from religious polemics and outdated anthropological theories "not yet decently interred." The very tradition that gives the magical amulet its power stems directly from the ideas expressed in the tablets, texts that express the ideas of their composers about the nature of life and death and about the relation of the individual to the world.

The gold tablets – texts produced for the audience of the deceased alone – serve to give expression in the traditional language of myth to the hopes and fears of the deceased as she left the world of the living and prepared to enter the world of the dead. The analysis of the obstacle-solution–result complexes expressed in these tablets has shown a variety of ways in which the deceased distances herself from the normal, locative order of the mortal world, be it the socio-political structure of the aristocratic clans or simply the ordinary mass of people, in favor of a utopian identification with a divine order, which harks back to the period when gods and men were not separated, but feasted and celebrated together, free from the cares and toils of everyday life. The claims to purity and divine lineage indicate a rejection of the normal standards and measures of status. Rather than defining her identity by her genetic ancestors and their place in the socio-political hierarchy, the deceased defines herself in terms of a lineage of the ritually purified and in terms of a link with the gods. Rather than explaining all the tablets simply as the products of a single (and anachronistic) 'Orphic' doctrine of original sin, analyzing the different ways in which these 'Orphic' tablets make use of traditional mythic elements to depict the journey to the underworld reveals the various modes of protest they are expressing against the world from which they came. Appreciation of these differences provides a more comprehensive view of the countercultural religious currents from which the tablets came, a few more pieces in the jig-saw puzzle.

## APPENDIX: GOLD TABLET SIGLA

| Siglum | Location | Date | Pugliese Carratelli | Colli | Janko | Kern | Bernabé & Jiménez |
|---|---|---|---|---|---|---|---|
| A1 | Thurii, Timpone Piccolo | 4th BCE | II.B1 | 4.A65 | — | 32c | L9/488 |
| A2 | Thurii, Timpone Piccolo | 4th BCE | II.A1 | 4.A66a | — | 32d | L10a/489 |
| A3 | Thurii, Timpone Piccolo | 4th BCE | II.A2 | 4.A66b | — | 32e | L10b/490 |
| A4 | Thurii, Timpone Grande | 4th BCE | II.B2 | 4.A67 | — | 32f | L8/487 |
| A5 | Rome | 260 CE? | I.B1 | 4.B31 | — | 32g | L11/491 |
| C | Thurii, Timpone Grande | 4th BCE | III.1 | 4.A68 | — | | L12/492 |
| P1 | Pelinna, Thessaly | end of 4th BCE | II.B3 | — | — | — | L7a/485 |
| P2 | Pelinna, Thessaly | end of 4th BCE | II.B4 | — | — | — | L7b/486 |
| B1 | Petelia, Italy | 4th BCE | I.A2 | 4.A62 | P | 32a | L3/476 |
| B2 | Pharsalos, Thessaly | 350–320 BCE | I.A3 | 4.A63 | Ph | — | L4/477 |
| B3 | Eleutherna, Crete | 2nd BCE | I.C1 | 4.A64 | K1 | 32b I | L5a/478 |
| B4 | Eleutherna, Crete | 2nd BCE | I.C2 | 4.A70a | K2 | 32b II | L5b/479 |
| B5 | Eleutherna, Crete | 2nd BCE | I.C3 | 4.A70b | K3 | 32b III | L5c/480 |
| B6 | Mylopetra, Crete | 2nd BCE | I.C4 | 4.A70c | K4 | — | L5d/481 |
| B7 | Eleutherna, Crete | 2nd BCE | I.C5 | 4.A70d | K5 | — | L5e/482 |
| B8 | Eleutherna, Crete | 2nd BCE | I.C6 | 4.A70e | K6 | — | L5f/483 |
| B9 | Thessaly | 4th BCE | I.C7 | 4.A70f | M | — | L6/484 |
| B10 | Hipponion, Italy | end of 5th BCE | I.A1 | 4.A72 | H | — | L1/474 |
| B11 | Central Sicily, Entella? | 3rd BCE | I.A.4 | — | — | — | L2/475 |
| Ph | Pherai, Thessaly | 4th BCE | II.C.2 | — | — | — | L13/493 |
| El | Eleutherna | 2nd BCE | II.C1 | — | — | — | L15/495 |

# 3 | Descent to the Depths of Comedy: The *Frogs* of Aristophanes

## INTRODUCTION

τίς δ'οἶδεν εἰ τὸ ζῆν μέν ἐστι κατθανεῖν, τὸ κατθανεῖν δὲ ζῆν;

"Who knows if life be death or death life?"[1]

The spring of 405 BCE was a time of uncertainty for Athens as it tottered on the brink of destruction. Aristophanes produced the *Frogs* at the Lenaia festival in competition with the *Muses* of Phrynichos and the *Kleophon* of Platon Comicus, roughly six months after the naval battle of Arginousai, the Athenians' last major victory in the Peloponnesian War, and six months before the fateful battle of Aigospotamai, where Athens lost its fleet to the Spartan forces. Not only did the *Frogs* take first prize in this contest, but the play also received the unprecedented honor of a second performance, probably in 404.[2] This exceptional play, performed

---

[1] A fragment of Euripides referred to in the *Frogs* at lines 1082 and 1477, quoted at Plato *Gorgias* 492e, cp. Euripides *Phrixos* fr. 833 and *Polyidos* fr. 638. I use the text from Dover's excellent edition and commentary (Dover 1993 – hereafter "Dover"). Translations, unless otherwise acknowledged, are my own.

[2] One of the preliminary notes to the play (Hypothesis Iᶜ) attributes to Dikaiarchos the knowledge that the *Frogs* was given a second performance. Modern scholars have debated when this second performance was held. Russo asserts that the second performance must have been held immediately: "It is clear, for technical, economical and administrative reasons alone, that the second performance must have involved the same actors and choreutai, choregos and didaskalos as the first.... The new production would have been practically identical to that deemed worthy of victory and repetition." (Russo 1994, pp. 202–203.) A second performance for the same audience at the Lenaia in 405 seems less likely than a new performance commissioned after the decree of Patrokleides (cp. And. i.77–79) in the fall of 405, which effected the recall of the exiles urged by Aristophanes in the parabasis. The case for Lenaia 404 is argued persuasively by Dover (pp. 73–76) and Sommerstein 1993.

111

at a crucial time in the history of Athens, is also the longest telling of a *katabasis* myth extant from the classical period and earlier. Although many myths of this type were told in many different genres, no complete telling of a journey to the underworld survives between the *Nekyia* in Homer's *Odyssey* and the myths of Plato. While only allusions and fragments of this tradition remain to us, it was quite familiar to Aristophanes' audience in 405, and, in this comedy, Aristophanes plays with the traditional elements of this kind of story, humorously distorting well-known motifs.

In contrast to the simple and fragmentary narratives of the gold tablets, the narrative of a journey to the underworld in Aristophanes' *Frogs* is not only complete but complex. Aristophanes does not merely make use of a few traditional motifs in his telling, he piles up as many as he can in the narrative, never content with a single allusion if he can make multiple ones. Nevertheless, Aristophanes' manipulations of the traditional mythic elements all serve similar functions. Throughout the *Frogs*, he employs the traditional mythic pattern of a journey to the realm of the dead to redefine the identity of Athens, negotiating the boundaries of his society to recreate an image of the city as a unified whole. In this chapter, I analyze three different sections of the *Frogs*, looking at different complexes of *obstacle, solution,* and *result,* each of which is familiar from other tellings of the *katabasis* myth: the water barrier, finding the way in the underworld, and the guardians of the underworld. In each section, Aristophanes makes use of elements from the mythic tradition familiar to his audience, manipulating these elements to create his effects. Earlier studies have either not appreciated or misunderstood the significance of Aristophanes' use of the mythic tradition, too often interpreting the *katabasis* pattern and Eleusinian elements as simply indicative of an initiation ritual. I first examine the previous scholarship on the *Frogs*, with special attention to the theories of Segal, Bowie, and the recent work by Lada-Richards. I then show how Aristophanes plays with the familiar *katabasis* story to present the tale of the salvation of his contemporary troubled Athens. In contrast to the gold tablets, which make use of the difference between the worlds of the living and the dead to mark the difference between the valuation of the deceased in life within society and her true worth in the ideal, divine realm, Aristophanes comically blurs the dichotomy between the worlds and then recreates it in his own terms. Aristophanes reformulates the boundaries of the polis through his deployment of mythic elements and patterns in the comedy, redefining the true citizens of the polis and excluding those he sees as harmful to the city.

## The Initiation of Dionysos: The Abuse of a Pattern

Although the question of 'Orphic influence' on Athens from the Eleusinian Mysteries is sometimes mooted, scholars have not spent as much time trying to trace the mythic elements in the *Frogs* back to an exclusively Orphic context as they have with the gold tablets.[3] The fact that Aristophanes' comedy was performed in the public festivals of Athens shows that, whatever their origin, the images of the afterlife presented in the *Frogs* must have been familiar to the general audience, not the secret heritage of an Orphic fringe. Rather, the major issue in the scholarship within the last hundred years has been the problem of the unity of the *Frogs*, and much of the critical work on the play stems from the attempt to find an element that unifies the literary *agôn* with the rest of the play. Dionysos's quest to retrieve Euripides from the underworld has seemed disjointed from the great literary contest between Euripides and Aeschylus, and scholars have proposed various theories of revisions or hasty joinings of unrelated plot patterns.[4] In the last forty years, however, beginning with Segal's influential article, one solution has won increasing acceptance: the initiation of Dionysos. As I have shown, however, this argument rests on a number of problematic bases, and this ritual interpretation of the *Frogs* distorts or obscures a number of important elements within the play.[5]

The initiatory interpretation is appealing, in the first place, because of the common equation of the *katabasis* story with a process of death and rebirth and the assumption that such a death and rebirth is always initiatory. As Eliade puts it: "Descending into Hades means to undergo

---

[3] cp., however, Elderkin 1955 and Graf 1974.

[4] Rogers claims of the *katabasis*: "It can hardly be said to be woven into the texture of the play at all; it is but loosely tacked on, and the stitches by which it is attached to the main fabric are quite visible to a careful observer." (Rogers 1919, p. xvi.) Russo argues that the fact that no reference is made to saving the city in the first part of the play proves that the story was radically revised and that the idea of bringing a poet back was not part of the original concept of the play. (Russo 1966, p. 1–13; 1994, esp. pp. 206–8.) Hooker too believes that the *katabasis* element is a last minute addition, worked in only after Aristophanes had obtained and read a copy of Euripides' posthumously released work, the *Bacchae*. (Hooker 1980, pp. 169–182; cp. Cantarella 1974.) I agree, however, with Dover, p. 9: "It is hard on a dramatist if his most striking and successful innovation in plot structure is to be treated by posterity, because his other plots are not so good, as the unhappy consequence of hasty revision."

[5] Edmonds 2003. The following section briefly summarizes my arguments there.

'initiatory death', the experience of which can establish a new mode of being."[6] The descent to the underworld fits into van Gennep's schema of the *rite de passage*, the three-part transition consisting of separation, liminality, and reaggregation.[7] The deceased separates himself from the world of the living, goes through a liminal period in the realm of the dead, and is finally brought back into the normal world as a new person. Such a pattern provides a coherent framework to unify a disjointed narrative, since the tripartite schema delineates a nice beginning, middle, and end that follow one another in logical sequence. The end result of such an initiatory sequence must be, in the logic of this argument, the creation of a new identity for the protagonist as he is reborn upon completing his passage through the realm of death. Hence, for these scholars, Dionysos progresses in the play toward a new and better definition of himself, abandoning the uncertain state in which he starts the play.[8] This metatheatrical idea that Dionysos represents the "Spirit of Comedy" permits a further connection of the *katabasis* with the *agôn*, since Dionysos's

---

[6] Eliade 1972, p. 27. See also Eliade 1958, p. 62: "From one point of view, we may say that all these myths and sagas have an initiatory structure; to descend into Hell alive, confront its monsters and demons, is to undergo an initiatory ordeal." Thiercy 1986, p. 305, discusses the initiation pattern he sees in Aristophanes as a cultural universal: "L'essentiel n'est pas pour nous attribuer une origine plus ou moins précise à cette notion d'initiation chez Aristophane, mais de constater que dans toutes les religions, les littératures et les civilisations, quels qu'en soient l'époque ou le niveau, la notion d'initiation est ancrée dans l'esprit humain, d'autant plus qu'elle répond toujours à un même scénario dont seuls les noms et les détails varient."

[7] Van Gennep 1960. Jane Harrison, in her *Themis*, was among the first to make use of van Gennep (originally published 1909) to understand myths of death and rebirth as initiatory. (Harrison 1912, pp. 19, 20.) Classicists, however, have for the most part still not availed themselves of more nuanced anthropological theories of initiation, preferring the simple Aristotelian schema of van Gennep. Indeed, the more complicated pictures of liminality provided by Turner and others would not serve the desired function of unification of the narrative, so they are, for the most part, ignored.

[8] For Whitman, "In the light of the deaths of Sophocles and Euripides, comedy puts on the buskin of high seriousness and the club and lion skin of heroic self-search, and undertakes the quest to recover poetic and political virility." (Whitman 1971, p. 236.) Segal notes the references to various aspects of the deity Dionysos throughout the play and sees the journey through the underworld as a gradual quest for self-awareness by Dionysos. (Segal 1961, p. 208.) For Segal, "Dionysus appears as the embodiment of the comic spirit seeking a stable definition of itself and its aims; and his search is presented primarily through the motifs of disguise and changeability." (Segal 1961, p. 211.) Contrast Stanford's assessment: "So supple, fickle, wayward, panicky, opportunistic, and unscrupulous is he that he rather resembles the oil which helps to blend a salad or lubricate a machine, than any solid substance." (Stanford 1983, p. xxix.)

initiatory journey results in the true definition of Comedy, just as the *agôn* redefines the proper nature of Tragedy.

However, the basic premises of this argument – the equation of *katabasis* with initiation, the idea that Dionysos gains a new identity, and the metatheatrical identification of Dionysos with the "Spirit of Comedy" – are all severely flawed, and the resulting argument, in all its incarnations from Segal 1961 to Lada-Richards 1999, presents a distorted picture of the character of Dionysos and his *katabasis* in the *Frogs*. In the first place, despite the authority of Eliade, a descent into the underworld is by no means necessarily an initiation. Initiation rituals do frequently make use of the imagery of death and rebirth (although not as frequently as has sometimes been claimed[9]), and the process of initiation is sometimes imagined or enacted as a journey through the realm of the dead. However, the pattern of action in which the protagonist leaves one status and gains a new status is not always connected with the journey to the realm of the dead, but other imagery (such as bathing or signs of physical maturation) may be used to express the same pattern of passage. Moreover, while a ritual of initiation may make use of the traditional mythic motifs associated with the journey to the realm of the dead to communicate the idea of a change in status for the initiand, the use of those motifs is hardly confined to initiatory ritual or even to narratives in which a death and rebirth is experienced by the protagonist.[10] Mythic narratives and rituals, in short, draw upon the same set of traditional images and patterns of action to convey their ideas, but the specific meaning of a given traditional pattern or image cannot be divorced from the way in which it is deployed within the narrative or ritual. A *katabasis* does not necessarily imply an initiation nor an initiation a *katabasis*.

The initiatory interpretations of the *Frogs* too often distort the text of the play in the attempt to fit the details into the pattern. A ritual makes use of traditional mythic elements in a different way than a narrative, following different patterns and logic. The presumption of a pattern of initiation in the play causes the commentators to go to great lengths to

---

[9] cp. Barry and Schlegel 1979, pp. 277–288.

[10] Thus, although Lada-Richards, for example, claims that "ritual liminality is a period deeply impregnated with the imagery of death" (Lada-Richards 1999, p. 57), she makes no argument to show that the imagery of death in many circumstances of ritual liminality is more than a particularly useful set of images in the context, neither that it appears only in *ritual* liminality (which it obviously does not) nor that ritual liminality always and exclusively makes use of the imagery of death.

squeeze the details of the plot into a van Gennepian sequence of separation, liminality, and reaggregation,[11] or into the specific sequence of the Eleusinian Mysteries.[12] Moreover, the presumption of character development for Dionysos also causes scholars to distort the descriptions of Dionysos's behavior in the text to fit in with whatever kind of development they suppose. Despite Segal's claim that Dionysos has changed from "the rather timorous and almost despicable figure of the first part of the play" to a worthy judge of a "contest with the gravest consequences," Dionyos remains an undignified buffoon throughout the literary contest, cracking rude jokes and relieving the seriousness of the conflict with silly remarks.[13] These distortions of character and plot obscure the subtle

[11] Moorton, for example, attempts to apply van Gennep's pattern to the end of the play: "Of the three rites required, the rite of separation is fully portrayed in the *Frogs*, the rite of transition is anticipated, and the rite of incorporation into Athens is left to our imagination." (Moorton 1989, p. 322.) Which is to say that while a motif of separation is present in the closing ode, the other two parts are not actually present, but can be imagined if the reader assumes that van Gennep's pattern is present.

[12] For example, Bowie unconvincingly attempts to relate the silence and immobility of the characters in Aeschylus's prologues to what he calls the *thronosis* ritual, but the allusion in the literary contest to someone sitting silently does not even fit into the place of the so-called *thronosis* in the sequence of the initiation as Bowie lays it out. (Bowie 1993, p. 247.) Following Burkert 1983, Bowie calls *thronosis* the ritual in which the initiate sat, with head covered, on a chair or stool. Depictions of the seated initiate appear on a number of vases, but the words, *thronosis* and *thronismos*, do not appear in Eleusinian contexts. On the contrary, Plato describes *thronosis* as a rite in which Corybantes dance wildly around the initiate, playing around and confusing him (*Euthyd.* 277d). Such a rite differs dramatically from the somber silences of the protagonist in Aeschylus's prologues. Bowie also tries to link the whipping contest, in which Dionysus and Xanthias try to avoid indicating that they are suffering pain, to the ritual requirement of silence for the Mysteries. (Bowie 1993, p. 236.) However, not only is the silence in the Mysteries connected with the awe at the moment of revelation (and secondarily with the importance of not revealing the Mysteries to the uninitiate) rather than with keeping silent under torture. In fact, neither Dionysus nor Xanthias ever actually keep silent; they are continually cracking jokes or trying to disguise their exclamations of pain as some other outburst. Moreover, the whipping ordeal, whether imagined as an allusion to the silence of the initiates at Eleusis or as a general ritual ordeal, comes *after* the encounter with the festival of the blessed initiates, instead of being a necessary step on the way to that final reward (as Lada-Richards admits, pp. 90, 86 n. 161).

[13] As Dover notes, Dionysos's responses are often coarse or bathetic, as in 980-991, 1074-1075, 1089-1098, 1149, 1279-1280, and 1308. As for his fitness to judge the contest, Dionysos himself admits in response to one of Euripides' subtle distinctions, "I have no idea what you're talking about!" (1169) Both Aeschylus and Euripides abuse him repeatedly for his stupidity and lack of good dramatic taste. Both accuse him of talking nonsense, 1136 and 1197, and they abuse his stupidity in 917-918, 933, and 1160. Whatever Aeschylus means in 1150, it is clearly not complimentary to Dionysos's taste and

use of the traditional mythic motifs and patterns that Aristophanes does make in the *Frogs*.

### Aristophanes and the Mysteries

The recent studies by Bowie and Lada-Richards uncover a wide range of the resonances that these familiar motifs and ideas would have had for Aristophanes' audience.[14] However, their attempts to fit all these elements into the initiatory pattern of action cause them to miss the full depth and richness of Aristophanes' use of these elements. The tradition on which Aristophanes draws includes both the many mythic tellings of journeys to the other world and the rituals associated with the Eleusinian Mysteries. Rituals are performances composed of a number of traditional actions set in a sequence that is itself traditional.[15] Like the elements of a myth, therefore, the elements and patterns of action of a ritual have a significance to their audience whose scope is determined by the range of meanings evoked by the familiar signs and limited by the context in which

good judgement. Riu also questions the development of Dionysos's character (Riu 1999, p. 130-134).

[14] While Lada-Richards 1999 excellently plumbs the depths and richness of the traditions available to Aristophanes' audience, in her attempts to align motifs with different aspects of the traditional picture of Dionysos, she neglects the arrangement and deployment of those motifs. She never argues how the audience would shift its interpretation of the character to choose among the axes of Heraklean and Dionysiac, Euripidean and Aeschylean, individual and civic. To make such choices, the audience would have to be guided by Aristophanes' specific manipulations of the mythic tradition within the play, that is, what he does with the familiar elements of Herakles' gluttony and strength or Dionysos's connection with the theatre and wine. Although Lada-Richards uncovers the mythic resonances of Aristophanes' images more thoroughly than her predecessors, like them she never extends her analysis to the level of Aristophanes' specific manipulations of familiar mythic elements. My analysis of the *Frogs* is likewise greatly indebted to Bowie's insights, especially on the importance of the Mysteries. Bowie, however, searches the details of the play, trying to find places in which the rituals are acted out, rather than taking Aristophanes' allusions to the Eleusinian rituals as a manipulation of the symbolic language of ritual that recalls the familiar rituals to the audience while reconfiguring the meaning of the element in the context of Aristophanes' story. Bowie assumes that the similarities between the elements in the ritual of the Mysteries and those Aristophanes uses in the *Frogs* simply imply the ritual pattern, and thus he reads the *Frogs* as an initiation of Dionysos.

[15] cp. Calame's definition of myth and ritual: "Ils sont tous deux des manifestations distinctes du même processus d'élaboration intellectuelle: construction et manipulation d'objets conceptuels par le moyen de la langue et de la narration dans un cas, travail conceptuel par l'intermédiaire du corps et des objects du monde naturel ou culturel dans l'autre." (Calame 1990, p. 29.)

they are arranged.[16] The Eleusinian Mysteries are a particularly evocative symbol for the life of the Athenian polis, since the ritual performance of the Mysteries was a way for the city to define its borders of territory, of community, and of influence.

As recent studies have shown, Eleusis was a part of the Athenian polis from its formation, and the sanctuary at Eleusis served as an important marker of the boundaries of Athens, both spatially and ideologically.[17] The ritual procession from the center of the city to the periphery at the Eleusinian sanctuary reinforced the unity of the Athenian polis.[18] A large portion of the Athenian population participated in the Mysteries, which were open not only to adult male citizens but also to groups of Athenians excluded from other civic institutions - women, metics, and slaves. Participation in the Mysteries cut across political factions as well as the barriers of gender and citizenship, so a group of initiates presented a very good way for Aristophanes to represent the group of Athenians, united in their celebration of a festival.[19]

---

[16] cp. Redfield's description of the intertwining of myth and ritual in a culture: "Myths and rituals are knitted together by a system of metaphorical transformations which constitute the practical logic of the culture. This is not a language because the signs are not arbitrary; the objects manipulated are found already constituted in nature. But as they are organized into a system of meanings, they are further formed and acquire new meanings; these in turn, by their coherence, prove to the native the truth of the system as a whole." (Redfield 1990, pp. 132-133.)

[17] cp. Osborne 1985; Parker 1996, pp. 13, 25; and particularly, Sourvinou-Inwood 1997. Earlier views that Eleusis was not integrated into Athens until the late sixth century are based upon a literalist reading of the myths of conflict between Eleusis and Athens as history and upon the assumption that the absence of explicit mention of Athens from the Homeric Hymn to Demeter implies that the hymn was written before Athens had conquered Eleusis in these 'historical' wars. (cp. Sourvinou-Inwood 1997, p. 143.)

[18] "The great paths that linked the urban centers with their principal peripheral sanctuary were constructed with particular care. These axes of the civic territory, tangible traces of the fundamental connection between the two poles of the city, constituted the stage upon which great processions took place. In these, at regular intervals, the social body as a whole performed for itself, parading from the town to the sanctuary and thereby periodically reaffirming its control over the territory." (de Polignac 1995, p. 40.) Although de Polignac did not see Eleusis as a peripheral sanctuary for Athens, Osborne 1985, pp. 172-82; Calame 1990, pp. 361-362; and, most thoroughly, Sourvinou-Inwood 1997 have convincingly demonstrated the applicability of his model.

[19] As Bowie notes, "The Mysteries have acted as a model for stable life in a *polis*: they are open to slave and free alike; they offer justice and proper treatment and equality to all as well as happiness in the afterlife; they exclude the incomprehensible barbarian and polluted criminal. They even offered peace in time of war: a truce from war of fifty-five days was traditionally declared." (Bowie 1993, p. 252.)

The importance of the Mysteries as a symbol of the unity of Athens can be seen from the seriousness with which the profanation of the Mysteries was treated.[20] The integrity of Eleusis stood for the the integrity of the Athenian state; the profanation of the Mysteries, therefore, was immediately interpreted as a political act, subject to prosecution, that many thought was a signal of an attempt to overthrow the democracy and replace it with a tyranny or oligarchy. In being accused of profaning the Mysteries in 415, Alcibiades was accused of trying to appropriate the celebration of the Mysteries to his own authority, instead of respecting the traditional authority that governed the celebration. In 407, therefore, two years before the performance of the *Frogs*, when Alcibiades led the traditional procession to Eleusis and had the curses of the Eleusinian priests reversed, this public celebration was meant to be symbolic of his devotion to Athens and its traditions.[21]

The Eleusinian Mysteries, moreover, represented Athens' claim to Panhellenic leadership, for Demeter's double gift of the Mysteries and grain made Eleusis a Panhellenic shrine, to which offerings came from all over the Greek world. This Panhellenic position could be used as justification for Athens' leadership of other Greek states, that is, for her position as an imperial power in the Greek world.[22] The Spartan occupation of Decelea since 413, which prevented the celebration of the Mysteries with full pomp, was more than an inconvenience to the Athenians; it was a symbolic deprivation of Athens' authority to rule her territories. The chorus of Mystai, celebrating their festivals in the other world, therefore, represented an ideal of Athens that is not only unified but also restored to potency with respect to her neighbors.

Aristophanes, however, depicts this chorus of Mystai in the realm of the dead, the other world, because in the spring of 405 the Athens of the real world was fraught with disunity and faction, deprived of much

---

[20] As Bowie 1993 points out, pp. 243–244. cp., Isoc. *De Bigis* 6.

[21] As Murray points out, "There is no evidence whatsoever that the Mysteries were parodied: all of our evidence shows that they were *performed*, that the ritual was followed accurately. Nowhere is there any suggestion, as a possible defence, that the occasions were jokes or ritually unreal in any way, that the Mysteries were not actually divulged – the performances were illegal, sacrilegious, and immoral, but not unreal." (Murray 1990, p. 155.) Alcibiades is not accused, in the contemporary texts, of not taking the Mysteries seriously, but rather of taking them for himself, which is a hubris of a different flavor, but one that better explains the fear of tyranny that the accusations raised. cp. And. 1.12, 16, 17; Lysias 6.51; Plut. *Alc.* 22; Isoc. 16.6; Thuc. 6.28.2.

[22] cp. Isoc. *Panegyricus* 28–9, 31; Lysias 6.50; Diod. Sic. XIII. 27.1; and Kallias' statement in Xenophon *HG* vi 3.6.

of her authority over other Greek states, and powerless even to conduct her festival of the Mysteries. Dionysos goes on a quest to the realm of the dead to bring back a fertile poet to an impotent Athens, venturing into a world where everything is different and strange to bring change to the familiar world. The contrasts between the realms of the living and the dead, provide a means by which Aristophanes can renegotiate the boundaries of the society, excluding those whom he sees as destructive to the city and recalling those whom the city needs to be whole. Each of the obstacles that Dionysos faces in his quest to bring back a poet to save the city is an opportunity for Aristophanes to play with the contrasts between good citizen and bad citizen, master and slave, Athenian and foreigner, and a wide array of other categorical distinctions that define the boundaries of the society.

## A CARNIVALESQUE REFLECTION

The contrast of the worlds of the living and the dead naturally serves as analogy for these distinctions, and we have seen how this contrast is manipulated in the tablet narratives to distance the deceased from her society. In the *Frogs*, however, Aristophanes also works to elide many of these distinctions by comically undermining the radical separation of the worlds of life and death. Even the traditional distinctions between the different fates of the dead in the afterlife are blurred in Aristophanes' comedy as he pleads for Athens to unify itself and reinvigorate itself at a crucial moment in its history. Aristophanes presents a world in which all of the normal boundaries are dissolved, in which life is death and death life, so that he can create new categories and new boundaries, defined through his manipulations of the mythic tradition.

Aristophanes presented his comedies at the city festivals for Dionysos, the Dionysia and the Lenaea, and this Dionysiac setting provides the comedies with the license to go beyond the ordinary boundaries of social order, to suspend the normal hierarchies and turn the world on its head. Whereas the Dionysiac setting of countercultural religous groups involves a permanent protest against the normal order, a lifelong suspension of ordinary values, the city festivals of Dionysos represent instead a temporary dissolution of restraints, a hiatus in the quotidian lifestyle rather than a permanent ending.[23]

The Bahktinian notion of the carnivalesque is helpful for understanding the setting in which Aristophanes put forth his ideas about the

[23] cp. Sabbatucci 1979, p. 51.

problems and salvation of Athens.[24] The comic festivals provide an opportunity for the poet, as Goldhill puts it, to "represent the city to the city," to put forth, in a competitive setting for the approval of the city, a model of the city that deliberately transgresses the ordinary norms of society.[25] Aristophanes' comedies derive their humor from their grotesquely distorted reflection of Athenian society, from the juxtaposition of the bizarre and twisted in the play with the audience's knowledge of the normal conditions of Athenian life. However, this disruption of ordinary categories is not merely a funny image, like a carnival mirror that shows a grossly elongated or compressed reflection, but the dissolution of the normal order also permits the possibility of a reformulation of boundaries within society. Goldhill's comments on understanding the way comedy functioned within Athenian society are important in this regard: "Comedy in and as performance tests - *negotiates* as well as *celebrates* - the possibilities of transgression."[26] Each play represents a different negotiation of the societal norms. In the *Frogs*, Aristophanes makes use of the comic genre to tell a story of the journey to the other world that does not simply depict an idealized model of the world in which the problems of life are rectified, as, for example, the myths in the gold tablets do. Instead of incorporating familiar elements from the tradition to produce a persuasive and authoritative model of the world, Aristophanes evokes the familiar elements to spin jokes off of them, deliberately distorting the traditional elements to create a humorous effect. The carnivalesque vision of the world that he produces by these manipulations depicts a world with all the normal boundaries disrupted, a world in which the order of society may be reformed. The carnivalesque nature of Old Comedy permits the kind of redefinition of the boundaries of society that Aristophanes is attempting in the *Frogs*.

### Dionysos's Comic *Katabasis*

Aristophanes' *Frogs* focuses not on Dionysos' passage from immaturity to maturity, as the ritualists would have it, but on his quest to return to the world of the living with a poet from the world of the dead to save

---

[24] The best discussion of Bakhtinian notions of the carnivalesque and Aristophanic comedy is Goldhill 1991, pp. 167-222. cp. Henderson 1990 on the dynamics of comedy within the political community of Athens and the works by Carriere 1979, Thiercy 1986, and Rösler in Rösler & Zimmermann 1991.

[25] Goldhill 1991, p. 185.

[26] Goldhill 1991, p. 188.

Athens from its dearth of cultural life. No more good poets remain in the city of Athens (for, despite the fact that they are gods, both Herakles and Dionysos are, for the purposes of the play, citizens and residents of the city of Athens[27]), and Dionysos wants to bring a clever (δεξιός) poet to fill the gap in Athenian life. Dionysos's desire for Euripides is not a purely personal longing, but, even at the beginning of the play, the absence of Euripides has a larger dimension. As Dover points out, δεξιός carries the sense of wise and understanding, as well as creative and clever.[28] When Dionysos rates the living poets unfavorably in comparison to the dead Euripides and announces his intent to seek a γόνιμος (creative or perhaps 'ballsy') poet in the land of the dead, Aristophanes is playing off the traditional motif of descent to the underworld to bring back wisdom beyond the mortal world.[29] Of course, speaking of the fertility of a dead man, coupled with Herakles' insinuations of necrophilia,[30]

---

[27] Hooker 1960 suggests that the house of Herakles should be identified with the temple of Herakles in Kynosarges, outside the city walls near the Diomeian Gate. While Xanthias does refer to the Heracleia in Diomeia (650f.) held at this temple, Hooker's attempts to map the action of the play onto the local topography of Athens seems strained. There is, however, no reason to suppose that the humor of the situations was derived from the audience's recognition of *specific* places around Athens rather than from the *general* juxtaposition of the extraordinary (Herakles, Dionysos, etc.) with the ordinary world of the city of Athens. The humor derives from the fact that Herakles and Dionysos converse like two regular citizens rather than from the fact that the specific temple of Herakles is depicted as an ordinary house. The latter sort of joke does appear to be made later in the transformation of the halls of Hades into an ordinary household. (See below in "Confrontation with the Powers of the Underworld.")

[28] "To be δεξιός is not simply to possess a perceptive intelligence, the capacity for quick and deep understanding; in many instances, it covers creative intelligence, skill, or expertise, and so overlaps with σοφός." (Dover, p. 14.) Euripides' poetic creativity could be seen as literally life-saving. Plutarch (*Vita Nic.* xxix. 2–3) tells how some Athenian survivors of the Sicilian disaster won food and drink or even release from slavery by reciting bits of Euripides' poetry to their Syracusan captors. Plutarch also relates that some Caunians, who were pursued by pirates, were allowed to enter the harbor of Syracuse because they could recite some choruses of Euripides.

[29] Most famously, Odysseus goes to the realm of the dead to consult the shade of Tiresias (Od. x 490–5, xi 100ff.) because only in the otherworld can he obtain the special knowledge he needs to return to his homeland. cp. Pausanias' account of the Trophonius oracle (Paus. IX 39.7–14) and Clark (1979, pp. 13–52) on the ancient Near Eastern predecessors of the *Odyssey Nekyia,* especially the epic of Gilgamesh. Clark carefully distinguishes this wisdom tradition of katabases from other descents connected with fertility cycles.

[30] Aristophanes, of course, plays with the meanings of desire, πόθος, which generally conveys the idea of longing for one who is absent, but can have both erotic and funerary connotations. The most basic meaning of Dionysos's πόθος is mourning at the absence of the deceased, but Herakles takes it as an erotic desire for a woman or a boy, or even

flavors the wisdom quest of the Odyssean type with a taste of the erotic pursuit of Orpheus or even Peirithoos and Theseus.[31] Still, the objective of bringing back wisdom to the city is implicit in Dionysos's critique of the living tragic poets and even in his disparagement of Aristophanes' rival comedians. Although references to 'saving' the city do not come until later in the play, Dionysos intends the return of a δεξιός poet to the city to bring relief to the current conditions.

The primary difficulty Dionysos faces is at once the cause of his journey and the biggest problem he must overcome, the fundamental distance between the worlds of the living and the dead. His desire for Euripides is caused by the fact that Euripides has died and is no longer present in the world of the living, yet the lengths he must go to recover Euripides (or a substitute) provide the narrative action for the entire play. This separation of the worlds of the living and the dead, however, provides Aristophanes with one of the main sources of humor throughout the play, as this basic fact of human existence is undercut, not only by the ease of transition between the worlds but also by the continual jokes about the similarity of the two worlds. Aristophanes takes Euripides' notorious line, 'who knows if life be death and death life?' and makes of it a leitmotif, or

a man (56–57). Even when he discovers that the object of desire is a dead man, he still takes it in an erotic sense, as necrophilia rather than mourning. Only Dionysos's declaration that he will go to Hades to bring Euripides back makes the comical confusion clear (66–70).

[31] Although the earliest evidence gives no clear indication whether Orpheus succeeded in his venture, the popularity of all the different versions of his story attests to the resonance with many audiences in the Greek tradition of this motif of recovering a lost loved one from death. (The earliest references to the story are in Eur. *Alcestis* 357 and Plato, *Symp.* 179d. Later references can be found in the Alexandrian poets Hermesianax and Bion, but the versions of Vergil (*Georgics* IV.453–527) and Ovid are the best known (*Met.* X.1–85); cp. the story of Alcestis, which plays with the idea of bridging the gap between living and dead for the sake of a loved one in different ways.) The tale of Theseus and Peirithoos, who attempt to carry off Persephone for Peirithoos, fall into this category of katabasis in search of a loved one, but while their heroic ability enables them to reach the underworld, they cannot succeed in their mission because Persephone is not simply a mortal who has passed over to the realm of the dead, but rather the very Queen of Death, a power at home in the underworld. Dionysos himself descends to the underworld in search of a loved one, according to one tale found in later tellings in the tradition. After attaining recognition of his godhead, in these stories, Dionysos goes to the realm of the dead to lead his mother Semele up to Olympus. As Dover suggests, the story of Dionysos's descent for Semele was probably well known to the audience, but "any reference to that would spoil much of the central importance of the comedy, especially the god's disguise as Herakles and his complete ignorance of the underworld." (Dover, p. 40.)

perhaps rather a running joke, throughout the play.[32] By assimilating the world of the dead to the world of the living, Aristophanes can tamper with the categorical distinctions that are made by the separation of the two worlds, distinctions between vital and impotent, familiar and strange, life and death.

In my analysis, I examine three of the complexes of obstacle, solution, and result Aristophanes employs within the play that are drawn from the mythic tradition. The first obstacle that Dionysos and Xanthias must get past is the water barrier, in this case the Acherusian lake, which serves as a border between the realms of the living and the dead. While Xanthias, as a slave who evaded naval service, is forced to walk around the lake, Dionysos rows like a citizen sailor in the ferryboat of Charon to the song of the mysterious frogs. Once into the underworld, the two must find their way to the halls of Plouto in order to find the poet to bring back with them. They join the revels of the chorus of Mystai, the Eleusinian initiates enjoying a blissful afterlife, who give Dionysos and Xanthias the directions that save them from wandering lost in the darkness of Hades. The pair encounter another obstacle in the form of guardians at the doors of Plouto's house, where the doorkeeper's various tests of their identity finally result in Dionysos's identity being confirmed by Plouto and Persephone while Xanthias remains out with the other slaves. Having bypassed all these obstacles, Dionysos engages in a comic *psychostasis* or weighing of souls to choose the poet he thinks can save Athens. In all of these narrative complexes, Aristophanes uses motifs from a wide variety of traditional myths and rituals, combining and twisting them to create his effects, and, as the chorus of mystai tells the audience, ultimately "to say many silly things as well as many serious, and, having played around and jested worthily for this festive occasion, to wear the ribbons as the victor."[33]

---

[32] Not only does Aristophanes play with the blurring of the boundaries of life and death, but in a *reductio ad absurdum* he turns the famous line against Euripides himself, when he complains that Dionysos is leaving him among the dead instead of bringing him back to the land of the living. Τίς δ' οἶδεν εἰ τὸ ζῆν μέν ἐστι κατθανεῖν', τὸ πνεῖν δὲ δειπνεῖν. τὸ δὲ καθεύδειν κῴδιον (1477–1478), "Who knows if to live is to be dead, if to breathe is to dine, and if to sleep is a fleece?"

[33] 389–393 – Καὶ πολλὰ μὲν γέλοιά μ' εἰπεῖν, πολλὰ δὲ σπουδαῖα, καὶ τῆς σῆς ἑορτῆς ἀξίως παίσαντα καὶ σκώψαντα νικήσαντα ταινιοῦσθαι.

## ENTERING THE REALM OF HADES

### Obstacle: Crossing the Acherusian Lake

Amusingly, Aristophanes takes Dionysos and his companion directly from the world of the living to the borders of the realm of the dead without spending any time on the journey that takes them from Athens to the lake of Acheron. Perhaps Aristophanes is suggesting that despite the separation of the realms of the living and the dead, Athens is not far from death – a grim reminder of Athens' precarious war situation in 405. Whether or not such a reference was intended, the rapid shift of scene moves the plot along, maintaining the intensity of the action. The obstacle that faces Dionysos and Xanthias is familiar from the mythic tradition, a water barrier that divides the two realms, specifically, the Acherusian lake.[34] The choice of the nature of the water barrier seems to depend on the nature of the solution envisioned; for an obstacle that can only be overcome by monumental heroic effort, a huge expanse of water that requires great time and effort to cross is appropriate, whereas if the solution is simply a ritual like burial or a deity's aid, the body of water has a symbolic function and need not seem physically impassable.

Aristophanes plays it both ways, wringing jokes out of both traditional elements. Herakles (137–139) describes a vast body of water (λίμνην μεγάλην . . . πάνυ ἄβυσσον) and a long journey (ὁ πλοῦς πολύς) in a tiny skiff (ἐν πλοιαρίῳ τυννουτῳί) over the abyss. Yet Dionysos crosses a marshy lake small and shallow enough for the song of the frogs along its banks to be heard throughout the relatively brief journey.[35] However,

---

[34] The water barrier takes various forms in the Greek tradition. In *Iliad* XXIII 69–74, Patroklos complains that he cannot cross the river until his body is buried, while the river that Odysseus must cross to reach the realm of the dead is the 'river' Ocean (*Odyssey* x 508, xi 11–9). In *Iliad* VIII. 369, Athena mentions how she helped Herakles cross the river Styx to get the hellhound. In other versions of the Herakles stories, Herakles, not being the sailor that Odysseus is, crosses the Ocean to the other world of Geryon by commandeering the golden cup of the sun. (Stesichorus 185 PMG, Pherecydes FGH 1.18, cp. Athenaeus 11. 469e, 470c, 781d; Eustathius *Od.* 1632.23.) Some sort of water barrier between the living and the dead is found in folktales around the world, cp. Haavio 1959.

[35] The discrepancy between the vast abyss Herakles describes and the shallow swamp that is the natural setting for the frogs has been mostly overlooked by the various scholars debating whether the frog chorus appeared on stage. Most commentators assume a shallow swampy setting that would provide the possibility of the frogs hopping about

although the lake in the *Frogs* recalls both the expanse of Ocean and the smaller streams of the mythic tradition, Bowie's comparison with the crossing of the Cephisus by the Eleusinian procession remains unconvincing.[36] Although rivers are a natural way of marking boundaries, not all boundaries are between the worlds of the living and the dead. The *gephurismos* ritual at the crossing of the Cephisus marks a different kind of transition, from one phase of the ritual to the next, from the city of Athens into Eleusis, but not from the land of the living into the realm of the dead; that is a transition reserved for a different part of the rite.[37]

### Solution: Dionysos Rows Charon's Skiff

Aristophanes also plays with the traditional solutions to the water barrier, evoking both the heroic effort required for a long trip across the Ocean and various other ritual or symbolic solutions for getting across the water. Both Patroklos and Elpenor beg for the ritual of burial to allow them to enter into Hades, and the ritual of burial remains one of the key solutions for crossing in later stories of the journey of the deceased to the realm

---

around the boat, but Allison points out that frogs would naturally be at the edges of a large body of water and remain invisible, but audible to travelers. (Allison 1983, p. 17.)

[36] Bowie 1993, p. 235. Bowie also tries to connect the insults of the chorus to various prominent Athenians with this *gephurismos* ritual. Although both the chorus's lampoons and the *gephurismos* involve obscene abuse directed at prominent Athenians, such abuse is a part of many rituals and occasions within the Athenian festival year, the comic competitions not the least of them. (cp. Rösler in Rösler & Zimmermann 1991, pp. 39–40.) Whereas the *gephurismos*, the ritual abuse heaped on the procession as it crossed the bridge over the Cephisus into the territory of Eleusis, plays an important transitional role in the structure of the Eleusinian festival, the various choral songs of abuse play no such role in the *Frogs*, recalling rather the sort of licensed scurrility at the Thesmophoria or the Haloa, carnivalesque settings in which transgressions of the social norms are given a controlled expression. To extrapolate the structural function of the choral abuse from the structural function of the *gephurismos* on the basis of the similarity of their content distorts the structure of the play, forcing it into the semblance of an initiation for Dionysos. cp. Henderson 1975, pp. 13–17, for an overview of obscenity in various cults. Henderson rightly denies that the comic abuse by the chorus is a *gephurismos* and connects it instead with Dionysiac processions where jesters improvised ribald abuse on passers-by. (Henderson 1975, pp. 15–16 and n. 49.)

[37] The bridge in the *gephurismos* also represents a different kind of solution than travel over the water. As a permanent structure over the water barrier, the bridge must present some other ordeal to test those attempting to cross. While later journeys to the other world sometimes represent the bridge as a narrow swordblade or other physically difficult thing to cross, the Eleusinian ritual creates the ordeal of ritual abuse directed at important members of the procession.

of the dead.[38] In Homer, the shade, once the body is buried, seems to be able to cross on its own, but other stories provide a ferryman to bring the souls across the water barrier. Although the *Frogs* is the first time this character, usually named Charon, appears in extant Greek literature, the figure of the ferryman of the dead is mentioned in a number of earlier sources, both literary and artistic.[39] So familiar does Charon become as the means to cross over into the realm of death that his ferry becomes a metonym for death itself, and Pindar refers to immortality as escape from the ferry of Acheron.[40] Whereas in some stories, Charon is savagely eager to transport any soul that comes to him, in others he demands payment for his services.[41]

Charon, in the *Frogs*, is a gruff old man who responds mechanically to Dionysos's greeting with a list of the ferry's destinations, just like any bored modern-day bus driver or train conductor who has gone over the same route endlessly for years and years.[42] As mundane and familiar an exchange as the overly bright greeting of a passenger and the weary response of the ferryman might have been, Aristophanes works jokes into both lines. Dionysos's greeting, Χαῖρ', ὦ Χάρων, ὦ Χάρων, χαῖρ', ὦ Χάρων, not only amuses with the word play between the cheery greeting

---

[38] Contra Sourvinou-Inwood: "In the fifth century the Homeric 'rule' that one could not enter Hades until after burial did not pertain." (Sourvinou-Inwood 1995, p. 310); cp. note 35 in my treatment of the *Phaedo* below, Chapter 4.

[39] Pausanias's reference to Charon in the epic Minyas as the model for him in Polygnotus's painting seem to be the oldest testimony, but black figure vase paintings and inscriptions appear around 500 BCE. cp., Sourvinou-Inwood LIMC s.v. Charon. Charon appears most often as an old man, frequently with an ugly face and tattered clothes. His ferryboat is small, propelled by a pole and/or oars, although a few testimonies make reference to a sail. The ferryman of the dead also appears in Near Eastern and Indo-European mythologies. cp. Lincoln 1991, pp. 62–75; and Cook 1992.

[40] Pindar fr. 143, cp. Theokritos 17.46–50. On Charon or his ferry as a metonym for death: Euripides *Alcestis* 252–257, 360–362, 439–444; *Herakles* 430–433; Aristophanes *Lysistrata* 605–607, *Plutus* 277–278 (with anagram of Charon and Archon); Timotheos fr. 786 PMG; Aesch. *Septem* 854–860; Theokritos 16.40–41; *Anth. Pal.* VII. 63, 66, 67, 68, 365.

[41] Although all the literary references are later than the *Frogs*, the practice of placing small coins in graves to pay the ferryman seems to go back to the beginning of the fifth century. Kallimachus, *Hecale* fr. 278 Pf.; *Etymologicum Magnum* s.v. δανάκης; Suda & Hesychius s.v. δανάκη; Juvenal 3.264–267; Apuleius *Met.* 6.18; Lucian *Luct.* 10, *Catap.* 18–21, *d. mort.* 22; Antiphanes Maced. *Garland of Philip* 8.6. While the archeological evidence reveals that the coins in graves vary widely in denomination and quantity, the literary references all mention a single small coin, usually a bronze obol, as the appropriate fee. cp. Stevens 1991, who points out, however, that the practice of putting coins in graves had other symbolic references than the 'Charon's obol' alone.

[42] cp. van der Valk 1981, p. 97 and nn. 8 & 9.

(χαῖρε - be well) and the name of the ferryman of death (as if O hello, Hell; O Hell, hello; O hello, Hell), but also evokes funereal situations from Homer through tragedy in which the dying one bids his or her companions farewell, χαῖρε.[43] The humor of Dionysos's greeting is complemented by Charon's mechanical listing of the stops on the route, each one either a well-known entrance to the underworld or a familiar expression for destruction.[44] In presenting Charon and his ferry route as a solution to the water barrier, Aristophanes mixes his mythic and proverbial references in the ferryman's list of his ports of call, all of which represent death.

Whereas Charon in other myths takes passengers indiscriminately from all ranks, Aristophanes uses Charon's ferry to make a distinction between citizens and slaves, just as Homer distinguishes between buried and unburied. Two obols suffice for Dionysos to use Charon's ferry as a solution to the water barrier, but only because he already has the status of a citizen.[45] Xanthias must find another solution. Charon tells Xanthias (191)

[43] cp. Sourvinou-Inwood 1995, pp. 388–392. She argues at length (pp. 180–216) that χαῖρε could not be said to an ordinary dead person in the archaic age, only to a living person, a god, or a heroized deceased, "for it characterized life and living in contrast to the dead" (p. 216). She begins to see exceptions to this rule by the end of the fifth century, and epitaphs beginning with χαῖρε appear frequently in the late fourth and third centuries. Even if she is correct about the archaic age, Aristophanes and his audience would have found the humor in Dionysos's line, especially since, as the scholiast *ad loc.* notes, Achaios had used the line in his *Aithon* (TrGF 20F11).

[44] Tainaros was the entrance used by Herakles, Orpheus, and others, while the land of the Kerberians appears as an alternate reading of Kimmerians at Homer, *Odyssey* xi.14, undoubtedly a reference to the hellhound. Κερβέριοι also appears in Sophocles fr. 1060. The word for stops, ἀναπαύλας, in conjunction with ἐκ κακῶν καὶ πραγμάτων, would mean something like 'eternal rest from ills and woes', a clear euphemism for death. The plain of Lethe or oblivion is metonymic for death already in Theognis (1215) and appears as a feature of the afterlife in Plato's myth of Er in the *Republic* (621a). cp., Theognis 1215 - "for we have a beautiful city, situated right by the plain of Lethe," πόλις γε μέν ἐστι καὶ ἡμῖν καλή. Ληθαίωι κεκλιμένη πεδίωι. Some of the B tablets mention two springs, one of which flows from the lake of Mnemosyne; the other presumably would flow from Lethe. Ὀνουπόκας or 'ass-shearings' were the results of a proverbially hopeless task, so εἰς Ὀνουπόκας is probably understood here as 'going nowhere fast'. Some commentators have preferred to read Ὄκνου πλοκάς as a reference to the figure of Oknos in Polygnotus's painting (Paus. 10.29.1–2), endlessly plaiting a rope that is being eaten by his donkey. Dover *ad loc.* suggests that Aristophanes built in the reference to Oknos just by using the proverbial expression with similar sounds. Likewise, going εἰς κόρακας meant literally that the corpse was unburied and devoured by the crows, but it was also a figurative expression best conveyed in English by 'going to the dogs'. So Dionysos' response, "Are we really going to the dogs?" is met with a surly, "Because of you we sure are'." ΔΙ. Σχήσειν δοκεῖς ἐς κόρακας ὄντως; ΧΑ. Ναὶ μὰ Δία σοῦ γ' οὕνεκα. (188–189) p. 607.

[45] Aristophanes is clearly relying on some traditional idea of the ferryman's fee, when he has Herakles tell Dionysos that the fee is two obols (140). Dionysos's shocked reaction at

that he cannot board the ferry unless he had won his freedom in the sea battle. Xanthias weakly pleads eye disease (192), no doubt a favorite excuse for those, both free and slave, who wanted to avoid military duty.[46] Naval service here, however, has a special significance for Xanthias. In 406, Athens launched a navy manned with slaves as well as free men, and those slaves who participated in the battle at Arginousai, the Athenians' last major victory against the Spartans, were given their freedom.[47]

the steep price is probably, like his reaction to the porter corpse (175ff.), a joke about the high prices for standard services in wartime Athens, but the διωβελία was also a public disbursement instituted after the fall of the oligarchy of the 400 in 411/410 by Kleophon. The exact nature of this payment is uncertain, but it seems to have been intended as some sort of relief for the poorer citizens during the war, introduced by the leader of the democratic factions, Kleophon, to win popularity among the people. Aristophanes alludes to the διωβελία as a popular democratic insitution by attributing the spread of the διωβελία to the underworld to Theseus, who was known in Athens not only for his heroic journey to the underworld, but also as the pre-founder of the democracy in Athens. Playing off the resonances of Theseus's role as democratic founder, Aristophanes makes him the originator of the διωβελία in the underworld, as the democrat Kleophon was in the realm above. Not only was Theseus thought to have accomplished the synoikism of Attica (Thucydides II.15.ii; Isoc. *Helen* 35; [Dem.] LIX.74–5; Marm. Par. 239a 20; D.S. IV 61.8), but Theseus was also given credit for having transformed his monarchy into a sort of democratic government that prefigured the post-Pisistratean democracy (Eur. *Supplices* 399–408, 350–353, 429–441; Isoc. *Helen* 34–37, *Panath.* 126–129; [Dem.] LIX 74–75, LX 28; Marm. Par. 239a 20; D.S. IV 61.8; Plut. *Theseus* 24.ii, 24.v–25.iii). cp., [Aristotle] *Ath. Pol.* 28.3. The scholiast at *Frogs* 140 claims that the διωβελία is jury pay, but Kleon had earlier raised the pay for jurors to three obols. Other scholars, such as Rogers 1919 and Pickard-Cambridge 1968, have conjectured that this διωβελία was the theoric grant, reimbursing citizens for attending festivals. Plutarch attributes this institution to Pericles (9.2–3), but as Rhodes notes, "Aristophanes and other contemporaries are suspiciously silent on the theoric fund in the late fifth and early fourth centuries," and the theoric grant may have been instituted later, either by Agyrrios as Harpokration (s.v. θεωρικά) says, or by Euboulos and Diaphantos around 350 as Rhodes argues. (Rhodes 1981, p. 492 *ap.* 41.iii, cp. *ap.* 43.i, 28.iii.) Rhodes *ap. Ath. Pol.* 28.iii (followed by Dover *ap. Frogs* 140) argues that the διωβελία was rather a grant for citizens in reduced circumstances who were not otherwise receiving money from the state. If the διωβελία did refer to the price of attending the theatrical festival, it would be a nice metatheatrical reference (as Rogers, Bowie, and others note), but even if διωβελία does refer to the theoric grant, the actual admission price for the theatre would have been lower.

46 On the use and suspicion of abuse of ophthalmia as an excuse, cp. Herodotus's story (VII.229–231) of the two Spartans at Thermopylae afflicted with ophthalmia, one of whom had himself led into the thick of battle anyway and thus perished nobly, whereas the other did not fight and was reviled as a coward.

47 cp. Xenophon *Hell.* I.6.24; Hellanikos FGrH 323a F25. Even if some slaves had previously served in the navy, the emancipation after Arginousai was a major political event and must have created a shift in attitudes in Athens. As Dover notes, "Confrontation, even if belated, of the fact that slaves were as good as free men when it came to winning a sea battle must have given Athenian assumptions a severe jolt, and Aristophanes created Xanthias precisely at the moment of its impact." (Dover, p. 49.)

The possibility of a slave gaining citizenship through fighting at Arginousai is a recurring theme throughout the play. Xanthias has already grumbled (33) that if he had fought at sea, he would not have to bear the heavy burdens (or perhaps to bear Dionysos's sophistic chattering about bearing and being borne). Moreover, in the parabasis, the chorus contrasts the slaves who gained liberty from the battle with the citizens of aristocratic family who were disenfranchised for their part in the oligarchic revolution of 411.

Isn't it unfair that, just for having been in one sea fight, slaves should have Plataian status, and be over men once free? Please, I'm not against their freedom in itself. I quite agree. They deserve it. That's the only thing you've done intelligently. Still, there are those others, men who also often fought at sea, by your side, whose fathers fought for us, akin by blood to you.[48]

The slaves who fought just once are contrasted with those who fought for generations in naval battles on behalf of the city. Naval service is used as a symbol of participation in the life of the city, both a privilege and a crucial necessity for this city on the brink of disaster. Like a rite of passage, naval service is here an experience that defines the identity of the individual with respect to the larger group.[49] Xanthias has not undergone (and perhaps even shirked) this experience, and so he is excluded from Charon's ferry as though he were an unburied corpse, like Elpenor or Patroklos, forbidden to cross the river into the realm of the dead.

Dionysos, however, can employ Charon's ferry to cross the water barrier for he is an Athenian citizen, although his record of naval service is somewhat dubious at best. He does conceive his longing for Euripides while reading the *Andromeda* on naval patrol, but the fact that Dionysos has leisure to read on board suggests he is not engaged in serious duties. Moreover, as his innuendos make apparent, Herakles views Dionysos's voyage with the effeminate Kleisthenes more as an opportunity for sexual encounters than military ones.[50] Dionysos himself protests to Charon

---

[48] 693–698, Lattimore translation. Καὶ γὰρ αἰσχρόν ἐστι τοὺς μὲν ναυμαχήσαντας μίαν καὶ Πλαταιᾶς εὐθὺς εἶναι κἀντὶ δούλων δεσπότας. Κοὐδὲ ταῦτ᾽ ἔγωγ᾽ ἔχοιμ᾽ ἂν μὴ οὐ καλῶς φάσκειν ἔχειν, ἀλλ᾽ ἐπαινῶ· μόνα γὰρ αὐτὰ νοῦν ἔχοντ᾽ ἐδράσατε. Πρὸς δὲ τούτοις εἰκὸς ὑμᾶς. οἳ μεθ᾽ ὑμῶν πολλὰ δὴ χοὶ πατέρες ἐναυμάχησαν καὶ προσήκουσιν γένει.

[49] cp. Clay 2002, p. 275.

[50] Dover notes that ἐπεβατεύειν, to fight as a marine on board ship, would suggest ἐπεβαίνειν, to mount sexually, and that Herakles' question, Κἀναυμάχησας, could be a euphemism for sexual penetration. cp. Herakles' confusion over Dionysos's object of desire (56–57) – was it a woman? a boy? a *man*? Was it *Kleisthenes* you "were together with"?

that he is no seaman: "Why, how am *I* to pull? I'm not an oarsman, seaman, Salaminian. I can't!"[51] He makes a comic display of his ignorance by sitting *on* his oar when Charon orders him to sit *to* it and by stretching out his hands without the oar when Charon tries to get him into rowing position. Like many an upper-class landsman from Athens forced by the necessities of the war to serve in the navy, Dionysos is out of shape (cp. Charon's insult, γάστρων, 'Tubby') and awkward at grasping the necessary means of overcoming the obstacle that faces him. Although, for most of the war, the upper classes of Athens served as armored infantry and scorned to serve as rowers, Athens' plight was such that men from all levels of Athenian society served on board ship at the battle of Arginousai, breaking down the earlier social stigma on the activity. To get across the water barrier of the Acherusian lake, Dionysos must row, just as the Athenians, the chorus says in the parabasis, when their city is "in the embrace of the waves" must "acquire all men as kinsmen and honored citizens who are willing to fight in the navy with us."[52] Charon promises that despite his incompetence, Dionysos will be able to row to the song of the wondrous swan-frogs, the chorus that gives the play its name. The confrontation of Dionysos with the frog chorus represents a comic complication in the solution to the water barrier.

Few aspects of the *Frogs* command less unity of scholarly opinion than this frog chorus. Disagreements range from the technical - were the frogs onstage or offstage? - to literary critical - are the frogs' lyrics an example of Aristophanes' best lyric style or a parody of his rivals excesses? Many commentators have assumed that the frogs are hostile to Dionysos and that their conflict must prefigure the coming contest between Aeschylus and Euripides. I propose to examine the frogs' function in the storyline, to see how they fit into the obstacle that Dionysos faces in the crossing of the lake of Acheron. Charon's ferry is a solution to the water barrier that contains a further ordeal within it, the rowing test. Dionysos must learn to be a good seaman to cross the infernal lake, and the humor of a rowing lesson for an inept Dionysos had already succeeded with Athenian audiences in Eupolis' *Taxiarchs*.[53] The frogs serve as the piper who kept

---

[51] 203–205, Rogers' translation. Κᾆτα πῶς δυνήσομαι ἄπειρος. ἀθαλάττευτος. ἀσαλαμίνιος ὢν εἶτ' ἐλαύνειν;

[52] τὴν πόλιν καὶ ταῦτ' ἔχοντες κυμάτων ἐν ἀγκάλαις. (704)... πάντας ἀνθρώπους ἑκόντες ξυγγενεῖς κτησώμεθα κἀπιτίμους καὶ πολίτας. ὅστις ἂν ξυνναυμαχῇ. (701–702.)

[53] Eupolis fr. 268, cp. 269, 272, 274. Dover mentions a fragment of a vase painting that seems to illustrate this scene in Eupolis, fig. 86 in Pickard-Cambridge 1968.

the time for the rowers in a trireme, and their song enables even the novice oarsman Dionysos to row across the Acherusian lake. Charon claims that the frogs' beautiful song (μέλη κάλλιστ') will enable Dionysos to row, and the frogs themselves claim they are beloved of the Muses, Pan, and Apollo.[54] Unused to hard naval service, Dionysos suffers blisters on his hands and rear from the unaccustomed activity, and he pleads for them to stop their relentless tune.[55] By the end of the chorus, however, Dionysos is ready to beat the frogs at their own game and claims that he too can keep up all day. Although the frogs control the pace at the beginning, making Dionysos row faster and longer than is comfortable, Dionysos is able to 'take' their song from them (251) and overpower them with the *koax*, suggesting that he controls the rhythm and pace of his rowing. Despite the conflict, then, the frogs help Dionysos cross the water barrier by teaching him to row like a good Athenian citizen who contributes to the salvation of his city by fighting in the sea battles.[56]

But why frogs? Scholars have postulated that the frogs represent some rivals of Aristophanes, or the primitive and bestial elements of comedy, or even the repressed Freudian libido, but frogs are appropriate creatures to provide music in the setting of a lake. Their invisible chorus can provide the rowing song in the marshy underworld lake, recalling the festivals

[54] "For the Muses of the lyre love us well; and hornfoot Pan who plays on the pipe his jocund lays; and Apollo, Harper bright, in our Chorus takes delight." 229–231 Rogers' translation. Ἐμὲ γὰρ ἔστερξαν εὔλυροί τε Μοῦσαι καὶ κεροβάτας Πάν, ὁ καλαμόφθογγα παίζων· προσεπιτέρπεται δ' ὁ φορμικτὰς Ἀπόλλων. Moorton compares these lines to the chorus of Euripides' *Iphigenia in Tauris*, in which the music of Pan and Apollo drives the rowers to bring Iphigeneia and Orestes home to Athens: "And in the rowers' ears Pan shall be sounding all his pointed notes, great mountains echoing to his little reed, and Phoebus on his lyre shall strike profound the seven strings and sing to you of Attica, shall sing to you of home and lead you there." (1125–1132, Witter Brynner translation in Grene and Lattimore edition.) συρίζων θ' ὁ κηροδέτας κάλαμος οὐρείου Πανὸς κώπαις ἐπιθωΰξει, ὁ φοῖβός θ' ὁ μάντις ἔχων κέλαδον ἑπτατόνου λύρας ἀείδων ἄξει λιπαρὰν εὖ σ' Ἀθηναίων ἐπὶ γᾶν. Moorton, however, sees the frogs as serving the opposite function in Aristophanes. (Moorton 1989, p. 314.)

[55] Stanford genteelly notes: "As amateur oarsmen soon learn, it is not only the hands that get sore in rowing... Experienced Greek oarsmen sat on a cushion (cf. Hermippus, fr. 54)" (Stanford 1983 *ap.* 222.)

[56] As Whitman notes, "They are genuine Athenian frogs, and above all, they teach Dionysus to row, whereas the sailors brought up on Euripides are good only at talking back to their officers. The rhythm of the frogs is the rhythm of the victorious Athenian fleets, and Dionysus learns it despite himself, to the sorrow of his blistered hands and backside." (Whitman 1971, p. 249.) cp. the reference to the degenerate character of the modern navy, 1071–1077. See now Clay 2002.

in the marshlands of Attica in which the audience would have heard the frog accompaniment.[57] The frogs, indeed, refer to the festival of the Pitchers in the Anthesteria, another festival of Dionysos celebrated earlier in the year than the Lenaia, at which the *Frogs* was performed.[58] While the actual sound of frogs has led commentators to suspect that the frogs' chorus must be a parody of some musical style Aristophanes disliked, nothing in the song itself indicates that Dionysos wants it to cease for any reason other than that it drives the rowing tempo.[59] Moreover, as Dover notes, "A culture which could think of the maddening noise of cicadas as the perpetual 'singing' of creatures dear to the Muses (Pl. *Phdr.* 259BC) could take in its stride and enjoy lyrics founded upon the cries of *Rana ridibunda.*"[60] Once more, Aristophanes creates humor by juxtaposing features of the mundane world of the living with the world of the dead. For these frogs are not simply the ordinary frogs that sing in the marshes

[57] I follow Allison's defense of the scholiast's assertion that the frog chorus never appeared on stage. While I can appreciate from experience Dover's comment about the difficulty of offstage choruses ("usually a disaster", p. 57 and n. 5), the inherent difficulty has not stopped composers from including offstage choruses. Russo, moreover, lists a number of other places in Aristophanes where the chorus is likely singing offstage, including the *Clouds*, the Hoopoe's song in the *Birds*, and the dialogues with offstage choruses in *Wasps* 144–173 and *Thesmophoriazeusae* 1056–1097.

[58] "We sing the Iacchos song we used to love in the Marshland up above, in praise of Dionysos to produce, of Nysaean Dionysos, son of Zeus, when the revel-tipsy throng, all crapulous and gay, to our precinct reeled along on the holy Pitcher day." 215–219 Rogers' translation modified. ἦν ἀμφὶ Νυσήιον Διὸς Διώνυσον ἐν Λίμναισιν ἰαχήσαμεν, ἡνίχ' ὁ κραιπαλόκωμος τοῖς ἱεροῖσι Χύτροισι χωρεῖ κατ' ἐμὸν τέμενος λαῶν ὄχλος. By singing an Iacchos song, the chorus of frogs aligns itself with the chorus of blessed Mystai that sings to Iacchos later. It should not be forgotten that the two choruses are, in fact, the same singers who appear in different guises.

[59] *Contra* Defradas, "Les grenouilles-cygnes doivent être considérées comme la réprésentation symbolique des poètes du Nouvelle Dithyrambe. Aristophane a composé une véritable parodie de ce genre musical." (Defradas 1969, p. 34.) Demand's ingenious suggestion is that the frogs symbolize Aristophanes' rival Phrynichos, along the pun of *phryne* = toad ≈ frog = *batrachos*. I would agree, however, with Campbell 1984 (p. 164): "This is too far-fetched: Aristophanes was certainly fond of that underrated form of humour, the pun, but his examples are straightforward and involve one step . . . Even Lycophron might have hesitated before foisting this on his readers." Demand 1970 is right, however, to emphasize the role of Phrynichos throughout the play, for Aristophanes mentions three different Phrynichos': the rival comedian (13), the tragedian whom Aeschylus surpasses (910, 1299), and the politician who led the oligarchs astray in 411 (689). In each case, Phrynichos represents an element of the city's past that is negative – tired and trite comic jokes, outmoded tragic style, or a misguided attempt at revolution.

[60] Dover, p. 56, n. 2. However, in Plutarch's much later *De Sera Num.* 567f, Nero is transformed into a frog in the afterlife, a fate befitting his pretensions to singing in life.

of Attica, but 'swan-frogs' (βατράχοι κύκνοι), whose song is amazingly beautiful. As befits pipers in the realm of the dead, their song is a 'swan-song', since the song of the swan is heard only at death.[61] Frogs themselves, as creatures that live in the two worlds of water and land, are appropriate creatures to facilitate the transition of Dionysos across the border between the worlds of living and dead.[62]

The spectacle of Dionysos rowing his way across the Acherusian lake would conjure up for the spectators not only the traditional mythic images of Charon's ferry, but also the image of Dionysos being carried by boat in the ritual procession at the Anthesteria.[63] Instead of being carried as a helpless shade in Charon's ferry or as a triumphant god in a ritual procession, Dionysos must row like a citizen soldier aboard one of the fleet that provides the last lifeline for the city. For the free ride expected from the traditional models, Aristophanes substitutes the comic spectacle of Dionysos trying to row to the chant of the marvelous swan-frogs.

Aristophanes elaborates upon the familiar traditional solutions to the water barrier that separates the world of the living from that of the dead and transforms the results of applying those solutions. In this way, Aristophanes weaves in the important theme of citizenship in Athens and the importance of Athens' navy. By having Charon bar any slave not freed by fighting at Arginousai and by making Dionysos do his own rowing instead of merely being carried by Charon, Aristophanes redraws the boundaries of the worthy Athenian. What good Athenians, slave or free, noble or poor, must do is serve in the navy, keeping the city afloat by pulling their own oars.[64] Aristophanes therefore introduces the chorus of frogs, whose

---

[61] For the idea that swans sing just before death, cp. Plato *Phaedo* 85b; cp. Aristophanes *Birds* 769-784; Euripides *IT* 1104.

[62] cp. Moorton on the liminality of frogs: "Aristophanes' amphibians incorporate a duality that embraces both life and death, and the ridiculous and the sublime, situated as they are on the dividing line between them. Likewise, the identification of the frogs with swans, which in popular belief sing only at the moment of death, is particularly appropriate to the frogs, singing eternally on the threshold of death." (Moorton 1989, p. 313.)

[63] cp. Pickard-Cambridge 1968, p. 12.

[64] The importance of naval service reappears in the contest between Aeschylus and Euripides at the end of the play. Aeschylus uses the metaphor of a lion cub he had applied to Helen in his *Agamemnon* to answer Dionysos's question about Alcibiades, saying that if the state has reared such a dangerous creature, its best hope is to do good seaman's service (ὑπηρετεῖν) to his ways. Aeschylus uses a verb that means to serve as a rower under the command of, a clear reminder of the importance of naval service throughout the play as well as an allusion to Alcibiades' brilliant successes as a naval commander, since Alcibiades' naval victory at Kyzikos in 410 even provoked an offer of peace from the Spartans.

swan-song serves as a rowing chant to help Dionysos learn to row like a good citizen.

### Result: Rendezvous at Withering Heights

The results of Aristophanes' tinkering with the traditional elements are Dionysos's rowing excursion and Xanthias's walk around the lake. However, although Dionysos does naval service while Xanthias toils through the muck, the difference between their fates is blurred because both cross the water barrier at almost the same time. Xanthias, barred from the boat, makes his way around the water barrier. Charon tells him to wait for Dionysos at the Αὐαίνου λίθον, Withering Heights, as Stanford renders it. This stone of withering may, as Dover suggests, reflect a current expression – 'wither away' – taking αὐαίνου as an imperative equivalent to 'go to hell', but the idea that the inhabitants of the realm of the dead are parched and withered appears in a variety of places in the mythic tradition.[65] Charon's instructions to Xanthias, therefore, humorously combine a dismissive snarl with an idea familiar from the tradition of the withered dead. Xanthias bewails his fate and disappears into the darkness during the scene of Dionysos with the frogs, but he reappears unscathed at the end of the scene. Aristophanes again undercuts the very divisions he has set up between the worlds of living and dead and between the routes of Dionysos and Xanthias. Although Xanthias was barred from the boat, he arrives at the other side of the lake almost as soon as Dionysos, blurring the difference between their routes. The water barrier turns out to be neither the vast Ocean that can only be crossed by herculean effort nor the magical water of other tellings that requires special ritual or divine aid to cross. Instead it is a smallish marshy lake that can be walked around as easily as rowing across. Xanthias apparently suffers not at all for his lack of privileged status. He has not shrivelled up at the stone of withering or

---

[65] The scholiasts to the *Frogs* note that certain dead are said to be dried up, and Lawson connects these unhappy dead with revenants, restless dead unable to settle down in Hades. Σ – τοῦτο ἀναπλάττει ἀπὸ τοῦ τοὺς νεκροὺς ξηροὺς εἶναι καὶ ἀλίβαντας. cp. Lawson 1926, on the vampire-like *alibantes*. In the gold tablets of the B series, the deceased all identify themselves as dried up: δίψηι δ' εἰμι αὖη καὶ ἀπόλλυμαι, I am parched with thirst and I perish. B1.8, cp. B2.9, B3-9.1, B10.11, B11.13. The thirst of the dead also appears in the shades' desire for blood in the *Odyssey Nekyia* (xi.36-7), and Tantalus, of course, is the ultimate example of one tormented by thirst in the underworld, but the motif of the thirsty dead is found all over the world (Deonna 1939).

drowned in the attempt to get past the water barrier without the proper solution. Aristophanes carefully sets up the division between the routes of Dionysos and Xanthias by playing off traditional motifs of differentiated fates for the dead in the afterlife, but he cheerfully undermines the distinctions for a further joke. The blurring of difference between the master and the slave recurs in the *Frogs* and provides the basis for much comic confusion as the master behaves slavishly in contrast to the bold and heroic behavior of the slave.

### FINDING THE PATH IN THE UNDERWORLD

### Obstacle: Lost in the Muck

Another danger for the traveler in the underworld is the possibility of becoming lost in the murky darkness. The underworld is full of unpleasant places like the ever-flowing rivers of filth or the rivers of boiling mud described in the myth in Plato's *Phaedo*.[66] Xanthias describes his detour around the lake as a route of "filth and darkness" (σκότος καὶ βόρβορος – 273). Aristophanes evokes this familiar image of an unhappy fate in the afterlife with Herakles' description of "weltering seas of filth and ever-rippling dung."[67] While according to Plato, poets reserve this fate for the uninitiated or the unjust, Aristophanes spells out the sort of misdeed that brings such retribution in the realm of the dead. "Whoso has wronged the guest-friend here on earth, or robbed his boylove of the promised pay, or smacked his mother, or profanely smitten his father's cheek, or sworn an oath forsworn, or copied out a speech of Morsimos."[68] Some of these crimes, such as oathbreaking and wronging a guest-friend or a parent, were depicted in the tradition as bringing forth Erinyes upon the wrongdoer to torment him in life or after death.[69] However, to the list

[66] *Phaedo* 111de, 113ab. Kingsley 1995, pp. 96 ff., argues plausibly that these elements were used in other myths before Plato. Indeed, the very name of the Pyriphlegethon in Homer (*Od*. x.513ff.) would suggest that such a motif goes far back in the tradition.

[67] 145–146, Rogers' translation. βόρβορον πολὺν καὶ σκῶρ ἀείνων·. This unpleasant fate for wrongdoers is mentioned by a number of authors, cp., Dem 25.53; Plato *Rep*. 363d, *Phd*. 69c, with Olymp *ad loc.*; Plotinos 1.6.6; Asios fr. 1.; for uninitiate: D.L 6.39, Julian 7.238; specifically as Eleusinian, Plut. fr. 178, Aristeides Or. 22.10; cp. Graf 1974, pp. 103–107.

[68] 147–151, Rogers' translation modified. εἴ που ξένον τις ἠδίκησε πώποτε, ἢ παῖδα κινῶν τἀργύριον ὑφείλετο, ἢ μητέρ' ἠλόησεν, ἢ πατρὸς γνάθον ἐπάταξεν, ἢ 'πίορκον ὅρκον ὤμοσεν, ἢ Μορσίμου τις ῥῆσιν ἐξεγράψατο.

[69] cp. e.g., Aeschylus, *Eumenides* 269–275; Homer, *Iliad* XIX.259.

of traditionally serious crimes, Aristophanes adds a bathetically untra-
ditional one, sneakily taking back the money given to a prostitute. He
compounds the joke by adding offenses of bad taste in drama, such as
copying out a speech from the tragedian Morsimos or learning the Pyrrhic
dance of Kinesias.[70] In the same way, Aristophanes takes the traditional
motif of wrongdoers wallowing in the muck in the underworld and gives
it a twist by having Xanthias identify the wretched sinners as the audience. Once again, he mixes up the worlds of the living and the dead, but,
in this case, the real world of the living outside the play is identified with
the world of the dead inside the play. Aristophanes thus humorously uses
the distinction between a happy lot and an unhappy lot in the afterlife to
redefine the models of acceptable behavior in Athenian society.

Dionysos and Xanthias must find their way through the unfamiliar
underworld to their destination, the halls of Hades, and avoid becoming
stuck in the wretched conditions of the unhappy dead. Moreover, the
chances of encounters with the fearsome denizens of the underworld increase for those who wander lost in the realm of the dead.[71] The problem
of finding the right path in the underworld is a traditional element that
occurs in a number of the mythic tellings.[72] Plutarch describes the experience of the underworld as being like an initiation: "wanderings astray
in the beginning, tiresome walkings in circles, some frightening paths in
darkness that lead nowhere."[73] The lost traveler in the underworld must
find some guide to reach his destination or wander astray in the perilous
shadows of Hades. Dionysos and Xanthias are astray in the underworld,
beset by the terrors (real or imaginary) of the monstrous inhabitants, and

---

[70] cp. Vaio, "The aesthetic sinner shares the same fecal bath as his moral counterparts. No
distinction is made between them regarding their punishment. They are judged alike,
and their juxtaposition points the way to the later criticism of drama on ethical as well
as stylistic grounds." (Vaio 1985, p. 98.) Aristophanes also mocked Morsimos in *Knights*
401 and *Peace* 802. The precise meaning of Dionysos's addition of learning the Pyrrhic
dance of Kinesias is uncertain. See Dover *ad loc.*

[71] The encounter, real or imaginary, with Empousa (290ff.) evokes the familiar motif of
monstrous beings in the underworld who bar the way of the traveler. Aristophanes'
choice of Empousa, rather than Eurynomos (Paus. X.28.7) or Kerberos, as the monster
may have Eleusinian resonances. cp. Brown 1991, pp. 42–43.

[72] cp., the choice of paths in the gold tablets (B1.1–5, B2.1–5, B10.2–7, B11.4–9), see
Chapter 2, pp. 46–50. In the *Phaedo*, Socrates reasons that the legends of daimonic guides
in the underworld must imply a multiplicity of paths. *Phaedo* 108a. See below, Chapter 4,
pp. 188–190.

[73] Plut. fr. 178. πλάναι τὰ πρῶτα καὶ περιδρομαὶ κοπώδεις καὶ διὰ σκότους τινὲς ὕποπτοι
πορεῖαι καὶ ἀτέλεστοι.

they only have the courage to squat down and hide when they hear the sounds of the approaching procession, despite the fact that Herakles has told them to ask the initiates about the way to the halls of Hades.[74]

### Solution: Join the Festivals of the Mystai

Relying on the instructions of Herakles, Dionysos and Xanthias have none of the other traditional solutions to finding their way in the realm of the dead. They have no written reminder, like the gold tablets, to direct them, nor have they the assistance of a god who can aid them, as Hermes or Athena aids Herakles.[75] They are not aided by a guardian spirit such as that alluded to by Socrates in the *Phaedo*.[76] Menander refers to such a daimon as a good mystagogue for every individual in life.[77] The reference to the mystagogue, who guided the initiand through the mysteries at Eleusis, suggests another possible solution to the problem of wandering lost in the underworld, initiation in the Eleusinian mysteries.

The chorus of Mystai who enter the scene are not explicitly labelled as Eleusinian initiates, but there can be no doubt that, for Aristophanes and his audience, the Eleusinian Mysteries were the primary reference.[78] Torchlit processions and night-time revels could be part of the many Bacchic mystery cults as easily as the Eleusinian, but the hymns to Iacchos and Demeter seem to indicate that the Eleusinian Mysteries are intended. While Demeter had many cults and festivals in her honor, Iacchos seems

---

[74] 161–163, cp. Xanthias's reminder when he hears the identifying Iacchos song: "I have it, master: 'tis those blessed Mystics of whom he told us, sporting hereabouts. They sing the Iacchos song through the marketplace'." (318–320, Rogers' translation modified.) Τοῦτ' ἔστ' ἐκεῖν'. ὦ δέσποθ'· οἱ μεμυημένοι ἐνταῦθά που παίζουσιν. οὓς ἔφραζε νῷν. Ἄδουσι γοῦν τὸν Ἴακχον ὅνπερ δι' ἀγορᾶς. Dionysos, however, is still not taking any chances.

[75] Athena claims to have helped Herakles, *Il.* VIII. 366–369, while Apollodorus refers to Hermes as the guide of Herakles in the underworld. Vase paintings depict one or both present in various scenes of Herakles carrying off Kerberos. cp. Boardman 1975, pp. 7–9; LIMC s.v Herakles 2553–2568, 2581–2603, 2605–2615.

[76] *Phaedo* 108a. Heraclitus refers to the same belief in a guardian spirit that guided each individual during life (and after death) in his famous dictum (B119), ἦθος ἀνθρώπῳ δαίμων, usually loosely translated as "character is fate." The Derveni Papyrus fragment mentioning a δαίμων γίνεται ἑκάστωι, a daimon is to each one, probably testifies to the same idea. (col. III.4 in Tsantsanoglou 1997.) cp. also [Heracl.] Epistle 9.6.

[77] ἅπαντι δαίμων ἀνδρὶ συμπαρίσταται εὐθὺς γενομένῳ. μυσταγωγὸς τοῦ βίου ἀγαθός. fr. 550 Kock.

[78] cp. Graf 1974, pp. 40–50; also Dover, p. 61; Bowie 1993, pp. 229–230.

to be an especially Eleusinian deity, particularly associated with the long procession from Athens to Eleusis.[79] Herodotus tells of the phantom Iacchos procession that traversed the plain just before Salamis; even though Athens was without a city, her power manifested itself in the Eleusinian procession, prophesying the great victory of Athens over the Persians.[80]

To be of the company of the initiates, however, was not for everyone; certain types of people were excluded from the rituals. The *Prorrhesis*, the ritual proclamation at the beginning of the Mysteries excluded barbarians (anyone who could not speak Greek) and anyone who was ritually impure from having spilled blood.[81] Potential initiates could include women and slaves as well as male citizens, but all these initiands had to undergo certain purifications before being initiated.[82] Those who had been deprived of citizen's rights could be barred from the Mysteries as they were barred from many other rituals.[83] For those who were initiated, however, great benefits were promised, both in life and after death. "Blessed is he among

---

[79] "Iakchos ist hier die eleusinische Sonderform des Dionyos." Graf 1974, p. 51. cp. his discussion of Iacchos and the Eleusinian elements in the *Frogs*, pp. 41–66; The chorus's reference to traveling the long road without tiring reinforces the Eleusinian atmosphere: καὶ δεῖξον ὡς ἄνευ πόνου πολλὴν ὁδὸν περαίνεις. (400–401), cp. untiring Bacchics in Eur. *Bacchae* 64ff., 161ff. Iacchos as an aspect of Dionysos: Soph. *Ant.* 1146–54, Eur. *Bacch.* 725ff. cp. the invocation at the Lenaia, Σ479 – Iacchos son of Semele, Σεμελήι' Ἴακχε. Mylonas denies that Iacchos was an aspect of Dionysos (p. 238), claiming that the confusion between the two arose later ("in Roman times," Mylonas 1961, p. 318, although he admits the Sophocles reference, p. 238 n.71). Clinton argues that "We must not speak of an 'identification' of Iakchos and Dionysus: 'Iakchos' was one of many names that could be given to Dionysus, but the Iakchos at Eleusis was a distinct god, born no doubt of the Dionysiac milieu in the mystic procession." (Clinton 1992, pp. 66–67.) To be sure, the names 'Iacchos' and 'Dionysos' are not interchangeable, but there is no reason to suppose that Iacchos was not the Eleusinian aspect of Dionysos and that the 'Dionysiac milieu' of the Iacchos procession was due to the presence of the Dionysiac deity. (I would speculate that the controversy over the identity of Iacchos and Dionysos is probably rooted in the turn-of-the-century desire to separate the Eleusinian and Bacchic Mysteries, especially among those for whom, as for Rohde, Dionysos was an outsider and latecomer to Greek religion.)

[80] Hdt. VIII.65.

[81] Isocrates *Panegyricus* 157.

[82] These seem to have included the Lesser Mysteries at Agrai, possibly some ritual taboos in the days preceding the Mysteries, and a purification ceremony known as 'Seaward, Initiates!' (ἅλαδε μύσται), in which the initiates immersed themselves and a sacrificial piglet in the sea before sacrificing the piglet. cp. Parker 1983, pp. 283–286; Bowie 1993, p. 239; on ἅλαδε μύσται: cp. *IG* II/III$^2$ 847.20; *IG* I$^2$ 94.35; Polyaenus 3.11.2; ΣAeschines 3.130; cp. Plut. *Phoc.* 28.6.

[83] Andokides was prosecuted for, among other things, having taken part in the Eleusinian Mysteries despite having been exiled. cp. Andok. 1.33, 71, 132; Lys. 6.9, 24, 52; Dem 21.58f,

men on earth who has seen these mysteries; but he who is uninitiate and who has no part in them, never has lot of like good things once he is dead, down in the darkness and gloom."[84] The benefits of this lot in the afterlife are not clearly specified for Eleusis, but some mystery cults seem to have promised a continuation of festivals into the afterlife.[85] The chorus of Mystai describes their blessed afterlife: "On us alone shines the sun and the holy light, on us who were initiated and conducted ourselves in pious manner towards both strangers and individuals."[86] Aristophanes here highlights the distinction drawn in the tradition between the blessed and the unhappy dead, separating his chorus of initiates dancing in flowering meadows from the wretches in the mud.[87]

The party in the realm of the dead is one facet of mystery cult tradition that looms large in Aristophanes' portrayal of the chorus of Mystai. Aristophanes gives neither a mocking parody nor an accurate, detailed picture of the Eleusinian rites, but the chorus of Mystai evokes a number of familiar elements for the Athenian audience of the *Frogs* in a humorous, slightly skewed way. The first hint of the approach of the chorus to Dionysos and Xanthias is the sound of festal flutes and the smell of mystic torches, but as they come closer Xanthias is enraptured, "O, what a jolly whiff of pork breathed o'er me!"[88] In Xanthias' reference to piglets, Aristophanes comically combines two familiar aspects of the Eleusinian

---

22.73, 24.181; Aesch. 3.176 and Σ. See Hansen 1976, pp. 54–98, esp. 62, on the prohibition of those deprived of citizens' rights from entry into the agora or any sanctuary.

[84] ὄλβιος ὃς τάδ' ὄπωπεν ἐπιχθονίων ἀνθρώπων· ὃς δ' ἀτελὴς ἱερῶν, ὅς τ' ἄμμορος, οὔ ποθ' ὁμοίων αἶσαν ἔχει φθίμενός περ ὑπὸ ζόφῳ εὐρώεντι. *Homeric Hymn to Demeter*, 480–482. cp. Pindar, fr. 137 and Sophocles fr. 837. cp. Isoc. iv.28.

[85] Plato, *Rep.* 363cd, speaks scathingly of cults that reward the initiate with everlasting drunkenness while others lie in the mud. cp. gold tablets P1.6–7 "You have wine as your fortunate honor. And rites await you beneath the earth, just as the other blessed ones. οἶνον ἔχεις εὐδ(α)ίμονα τιμὴ(ν). κἀπ(ι)μένει σ' ὑπὸ γῆν τέλεα ἅσσαπερ ὄλβιοι ἄλλοι. cp. P2.5 and perhaps B1.10.

[86] 454–459, Rogers' translation: "O, happy mystic chorus, the blessed sunshine o'er us on us alone is smiling in its soft sweet light: on us who strove for ever with holy pure endeavour, alike by friend and stranger to guide our steps aright." Μόνοις γὰρ ἡμῖν ἥλιος καὶ φέγγος ἱερόν ἐστιν. ὅσοι μεμυήμεθ' εὐσεβῆ τε διήγομεν τρόπον περὶ τοὺς ξένους καὶ τοὺς ἰδιώτας.

[87] Many features of the chorus's environment correspond with the traditional descriptions of paradise for the blessed dead. The flowery meadows (cp. 326, 344, 373–374, 448ff.) recall Pindar's descriptions of paradise (O. II.70–5, fr. 129) as well as the λειμών which appears in the underworld from Homer (x.509, xxiv.14) to Plato (*Rep.* 614e) and the gold tablets (cp. A4.6 and the tablet from Pherai).

[88] 338, Rogers' translation. ὡς ἡδύ μοι προσέπνευσε χοιρείων κρεῶν.

Mysteries. The piglet does recall the preliminary sacrifice at the "Seaward, Initiates" ritual, which would have concluded in a tasty feast of pork, but the word for piglet, χοῖρος, also was used for female genitalia, and Xanthias anticipates not only gustatory but also sexual pleasures from the festive celebrations.[89] The chorus repeatedly describes its actions with verbs of playing,[90] and the pleasures of the festival it describes are not just dancing in the meadows of paradise, but in particular revelling with women. Dionysos and Xanthias get up and join the dancing after the chorus describes the pretty girl whose breast has popped out of her torn shirt (409–415), and the chorus goes off to an all-night revel of playing in the flowering groves with the maidens and women (440–446).[91] Aristophanes emphasizes the party aspects of the Mystery rites and of the traditional mythic descriptions of the blessed afterlife, playing up the sexual element for comic effect.

While the Mystai happily welcome anyone who is ready to frolic, these initiates, like the Eleusinian Mysteries, do ban from their revels certain types of people. Their comic *prorrhesis* limits and defines the membership of their group just as the Eleusinian *prorrhesis* does, and the chorus continues to draw distinctions throughout the parodos and its next appearance in the parabasis. The categories of the included and excluded are carefully tailored by Aristophanes for his social and comic purposes as he manipulates the traditional distinction between the fates of the blessed dead and those of the unhappy dead to redefine the boundaries of his ideal of Athenian society. Those who are unable to understand their language and who are impure of mind are banned from the chorus's celebrations in the realm of the dead, just as barbarians and polluted persons are banned from the Eleusinian Mysteries, but the definition of barbarian and impure are twisted by Aristophanes.[92]

---

[89] cp. Dover, ad 338f. Aristophanes makes the same kind of joke in *Ach.* 764ff. where a Megarian sells off his daughters as "piglets for the mysteries" (χοῖρους μυστικάς), and the string of sexual jokes makes clear the double meaning. As Dover notes, Dionysos's reply to Xanthias, concerning 'sausage', reinforces the sexual aspect of the joke.

[90] cp. 333, 375, 388, 392, 407b, 411, 415, 442, 452.

[91] On the questions of whether the chorus is divided into groups of men and women and whether any part of the chorus actually leaves the stage, see Dover, pp. 63–69. I would argue that the chorus retains its Eleusinian character even after its exit and return, *contra* Dover, p. 68: "This section is their last utterance as initiates, and from now on they are simply the chorus necessary to an Old Comedy, divested of any distinctive character."

[92] cp. Bowie 1993, pp. 239–244, on the application of the categories of the Eleusinian *prorrhesis* to the chorus's comments. My analysis differs somewhat from Bowie's, however.

Real barbarians, for Aristophanes, are those who are unfamiliar with the celebrations of the Muses or the comedies of Kratinos, or those who laugh at bad jokes made at the wrong time (356-359). Also in this excluded group of those who are unversed in the proper language are bad comedians like Kinesias and politicians who are so resentful of being mocked in comedy that they try to reduce the fees paid to the comic poets (366-368).[93] The comic abuse resented by the politicians is described as "in the rites of Dionysos established by our forefathers" (ἐν ταῖς πατρίοις τελεταῖς ταῖς τοῦ Διονύσου), with the reminder that such festivals comprise part of the religious tradition of Athens, not to be broken up or attacked for personal gain.

The impure are not those who have committed murder or some other serious crime that has led to their banishment from the state, as in the Eleusinian Mysteries.[94] The chorus instead banishes all those whom Aristophanes sees as disrupting the unity of Athens: those who do not make the effort to get along with their fellow citizens and who foster faction in the city.[95] Particularly condemned are all those who exploit the circumstances of Athens' distress for personal profit, those who take bribes in office or betray military outposts or ships to the enemy. A certain Thorykion, otherwise unknown, is accused of smuggling naval supplies from Aigina to Epidauros. Such smuggling may also be the target of the next attack, on those who try to get supplies for the enemies' ships. All those who do not help save the city while it is weathering the storm (τῆς

---

[93] The scholiasts suggest that Archinos or Agyrrios are intended here. Kinesias is mocked by Aristophanes in the *Birds* 1403 and, probably for having stained his clothing, in *Eccl.* 329f.

[94] Scholars have debated the importance of moral vs. formal requirements for a positive afterlife in Eleusinian theology. Graf concludes that, by the time of Aristophanes, moralizing notions have crept in from Orphic sources to supplement the formal requirement of initiation. (Graf 1974, pp. 79-126.) I would argue that some moral notion was probably always implicit in the discrimination between those who received good afterlives and those who received bad afterlives. As the conceptions of morality shifted, however, the sacrifices and purifications involved with initiation were no longer considered as important as other realms of behavior. The Platonic and Cynic critiques of initiation reflected the increasing gap between the religious institutions and the current moral debates (*Rep.* 363c-366a; the story of Diogenes in Plut. *Quom. Adul.* 21ef, cp. D.L. vi.39, Julian *Or.* vii.25). The issue was no doubt popular in late nineteenth and early twentieth century scholarship because of its implications for the Protestant moralizing critique of Catholic formal ritual.

[95] cp. description of Euripides as εὔκολος (82), whereas Aeschylus never got along with the Athenians (807).

πόλεως χειμαζομένης) but instead take advantage of its troubles are assimilated to the murderers of the Eleusinian *prorrhesis* and expelled from the paradisal revels.

The chorus then takes the opportunity, as the parodos continues, to abuse several prominent politicians, casting aspersions on their right to be leaders of the city. Archedemos, a leading politician who may have played a major role in the prosecution of the generals after Arginousai, is accused of being the ace of corruption in Athens (τὰ πρῶτα τῆς ἐκεῖ μοχθηρίας), most likely a charge that he is abusing his leadership position for personal gain.[96] His legitimacy and citizenship are cast into question by the insinuation that he had not been introduced to his phratry at the appropriate age.[97] The next target, Kleisthenes or his son,[98] is characterized as a passive homosexual, longing for his dead lover with the unlikely name of Sebinos of Anaphlystia.[99] For an adult male citizen to submit willingly to be the passive partner in sex was tantamount to accepting the position of a woman or a slave and was thus grounds for disenfranchisement.[100] Kallias, notorious for squandering his substance on womanizing, is mocked as wearing the trophy of his conquests.[101] His sea battles are, like those Herakles assumed of Dionysos in the first scene, sexual rather than military, and he pursues his personal pleasures instead of the needs of the community.[102] Not only does Aristophanes suggest through his insults that these figures be excluded from leadership in politics, but he again deploys the comic confusion of the worlds of the living and the dead to isolate them further from the true and living world of

[96] cp. Lysias xiv.25, which refers to Archedemos as an embezzler.

[97] cp. Dover *ad loc.*

[98] Dover takes τὸν Κλεισθένους as referring to an unknown son of Kleisthenes, whereas earlier editors read it as referring to Kleisthenes. The characterization fits with Aristophanes' previous abuse of Kleisthenes, but that does not rule out a reference to his son instead.

[99] cp. Dover, on 423, 425, and 427. "'Sebinos', suggestive of βινεῖν, 'fuck' is improbable as a Greek name...its bearer may have been not a contemporary but a proverbial figure; at any rate 'Sebinos the Anaphlystian' is alluded to thirteen years later, in *Ec.* 979f."

[100] "It is not only by assimilating himself to a woman in the sexual act that the submissive male rejects his role as a male citizen, but also by deliberately choosing to be the victim of what would be, if the victim were unwilling, hubris.... To choose to be treated as an object at the disposal of another citizen was to resign one's own standing as a citizen." (Dover 1978, pp. 103–104.)

[101] Dover renders it as wearing "a pussy-skin," rather than, like Dionysos, a Heraklean lion skin. For Kallias, cp. Aesch. 1.30-2, 94-105, 154; Andok. 1.124-7; Kratinos frr. 12, 81.

[102] The comic distortion of his patronymic, Ἱππονίκου τὸ Ἱπποβίνου, suggests where he is spending his paternal resources.

Athens. Archedemos is the leading demagogue among the dead above (420- ἐν τοῖς ἄνω νεκροῖσι), whereas Kleisthenes spends his time among the graves (423 – ἐν ταῖς ταφαῖσι). Both belong in the world of the dead instead of the world of the living, like the politicians whom Plouto calls for when he sends Aeschylus back up to the world of the living (1505ff.). The chorus's comic attacks create an in-group of true and good Athenians by characterizing those whom Aristophanes sees as detrimental to the unity of the city as outsiders, barred from the community of initiates.

The chorus continues in this vein during the parabasis, in which it couples attacks on two prominent politicians with some metaphoric advice on bringing unity to the troubled city. Kleophon, one of the major opponents to peace with the Spartans, is called a barbarian and an outsider, despite the fact that his father had been a general for the city.[103] The chorus condemns him for being less concerned with the honor of Athens than the average citizen in the theatre.[104] Even though Kleophon leads the war effort to preserve Athens' empire, the chorus is claiming that Kleophon too is more concerned with his own interests than the glory of his city. Kleigenes is not a peaceful man (οὐκ εἰρηνικὸς), and the chorus prophesies that he will receive the recompense for his way of life. Not only does he cheat his fellow citizens, but he distrusts them so much that he is always on guard and ready to lash out at them.[105] Aristophanes reduces Kleigenes' violence and distrust of his fellow man to a ridiculously low

---

[103] Kleophon opposed peace after the Athenian victory at Kyzikos and possibly also after the battle of Arginousai (although see Rhodes 1981, p. 424). He even opposed peace negotiations after the Athenian defeat at Aigospotami. Kleophon's father, Kleidippes, son of Deinias, from Acharnai, was a general in 428, cp. Thuc. iii.3. According to the Σ on 681, Plato Comicus also alleged that Kleophon's mother was Thracian, perhaps in his *Kleophon* which was in competition with the *Frogs*.

[104] 676–678 σοφίαι μυρίαι κάθηνται φιλοτιμότεραι Κλεοφῶντος. cp. Dover *ad loc.*, "We must, however, distinguish between a desire to achieve high status by inspiring fear (whatever people may really think) and a desire to achieve it by courage and generosity which deservedly win admiration and respect... An alternative possibility (Dn) is that Kleophon (like Demosthenes) constantly professed devotion to the honour of Athens, and the chorus is saying that the average Athenian was more genuinely concerned with that than Kleophon."

[105] Beyond a general accusation of fraud and a disposition to cheat his fellows, the significance of the accusation that Kleigenes mixes ash into his soaps is unclear. Bowie's suggestion that it refers to some kind of ritual impurity seems unlikely, especially since the primary association for bathkeepers was with prostitutes (cp. *Knights*, 1403). I suspect that the language of ruling over earth (κρατοῦσι κυκησίτεφροι ψευδολίτρου τε κονίας καὶ Κιμωλίας γῆς – 710-12) refers to some abuse of an administrative position in the Athenian-controlled islands, but no certain conclusion can be drawn since all that is

level, walking home armed lest someone steal his clothes, but the suspicion and war-mongering that Aristophanes condemns are not only on the personal level but on the political level as well.

The chorus also uses the parabasis to make two constructive suggestions for promoting the unity of Athens and building the strength of the group. They plead for the restoration to citizenship of those exiled for their part in the oligarchic revolution of 411. The chorus argues that the one slip-up of these oligarchs in trying to overthrow the democratic government is less important than the generations of service they have shown to the polis, with the implication that they intended the good of Athens, but that the deceptions of Phrynichos led them astray.[106] Athens should accept as citizens all who are willing to fight on behalf of the city. Drawing on the familiar myth of the autochthonous origin of the Athenians, which defined all Athenians as coming from the same family sprung from the soil of their country, the chorus suggests that whoever proves willing to be a good citizen should be recognized as part of this same family of Athenians.[107] The myth of autochthony defines Athens as a group of people related genetically to each other and to the land they possess.

With the famous metaphor of coinage, the chorus urges the Athenians to make use of the true-born (εὐγενεῖς) citizens as leaders, not the foreigners and red-haired Thracians (ξένοις καὶ πυρρίαις) whose value has not been tested (κεκωδωνισμένοις).[108] Whereas the former, the beautiful and the good (καλούς τε κἀγαθοὺς), have been trained to respect the traditional games and festivals of the city, the latter are late-comers (ὑστάτοις ἀφιγμένοισιν), barely fit to be expelled with ceremony from the city. Throughout the parodos and the parabasis, the chorus continually speaks in terms of inside and out, defining the boundaries of the ideal Athens by excluding those whom Aristophanes opposes as foreigners and

---

known of Kleigenes is that he (probably) was first secretary of the Council in 410/9 (*IG* i$^3$.375.1).

[106] As Dover wryly notes, "One's own misdeeds and those of one's friends are συμφοραί; other people's are crimes." (Dover, p. 73 n.12.) The politician Phrynichos is one of the three Phrynichos's criticized in the play (cp. n. 59). Each one represents the negative aspect of the past tradition: in politics, in tragedy, and in comedy.

[107] e.g, Demosthenes Epit. 4; cp., Loraux 1986, esp. pp. 146-151, 277-278, for interpretation of the political uses of the myth of autochthony.

[108] cp. Iophon must be tested to see if he can write good tragedy with Sophocles gone (79). Euripides' gods are described as of his own new minting, like the leaders the chorus condemns here (889).

barbarians, strangers who seek their own profit at the expense of troubled Athens. By assimilating the chorus's distinctions to the traditional difference between the lots of the blessed and the unhappy dead, Aristophanes urges changes in the way Athenian society defines its own boundaries.

### Result: Guidance to the House of Hades

The Mystai direct Dionysos and Xanthias, not to the spring of Memory or the Elysian Fields, but rather to the house of Hades, which comically is not at all difficult to find, but in fact right in front of them. The chorus provides the humorously simple solution to the obstacle facing Dionysos and Xanthias lost in the underworld. The chorus of initiates in the *Frogs*, like the specially privileged or initiate in the mythic tradition, has special knowledge of the underworld that enables it to direct the lost traveler to the proper destination, and, like other initiate groups, it carefully restricts participation in its group. Although Dionysos and Xanthias are accepted immediately into the revelry and dance, the Mystai make a variety of exclusions from their group, which Aristophanes presents as a kind of idealized Athens, the truly living Athens in contrast to the dead above. If the real Athens were to make the same kind of exclusions and inclusions, the true Athenians might enjoy the same kind of blissful existence as the Mystai enjoy, endlessly celebrating the festivals. The identity of this chorus thus supports a crucial theme in the play: the connection of the salvation of Athens with the continuation of the traditional Athenian festivals and rituals. The chorus calls upon Soteira to preserve Athens from season to season, despite the traitorous activities of such as Thorykion (377–382), and they beseech Demeter to preserve her chorus so they can play and dance all day (385–388).[109] The continuation of the traditional rituals represents the continuation of the whole life of Athens, political and cultural, socio-economic and religious. Aristophanes' portrayal of a chorus of Eleusinian initiates in festal procession praying for the continuation of their festivities surely reminded his audience of the real Eleusinian

---

[109] Commentators have argued whether Soteira refers to Athena Soteira or to Persephone/Kore. Although Kore has the epithet Soteira in a variety of places (Attic deme Korydallos, Arkadia, Lakonia, certain coins of Kyzikos; cp. Ammon. *Diff.* 279, Paus. VIII.31.1 and III.13.2.), the scholiasts identify this Soteira as Athena. The Eleusinian context does not demand that Kore be given a hymn, nor that Athena should not be honored. Rather, the presence of Athena reinforces the identification of the Eleusinian rituals with the life of Athens.

procession, which the Spartan occupation of Decelea had discontinued. Only Alcibiades, in 407, had renewed the ancestral ritual, leading the Eleusinian procession in the face of the Spartan threat, proclaiming the vitality of Athens as well as his own innocence against the charges that he had profaned the Mysteries.[110] The double symbolism of this gesture reveals the crucial symbolic importance of the Eleusinian Mysteries to the Athenians, not merely within the play but in historical reality. Not only was Eleusis the most important border sanctuary, defining the bounds of Athens' home territory, but, because of its Panhellenic status, Eleusis also represented Athens' claim to leadership among the Greek states and thus to empire. Alcibiades' performance is the same sort of symbol of the unity and strength of Athens that Aristophanes is evoking with the chorus of Eleusinian initiates, and the chorus of the *Frogs* recalls Alcibiades' gesture in the time of Athens' troubles when Alcibiades has again been exiled.[111]

### CONFRONTATION WITH THE POWERS OF THE UNDERWORLD

#### Obstacle: The Doorkeeper at the Gate

Having found the halls of Hades, Dionysos and Xanthias are confronted with the problem of getting past those who guard its doors, a problem that has many resonances in the mythic tradition. As early as Hesiod, dangerous guardians appear at the gates of the house of Hades, "a fearful hound guards the house in front, pitiless... a monster not to be overcome and that may not be described, Kerberos who eats raw flesh, the brazen-voiced hound of Hades, fifty-headed, relentless and strong."[112] This watchdog of Hell, Kerberos, is Herakles' objective in his journey to

---

[110] Xenophon *Hellenika* I. 4.20–1; cp. Plut. *Alc.* 34.3–7. cp. Murray 1990, esp. p. 156.

[111] cp. Hatzfeld's commentary, "Très adroitement, le poète a su, dès la première partie de la comédie, créer pour lui un climat favorable. Ce n'est pas sans raison que le choeur des Initiés d'Éleusis évoque la prairie, où sans danger, l'on arrive le soir, et où l'on danse en toute sécurité à lumière des torches, après les gaillardisses échangées dans l'après-midi auprès du pont du Céphise – prairie, danses, joyeux brocards que, depuis huit ans, on n'avait revus qu'une seule fois: lors de la glorieuse journée où Alcibiade avait mené la procession par la Voie sacrée au nez de la garnison de Décélie." (Hatzfeld 1951, pp. 329–330.)

[112] *Theog.* 769–70, 310–312 – δεινὸς δὲ κύων προπάροιθε φυλάσσει νηλειής.... ἀμήχανον, οὔ τι φατειὸν Κέρβερον ὠμηστήν, Ἀίδεω κύνα χαλκεόφωνον, πεντηκοντακέφαλον, ἀναιδέα τε κρατερόν τε. Hesiod describes the hound as friendly to those entering, but preventing anyone from leaving.

the halls of Hades, and, in many versions, Herakles must fight to get the dog.[113] In other tellings, however, Herakles can obtain the dog merely through the good will of Persephone.[114] In the B series of gold tablets, guardians stand near the halls of Hades, interrogating those who come for a drink at the fountain of Memory.[115] The tablets' guardians are unnamed, but later tradition often has Aiakos as the keeper of the keys to the halls of Hades.[116]

The doorkeeper in the *Frogs* is not named in the text, nor did any early manuscript list his name as Aiakos, but if the doorkeeper of Hades were recognizable somehow as Aiakos, the comic transformation would

[113] The *Iliad's* references (V.395ff.) to the fight at the gates of Hades, in which Herakles wounds Hades himself, allude to this episode, as do a number of vase illustrations showing conflict between Herakles and Hades and/or Kerberos. LIMC s.v. Herakles 2553, 2559, 2566, 2567, 2570, 2581–2582, 2584, 2586, 2605, 2608.

[114] cp. Boardman 1975, pp. 3–10, who lists a number of vase illustrations and suggests that the shift in the mode of telling is due to the introduction of Herakles as the archetypal initiate at Eleusis in the Lesser Mysteries. cp. LIMC s.v. Herakles 2554–2558, 2562, 2574, 2592, 2599, 2600, 2602, 2607. Herakles the initiate appears in Euripides *Herakles* 605–612.

[115] B10.7–9 φύλακες δ' ἐπύπερθεν ἔασιν. οἳ δέ σε εἰρήσονται ἐν(ὶ) φρασὶ πευκαλίμασι ὅτ(τ)ι δὲ ἐξερέεις Ἄιδος σκότος ⟨ἠε⟩ρόεντος. "But guardians are nearby. They will ask you, with sharp minds, what you seek in the misty shadow of Hades." cp. B1, B2, B11. B3–9 imply the presence of these guardians with the questions that are asked.

[116] Aiakos as κλειδοῦχος appears in Apollodorus III.12.6, some late inscriptions (CIG iii.6298; Epig. Gr. 646), and an invocation in the Greek Magical Papyri (PMG IV.1264), cp. πυλαουρέ in a second BCE inscription (GVI i,1179.7). The less dignified position of doorkeeper is his usual role in Lucian – d. *Mort.* 13.3, 20.1, 6, 22.3, *de Luct.* 4, *Philops.* 25; cp. Philostr. *V.Ap* 7.31. Isocrates, however, makes him simply a special attendant (πάρεδρος) of Hades and Persephone, without specific reference to his duties. (Isoc. 9.15.) Herodotus reports that he had a temple in Athens (V.89.3). Plato makes him one of the judges in the underworld who judge the newly arrived souls (*Apol.* 41a, *Gorgias* 524a) as do some strands of the Roman tradition (Horace C. II.13.22; Ovid *Met.* XII.25; Seneca *Apoc.* 14.1–4), but the role of doorkeeper remains attached to Aiakos in tellings that are less directly influenced by Plato. Kritias' *Peirithoos* (TrGF i.43 F1–14) may have depicted Aiakos as a lowly doorkeeper, but the fragments that remain of the play make any certainty impossible, nor can it be securely dated before the *Frogs*. cp. Dover's discussion pp. 54–55. The controversy over the identification of him with Aiakos begins already in the scholia. The transformation of Aiakos from revered hero granted priestly honor in the service of Pluto and Persephone to a doorkeeper with slave status is not impossible as early as Aristophanes or Kritias; but, since nothing in the text identifies the doorkeeper as Aiakos, the identification is probably the interpretation of a later scholiast, especially because Aiakos, unlike Herakles, is not immediately recognizable from visual characteristics like the lion skin and club. cp. Dover, "It may not be wholly wide of the mark to suggest that a slow change in the common perception of Aiakos was a reflex of metaphor; compare the long tradition of jokes about St. Peter, derived ultimately from Matt. 16:19." (p. 53.)

certainly be in keeping with the rest of Aristophanes' treatment of the house of Hades, for he consistently treats the dreaded dwelling of the lord of the dead as if it were an ordinary Athenian household.[117] Despite Dionysos's fear lest the local inhabitants have some strange way of knocking at doors, his timid call for the slave to open the door is met with a doorkeeper slave (460–464). The household is supplied with kitchen slaves whom the mistress of the house, Pherrephatta (the Attic name for Persephone), supervises, as well as a retinue of household slaves of various sorts. The house of Hades seems to be located along an ordinary street, for two women who keep a local inn pass by as Dionysos and Xanthias are waiting by the doors. So like quotidian Athens is this underworld scene that these women even threaten to bring the orators, Kleon and Hyperbolos, to prosecute those who have done them wrong. Aristophanes sets up a traditional scene of an obstacle facing the hero in the underworld, the ominous gates of Hades, but instead of a hideous monster or keen-witted guardians, Dionysos and Xanthias are faced with an ordinary Athenian household. How can one tell if life be death or death life, if even the halls of Hades in the realm of the dead are just like the house of an ordinary Athenian citizen?

### Solution: Declaration of Identity – Herakles, Slave, or Dionysos?

Dionysos tries to get past this obstacle of the gates of Hades by proclaiming his identity as Herakles. The declaration of identity is a familiar feature in the mythic tradition, and a special identity is often the solution to bypassing this obstacle. In the B series of gold tablets, the deceased declares to the guardians, "I am the child of Earth and starry Heaven," an identification that is sufficient for the guardians to permit the deceased to quench her thirst at the fountain of Memory.[118] Herakles' identity as an initiate in the Eleusinian Mysteries seems to be the key to the favorable

---

[117] In the same way, if Aiakos was thought of as the judge of the dead (for which there is no evidence before Plato), then Thiercy's ingenious observation that Aiakos is transformed into a slave just as Dionysos is transformed from a slave to a judge would apply. "C'est alors Dionysos qui prend en quelque sort une des functions d'Éaque, celle de juge des âmes des morts, puisqu'il va avoir à choisir entre Eschyle et Euripide dans cette espèce de *psychostasie* où il va devoir décider quelle sera l'âme qui restera dans le royaume des ombres, et quelle sera celle qui retournera à la lumière." (Thiercy 1986, p. 363.)

[118] B1.5 Γῆς παῖς εἰμι καὶ Οὐρανοῦ ἀστερόεντος. cp. the A series of tablets, in which a proclamation of identity is the key to a slightly different obstacle. See above, Chapter 2, pp. 64–82.

reception he receives in some versions of his quest for Kerberos.[119] In other versions, of course, Herakles relies on his standard solution for most of the situations he encounters in his labors – violence. Aristophanes plays off both kinds of traditional solution in his depiction of Dionysos and Xanthias at the gates of Hades.

Throughout the play, Dionysos presents a ridiculous spectacle, for he has combined the costume that marks his own identity, the effeminate yellow robe and tragic buskins, with a costume that marks the identity of the heroic Herakles, the lion skin and club. The sight is so ludicrous that Herakles cannot keep from laughing at the sight, and the contrast of the cowardly and weak Dionysos and his disguise as Herakles must have provided a running sight gag for the audience throughout the play. Up to this point, however, little has been made of his disguise.[120] If the choruses of frogs and initiates fail to recognize the Dionysos whom they are hymning in various aspects, they also fail to recognize him as Herakles.[121] Charon and Empousa show no signs of being impressed with the hero's lion skin. Dionysos chooses to claim the identity of Herakles, however, because he wants to benefit from the guest-friend relations that Herakles had created on his journey, and the house of Hades is where those relations are first tested, with comically catastrophic consequences.

Dionysos's solution to the obstacle of the guardians at the gate of Hades is to disguise himself as Herakles.[122] The identity of Herakles brings

---

[119] Such an initiation would establish his special relation with Persephone, a relation that may have been interpreted in other ways in comic treatments of the story. "It is quite possible that in vulgar belief Persephone fancied Herakles, and that in this scene Aristophanes is quite deliberately, and rather daringly, giving a touch of Stheneboia to Persephone." (Dover, p. 257.)

[120] Excepting, of course, Herakles' first sight of Dionysos (41–47) and Xanthias's appeal to Herakles/Dionysos in the Empousa scene (298).

[121] The choruses' failure to recognize Dionysos or for the disguised Dionysos to respond to their hymns to various aspects of Dionysos is one of the major foundations for Segal's argument about Dionysos seeking his own identity. Dionysos fails to respond because he "has not yet attained the unified conception of himself which he is seeking." (Segal 1961, p. 213.) cp. Thiercy's idea that Dionysos does not realize that he is the Iacchos hymned by both choruses because, "la perte de son identité de Dionysos lui fait perdre en même temps celle de Iacchos." (Thiercy 1986, p. 317.) Aristophanes, however, has Dionysos conceal his identity because he wishes to benefit from the identity of Herakles, not because he is having an identity crisis. See further Edmonds 2003.

[122] Dionysos's disguise as Herakles is, first and foremost, his strategy for overcoming the perils of the journey to the realm of the dead to accomplish his quest. Because of Herakles' previous experience in the journey to bring back Cerberus, Dionysos asks Herakles to provide him with information about guest-friends on whom he can

Dionysos only negative reactions from the inhabitants of the underworld when he expects positive ones, but Xanthias disguised as Herakles gets the positive reactions Dionysos had planned on. Throughout this scene, Aristophanes assumes knowledge of the tales of Herakles' katabasis to set up all of the comic reversals. The hostile reaction of the doorkeeper is provoked by Herakles' theft of the dog, the very purpose of his traditional journey. Dionysos, hoping to reap the rewards of Herakles' last visit by claiming his identity, must instead pay the penalty for the relations Herakles established. The doorkeeper threatens all the gruesome torments of Hades, but then, comically bringing Hades back to the level of quotidian Athens, he goes off to fetch a policeman. Instead of the hellhounds of Kokytos, Echidna, the Tartessian Eels, and the Gorgons – all good mythological monsters – the doorkeeper brings some Scythian policemen with comic names.[123]

When Dionyos tries to escape the negative consequences of the Heraklean identity by passing off the disguise to Xanthias, Herakleioxanthias reaps the very rewards of being Herakles that Dionysos had wanted. Playing with the tradition, in earlier tellings, that Herakles had sacrificed a whole ox during his visit to the underworld, Aristophanes has a kitchen slave come out to invite 'Herakles' to another feast of ox, along with a whole catalogue of delights calculated to attract the hero, who was notorious as a glutton for food and sex. Xanthias yields to the temptation to try to cull the benefits of his role when the slave mentions sexual attractions

make claims during his journey. ἵνα μοι τοὺς ξένους τοὺς σοὺς φράσειας. εἰ δεοίμην. οἷσι σὺ ἐχρῶ τόθ'. ἡνίκ' ἦλθες ἐπὶ τὸν Κέρβερον. τούτους φράσον μοι, λιμένας, ἀρτοπώλια, πορνεῖ', ἀναπαύλας, ἐκτροπάς, κρήνας, ὁδούς, πόλεις, διαίτας, πανδοκευτρίας, ὅπου κόρεις ὀλίγιστοι (109–115). "You can tell me about your friends who put you up when you went *there* to fetch the Cerberus dog. Well, I could use some friends, so tell me about them. Tell me the ports, the bakery shops, whorehouses, parks and roadside rests, highways and springs, the cities, boarding houses, and the best hotels scarcest in bedbugs" (Lattimore translation). Aristophanes transforms Dionysos's inquiry into an ordinary traveler's questions about his prospective route. Showing a characteristic interest in pleasures of the flesh, Dionysos wants to know about the everyday comforts he can look forward to on his journey. cp. Xanthias's characterization of Dionysos as concerned only with sex and drinking (740). That he asks about inns and bakeries as well as brothels and springs shows that he does not entirely neglect eating and sleeping.

[123] Kokytos is one of the rivers of Hades from Homer on (Od. x.513, etc.). Echidna appears in Hesiod as the mother of many monsters (Theog. 295–332). Tartessos recalls the familiar underworld pit, Tartaros, but eels from Tartessos in Iberia were considered a delicacy. cp. Pollux vi.63 and Varro *ap.* Gell. vi.16.5. A gorgon appears as a threat in the underworld in the *Odyssey* (xi.635), but the epithet Teithrasian is doubtless a joke at the expense of the women of the Attic deme of Teithras. cp. Dover *ad loc.*

in addition to the culinary ones, a flute girl and some dancing girls. When Dionysos takes back the role of Herakles in order to enjoy the food and hospitality that the identity of Herakles won in the house of Persephone, he is faced once again with paying the penalty for the deeds of Herakles, who abused the hospitality of the innkeepers and stole their food. When Dionysos tries once again to get Xanthias to take the consequences of being Herakles, Xanthias denies the identity of Herakles, claiming that although he looks like the hero who wreaked such havoc in the underworld, he has never before visited the place. To prove his claim, he offers Dionysos as a slave to be tortured. Dionysos, in adopting the identity of a slave to avoid the consequences of being Herakles, has been tricked into receiving the consequences of being a slave.

Dionysos, who is not only a free man but actually a god, behaves with the utmost cowardice, soiling himself with fright at the idea of actually having to live up to the heroic identity he assumed.[124] He abases himself before Xanthias, pleading with him and promising to let himself be beaten without complaint if he tries to take the role of Herakles back. The chorus comments that his attempts to assume the identity that will bring the most reward at any given moment and his ability to wriggle out of any role that has negative consequences are like the famed skills of the politician Theramenes. Theramenes had been a leader in the oligarchic coup of the Four Hundred in 411, but managed to stay in favor during the restoration of the democracy by leading a pro-democratic faction of the Four Hundred. He was one of the two trierarchs who should have picked up the dead and wounded at Arginousai, but, by pressing for charges against the generals, he escaped the consequences of the disastrous aftermath of that victory, while the generals were executed after an unconstitutional mass trial.[125] Dionysos mentions Theramenes' adeptness at political survival when Euripides has claimed him as a disciple, along with the sophist Kleitophon (967–970). Theramenes and Dionysos are accused (534–548)

---

[124] As he did in the encounter with Empousa (308). In this scene, Dionysos cracks a joke about his reactions, distorting the ritual formula from the Lenaia, Ἐγκέχυται· κάλει θεόν, "the libation is poured, call the god." The scholiasts *ad loc* say that the torchbearer of Dionysos speaks the formula, at which all call out, "Iacchos, son of Semele."

[125] cp. Thuc. VIII 68.4, 89.2–94.1; Xen. *HG* I 6.35, 7.5–8. Lysias attacks Theramenes (12.62–80), but the Aristotelian *Ath. Pol.* (28.5) praises him for moderation. He became one of the Thirty Tyrants, but was executed by Kritias when he attempted to oppose the extreme policies of the Thirty and escape the consequences of his political choices once again. Xenophon (*Hellenika* 2.3.31) relates that he was known as 'Kothornos', because, like that kind of boot, he would fit on either foot.

of not staying with a single form (σχῆμα), but always shifting to the softer side (πρὸς τὸ μαλθακώτερον). Xanthias, on the other hand, though he is a slave and a mortal (531, cp. 583), has the courage (λῆμα) that goes along with the form and appearance (σχῆμα) of Herakles.[126] Dionysos emphasizes the contrast between Xanthias's appearance as a divine hero and his true identity as a slave with his joke about Xanthias looking like the rogue of Melite (Μελίτης μαστιγίας), instead of the expected 'god of Melite'.[127] The chorus threatens that if Xanthias does not live up to the part, but lets fall something soft (τι μαλθακόν) in the manner of Dionysos, he will lose his heroic identity and become a slave carrying the baggage once more. Xanthias plays his part as Herakles well, borrowing the hero's tactic of violence to hold off the men coming to punish him for stealing Kerberos (607). However, his adoption of Heraklean violence is only temporary; he evades the consequences of his Heraklean identity by exploiting instead the consequences of Dionysos's adoption of slave identity and transferring the violent retributions to him.

Xanthias's manuever leads to the final test of identity at the gates of Hades, the test by whipping. Although this whipping might have had resonances from various rituals which may have been familiar to Aristophanes' audience, whipping is a punishment appropriate for a slave, and the test is to determine which of the two is a slave and which a god.[128] Hoping to avoid the consequences of the slave identity, Dionysos has claimed his true identity as a god, but Xanthias traps him by insisting that a real god would not feel the pain of whipping as a slave would. In contrast to his reasoning for the doorkeeper, Xanthias figures that as a slave accustomed to beatings, he himself will be better able to bear the pain than his soft and cowardly master, thus earning himself the identity

---

[126] Xanthias urges Dionysos to match his λῆμα to the σχῆμα he bears before knocking (464). Dionysos gives him the lion skin because he has the courage (λημ", ιᾶς) to match the role (494), and Xanthias boasts that he has the λῆμα for the part (500).

[127] Note the emphasis on the slave as one who is whipped, since citizens could not legally be beaten. cp. Dover, *ad loc.* The scholiast thinks the joke is referring to Kallias (cp. 428–430), but the allusion seems strained.

[128] The whipping scene in the villa of Mysteries at Pompeii and the whipping contest at the sanctuary of Artemis Orthia in Sparta are mentioned by Bowie 1993 (p. 236) as mystery cult parallels, but the evidence is quite late in both cases. Σ ad 622 mentions a ritual in which boys were beaten with leek or onion, cp. Theoc. 7.106, Hipponax 6.2. Such a symbolic flagellation, perhaps for purification (cp. Hesych. s.v. *katharthenai - mastigothenai*), is ruled out by Xanthias (621); he wants whatever is done to his master to hurt.

of a god through his experience as a slave. This leap of logic transforms the test of identity from the question of Herakles and the consequences of his identity to one of the identity of slave and master. Comically, both Xanthias and Dionysos manage to conceal the pain they feel, blurring the lines between master and slave even further, and the doorkeeper finally proposes an infallible test of identity, a consultation of Persephone and Plouto. Aristophanes tops off the slapstick humor of the beating contest by making all these solutions needless in the face of the real test, the traditional confrontation with the real lords of the the underworld.

### Result: Put in One's Place

The result of all these trials of identity is that Dionysos enters the house to meet with Plouto and Persephone, while Xanthias stays outside to hobnob with the doorkeeper. The differentiation of their fates according to status and relation to the gods is familiar from the mythic tradition, but Aristophanes, of course, gives it a comic twist. On the gold tablets from Thurii, the deceased claims privilege in the underworld because she is related to Persephone: "I claim that I am of your blessed race."[129] In the *Odyssey*, Menelaus has the privilege of going to the Elysian Field simply because he married Helen and thus has acquired Zeus as a father-in-law.[130] Dionysos, as a son of Zeus, can claim relation to both Plouto and Persephone, and this identity as Dionysos, the son of Zeus, wins him entrance into the halls of Hades and even, it would seem, the permission of Plouto to return to the upper world with a poet to save the city.[131] Dionysos' attempts to disguise his identity bring him nothing but comic

---

[129] A1.4 – καὶ γὰρ ἐγὼν ὑμῶν γένος ὄλβιον εὔχομαι εἶμεν. cp. A2, A3. The claim to be the child of Earth and starry Heaven in the B tablets is likewise a claim of kinship with the gods. See above, ch. 2, pp. 76–80.

[130] iv.561–570.

[131] Contrast Dionysos's comic patronymic in line 22, Διόνυσος. υἱὸς Σταμνίου, with his claim in 631 to be the immortal son of Zeus, Ἀθάνατος εἶναί φημι. Διόνυσος Διός. Dionysos must reveal his mission to Plouto during the offstage conference before the agon of Aeschylus and Euripides, for Plouto knows of it at line 1414. While it is unwise to press too far in the pursuit of dramatic logic in Aristophanes, nothing suggests that Plouto would be opposed to Dionysos's project once Dionysos contacts him, despite the use of ἀποδιδράσκειν at 81 for the description of Euripides getting out of Hades.

trouble, and his true identity is not believed until he meets with Plouto and Persephone.[132]

Xanthias, on the other hand, after proving himself brave and heroic when dressed as Herakles, is relegated to the outside with the other slaves fearing that the affairs of their masters will only result in further beatings for them (812–813). Aristophanes, however, makes fun of the distinctions drawn between the slavish slaves and the noble nobles in the discussion between the doorkeeper and Xanthias about Dionysos. "By Zeus the Saviour, quite the gentleman your master is," says the doorkeeper, echoing the term that both he and Dionysos have applied to Xanthias.[133] Xanthias is quick to put Dionysos in his proper place with his own definition of what it means to be a 'gentleman', someone who knows nothing but sex and drinking.[134] This exchange, following right on the heels of the chorus's parabasis advice about choosing the noble and good to be leaders of the city (719, 728, 734), puts the parabasis in the perspective, as it were, of the post-Arginousai Athens. The freeing of the slaves who fought in the battle demonstrated that even slaves might prove themselves worthy of the city, whereas the debacle of the generals and their trial proved that the leaders of the city were not always the most noble.[135] However, Aristophanes merely touches on this message of the possible unworthiness of masters and the worthiness of slaves, and he continues the scene with a series of jokes that reinforce the outside status of the slaves, who share their own pleasures and swear by their own special epithets (750, 756). Aristophanes is not seeking emancipation for all slaves, but is rather concerned with defining who is worthy to be counted among the members of the Athenian polis in its time of trial. His concern with the slaves without citizens' rights is overshadowed by his concern for

---

[132] Not only does the doorkeeper not believe him and subject him to the whipping test, but the two innkeepers, in a wonderfully comic moment, mistake the signs of his true identity, the tragic buskins and yellow robe, for a disguise. "O, you thought I shouldn't know you with your buskins on!" – Οὐ μὲν οὖν με προσεδόκας, ὅτι ἡ κοθόρνους εἶχες, ἂν γνῶναί σ'ἔτι. (556–557, Rogers' translation.)

[133] 738–739, Rogers' translation: Νὴ τὸν Δία τὸν σωτῆρα, γεννάδας ἀνὴρ ὁ δεσπότης σου. cp. 640 (γεννάδας ἀνήρ) and 179 (χρηστὸς εἶ καὶ γεννάδας.).

[134] 739–40, Πῶς γὰρ οὐχὶ γεννάδας, ὅστις γε πίνειν οἶδε καὶ βινεῖν μόνον; cp. Goldhill 1991, p. 204.

[135] As Bowie suggests, "The relationship between Dionysus and Xanthias in the play thus provides an articulation of the relations between citizens and non-citizens in the state." (Bowie 1993, p. 243.)

the disenfranchised citizens whom he thinks are essential to the survival of the city and by his contempt for the leaders of the people whom he thinks have shown themselves to be no true citizens of the city by their self-serving behavior.

## CONCLUSION

> O unwise and foolish people, yet to mend your ways begin;
> use again the good and useful: so hereafter, if ye win
> 'twill be due to this your wisdom: if ye fall, at least
> 'twill be not a fall that bring dishonor,
> falling from a worthy tree.[136]

The chorus ends the parabasis with this plea for change in Athenian society at a desperate point in Athenian affairs. Aristophanes' chorus of blessed initiates in the underworld, which draws on the symbolic value of the Eleusinian Mysteries to depict them as an idealized vision of the Athenian people, is one of the major ways in which Aristophanes makes use of the traditional language of myth and ritual to plead his case. Rather than the traditional pattern of the journey to the other world signaling an initiation of Dionysos into maturity, the pattern provides Aristophanes with a number of opportunities to renegotiate the boundaries of the categories that define Athenian society. In each of the scenes I have examined, Aristophanes plays with elements familiar to his audience from traditional myths and rituals, humorously twisting the details to evoke familiar resonances with his own peculiar ring to them. Not only does the underworld setting let him play with the traditional distinction between the blessed dead and those who suffer a worse fate in the underworld, but the motif of crossing from one world to the next presents the dichotomy of the living and the dead for his manipulations. While Aristophanes does use the differentiated lots in the underworld to draw distinctions between those he feels belong in Athenian society and those whom he would exclude, he also repeatedly uses the separation of the living and the dead in a more complex and humorous way. By both insisting upon and undermining the fundamental separation of the living and the dead, Aristophanes creates in the *Frogs* a carnivalesque world in which one may

---

[136] 734–737, Rogers' translation. Ἀλλὰ καὶ νῦν, ὠνόητοι, μεταβαλόντες τοὺς τρόπους χρῆσθε τοῖς χρηστοῖσιν αὖθις· καὶ κατορθώσασι γὰρ εὔλογον, κἄν τι σφαλῆτ', ἐξ ἀξίου γοῦν τοῦ ξύλου, ἤν τι καὶ πάσχητε, πάσχειν τοῖς σοφοῖς δοκήσετε.

truly question with Euripides whether life is death or death life. Aristophanes breaks down some of the familiar categories of master and slave, citizen and noncitizen, familiar and strange, along with the difference between the world of the living and the realm of the dead. By dissolving the familiar distinctions, Aristophanes opens the space to create his own definitions of what is a worthy member of the Athenian polis and what the city needs to rescue her from the perilous seas in which she swims.

Aristophanes calls for the city to put aside its factional squabbling and to unite behind the leadership of the noble families. The criterion for a true member of the Athenian family, however, must be the willingness to serve the needs of the polis, specifically in the navy that is Athens' last military resource. Naval service is a theme that recurs throughout the *Frogs*, from Dionysos's laughable rowing lesson to Aeschylus's grim lion metaphor, and the test of naval combat can prove even slaves worthy of citizenship. Aristophanes is happy to elide the boundaries between master and slave, between ally and kinsman, if by doing so Athens can unite itself and be saved. The parabasis includes a special plea for the oligarchs disenfranchised in the revolt of 411. If fighting in sea battles is worthy proof of good citizens, then surely, pleads the chorus, these oligarchs deserve to be reconsidered if they can serve their city in its time of need. Various scholars have classified Aristophanes' political advice along a spectrum as widely varied as their own, but his sympathies with this group of oligarchic politicians come out strongly in this chorus passage.

This parabasis, according to Dikaiarchos, won the *Frogs* the unprecedented honor of a second performance.[137] Dover and Sommerstein convincingly argue that the most likely occasion for this second performance would have been at the Lenaia 404, after the decree of Patrokleides in the autumn of 405 put into action at least part of what Aristophanes had suggested, recall and amnesty for the exiled oligarchs.[138] By this time, however, Athens had suffered a crushing defeat by Sparta at the battle of

---

[137] Hypothesis I$^c$. See note 2.

[138] Sommerstein argues that such a performance would not have been authorized much later than 404. "A decree passed under the Thirty would have been destroyed at the restoration of the democracy, and would not have been available to Dikaiarchos; while the restored democracy itself would certainly not have honored Aristophanes for having been among the first to advocate a measure which, whatever its merits as an act of reconciliation, had conferred civic and political rights on men who within a few months had used them to overthrow the constitution and install the Thirty." (Sommerstein 1993, p. 465.)

Aigospotamai, and Aristophanes' advice about using the navy could not be implemented, since Athens no longer had a navy. Within a few months of the exiles' recall, the oligarchic factions in Athens installed the Thirty Tyrants and dismantled the democracy. Kleophon, one of Aristophanes' main targets in the *Frogs*, was put to death, possibly soon after the second performance of the play that ended with the god of death extending an invitation to a number of Athenian politicians. Aristophanes can certainly not be blamed for the execution of Kleophon and the rise of the Thirty, but his call in the play for change in Athenian society produced results in the real world.[139] Aristophanes' manipulations of the mythic tradition in telling his tale of Dionysos's search for a poet to reinvigorate the city produced poetry clever (δεξιός) enough that some of his advice (νουθεσία) was taken seriously.

[139] cp. Sommerstein on the possible addition of the advice to change leaders into the second performance: "The introduction of 1442-50 has another effect as well. As the end of the play approaches, the message of the parabasis, the demand for a change of leaders, is recalled and reinforced. To say the least, the substitution will not have displeased the anti-democratic conspirators. And it may make one wonder whether Aristophanes may after all have been aware of how he was being used." (Sommerstein 1993, p. 475.)

## 4 | The Upward Path of Philosophy: The Myth in Plato's *Phaedo*

### INTRODUCTION

#### Socrates' Final Myth of Hades

"And that, Echecrates, was the end of our companion, a man, who, among those of his time we knew, was – so we should say – the best, the wisest too, and the most just."[1]

Plato's *Phaedo* ends with this encomium of Socrates, and the dialogue is an illustration of these claims, portraying Socrates as a hero of philosophy who pursues its ideals up to the final moments of his life. Plato's character of Socrates in the *Phaedo*, whatever its relation to the actual historical Socrates,[2] provides a model for the philosophic way of living that Plato advocates. The details of his last day of life, especially his conversations with his closest friends, serve as a medium for Plato to outline the nature and importance of what he calls philosophy. Socrates, as he contemplates the fate of his own soul after death, serves as a model for the philosophic life, a life concerned always with the realm of the unseen (τὸ ἀιδές).

A philosopher to the end, Socrates spends his final hours in philosophic debate with his closest companions, discussing the nature of the soul and attempting to prove its immortality. After engaging in a series of fairly abstract dialectic arguments concerning the nature of the soul, Socrates concludes his arguments with a myth, a narrative describing the fate of the soul after death, as it tries to make its journey to the realm of the dead

[1] Ἥδε ἡ τελευτή, ὦ Ἐχέκρατες, τοῦ ἑταίρου ἡμῖν ἐγένετο, ἀνδρός, ὡς ἡμεῖς φαῖμεν ἄν, τῶν τότε ὧν ἐπειράθημεν ἀρίστου καὶ ἄλλως φρονιμωτάτου καὶ δικαιοτάτου (118a15–17). All translations from the *Phaedo* come from Gallop 1975 edition, unless otherwise noted.

[2] cp. the comment in the Platonic Second Letter about the dialogues as the work of a Socrates 'made young and beautiful' (314c).

159

("Αιδου). How does this myth fit in with the dialectic arguments? Many modern scholarly philosophical treatments of the dialogue simply ignore the final myth, treating it as a kind of optional extra, devoid of serious philosophical content.[3] Some commentators, on the other hand, have seen the myth as essential to the discussion in the dialogue, but claim that the myth is important because only in myth could a subject such as the immortality of the soul be treated. "The description of what is hoped for must assume a mythic form since the goods to be described reside in the next life."[4] For these commentators, the subject matter dictates Plato's choice of form in the dialogue. Neither approach does justice to the function of the myth within the dialogue, since the former neglects the important ideas embedded in the myth, whereas the latter suggests that the important difference between the myth and the argument lies in content rather than in form. The fate of the soul after death is not treated only in myth, but, on the contrary, most of the dialectic argument centers around issues that some commentators claim are only accessible by myth. The invisible soul and the unseen world are discussed both dialectically and in mythic narrative. I suggest that the difference between the myth and the argument lies not so much in the content of the discussion – the soul and what happens to it after death – as in the form of the discussion – by narrative description or by dialectic questioning.

What, then, is Plato's purpose in depicting his philosophic hero, Socrates, as employing myth in his discussion of the soul, the final, crucial philosophic discussion of his life? Plato uses the traditional myth of the journey of the soul to the realm of the dead ("Αιδου) as a vehicle to discuss the philosopher's quest for understanding of the unseen realm (τὸ ἀιδές), the level of reality perceivable only by the intellect, which Plato regarded as the underlying true being which shaped all things. By identifying the unseen noetic realm of the Forms with the traditional Hades, Plato carefully crafts the myth Socrates tells of the soul's journey after death to highlight important ideas raised in the earlier arguments, shaping the traditional tale to expand and reinforce these arguments. Plato manipulates the traditional narrative patterns and elements of the myth of the

---

[3] cp., e.g., Bostock 1986, which entirely ignores the myth, and Gallop's edition, in which only two of the 151 pages of commentary deal with the myth. Annas 1982 makes a start at redressing this problem.

[4] White 1989, p. 41. cp. "Since the *Phaedo* talks about death, and since only the language of myth can speak about that which is beyond the limit, this is a first suggestion as to the connection between this life and the beyond." (Friedländer 1969, pp. 182–183.)

journey to the underworld in order to contrast the life of philosophy with that of the unphilosophic. The myth is interwoven with carefully placed allusions to the earlier arguments, and Plato manipulates the traditional mythic material to lend richness and vividness to his images as well as to ground his advocacy of the philosophic life in the authority of the tradition.

In my analysis of Plato's use of the traditional elements and story patterns from the myth of the journey to the underworld, I break down the narrative of the journey into narrative cruxes, which I see as providing the dramatic action of the story. The myth that Socrates relates in the *Phaedo* contains three such complexes of *obstacle*, *solution*, and *result*, drawn from traditional mythic ideas of the journey to the underworld: leaving the realm of the living, finding the way in the underworld, and confrontation with the powers of the underworld. In each case, I examine the traditional elements of this narrative complex that would have been familiar to Plato and his audience, not looking for specific sources of Plato's myth, but rather outlining the set of traditional elements available to him. I then show how Plato manipulates these elements to fit his own definition of the obstacle, his own suggestions for the solution, and his own explanation of the result. The philosophic life is identified with ideas and practices sanctioned by the tradition: firstly, with the funeral rituals that prevent the deceased from becoming one of the restless dead, secondly, with the daimon that guides the souls, and finally, with the virtuous and heroic deeds that bring a privileged afterlife. By transforming the traditional tale of the journey to the underworld, Plato enriches his discussion of the philosophic life as the quest for the understanding of the fundamental reality underlying the perceptible world, a reality which Plato locates in the unseen realm perceivable only by the mind.

### Mythos and Logos in Plato's Dialogues

Plato's dialogues present a challenge to any reader, for they are constructed on many levels: as philosophical discussions between a number of interlocutors, as a narration of such a discussion between another set of characters, and ultimately as a communication between the absent author, Plato, and his audience. Platonic myth poses a particular problem because the presented myths are told by a specific character who shapes the myth for his audience within the dialogue, while at the same time, Plato is the one manipulating the form of the myth for the audience of the reader of the dialogue. Any understanding of Plato's use of myth must therefore take into account both levels of myth-telling. In the *Phaedo*, the narrator of the myth within the dialogue is the character Socrates, the most privileged of all the speakers in Plato's dialogues, who closes off the philosophical discussion with an extended myth that describes the journey of the soul to the realm of the dead.

Particularly in light of the critique of poetry in the *Republic*, however, scholars have questioned whether the myths can be regarded as serious parts of the arguments in which they are presented. The status of the myths as part of the dialogues is the central problem in the scholarship on Platonic myth, and Plato himself signals the problematic status of the myths within his dialogues. In each of the dialogues with an eschatological myth, the interlocutors raise the issue of the valuation of mythic discourse. In the *Phaedo*, Socrates compares his myth to a charm used to allay the fears of children, leading some commentators to conclude that myth is an inferior form of discourse suitable only for children or childish adults (cp. 77e–78a; 114d). Nevertheless, Socrates claims that he and his closest philosophical friends with him at his death should repeat such charms to themselves. Similar kinds of hedging appear around many of the presented myths throughout the dialogues. Socrates introduces the myth in the *Gorgias* by claiming that, while Kallikles may consider the following tale a μῦθος, it is really a λόγος (523a1–2). Clearly, he is drawing a dichotomy in which μῦθος is devalued in comparison to λόγος, but, just as clearly, he is claiming the superior status for his myth of the judgement in the afterlife. Particularly troubling is the paradox of the end of the *Republic*, where Plato's most elaborate myth follows hard on the heels of his most severe pronouncements against the creators of myth. Socrates banishes the tellers of myths from his ideal state, but he concludes the arguments of the dialogue by telling the myth of Er and his fantastic journey. Socrates even claims that if he and his interlocutors are persuaded by the myth, they will be saved.[5]

For the most part, scholars have attempted to understand Plato's use of myth in the dialogues in terms of the dichotomy between two types of discourse, μῦθος and λόγος.[6] As it is generally understood in epistemological

---

[5] Rep. 621d. For the hedges that mark the myths in other dialogues, see Murray 1999, esp. pp. 255–258.

[6] The best critique of this dichotomy is probably Lincoln 1999, esp. 3–43 (an expansion of Lincoln 1997). For further history of mythos and logos, cp. Most 1999. Morgan 2000 and

terms, however, this overworked dichotomy provides little help in understanding Plato's use of myth. Μῦθος is generally defined as irrational, unverifiable, or simply speculative discourse in opposition to λόγος, which is thus rational, verifiable, and properly philosophic. Most often, μῦθος is understood as inferior to λόγος; it is a discarded relic of the past, a remnant of Orphic superstition or childish fancy. As a result, the myths are ignored or devalued in the analysis of the dialogues, regarded as sops thrown in to entertain or distract the vulgar mob who is unable to comprehend real philosophy.[7] At best, the myths serve as some sort of child's primer to assist those willing but incapable of following the logical arguments.[8] Some scholars, more critical of Plato, see the myths as Plato himself slipping into superstition or patching over the failures of his logic with the inferior substitute of myth.[9]

Other scholars, drawing the same distinction between μῦθος and λόγος, rate μῦθος higher than λόγος, claiming that Plato uses myth to convey truths beyond the grasp of reason. Akin to the early Symbolist and

Rowe 1999 both argue that the distinction of mythos and logos is not central in Plato because of the fallibility of all human discourse. "A sense of the 'fictionality' of human utterance, as provisional, inadequate, and at best approximating the truth, will infect Platonic writing at its deepest level, below other and more ordinary applications of the distinction between mythical and non-mythical forms of thought." (Rowe 1999, p. 265.)

[7] cp. Schuhl, who sees myth as that "qui permettent de faire comprendre au vulgaire même des relations abstraites, mais non plus hautes, que le raisonnement seul peut faire connaître." (Schuhl 1968, p. 26.) Popper 1945, writing shortly after the Second World War, sees the myths as propaganda of the worst kind, lies by which the archfacist intends to inflict the closed state upon the hapless citizens.

[8] Elias refers to this as 'the weak defense' of myth in Plato: myths have a positive role, but only for the unphilosophic person or parts of the soul. (Elias 1984, p. 38.) cp. Hitchcock 1974 and Edelstein 1949, who see myth as about or directed to irrational parts of the soul. Scholars such as Brochard 1900, Stöcklein 1937, and Voegelin 1978 consider myth operating on the level of opinion in contrast to dialectic knowledge. cp. Frutiger and Edelstein, who both claim that only some of Plato's myths deal with matters on the level of opinion, although they disagree significantly as to which passages fall into this category. (Edelstein 1949, pp. 467-72; Frutiger 1930, pp. 209-225.)

[9] cp. Zeller's condescending assertion that the myths "betray the boundaries of his methodological thought. However admirable in themselves, therefore, they are, in a scientific point of view, rather a sign of weakness than of strength; they indicate the point at which it becomes evident that as yet he cannot be wholly a philosopher, because he is too much a poet." (Zeller 1888, p. 163.) This idea that myths betray the limits of Plato's philosophic ability goes back to Hegel (1963, pp. 19-20). Although Annas 1982 makes a good critique of the *logos/muthos* distinction and the general neglect of the myths, she nevertheless treats the myths as if they articulated moral ideas about the nature of justice that Plato cannot defend.

Romantic interpreters of myth like Creuzer, these scholars see myth as a peculiar form of discourse that somehow expresses deep inner truths. Stewart, whose *Myths of Plato* revived the serious consideration of the myths of Plato in this century, describes the myths as evoking Transcendental Feeling, while more recently, Elias expresses his point more mundanely, claiming that Plato embeds his fundamental axioms in his myths.[10] Plato's own expressions about the problems of language for expressing important ideas often serve as the basis for these scholars' arguments that myth can express poetically what dialectic cannot convey.[11] Friedländer, most influentially, argues that the myths are necessary for Plato to discuss the soul and things beyond the realm of the living.[12]

Many scholars see the myths, particularly the eschatological ones, as the products of Orphic influence in Platonic writing; Frutiger, after his investigation of the traditional elements in the Platonic myths says categorically, "Tous les éléments essentiels des mythes eschatologiques sont empruntés à la tradition orphico-pythagoricienne."[13] Plato's debt to

---

[10] Stewart 1960; Elias 1984.

[11] cp. Levi 1937 and 1946, Hirsch 1971, Gregory 1968, Gaffney 1971, Moors 1982. Morgan 2000 provides a different interpretation of Plato's reservations about the problems of language. Since language remains grounded in the material world, all forms of language, including philosophic dialectic, remain vulnerable. Nevertheless, Morgan points out that Plato specifically rejects the idea that myths should present undefended axioms (Morgan 2000, p. 180).

[12] "Since the *Phaedo* talks about death, and since only the language of myth can speak about that which is beyond the limit, this is a first suggestion as to the connection between this life and the beyond.... When Socrates employs a myth in the later dialogues, this means that he cannot express himself in any other form." (Friedländer 1969, pp. 182–183, 176.) cp. Hirsch 1971, White 1989.

[13] Frutiger 1930, p. 260. Of Frutiger's conclusions, Hitchcock notes, "The resulting similarities are impressive until one begins to examine them." (Hitchcock 1974, p. 125 n. 13.) Contrast the arguments by Thomas 1938 (pp. 6–24) and Dodds 1959 about the difficulties of assigning these traditional elements to an exclusively 'Orphic' context. These problems notwithstanding, many scholars argue for Orphic influence on the basis of the eschatological concerns thought to be exclusive to Orphism. Windelband argues that Plato tries to ground the religious ideas of Orphism in scientific reasoning, but puts in the myths "the graphically living form which the thoughts had received, whether in the sect and its cult or in his own imagination freely dealing with this material." (Windelband 1923) Morgan too presents myths at times as the undefended (if not indefensible) beliefs of Socrates, his flashes of synoptic philosophical insight: "Sokrates' myths of the soul thus have a special status as expressions of his own beliefs and philosophical intuition. Yet this intuition (symbolised by his divine voice, the *daimonion*) is grounded in argument and is the result of a life of enquiry. If it were not so grounded, Sokrates would merely be a member of a belief-group along Pythagorean lines, taking the immortality of the soul as an article of faith and devoting itself to ethical purity." (Morgan 2000, p. 186.)

Orphism or Pythagoreanism is, however, evaluated differently by these two camps. For those who see Plato's myths as unfortunate evidence that "as yet he cannot be wholly a philosopher, because he is too much a poet," the sources of Plato's poetic strayings can be attributed to the Orphic influence that Plato, a child of his time, could not wholly escape.[14] Others regard Plato's use of 'Orphic' or Pythagorean ideas of the soul or the nature of god as a crucial step in the transformation of Greek religion into Christianity or true philosophy (whichever of the two they prefer).[15]

Both types of interpretation of the myths depend on the strongly valorized distinction between μῦθος and λόγος. Not coincidentally, the definition of what is μῦθος and what is λόγος frequently depends on whether μῦθος is better or worse than λόγος. Thus, the theory of recollection is often regarded as λόγος by those who see λόγος as superior, but as μῦθος by those who see μῦθος as the vehicle for Plato's most important ideas. Elias includes it among his "Methodological Myths" while Gallop and Bostock, among others, discuss it as the "Recollection Argument." Frutiger lists it among those "passages faussement considérés comme mythiques."[16] Anything from the nature of the soul to the Theory of Forms to the bulk of the *Timaeus* may be considered mythical, depending upon the commentator's evaluation of myth.

Other scholars try to avoid such a subjective evaluation of myth in relation to dialectic by drawing the distinction on the basis of Plato's own terminology, classifying as myth anything labeled μῦθος rather than λόγος. Plato, however, while he does in places draw a specific distinction between μῦθος and λόγος, does not make a systematic distinction, and the attempt to create a rigid difference leads to peculiar distortions. Zaslavsky,

---

[14] Zeller 1888, p. 163, see note 9 above.

[15] Guthrie quotes, but unfortunately does not cite, Cornford: "We find one scholar (Professor Cornford) saying of the Orphic religion that it 'made the alliance of Platonism with the religion of Christ and Saint Paul' - which is high praise indeed." (Guthrie 1952, p. 195.) cp. Jaeger: "The Orphic conception of the soul marks an important advance in the development of man's consciousness of selfhood. Without it Plato and Aristotle could never have developed the theory that the human spirit is divine, and that man's sensual nature can be dissociated from his real self, which it is his true function to bring to perfection." (Jaeger 1945, pp. 168–169.) Guthrie also describes the Orphic idea of the assimilation of the human soul to divinity as the bridge between religion and philosophy, Guthrie 1975, pp. 206ff. cp. Cornford 1952, pp. 107–126, Vernant 1983, pp. 354–364. In histories of philosophy, the Pythagoreans often appear as the link between the Orphic religious tradition and real philosophy.

[16] Elias 1984, pp. 194–198; Bostock 1986; Gallop 1975; Frutiger 1930.

for example, must exclude from the category of myth Socrates' tale in the *Gorgias*, since Socrates calls it a λόγος, but the entire *Republic* becomes a myth, since it is called a μῦθος in the *Timaeus*.[17]

The μῦθος/λόγος dichotomy hinders an understanding of Plato's use of myth in relation to his own critiques of myth. Defining myth instead as a traditional tale avoids the problems of both the subjective definitions according to value judgement and the arbitrary definitions according to word usage.[18] Moreover, examination of the two essential parts of the definition, *traditional* and *tale*, illuminates both Plato's use of myth and his critique of others' myths.

The narrative form, the *tale*, has two specific features that Plato makes use of in his dialogues. First of all, the narrative structure of the tale can be used to illustrate the ideas discussed in the dialectic, displaying the relations between them. The pattern of action of the myth and the relations of the elements to one another can be used to convey meaning on a structural level beyond the meaning of the component parts.[19] Plato makes use of this feature of the narrative to convey some of the complex ideas of the dialogue in a briefer, more condensed form.[20] Another attribute of mythic discourse as narrative is the power of persuasive imagery. The myths are more memorable for the reader or interlocutor than the arguments because of the imagery and the narrative logic that holds the ideas together. This power of persuasive imagery is something against which Plato protests, but his objection is more to the way this power is misused

---

[17] cp. *Gorgias* 523a1-2 and *Timaeus* 26cd. Zaslavsky 1981; cp. Moors 1982, Murray 1999. Brisson 1982, on the other hand, does consider words other than μῦθος-related terms in his analysis of Plato's myths, and his list of μῦθος terms takes account of the context in determining the meaning.

[18] Brisson 1982 is the first to consider the importance of the tradition in understanding Plato's use of myth, but he nevertheless resorts to the distinction between myth as *discours invérifiable* and logos as *discours vérifiable* to discuss Plato's attempts to take control of the traditional discourse. Brisson cites Plato's list in *Republic* 392a3-9 of the topics of myth: gods, daimons, heroes, things in Hades, and humans, but he elides the inclusion of human things and concludes that myth must have a supernatural or unverifiable subject. "Le mythe est un discours invérifiable, car son référent se situe soit à un niveau de réalité inaccessible aussi bien à l'intellect qu'aux sens, soit au niveau des choses sensibles, mais dans un passé dont celui qui tient ce discours ne peut faire l'expérience directement ou indirectement." (Brisson 1982, pp. 127-128.) Morgan 2000 points out Plato's concern that argument itself is often unverifiable but does not address the particularly traditional or narrative aspects of mythic discourse in Plato.

[19] Hitchcock 1974 discusses the ways in which a narrative can illustrate or symbolize important ideas through its internal logic, pp. 68-70. cp. Frutiger 1930, pp. 190-193.

[20] For myth as a 'shortcut' for Plato, cp. Morgan 1991, pp. 315, 323.

by ignorant poets than to the power itself. His distrust of it, however, even in his own use of it, may be seen from the comparisons of myths to magic. The tale is thus a useful device for communication, a form with its own particular strengths for transmitting Plato's message to his audiences.

Plato, however, uses myths not only because they are tales but because they are *traditional* tales. The myth's connection with the tradition has two important effects – polyvalence and authority. Myth, as a system of symbols, each of which can evoke a ranges of resonances for the reader familiar with the tradition, permits particularly dense communication.[21] The use of traditional motifs, names, etc., allows a rich discourse on multiple levels as Plato exploits the associations and resonances connected with, for example, Tartarus or Minos. Plato also uses myth, even citing other poets' versions in support of his own, because mythic discourse is one of the primary forms of authoritative discourse in Plato's society.[22] By including elements that are recognizable to the audience as being part of the common cultural ground, the account seems to fit with that which is already accepted by all.[23] The authoritative status of mythic discourse makes it a particularly effective mode of communication.

This very effectiveness makes mythic discourse a target of Plato's criticism, in the *Republic* and elsewhere. As a moral reformer, Plato must concern himself with the influence of his tradition on the present, since the traditional tales provide the models for ethical judgements.[24] Perhaps

---

[21] Aristotle remarks on the usefulness of mythic references in rhetoric, since one need only refer to a well-known myth to make one's point. "One need only make mention of well known things. Because of this, most people have no need of narrative, if you wish to praise Achilles, for everyone knows his deeds." δεῖ δὲ τὰς μὲν γνωρίμους ἀναμιμνήσκειν· διὸ οἱ πολλοὶ οὐδὲν δέονται διηγήσεως. οἶον εἰ θέλεις Ἀχιλλέα ἐπαινεῖν (ἴσασι γὰρ πάντες τὰς πράξεις). (*Rhetoric*, III.xvi.3.)

[22] Plato employs three main modes of incorporating the tradition: allusion to a recognizable motif or pattern of action, direct citation or quotation of a familiar poet, and the contestive device of the priamel, in which Plato brings up a rival version or versions to contradict them. This device nevertheless folds Plato's version into the traditional discourse as it acknowledges the rival versions and places itself into the familiar contest with them. cp. Griffith 1990. See Lincoln 1999 for discussion of Plato's manipulation of the authority of mythic discourse.

[23] Again, Aristotle, in his *Rhetoric* (II.xxi.11), advocates the use of well-known proverbs and stories that are from the common tradition, "for because they are common, they seem to be correct, since everyone agrees upon them." διὰ γὰρ τὸ εἶναι κοιναί. ὡς ὁμολογούντων πάντων, ὀρθῶς ἔχειν δοκοῦσιν.

[24] "Plato is no exception to the rule that speaking of tradition always refers to the present. If there were no crisis in the city and its value system, it would not be necessary to conjure up, more than the *paideia* or the scholarly transmittal of knowledge, accepted truths (*ta*

the most striking statement of the problem as Plato sees it comes in Adeimantus's speech in the *Republic*:

Well, if there are no gods, or they do not concern themselves with the doings of men, neither need we concern ourselves with eluding their observation. If they do exist and pay heed, we know and hear of them only such discourses and from the poets who have described their pedigrees. But these same authorities tell us that the gods are capable of being persuaded and swerved from their course by 'sacrifice and soothing vows' and dedications. We must believe them in both or neither. And if we are to believe them, the thing to do is to commit injustice and offer sacrifice from the fruits of our wrongdoing.[25]

As Adeimantus makes clear, the danger is not just for children or the unphilosophic, but precisely for those who are most capable of analyzing the messages conveyed by the traditional tales. "What do we suppose they do to the souls of young men who hear them? I mean those who have good natures and have the capacity, as it were, to fly to all the things that are said and gather from them what sort of man one should be and what way one must follow to go through life best."[26] The mythic tradition is the primary source of authoritative teaching in Plato's society, and if he wishes to effect change in his society, he cannot merely ignore it as a mode of discourse epistemologically inferior to his philosophic method.

Plato therefore raises a variety of protests against the ways poets have used myth and the consequences of such authority residing in a discourse that does not conform to the ethical ideas he holds as most important. One of Plato's important tasks in his writings is thus the replacement of the poetic and mythic tradition with philosophy as the primary form of authoritative discourse. Lincoln describes Plato's attack on rhetoric and poetry in various of the dialogues: "At this point the audacity of Plato's endeavor becomes clear: it is nothing less than an attempt to subordinate

*nomizomena*), custom and ancestors (*ta patria*), that is to say the 'aural' (*akoe*), what is said from mouth to ear but comes from the ancients." (Detienne 1986, p. 85.)

[25] οὐκοῦν, εἰ μὲν [θεοί] μὴ εἰσὶν ἢ μηδὲν αὐτοῖς τῶν ἀνθρωπίνων μέλει, τί καὶ ἡμῖν μελητέον τοῦ λανθάνειν; εἰ δὲ εἰσί τε καὶ ἐπιμελοῦνται, οὐκ ἄλλοθέν τοι αὐτοὺς ἴσμεν ἢ ἀκηκόαμεν ἢ ἔκ τε τῶν νόμων καὶ τῶν γενεαλογησάντων ποιητῶν, οἱ δὲ αὐτοὶ οὗτοι λέγουσιν ὡς εἰσὶν οἷοι θυσίαις τε καὶ εὐχωλαῖς ἀγανῇσιν καὶ ἀναθήμασιν παράγεσθαι ἀναπειθόμενοι, οἷς ἢ ἀμφότερα ἢ οὐδέτερα πειστέον. εἰ δ' οὖν πειστέον, ἀδικητέον καὶ θυτέον ἀπὸ τῶν ἀδικημάτων. (Rep. 365d6–366a1.)

[26] τοιαῦτα καὶ τοσαῦτα λεγόμενα ἀρετῆς πέρι καὶ κακίας. ὡς ἄνθρωποι καὶ θεοὶ περὶ αὐτὰ ἔχουσι τιμῆς. τί οἰόμεθα ἀκουούσας νέων ψυχὰς ποιεῖν. ὅσοι εὐφυεῖς καὶ ἱκανοὶ ἐπὶ πάντα τὰ λεγόμενα ὥσπερ ἐπιπτόμενοι συλλογίσασθαι ἐξ αὐτῶν ποῖός τις ἂν ὢν καὶ πῇ πορευθεὶς τὸν βίον ὡς ἄριστα διέλθοι; 365ab.

those forms of discourse and practice that previously enjoyed greatest authority and respect throughout the Greek world and to encompass them within philosophy."[27] Plato co-opts the mythic tradition, manipulating it to his own philosophic purposes, and insists that the myths told must reflect the ethical ideas that he considers the proper models of and for behavior, not stir up passions and promote actions he sees as destructive to human welfare. As Frutiger puts it, "La fiction, chez lui, n'est qu'un moyen, jamais un but; loin de d'obnubiler la raison, elle lui aide à mieux saisir les essences, toute au rôle modeste, mais utile qui lui est assigné: celui d'une ancilla philosophiae."[28] Myth is indeed for Plato the handmaid of philosophy, very useful if kept in her place.

Plato uses the myths in his dialogues to carry out this re-placing of the mythic tradition with regard to philosophy. By placing his myths in dialogues that discuss moral and philosophical issues and by linking the ideas of the argument directly with the myth, Plato guides the interpretation of the myth along the lines of the philosophical ideas of the dialogue. Not only does he craft the arguments of the dialogue to engage the reader in a process of philosophic inquiry, but he also designs the myths so that the reader interprets them along the same lines of inquiry.[29] Plato thus tries to control the possibility for multiple interpretations of the same tale, the same polyvalence that makes myth such a powerful and enduring kind of discourse within his society.[30]

[27] Lincoln 1993, p. 241. cp. Redfield: "This does not mean that poetry must be rejected; it means only that it must be re-evaluated and the poets deprived of any independent authority vis-à-vis the philosopher. For Socrates (as Plato represents him) all valid activities are one with dialectical philosophy and therefore can be included within it … If the poet is to have the status of teacher, he must be judged as a teacher; we should not praise him for being moving, or charming, or full of pictures of life. Furthermore, the status of teacher is really the only status worth having. This leaves the poet no special place to stand; he is (like the rest of us) a philosopher or nothing." (Redfield 1994, pp. 44–45.)

[28] Frutiger 1930, p. 269.

[29] I would agree with, e.g., Kahn 1996, Elias 1984, and others that the dialogues are not intended to convey precise arguments but rather to induce the reader to philosophic activity. I do not think, however, that Plato puts in the myths ineffable truths he cannot express in his representation of dialectic argument. As Morgan 2000 has shown, Plato's representation of mythic narration suffers from the same limitations of written speech as the rest of the dialogues. The myths, with the strengths of the tradition and the narrative form, can convey ideas in ways that dialectic reasoning cannot, but they are not a purer vehicle for truths beyond the scope of dialectic.

[30] The most glaring example of a problematically reinterpreted myth is the Hesiodic tale of the succession of the gods, involving the castration of Ouranos by his son Kronos and the binding of Kronos by his son Zeus. Whereas Hesiod uses the tale to depict the

Not only does Plato try to restrict the interpetation of the myth by placing it within a philosophic discourse, he also designs the myth to convey the superiority of philosophy. The myth Socrates tells in the *Phaedo* replaces the figures valorized in the tradition – be it the heroes sent to the Isles of the Blessed or simply those who have been given the traditional funeral rituals – with the philosopher as the model for how one ought to live.[31] The philosopher is no longer a marginal figure, like the caricature of Socrates in Aristophanes' *Clouds* or the Pythagoreans mocked in other comedies, but is instead the most valuable and respectable member of the society. In the *Phaedo*, Socrates not only presents the myth that advocates the life of the philosopher but he represents, by the example of his life, the way a philosopher should live. Plato uses the myth to mark the life of the philosopher as the best life, invoking the authority of the mythic tradition to support his claim. In this myth, the effects of the philosopher's focus on the intelligible rather than sensible world are illustrated in terms of the traditional motif of the restless dead who are unable to free themselves from the land of the living and complete the journey to the realm of the dead. The lives of the philosopic and unphilosophic are depicted in greater detail through the traditional ideas of the happy and unhappy dead. The myth reinforces the arguments in the dialogues, and Plato carefully tailors the details of the myth to match the specific concepts discussed by the interlocutors. In the *Phaedo*, Plato uses the vividness and authority of myth to provoke his readers into practicing philosophy, into conducting their lives according to the values that he regards as most important.

---

transformation of the world from violence and chaos to justice and order, later interpreters could take it as the story of sons offering violence instead of respect to their fathers. cp. the arguments of Euthyphro in Plato's *Euthyphro* 5e. Socrates' solution in the *Republic* is to limit the transmission of the tale to those who can be trusted not to interpret it immorally. οὐδ' ἂν εἰ ἦν ἀληθῆ ᾤμην δεῖν ῥαδίως οὕτως λέγεσθαι πρὸς ἄφρονάς τε καὶ νέους. ἀλλὰ μάλιστα μὲν σιγᾶσθαι. εἰ δὲ ἀνάγκη τις ἦν λέγειν. δι' ἀπορρήτων ἀκούειν ὡς ὀλιγίστους. θυσαμένους οὐ χοῖρον ἀλλά τι μέγα καὶ ἄπορον θῦμα. "Even if they were true I should not think that they ought to be thus lightly told to thoughtless young persons. But the best way would be to bury them in silence, and if there were some necessity of relating them, only a very small audience should be admitted under a pledge of secrecy and after sacrificing, not a pig, but some huge and unprocurable victim" (Rep. 378a2–3). The pig was the customary sacrifice made by initiates at the Eleusinian Mysteries. Even if such a myth did contain moral truth, it would only be apparent to the initiate few, and the rest would be led astray.

[31] Admittedly, Plato does not think that everyone is capable of living a philosophic life, but then again not everyone is capable of living up to the Homeric ideal of Achilles or Odysseus either.

Plato proves a highly effective manipulator of myth. Although he did not succeed in entirely replacing the discourse of myth with philosophy nor in limiting the interpretation of his own myths (as the series of reinterpretations from the Neoplatonists to the NeoKantians confirms), nevertheless he had a profound impact on the shape of the Greek mythic tradition and on the ways myths have been evaluated ever since. Not only have his own tellings survived and provoked thought for thousands of years while others' tellings have been lost, his efforts to establish the authoritative status of philosophy over myth still shape the discourse of academia today.[32]

### ENTERING THE REALM OF HADES

The first difficulty facing the deceased is the transition from the world of the living to the world of the dead. In the *Frogs*, Herakles and Dionysos joke back and forth about the various types of suicide that would enable Dionysos to travel quickly to the realm of the dead, but Aristophanes brings Dionysos and Xanthias to the boundary of the underworld without either an Odyssean journey or a painful death. In the gold tablets, the narrative begins in the underworld after death. In the *Phaedo* myth, however, Plato makes this transition into a crux in the narrative; the deceased must overcome obstacles in order to complete the transition successfully. While the event of death might seem to cause this transition to occur immediately, the idea that the deceased might not be fully able to leave the world of the living appears in a number of sources in the Greek mythic tradition. The attempt of the deceased to depart from the world of which it had been a part as a living person and to overcome the obstacles preventing it from entering the realm of the dead is a familiar story pattern in the tradition. Plato makes use of the idea that certain dead cannot complete the transition to the realm of the dead, but he substitutes his own reasons for this failure in place of the ones in the tradition. Plato likewise rejects the traditional solutions to this problem, the funeral rituals, and replaces them with the practices of philosophy. He then redefines the traditional results of the failure to complete the transition to the land of the dead in terms of his metaphysical distinction between the sensible world and the knowable world. The traditional fate of the wandering soul becomes the fate of the unphilosophic both after death and before it, while the

---

[32] Ironically, the biggest obstruction to an understanding of Plato's use of myth, the μῦθος/λόγος dichotomy, may be considered one of his legacies.

philosopher overcomes the obstacles in the journey to the realm of the unseen, both in life and after. Plato thus uses the traditional distinction between successful and unsuccessful journeys to the realm of the dead and the fate of the pure or impure souls to illustrate his argument for living the philosophic life.

### Obstacle: Departure from the Mortal World

In the Greek mythic tradition from which Plato was drawing the material for his own myths, three types of dead had difficulty fully making the transition from the world of the living to the world of the dead: the ἄταφοι or unburied dead, the ἄωροι or untimely dead, and the βιαιοθάνατοι or those killed violently. In each case, some link to the land of the living prevented the deceased from being able to complete the journey to the world of the dead. The result of this difficulty in the transition was expressed in a variety of ways in the mythic tradition – ghosts, curses, avenging spirits, etc. – but these three types of obstacle to the transition always created some problem for the spirit trying to separate itself from its mortal life.

The first group of restless dead were the ἄταφοι, those for whom the final rituals of burial had not been performed. Without these final markings of the end of life, the deceased could not be fully severed from the land of the living. This mythic motif is well known from Homer on through tragedy. In the *Iliad*, the ghost of Patroklos pleads with Achilles to give him a funeral so that his shade can cross the river and enter into the kingdom of Hades.[33] Patroklos returns as a ghost to the world of the living until the funeral ritual enables him to pass over the river and join the other spirits of the dead who now bar his entrance.[34] Plato and his audience,

---

[33] θάπτέ με ὅττι τάχιστα πύλας Ἀΐδαο περήσω. τῆλέ με εἴργουσι ψυχαὶ εἴδωλα καμόντων, οὐδέ μέ πω μίσγεσθαι ὑπὲρ ποταμοῖο ἐῶσιν, ἀλλ᾽ αὔτως ἀλάλημαι ἀν᾽ εὐρυπυλὲς Ἄϊδος δῶ. καί μοι δὸς τὴν χεῖρ᾽ ὀλοφύρομαι, οὐ γάρ ἔτ᾽ αὖτις νίσομαι ἐξ Ἀΐδαο, ἐπήν με πυρὸς λελάχητε. *Iliad* XXIII 70-76. (Translations from Homer are from the Lattimore editions.) "Bury me as quickly as may be, let me pass through the gates of Hades. The souls, the images of dead men, hold me at a distance, and will not let me cross the river and mingle among them, but I wander as I am by Hades' house of the wide gates. And I call upon you in sorrow, give me your hand; no longer shall I come back from death, once you give me my rite of burning."

[34] As Odysseus, in the *Odyssey*, prepares to enter the underworld in search of Tiresias, he encounters the shade of his companion Elpenor who begs his former companions to bury his body so that he may finally enter the halls of Hades. (xi. 51-78.)

then, would have been familiar with a long tradition of myths in which the lack of burial presented an obstacle for the deceased spirit trying to enter the realm of the dead.[35]

The second category of dead unable to separate from the world of the living are those untimely dead, the ἄωροι. Numerous funeral monuments attest to the unease felt about those who died too young.[36] While infant dead might be considered in this class, the problem most often for the untimely dead was the fate of death before marriage.[37] Sophocles' Antigone laments her untimely end, "Ill fated past the rest, shall I descend, before my course is run. . . . No marriage-bed, no marriage-song for me, and since no wedding, so no child to rear."[38] The ritual of marriage provided a kind of fulfillment of life, especially for women, and to die before reaching

[35] Sourvinou-Inwood argues that, "In the fifth century the Homeric 'rule' that one could not enter Hades until after burial did not pertain." (Sourvinou-Inwood 1995, p. 310.) She sees a shift in the concept of the soul's journey to Hades, and points out that, in tragedy, lack of burial does not mean that the soul cannot enter into Hades at all (as in Homer), but rather that the unburied dead had a 'bad' death. I would argue that, even in tragedy, although the soul of the unburied may go down to the underworld (and even bargain with the powers there), it cannot remain in the underworld and be fully a part of the realm of the dead. Rather, the unburied dead remain restless, returning to cause problems in the realm of the living, a sign that they are not separated from the world of the living and integrated into the land of the dead. The description of the specific *result* of failing to overcome the *obstacle* differs, but the *obstacle* remains the same, the need to separate fully from the world of the living. While in Homer, the barrier to the unburied dead is specifically described as the river and the legion of other souls, in other myths the barrier that prevents the unburied dead from entering is not explicitly described.

[36] Lattimore discusses the epitaphs for the untimely and childless dead (Lattimore 1962, pp. 183-198.) Rohde 1925 also cites Epig Gr. 12; 16; 193; 220, 1; 221, 2; 313, 2-3.

[37] Euripides' Alcestis prays that her children may not die as untimely as she will, "Give the little girl a husband, give the little boy a generous wife; and do not let them die like me, who gave them birth, untimely. Let them live a happy life through to the end." τέκν' ὀρφανεῦσαι τάμά· καὶ τῷ μὲν φίλην σύζευξον ἄλοχον, τῇ δὲ γενναῖον πόσιν. μηδ' ὥσπερ αὐτῶν ἡ τεκοῦσ' ἀπόλλυμαι θανεῖν ἀώρους παῖδας, ἀλλ' εὐδαίμονας ἐν γῇ πατρῷᾳ τερπνὸν ἐκπλῆσαι βίον. (165-169, Lattimore translation.) In the *Odyssey*, unmarried men and women are among the souls Odysseus encounters outside the border of Hades, "brides, and young unmarried men, and long-suffering elders, virgins, tender and with the sorrows of young hearts upon them." νύμφαι τ' ἠΐθεοί τε πολύτλητοί τε γέροντες παρθενικαί τ' ἀταλαὶ νεοπενθέα θυμὸν ἔχουσαι. (*Odyssey* xi 38-39.) Many scholars have argued that although they are not explicitly labelled as unable to complete the transition into the realm of the dead, these souls approach Odysseus first because, like Elpenor, who is among them, they have not yet fully entered the underworld. See Johnston 1994, p. 139, and her citations, n. 9. She argues that the long-suffering elders may be the spirits of unhappy suicides. cp. also Odysseus' curse to Antinous (xvii, 476).

[38] ὦν λοισθία 'γὼ καὶ κάκιστα δὴ μακρῷ κάτειμι, πρίν μοι μοῖραν ἐξήκειν βίου....ἄλεκτρον, ἀνυμέναιον, οὔτε του γάμου μέρος λαχοῦσαν οὔτε παιδείου τροφῆς. (895-6; 917-8.)

that point of completion was to leave unfinished business in the world of the living. Even those women who lived until marriage, but died before producing children were considered to have died untimely, having left a crucial task in life unfinished, since the bearing and raising of children were considered the essential functions of women.[39]

The βιαιοθάνατοι too could not complete their transition to Hades, for they were also cut off before they were ready to leave the world of the living. For the most part, the βιαιοθάνατοι are the murdered dead, suicides, and executed criminals, since the most common form of violent death, death in battle, was a glorious rather than a problematic way of dying.[40] The murdered and executed were put to death against their wills, torn from the world of the living abruptly without the chance to live out their allotted span.[41]

The spirits of executed criminals, a subcategory of the βιαιοθάνατοι, were frequently thought to lie uneasy due to the violence with which their lives were ended. Westerink, in his analysis of all the uses of the term cited in the LSJ, concludes, "The general meaning, that of violent death, can be narrowed down to either suicide or death by execution."[42] Vergil includes the unjustly executed among the βιαιοθάνατοι in his description of the underworld (VI, 430ff.), but this classification is unlikely to have originated with him, stemming rather from the fact that both murder

[39] cp. Epig Gr. 336, 2; cf. 372, 32; 184, 3; CIG 5574 for the ἄτεκνος ἄωρος. Johnston 1994 comments on the status of women untimely dead before marriage or childbirth, pp. 366–370. See also Johnston 1999, pp. 161 ff.

[40] cp. Johnston 1999, pp. 148–155, on the idea that the βιαιοθάνατοι suffered not just from an untimely death, but, more importantly, from a dishonorable death.

[41] Aeschylus' *Oresteia* provides a number of illustrations of the mythic idea that the spirit of one who is murdered cannot rest. In the *Choephoroi*, the chorus tells Electra and Orestes that the spirit of a murdered man does not rest after the flames of the pyre destroy his body, but that his wrath appears later to harm his slayer. τέκνον, φρόνημα τοῦ θανόντος οὐ δαμάζει πυρὸς μαλερὰ γνάθος, φαίνει δ' ὕστερον ὀργάς· ὀτοτύζεται δ' ὁ θνῄσκων, ἀναφαίνεται δ' ὁ βλάπτων (323–327). In the *Eumenides*, the ghost of Clytemnestra urges on the Furies, claiming she is dishonored among the dead because her murder has not been avenged. ἐγὼ δ' ὑφ' ὑμῶν ὧδ' ἀπητιμασμένη ἄλλοισιν ἐν νεκροῖσιν ὧν μὲν ἔκτανον ὄνειδος ἐν φθιτοῖσιν οὐκ ἐκλείπεται, αἰσχρῶς δ' ἀλῶμαι· (94ff.). Plato himself, in his discussion of murder in the *Laws*, refers to an ancient myth that describes the anger and horror of a murder victim when his spirit sees his murderer walking around in his familiar haunts (865e).

[42] Westerink 1976–1977, p. 346, n. 11. While early sources do not provide widespread evidence for this classification, Tertullian (*De Anima*, 56.8) provides evidence for its existence by vehemently arguing against this classification and trying to refute the traditions that class the executed among the βιαιοθάνατοι.

victims and executed criminals are put to death by other men. Of course, the body of the executed criminal was often not properly buried, but thrown into a pit with the bodies of other criminals.[43] This lack of proper burial might contribute to the idea of a restless spirit, but it was the violent death of the executed criminal that put him in the category of the βιαιοθάνατοι, along with the suicides and the victims of murder.

In the mythic tradition, then, three types of dead are thought to face difficulty in completing their transition from the world of the living to the land of the dead. This difficulty is not always expressed spatially, as it is in the *Iliad*, in terms of the deceased being unable to cross the river into the realm of Hades, but the idea that the transition from living to dead is somehow incomplete manifests itself in a variety of ways in the mythic tradition.

In the *Phaedo*, Plato plays with these traditional mythic ideas which express the potential difficulties in completing the transition from the world of the living to the world of the dead. While he makes reference to the three traditional classes of restless dead, he at the same time makes use of his own definition of death as the separation of body and soul (64c4–8) to develop a new kind of obstacle that prevents the departure of the soul from the land of the living to the realm of the dead. Plato employs two kinds of images to describe the soul's difficulty in leaving behind the body and its world for the realm of the dead. The first image is the much-disputed φρουρά, the idea of the soul somehow imprisoned in the body. This prison prevents the separation of body and soul that is defined as death. Plato also uses the image of the impurity of the soul as an obstacle; the soul that is contaminated by the body is mixed in with it and cannot completely separate itself. The impure soul therefore cannot entirely enter the realm of the dead, but it remains a part of the world of the living, the physical world of the body. Both of these obstacles described in the *Phaedo* stand in contrast to the traditional obstacles of lack of burial, untimely death, or violent death.

By incorporating the traditional motifs of the restless dead, Plato evokes the traditional pattern of action of the journey to the land of the dead. Crito is concerned about how he should bury Socrates after his death (115c), raising the possibility that Socrates might remain unburied. While Socrates could hardly be considered among the ἄωροι who die too

---

[43] cp. Rohde 1925, p. 604, on the πολυάνδριοι as the spirits of mass-buried executed criminals used in Cypriot defixiones.

young or before marriage, since he is not only over seventy years of age, but has married and sired a number of children, his execution nevertheless cuts short his life.[44] Moreover, as an executed criminal, Socrates could fall into the class of the violently killed, especially since, from Plato's perspective, he was executed unjustly.[45] The prison official remarks how other condemned men cursed him as responsible for their deaths, but Socrates curses neither the official nor those who sentenced him to death (116c). Plato uses the example of Socrates, who might in traditional mythic terms be thought to face obstacles in his departure to the realm of the dead, to redefine the obstacles that the deceased faces in his journey from the land of the living. Socrates is concerned with his transition to the realm of the dead, but not for the traditional reasons.

In explaining the prohibition against suicide, Socrates refers to the account in the mysteries that men are in some kind of prison under the supervision of the gods. "The reason given in the mysteries on the subject, that we men are in some sort of prison, and that one ought not to release oneself from it or run away, seems to me a lofty idea and not easy to penetrate."[46] Controversy has raged over the meaning of the word, φρουρά, which could indicate either a prison or a garrison post.[47] In the latter case, the soul's sojourn in the body would be regarded as a kind of civic obligation in the service of the gods, a frontier tour of duty from which it would be wrong to go AWOL. Such a sense presents a more positive image of the body than the idea of the body as a prison, which carries the connotation of a punishment for wrongdoing rather than simply an obligation that must be fulfilled. The idea of the body as a

---

[44] In the *Apology*, Socrates tells the jury to have patience, for in a few years they could be rid of him by natural death, rather than cutting his life off by execution (38c).

[45] While the death is forced upon Socrates by the Athenian legal system, Plato goes out of his way to stress Socrates' choice in the matter, pointing out his rejection of the opportunity to escape (98e-99a). Moreover, Plato de-emphasizes the violence of Socrates' death in his description of the action of the poison. Various scholars have argued whether the symptoms of hemlock poisoning correspond to Plato's description of the death, which shows Socrates completely in control of his bodily functions and quietly succumbing to the loss of sensation. cp. Gill 1973, who claims a more violent death would have occurred; *contra* Burnet 1911, Appendix I. Most recently, however, Bloch 2002 claims that Gill and others base their claims for more violent symptoms on the wrong type of hemlock plant.

[46] ὁ μὲν οὖν ἐν ἀπορρήτοις λεγόμενος περὶ αὐτῶν λόγος, ὡς ἔν τινι φρουρᾷ ἐσμεν οἱ ἄνθρωποι καὶ οὐ δεῖ δὴ ἑαυτὸν ἐκ ταύτης λύειν οὐδ' ἀποδιδράσκειν, μέγας τέ τίς μοι φαίνεται καὶ οὐ ῥᾴδιος διιδεῖν· (62b2–5).

[47] Plato uses the word to mean 'prison' at *Gorgias* 525a; but at *Laws* 762b, it has the more frequent meaning of 'garrison post.'

prison for the soul recalls the etymology Socrates attributes in the *Cratylus* to 'those around Orpheus', who believed that the soul is kept or preserved (σῴζηται) in the prison of the body (σῶμα) because it has a penalty to pay.[48] The mysteries (ἀπορρήτοι) to which Socrates refers may allude to secret doctrines of these people who make use of the poems of Orpheus or they may refer to some other religious group with a similar idea of the relation of the soul to the world.[49] It is quite likely, of course, that Plato chose the word φρουρά precisely because of its ambiguity, because it enabled him to convey the image of imprisonment of the soul in the body while tempering it with the more positive connotations of garrison duty that is owed to the gods.[50]

Given, however, that the setting of the dialogue is the prison in which Socrates is being held prior to his execution, the meaning of φρουρά as prison is most probably the primary significance. Socrates is repeatedly described as being in δεσμωτήριον, in a prison (57a2, 58c5, 59d4, 59d5, 59e1) from which he will be released at his death. Likewise, the souls that go to the upper realms are described in the closing myth of the dialogue as being released as if from prisons, δεσμωτηρίων (114c1). Just as Socrates is released at the beginning of the dialogue from his fetters (60c6), so the soul is released at death from the fetters of the body (67d1). These chains that hold the soul to the body, Socrates explains, are pleasures and pains. "Each pleasure and pain fastens the soul to the body with a sort of rivet, pins it there, and makes it corporeal, so that it takes for real whatever

---

[48] δοκοῦσι μέντοι μοι μάλιστα θέσθαι οἱ ἀμφὶ Ὀρφέα τοῦτο τὸ ὄνομα, ὡς δίκην διδούσης τῆς ψυχῆς ὧν δὴ ἕνεκα δίδωσιν, τοῦτον δὲ περίβολον ἔχειν, ἵνα σῴζηται, δεσμωτηρίου εἰκόνα (400bc). The controversy surrounding this passage mostly revolves around the issue of whether οἱ ἀμφὶ Ὀρφέα also provide the etymology of σῶμα/σῆμα, the body as the tomb of the soul, which, on the strength of this passage, has been declared a central tenet of the 'Orphic faith' by some modern scholars. I follow Wilamovitz and Linforth 1941, p. 148 in reading the passage as drawing a distinction between the etymology of οἱ ἀμφὶ Ὀρφέα and the unnamed τινες who provide the σῶμα/σῆμα derivation. Nevertheless, the σῶμα/σῆμα idea must come from a religious movement very similar to that which supports its ideas with the poems of Orpheus, the 'Orphics' in the strictest sense.

[49] cp. Empedokles' imprisonment in the body for crimes of bloodshed, fr. 115. For the development of the idea of imprisonment, see also Seaford 1986.

[50] Especially in light of the importance of the service to the gods in the discussion of suicide, the song of the swans, and the myth of the afterlife. (See further below.) Loraux likewise questions the necessity of the debate over one meaning rather than another. "Pourquoi, dès lors, refuser d'admettre qu'il faut dans ce mot condenser trois images: celle de la prison, celle de la geôle, pour des esclaves - en l'occurrence l'humanité entière - qui ont les dieux pour maîtres, celle du service de garnison qu'on ne saurait rompre par la fuit?" (Loraux 1982, p. 33.)

the body declares to be so."[51] These links forged by pleasure and pain as the body experiences them in turn[52] create the prison of the soul.[53] The captive participates in his own imprisonment, forging the chains of desire that bind him to the world of the body. So strong are these fetters that the soul is unable to separate itself from the body at death, but it remains connected to the material, sensible, visible world of the living.

Plato combines this image of the body as the prison of the soul with that of the body causing impurity in the soul. Impurity is the result of mixture, and the mixture of body and soul prevents the soul from being able to detach itself completely from the body. The soul is not unsullied (εἰλικρινῆ) by its contact with material things and cannot depart alone by itself (αὐτὴν καθ' αὑτὴν) (81c1-2). The soul in contact with the body during life grows to resemble it and becomes mixed up with it. Plato describes the effect of this mixture of the body with the soul in a variety of ways. The soul becomes σωματοειδῆ, corporeal or body-like.[54] It becomes subject to all the afflictions of the body and is confused by the multiplicity of things it perceives through the senses. Moreover, since the body's senses perceive only the visible realm, the soul cannot reach the invisible realm, the realm of Hades. Weighted down by the body, it remains in the visible world even after death.

Plato specifically emphasizes the contrast between the visible world that the senses perceive and the invisible world. Socrates sets up the dichotomy,

---

[51] Ὅτι ἑκάστη ἡδονὴ καὶ λύπη ὥσπερ ἧλον ἔχουσα προσηλοῖ αὐτὴν πρὸς τὸ σῶμα καὶ προσπερονᾷ καὶ ποιεῖ σωματοειδῆ, δοξάζουσαν ταῦτα ἀληθῆ εἶναι ἅπερ ἂν καὶ τὸ σῶμα φῇ (83d).

[52] This theme of the connection between pleasure and pain, prominent throughout the dialogue, appears when Socrates comments how pleasure follows pain with the removal of his fetters. He suggests that Aesop might have made a fable in which pleasure and pain were bound together (60c1-7). Here Plato brings together the motifs of pleasure and pain with that of fetters, foreshadowing their connection later in the dialogue.

[53] "The soul has been literally bound and glued to the body and is forced to view the things that are as if through a prison, rather than alone by itself; and [that] it is wallowing in utter ignorance. Now philosophy discerns the cunning of the prison, sees how it is effected through desire, so that the captive himself may co-operate most of all in his imprisonment." διαδεδεμένην ἐν τῷ σώματι καὶ προσκεκολλημένην, ἀναγκαζομένην δὲ ὥσπερ διὰ εἱργμοῦ διὰ τούτου σκοπεῖσθαι τὰ ὄντα ἀλλὰ μὴ αὐτὴν δι' αὑτῆς, καὶ ἐν πάσῃ· ἀμαθίᾳ κυλινδουμένην, καὶ τοῦ εἱργμοῦ τὴν δεινότητα κατιδοῦσα ὅτι δι' ἐπιθυμίας ἐστίν, ὡς ἂν μάλιστα αὐτὸς ὁ δεδεμένος συλλήπτωρ εἴη τοῦ δεδέσθαι (82e2-83a1).

[54] cp. 81b5, c4, e1; 83d5.

"Would you like us to posit two kinds of beings, the one kind seen, the other invisible?... And the invisible is always constant, whereas the seen is never constant?"[55] The visible is accessible to the senses, while the invisible can only be grasped by the reasoning of the mind. By referring to the invisible as τὸ ἀιδές, Plato sets up the identification of the invisible world proper to the soul with the traditional mythic idea of the realm of Hades, Ἅιδου (80d6). This connection of Hades and the unseen is part of the mythic tradition at least as early as Homer,[56] and Plato refers to it in the *Cratylus* as well, where he makes the etymology of Hades not from ἀειδές (not-visible) but rather from εἰδέναι (to know) (404b, cp. 403a). In the *Phaedo*, it would seem, Plato is toying with both associations, since the unseen world is that which is accessible only to the mind – it is that which is known rather than sensed.[57] By associating the world of the soul with the unseen world of Hades, Plato justifies his idea that the soul that is too mixed with the body and the visible world cannot fully enter Hades, the realm of the dead.

Incorporating the familiar mythic idea of certain dead who are unable to depart from the land of the living, Plato redefines the obstacle that prevents their departure to suit his metaphysical arguments about the contrast between the sensible and knowable worlds. Rather than depicting Socrates as concerned about lack of burial or his untimely and violent death, the traditional obstacles facing the deceased at death, Plato has Socrates discuss the potential problems of a soul that has become too mixed with the body and cannot break out of its prison, but remains trapped in the visible world of the living.

---

[55] Θῶμεν οὖν βούλει, ἔφη, δύο εἴδη τῶν ὄντων, τὸ μὲν ὁρατόν, τὸ δὲ ἀιδές; . . . Καὶ τὸ μὲν ἀιδὲς ἀεὶ κατὰ ταὐτὰ ἔχον, τὸ δὲ ὁρατὸν μηδέποτε κατὰ ταὐτὰ (79a6–10).

[56] cp. *Iliad* V 85, where Athena borrows the helmet of Hades so that she will not be seen by Ares.

[57] Although Plato does not actually stress this pun, it is tempting to suspect that, just as the realm of Hades, ἀιδου, is explicitly connected with the invisible, ἀιδῆ (80d6), so too Plato may be connecting Hades with the absence of pleasure, ἀηδές, since pleasures are the chains that prevent the soul from going to Hades. The description of the singing (ἀιδειν) of the ἀηδών, the nightingale, as a joyful song like that of the swan foreseeing death does make the reader suspect that Plato is deliberately engaging in egregious wordplays to associate a number of different ideas. Certainly such a pun is intended when Plato uses the unusual word ἀίδιον to refer to the everlasting, although a connection with ἀδεῶς, fearlessly, in describing how Socrates met his end (58e4), may be stretching the wordplay too far, even for Plato.

### Solution: Philosophy Replaces Funeral Ritual

Rituals often provide the solutions to the problems posed in the myths of a society. Both myths and rituals draw on familiar elements of the cultural tradition to express their essential ideas, but, whereas a myth usually describes a situation fraught with danger or *anomie*, a ritual, by its performance, successfully creates the state desired by the participants as, for example, in a wedding when the couple is united or in a sacrifice when the sharing of the offering establishes the relations among the participants. The most important solution to the potential problem of the deceased being unable to make the transition from the world of the living to the realm of the dead is the funeral of the deceased. The funeral ritually enacts the transition, symbolically effecting the removal of the deceased from his former place among the living to the new position among the dead. The washing and anointing of the corpse purify the deceased and prepare him for the separation from his former life.[58] Often the deceased is given a crown or some other token of his special, pure status.[59] The female relations of the deceased lament, chanting ritual songs of mourning. Friends and relations of the deceased visit the corpse at its laying-out, πρόθεσις. One important offering made to the deceased is the ceremonial clipping of hair.[60] After the πρόθεσις, the deceased is carried in procession to the grave, the ritual procession enacting the journey of the deceased from one realm to the other. Such rituals are intended to grant the deceased a successful passage, to smooth the difficult transition caused by death.

[58] cp. Damascius' interpretation of the ancient Attic funeral rituals. "What do the ancient Attic death-rites symbolize? – The closing of the eyes and mouth signifies the end of outward activity and reversion to the inner life; the laying down on the earth is a reminder that the soul should unite itself with the universe; the washing means purification from the world of process; the unction a disengaging from the mire of matter and a calling forth of divine inspiration; cremation transference to the higher, indivisible world; inhumation union with intelligible reality." (Damascius, II 150 in Westerink.) These interpretations show a clear Neoplatonic bent, but they neverthless indicate the role of the funeral rituals in the separation of the deceased from the world of the living.

[59] cp. Parker 1983, "Thus the dead man was made pure, in despite of the contamination all around him; of all those present at the wake, he alone wore the crown, emblem of purity." p 35. For the funeral rituals, cp. Rohde 1925, pp. 162–166; Ginouvès 1962, pp. 239ff.; also Garland 1985, pp. 21–37; the bibliography in Vermeule 1979, pp. 261–262.

[60] Van Gennep 1960, pp. 166–167, suggests that this ritual served as a symbolic separation of the living mourner from the deceased who had been a part of the mourner's life. The mourner symbolically detaches the deceased from himself by cutting off a piece of himself which thus belongs to the deceased. cp. Redfield 1994, pp. 181–182.

The unburied dead, the ἄταφοι, lack the assistance of these rituals, and thus are in danger of failing to make the transition.

Even more at risk are the ἄωροι and the βιαιοθάνατοι, who need extra assistance in their transitions. The unmarried ἄωροι are often dressed in wedding garments and wreaths and given a symbolic marriage to Hades in place of the marriage that they failed to make in life.[61] The structural similarities between the wedding and funeral rituals could be exploited to make the funeral serve as a kind of wedding for the deceased unfortunate enough to have perished before reaching this τέλος.[62] A λουτροφόρος, the jar used to hold the water for the prenuptial purifications, is often placed as a marker on the grave of one who died untimely.[63] For the deceased whose life was ended by violence, the only aid to ease the transition for the troubled spirit is revenge upon those responsible for the killing. Such vengeance is a sacred obligation of the relatives of the deceased, like the funeral itself. The theme of the duty of the relatives to prosecute the murderer as the proper vengeance within the laws of the polis appears frequently in the legal speeches of classical Athens.[64] For example, in Antiphon 1, a young man prosecutes his stepmother for the poisoning of his father, despite his almost total lack of evidence, simply in obedience to his father's last wish for vengeance. As Rohde notes, the duty of vengeance for the murder victim goes back to Homer in the written tradition and is undoubtedly one of the oldest features of Greek religion and society.[65]

While the Greek tradition provides several solutions to the obstacles facing the deceased in their transition from the world of the living to the realm of the dead, Plato has Socrates reject these traditional solutions to the problems of the journey to the realm of the dead and, in the *Phaedo*, substitutes instead the practice of philosophy as the proper preparation for the journey. Rather than rituals that need to be performed *after* death,

---

[61] cp. Rose 1925, pp. 238–242; Fontinoy 1950, pp. 383–396.

[62] cp., e.g., Seaford 1987, p. 106.

[63] Ginouvès 1962, pp. 257–258. Some have disputed this special significance of the λουτροφόρος, arguing it may have been used to mark tombs of others as well. cp. Kurtz and Boardman 1971, pp. 151–152, 161. The main evidence comes from Demosthenes, XLIV 18, 30, but it is supported by scholia on Euripides' *Phoen.* 347, Eustathius on *Iliad* XXIII. 41, and Hesychius s.v. λουτροφόρος.

[64] cp. various of Antiphon's speeches, particularly the *Tetralogies*; Lysias 12, in which Lysias prosecutes one of the Thirty Tyrants for his role in the death of Lysias's brother.

[65] Rohde 1925, pp. 174–179. Of course, due care should be observed in accepting Rohde's conclusions about the origins of this practice in the primitive worship of one's dead ancestors.

Plato emphasizes solutions to the potential problems of the transition that must be performed *before* death. The philosophic life, as the daily effort of separating the mind from the physical world, is the highest form of this practice for death, μελέτη θανάτου (81a1, cp. 64a6, 67e5).

Socrates rejects the traditional lamentations associated with the funeral ritual. He sends the women away at the beginning of the dialogue (60a7) when Xanthippe begins to wail, and he rebukes his friends at the end, when they lament like women after he drinks the poison (117d5–e2). Socrates likewise rejects the significance of his burial, the most important of the traditional solutions. When Crito asks him how he wishes to be buried, he denies that Crito can actually bury *him*, rather than merely his body (115c). By identifying himself with his departing soul rather than with the corpse, Socrates denies the importance of the traditional burial rite for the journey of the spirit to the land of the dead. He warns Crito against identifying the corpse with the departing soul, lest by mentioning the identification, he might somehow hamper the departure of the soul (115e). As for the burial rites, Crito may do whatever he likes with Socrates' body. For Socrates, the burial comes too late to help in the departure of the soul.

To signal the importance of not waiting until after death, Socrates explicitly moves two of the funeral rituals traditionally performed after death to before his death. He tells Phaedo not to shear his hair in mourning for him tomorrow, but rather to shear it immediately if they cannot prove the immortality of the soul and let the argument die (89bc). Socrates' decision to bathe before he drinks the poison conveys the same message. "It really seems better to take a bath before drinking the poison, and not to give the women the trouble of washing a dead body."[66] For Socrates, the purificatory washing in the funeral rituals comes too late; it only washes the body and fails to help the soul depart from the land of the living. Socrates' bath is not some strange 'Orphic' ritual, as some have suggested, but rather his symbolic rejection of the importance of the traditional funeral rites in favor of a life of purification through philosophy.[67]

---

[66] δοκεῖ γὰρ δὴ βέλτιον εἶναι λουσάμενον πιεῖν τὸ φάρμακον καὶ μὴ πράγματα ταῖς γυναιξὶ παρέχειν νεκρὸν λούειν (115a6–7).

[67] Stewart 1972 is often cited in support of the bath as an Orphic ritual, but Stewart's article offers no proof of an Orphic origin for the idea of bathing before death. The only parallel he cites is Euripides' Alcestis, who, in effect already dead, performs a number of the normal funeral rituals in advance of her actual death. Tragedy contains a few more examples of those who perform their ritual bath before death; in each case, it is someone,

Just as Socrates defines death as a separation of soul from body, so too he defines purification as a process of separation that undoes the mixture of soul and body.[68] Rather than the ritual purifications of the funeral ceremony that finally separate the departing soul from the body, the philosopher relies on the purifications of the philosophical life as Plato defines it in the *Phaedo* to separate the soul from the body on a continuous basis. The philosopher must separate himself from the concerns and afflictions of the body and the multiform world of the senses and concentrate upon exercising the mind. Philosophy thus serves both as a purifying ritual (καθαρμός) to dissolve the mixture of body and soul and as a release (λύσις) from the prison of the body (82d6, cp. 65a1, 67d7, 84a3).

To release his soul from this prison, Socrates argues, the philosopher withdraws his interest from the physical pleasures: food and drink, sex, bodily adornments, and all other things that affect the body (64d–65a). Because these pleasures and their attending pains are of little concern to him, the virtues he practices are not for the sake of pleasure and pain, as are the so-called virtues of the unphilosophic, who are brave through fear of death and temperate from the desire for other pleasures (68d–69b). Rather, the philosopher's virtuous behavior stems from his desire for wisdom, for an understanding of the things that truly are (82cd). Such a practice dissolves the chains of pain and pleasure that bind the soul to the body (83d4–6), for the pleasures and pains cease to appear real in contrast to the things that the soul apprehends by reasoning. As Socrates explains, "The soul of every man, when intensely pleased or pained at something, is forced at the same time to suppose that whatever affects it in this way is most clear and most real, when it is not so."[69] The prison of the soul

---

like Alcestis, Oedipus at Colonus, Polyxena, etc., who, knowing that death is imminent and unavoidable, accepts death, symbolically joining the ranks of the dead by performing the rituals for the corpse. Among modern commentators, Loraux 1982 recognizes the nature of the bath before death, but the idea even appears in Damascius' fifth century CE commentary. – "Why does Socrates not adhere to tradition? – Perhaps it was not customary to wash those who died a violent death. Rather, it is suggested that even the body should be cleansed voluntarily and before death." (Dam. II 151, p. 368, Westerink.) Incidentally, this passage also recognizes the potential for Socrates to be among the βιαιοθάνατοι.

[68] 67c5–6, cp. *Sophist* 227d.

[69] Ὅτι ψυχὴ παντὸς ἀνθρώπου ἀναγκάζεται ἅμα τε ἡσθῆναι σφόδρα ἢ λυπηθῆναι ἐπί τῷ καὶ ἡγεῖσθαι περὶ ὃ ἂν μάλιστα τοῦτο πάσχῃ, τοῦτο ἐναργέστατόν τε εἶναι καὶ ἀληθέστατον, οὐχ οὕτως ἔχον· (83c5–8).

that the unphilosophic person creates for himself from his desires (cp. 82e5-6) melts away for the philosopher as he perceives the reality of the unchanging, invisible, divine world.

The philosopher strives to brings his soul into contact with the invisible objects of knowledge, objects that Plato associates in a double pun with the realm of Hades – τὸ ἀιδές – εἰδέναι – Ἅιδου. "It departs yonder towards that which is pure and always existent and immortal and unvarying, and in virtue of its kinship with it, enters always into its company."[70] By this contact, the philosopher seeks to undo the mixture of body and soul that could prevent his soul's pure departure from the body at death. The soul makes use of the mind's power of knowing (εἰδέναι) to apprehend the invisible (τὸ ἀιδές), thus preparing it to be in the realm of Hades (Ἅιδου). Nurtured by this intellectual vision of the invisible, the soul of the philosopher grows into its own nature, coming more and more to resemble the uniform, unvarying, and divine.[71] Since the divine is naturally fitted to be the ruler of the mortal, the soul thus comes to rule more completely over the body, instead of being subject to it (80a1-9). No longer inextricably entwined with the body, the soul can guide the body rather than be led astray by it.

Just as Plato depicts the obstacle facing the soul in its departure as a prison of the body or as the impure mixture of body and soul, so too he depicts the philosophic life as dissolving this prison and purifying the soul. Plato portrays his philosophical solutions as superior to the traditional ritual solutions for overcoming the obstacles to the journey of the soul from the land of the living. The funeral ceremonies only help the soul separate from the body after death, whereas the philosophic life is a continuous practice of dying, an ongoing separation of the soul from the body.

## Result: Ghosts in the Graveyard

If the traditional ritual solutions are not performed by the friends or relatives of the deceased, the unburied or untimely or violently dead may be compelled to wander outside the gates of the realm of Hades, trapped

---

[70] ἐκεῖσε οἴχεται εἰς τὸ καθαρόν τε καὶ ἀεὶ ὂν καὶ ἀθάνατον καὶ ὡσαύτως ἔχον, καὶ ὡς συγγενὴς οὖσα αὐτοῦ ἀεὶ μετ᾽ ἐκείνου τε γίγνεται (79d1-4).

[71] 80b1-5, similarity of the soul to the divine; 84a8-b5, the soul nurtured by the contemplation of the unseen world.

between the world of the living and that of the dead. Often, as in the famous case of Patroklos, the restless dead appear as ghosts in the land of the living, visible but immaterial phantoms. Sometimes these spirits appear, like Patroklos or Polydoros in Euripides' *Hekabe*, in dreams, but they could also appear to the waking eye.[72]

The deceased stranded in this liminal zone between life and death not only are not only miserable themselves, since they are unable to find rest in one world or the other, but also present a grave danger to the living, either through the retribution wreaked by spirits angry at being deprived of rest or by the manipulation of these spirits by necromantic magicians.[73] The lack of burial prevents the deceased from fully leaving the world of the living, and this disruption of the proper order brings about the anger of the gods, an anger that takes a number of gruesome forms in the tradition.[74] As Isocrates notes in his funeral oration, as bad as the lack of proper burial is for the deceased stranded in the liminal zone, the repercussions on the living may be even worse.[75]

---

[72] Pliny (VII.27) relates the story of a haunted house at Athens, in which the spectre of an old man appeared at night to the occupants, rattling his chains and driving them to death by depriving them of their sleep. Finally, the ghost was laid to rest when someone followed it, discovered the fettered bones of the deceased, and gave them a proper burial. Phlegon of Tralles (*Mirabilia* 1) relates the tale of Philinnion, a girl of Amphipolis who died soon after marriage but came back as a ghost to seduce a guest in her father's house. When exposed as a ghost, she died again, and her doubly dead corpse was burned outside the city's boundaries.

[73] In Sophocles' *Antigone*, Tiresias tells Creon of the danger he has created by refusing to permit the burial of Polyneices. "You've confused the upper and lower worlds. You've sent a life to settle in a tomb; you keep up here that which belongs below, the corpse unburied, robbed of its release.... You rob the nether gods of what is theirs. So the pursuing horrors lie in wait to track you down. The Furies sent by Hades and by all gods will even you with your victims." νέκυν νεκρῶν ἀμοιβὸν ἀντιδοὺς ἔσῃ, ἀνθ' ὧν ἔχεις μὲν τῶν ἄνω βαλὼν κάτω, ψυχήν τ' ἀτίμως ἐν τάφῳ κατῴκισας, ἔχεις δὲ τῶν κάτωθεν ἐνθάδ' αὖ θεῶν ἄμοιρον, ἀκτέριστον, ἀνόσιον νέκυν. ὧν οὔτε σοὶ μέτεστιν οὔτε τοῖς ἄνω θεοῖσιν, ἀλλ' ἐκ σοῦ βιάζονται τάδε. Τούτων σε λωβητῆρες ὑστεροφθόροι λοχῶσιν Ἅιδου καὶ θεῶν Ἐρινύες, ἐν τοῖσιν αὐτοῖς τοῖσδε ληφθῆναι κακοῖς. (1067–1077, Lattimore translation.)

[74] The specific *source* of the danger varies in the different sources – the gods, the Furies, the dead spirit. As Parker cautions, "Even where the idea of danger is certainly present, however, it is not necessarily derived from the dead man's anger." (Parker 1983, p. 109.) The *cause* of the danger in all cases, however, is that the deceased has not been able to complete the transition.

[75] Isocrates XIV, 55. This idea of danger to the living from the failure to ensure that the deceased can successfully complete the journey to the land of the dead goes back as far as Homer. Patroklos may plead with Achilles on the basis of their friendship, but Elpenor reminds Odysseus of his duty to provide the burial rites for him and warns that he may

The same is particularly true for the βιαιοθάνατοι, the victims of murder or execution. Antiphon, in his *Tetralogies*, refers often to the wrath of the deceased and the avenging powers it will unleash, but mention is never made of the miserable condition of the deceased who is bringing forth such a visitation on the world of the living.[76] The spirits of the βιαιοθάνατοι are particularly dangerous and relentless in their hauntings, because they seek the revenge that would permit their spirits to rest.

The untimely dead, too, could be dangerous if the traditional solutions to ease their transitions were not employed. A host of dreadful spirits were thought to come from women who had died before marriage or childbirth. Deprived of their natural fulfillment in life, these women were thought to come back as monsters to steal and destroy the babies of other women.[77] Creatures such as Mormo, Gello, Lamia, and perhaps Empousa belonged

become a curse upon him if he neglects the burial. (*Od.* xi. 72-3, cp. Hector to Achilles *Il.* XXII 355.)

[76] In tragedy, the βιαιοθάνατοι were often depicted as wreaking harm, either personally or more often through the agency of the Furies. cp. Johnston 1999, p. 142-148, for a treatment of the various forms in which the anger of the violently dead might be manifested. In the *Eumenides*, Clytemnestra refers to herself as 'wandering dishonored' (ἀπητιμασμένη . . . αἰσχρῶς δ ἀλῶμαι), but the vengeance she calls upon the Furies to wreak on Orestes is far more horrific, "Let go upon this man the stormblasts of your bloodshot breath, wither him in your wind, after him, hunt him down once more, and shrivel him in your vitals' heat and flame." σὺ δ αἱματηρὸν πνεῦμ᾽ ἐπουρίσασα τῷ, ἀτμῷ κατισχναίνουσα, νηδύος πυρί, ἕπου, μάραινε δευτέροις διώγμασιν. (137-139, Lattimore translation.) Plutarch relates the story of Cleonice, who was accidentally murdered by Pausanias (*Cim.* 6). Her spirit continued to haunt him, tormenting him in his dreams at night. Finally Pausanias called up her spirit at the oracle of the dead at Heracleia, begging for pardon, but she merely told him he would be delivered from his troubles when he returned to Sparta - where he was killed, a satisfaction for the ghost. cp. Paus. III.17.7-9.

[77] Although more of these myths deal with women, men who died without the satisfaction of marriage were also thought to return in search of a substitute. The spirit of Achilles, cut off before he could marry a desirable bride, demands the sacrifice of the Trojan princess Polyxena. cp. Euripides, *Hecuba* 35-44. Later versions are explicit about a romantic connection, even inventing a previous marriage contract. cp. the summaries in Gantz 1993, pp. 628, 657-659. While Achilles was satisfied with a single sacrifice, the ghost of one of Odysseus's companions who was killed at Temesa for attempting to rape a local girl was more difficult to satisfy. According to Pausanias, this ghost wreaked havoc at Temesa until the inhabitants offered a yearly sacrifice of the fairest maiden in Temesa as a bride for the ghost. This sacrifice continued for years until the Olympic victor, Euthymos, fell in love with the girl of the year and fought with the ghost, driving it into the sea. (Pausanias V.6.7-10.) Pausanias relates that Euthymos won the crown for boxing in the 76th and 77th Olympic games, around 472 and 468 BCE. This ghost falls into all three categories, for he was an executed βιαιοθάνατος (by stoning) left unburied who died without the satisfaction of marriage.

to this category of child-stealing monsters.[78] Such monsters were a terror to children, the traditional Greek equivalent to the modern bogeyman.[79]

All three types of restless dead may return to the land of the living because they are unable to complete their journey to the realm of the dead. Their ambiguous status, stranded 'betwixt and between' the world of the living and the world of the dead makes these spirits particularly vulnerable to the magician. These spirits could be compelled to return to the land of the living and bring harm to the living. Numerous curse tablets and magical papyri refer to the unburied, untimely, and violently dead as the spirits summoned to effect the curse.[80] These hauntings may only be checked if the deceased can overcome the obstacle preventing it from remaining in the underworld, by getting a proper burial or revenge on its murderer.

Plato makes use of this traditional idea of the restless dead who suffer because they cannot complete their transitions to Hades, but he tailors his description of the results of this failed transition to fit with his redefinition of the obstacles the soul faces and the solutions that are needed. For Plato, the unprepared soul cannot detach itself entirely from the body, but is linked by it to the realm of the visible instead of being able to dwell in the invisible realm of Hades. Socrates explains, "And one must suppose, my friend, that this element is ponderous, that it is heavy and earthy and is seen; and thus encumbered, such a soul is weighed down, and dragged back into the regions of the seen." The material weight of the soul that is mixed with corporeality draws it into the visible realm, and so this impure soul haunts graveyards as a ghost. "It roams among tombs and graves, so it is said, around which some shadowy phantoms

---

[78] Johnston examines the myths of the origins of these various monsters and concludes, "All of these *aitia* express the belief that child-killing demons have their origin in mortal women who failed to bear and nurture children successfully." (Johnston 1995, p. 368.) The story of Gello, as related by Zenobius explaining an expression used by Sappho, best illustrates the idea. "'Fonder of children than Gello' is a saying used of those who died prematurely, or of those who are fond of children but ruin them by their upbringing. For Gello was a virgin, and because she died prematurely, the Lesbians say that her ghost haunts little children, and they attribute premature deaths to her." Zenobius *Prov.* 3.3 = Sapph. frg. 178 Campbell, cited in Johnston 1995, p. 367. Deprived of the chance for children in life, Gello, like Lamia, Mormo, and other such spirits of the untimely dead, haunts the earth endlessly trying to make up her lack.

[79] cp. Cebes' reference to the fear of death being like the child's fear of the Mormolukeia (77e6–8).

[80] cp. the discussions in Johnston, 1994, pp. 138–139; Rohde 1925, Appendixes II, III, VI, VII, and XII, pp. 582–588, 590–595, 603–605.

of souls have actually been seen, such wraiths as soul of that kind afford, souls that have been released in no pure condition."[81] By alluding to the impure condition of the souls that must wander without entering Hades, Plato connects his idea of souls impure through mixing with the body to the traditional motifs of ghostly hauntings by souls impure through lack of burial or violent and untimely deaths. Plato's story of the fate of the soul that cannot depart from the land of the living thus produces the same result as the traditional stories, even though Plato has differently defined the obstacles that face them and the solutions they must employ.

Taking the traditional idea that the problematic dead are restless, reappearing in the land of the living as ghosts, Plato redefines what makes such dead problematic as well as the solutions for their problems. He uses the vivid images of ghosts to evoke this traditional pattern of action, this familiar story line. The philosophic care of the soul is assimilated to the funeral rituals that traditionally are effective at preventing the dreadful fate of the restless dead. Plato transforms the traditional motifs he uses to relate the traditional story of the journey of the soul to the land of the dead, crafting his own vivid images that both resonate with the tradition and fit precisely into the philosophical framework he has devised. The ghosts that linger around graveyards both evoke the traditional ghost stories and illustrate his idea of the mixture of body and soul, of visible and invisible. The unphilosophic person becomes the liminal figure of the ghost who cannot free himself from his mortal life, who presents a threat to the community through his disruption of the normal categories, while the philosopher is released from his mortal prison into the invisible world.

FINDING THE PATH IN THE UNDERWORLD

### Obstacle: Wandering Astray in Hades

"So the journey is not as Aeschylus' Telephus describes it: he says it is a simple (ἁπλῆ) path that leads to Hades, but to me it seems to be neither

---

[81] Ἐμβριθὲς δέ γε, ὦ φίλε, τοῦτο οἴεσθαι χρὴ εἶναι καὶ βαρὺ καὶ γεῶδες καὶ ὁρατόν· ὃ δὴ καὶ ἔχουσα ἡ τοιαύτη ψυχὴ βαρύνεταί τε καὶ ἕλκεται πάλιν εἰς τὸν ὁρατὸν τόπον φόβῳ τοῦ ἀιδοῦς τε καὶ Ἅιδου, ὥσπερ λέγεται, περὶ τὰ μνήματά τε καὶ τοὺς τάφους κυλινδουμένη, περὶ ἃ δὴ καὶ ὤφθη ἄττα ψυχῶν σκιοειδῆ φαντάσματα, οἷα παρέχονται αἱ τοιαῦται ψυχαὶ εἴδωλα, αἱ μὴ καθαρῶς ἀπολυθεῖσαι ἀλλὰ τοῦ ὁρατοῦ μετέχουσαι, διὸ καὶ ὁρῶνται (81c8-d3).

simple nor single."[82] Socrates describes the next obstacle facing the soul on its way to Hades as one version of the familiar motif of finding the way in the underworld, a choice among the multiple paths and forkings, the twists and turns on the road. This motif of many paths is explicitly borrowed by Plato from the tradition. "It probably has many forkings and branchings; I speak from the evidence of the rites and observances followed here," says Socrates.[83] The problem of finding one's way in the underworld confronted Dionysos in the *Frogs*, and the specific motif of the fork in the road to the other world appears in the gold tablets. The idea that the choice of paths represents a moral choice can be seen in the tellings of Hesiod and Parmenides and recurs in the tradition through Prodicus' fable of the Choice of Herakles and beyond.[84] Plato adapts both of these traditional motifs in his own version of the journey of the soul from the land of the living.

For, just as the soul is confronted after death with a multitude of paths by which to reach Hades, so too the soul is confronted in life with a multitude of sense impressions by which it tries to figure out the way to go in life. Throughout the dialogue, Plato plays off the contrast between the confusing multiplicity of the mortal world of the senses and the simple singleness connected with the world of Forms perceived not by

[82] ἔστι δὲ ἄρα ἡ πορεία οὐχ ὡς ὁ Αἰσχύλου Τήλεφος λέγει· ἐκεῖνος μὲν γὰρ ἁπλῆν οἶμόν φησιν εἰς Ἅιδου φέρειν, ἡ δ' οὔτε ἁπλῆ οὔτε μία φαίνεταί μοι εἶναι (107e4–108a2).

[83] νῦν δὲ ἔοικε σχίσεις τε καὶ τριόδους πολλὰς ἔχειν· ἀπὸ τῶν θυσιῶν τε καὶ νομίμων τῶν ἐνθάδε τεκμαιρόμενος λέγω (108a4–6) The MSS have περιόδους for τριόδους, which is found in Olympiodorus and Proclus, but the latter corresponds with the split in the road known from Plato's other two eschatological myths in the *Gorgias* and the *Republic*, the gold tablets, and the *Prooimion* of Parmenides, as well as the sacrificial spot sacred to Hekate. Some MSS have ὁσίων instead of θυσιῶν, but the sense is similar in either case. I cite the text from the TLG.

[84] Although there is no fork in the road, Aristophanes takes advantage of the wanderings of Xanthias and Dionysos to put different areas of the underworld on view to the audience. Tablet A4 implies a choice with its instruction to "keep to the right," while the long versions of the B series of tablets all imply the choice between the road leading to the first spring and that leading to the second (see above, pp. 49–51). Parmenides labels the roads as the paths of Being and Non-Being. cp. Hesiod *W&D*, 290–292; Prodicus in Xen. *Mem* 1.22. The crossroads in the afterlife appears in Plato's other eschatological myths as well. See also for this motif, Feyerabend 1984. Plato's audience might also think of the traditional tale of Theseus in the Minotaur's labyrinth, since finding the way through a bewildering set of paths is crucial to the hero's success in the story. Although Plato builds in several allusions to Theseus's journey to Crete and his salvation from danger, which might suggest the story, he does not seem to make explicit reference to the labyrinth in his discussions of the multiplicity of the phenomenal world.

the body's senses but by the mind. The Forms are μονοειδές, uniform in nature (cp. 78d5, 83e2), and the soul is similar to these in its uniformity (80b2). By contrast, the world of phenomena is full of a myriad different things, each of which presents itself to the senses as truly real. But sense impressions are never perfectly accurate; they always misrepresent reality. Socrates asks his interlocutors: "Do men ever find any truth in sight or hearing, or are even the poets forever telling us that we do not see or hear anything accurately?"[85] Despite the conflicting and contradictory evidence of the senses, however, the soul is always tempted to believe that the pleasures and pains its body experiences are clear and true, so it perceives a constantly different set of false realities before it, an ever-shifting set of paths to truth.[86] Like the soul faced with the choice of paths in the underworld, the living soul must choose how to proceed when confronted with this variety of options.

**Solution: Following the Guide on the Simple Path**

In the myth, Socrates supports his refutation of Aeschylus's simple path to Hades with an appeal to the idea of a daimonic guide. "For then there would be no need of guides; since no one, surely, could lose the way anywhere, if there were only a single road."[87] In Socrates' myth, the solution to the choice of paths is simply to follow the guide, for every soul has an appointed daimon that guides it to the realm of the dead.[88] This idea of a personal daimon that watches over each individual and guides his fate appears in the Greek mythic tradition before Plato, although its ultimate origin is unclear. "To every man when he is born," claims a character in a lost play of Menander, "a daimon is appointed straightaway as a myst-agogue for life." Lysias, in his *Epitaphios*, refers to the daimon allotted to each of us, and Heraclitus's famous dictum, ἦθος ἀνθρώπῳ δαίμων, "for

---

[85] 65b1–4 ἆρα ἔχει ἀλήθειάν τινα ὄψις τε καὶ ἀκοὴ τοῖς ἀνθρώποις, ἢ τά γε τοιαῦτα καὶ οἱ ποιηταὶ ἡμῖν ἀεὶ θρυλοῦσιν. ὅτι οὔτ' ἀκούομεν ἀκριβὲς οὐδὲν οὔτε ὁρῶμεν; The failure of sight and hearing shows *a fortiori* that the other senses must be even more deceptive.

[86] For the idea that particulars never in any way remain the same as themselves or in relation to each other, cp. 78d; cp. 83c.

[87] οὐδὲ γὰρ ἂν ἡγεμόνων ἔδει· οὐ γάρ πού τις ἂν διαμάρτοι οὐδαμόσε μιᾶς ὁδοῦ οὔσης (108a2–4).

[88] τελευτήσαντα ἕκαστον ὁ ἑκάστου δαίμων. ὅσπερ ζῶντα εἰλήχει, οὗτος ἄγειν ἐπιχειρεῖ εἰς δή τινα τόπον (107d6–7). Plato uses this idea in his myth in the *Republic*, with the crucial difference that in the *Republic*, the soul chooses the daimon rather than having the daimon allotted to him (*Rep.* 617e1).

a man, his character is his daimon," may refer to the same idea.[89] All the soul need do is follow this guide to Hades, for this divine entity can lead the soul down the correct path to its appointed place.

Plato uses the same language of guidance to describe the philosopher who is led by his reason to knowledge (εἰδέναι) of the unseen world (τὸ ἀιδές). Whoever makes use of reasoning (διανοία) alone, without becoming distracted by the false paths of sense perceptions, "will not that man reach reality,...if anyone does?"[90] The soul must guide the body, rather than vice versa, for the soul is more divine, and the divine is naturally appropriate to rule and guide (ἡγεμονεύειν) the mortal.[91] The reasoning of the mind alone can find a simple path (ἀτραπός) to the true reality of the unseen world, and Socrates describes to his companions how he now rejects all the confusing explanations of causes that are based on phenomena but clings simply (ἁπλῶς) to explanations based on the Forms.[92] The philosopher should follow his reason along the simple and single path to the unseen world (ἀιδές), just as the soul should follow its daimon along the path to Hades. Only by this solution can they overcome the obstacle of the choice among the multiple paths.

### Result: Soul Goes to Its Appointed Place without Wanderings

The failure to employ this simple solution results in a wandering soul which is unable to reach its place in the unseen world. Plato again makes use of traditional ideas of the restless dead to illustrate the fate of the unphilosophic soul. Not only could the mixture of the seen and unseen worlds in the impure soul result in visible ghosts who linger around their

---

[89] Menander, fr. 550 Kock ἅπαντι δαίμων ἀνδρὶ συμπαρίσταται εὐθὺς γενομένῳ μυσταγωγὸς τοῦ βίου. Note the use of the terminology of the Mysteries in the description of the daimon's role. Plutarch, in citing this fragment (*de tranq. anim.* 474b), also cites Empedokles (B122) for the idea that every person gets two daimons at birth. Lysias, *Epitaphios* 78. ὅ τε δαίμων ὁ τὴν ἡμετέραν μοῖραν εἰληχώς. Heraclitus fr. 119. The better known translation of 'character is fate' obscures the connection with the traditional idea of a personal daimon. Detienne 1963 attempts to trace the evolution of this notion of a daimon as a personal spirit within the Pythagorean tradition, but the pre-Platonic evidence is desperately slim and the post-Platonic evidence is, for the most part, late and highly suspect.

[90] ἆρ' οὐχ οὗτός ἐστιν, ὦ Σιμμία, εἴπερ τις [καὶ] ἄλλος ὁ τευξόμενος τοῦ ὄντος (66a7–8).

[91] 94e4–5, cp. the verb ἡγεμονεύειν in 94c7 and 10. 80a3–5 ἢ οὐ δοκεῖ σοι τὸ μὲν θεῖον οἷον ἄρχειν τε καὶ ἡγεμονεύειν πεφυκέναι.

[92] Κινδυνεύει τοι ὥσπερ ἀτραπός τις ἐκφέρειν ἡμᾶς 66b3. Socrates claims that he is confused (ταράττομαι) by explanations that something is beautiful because of brightness or color or shape, or anything but Beauty (100d).

graves, but these impure souls could roam restlessly about the world, unable to find their way to their final rest in Hades.[93] Again, this dreadful fate was not only lamentable for the deceased, but dangerous for the community, for the souls of the miserable untimely dead were thought to roam at night with the black daimons of Hekate, bringing terror and destruction in their wake.[94]

Plato describes the wanderings of the soul in terms of the contrast between the multiple and the simple. Like the soul in life that is governed by the body in the visible and mortal world, the impure soul faces after death a bewildering multitude of choices without an understanding of the correct simple and single path that will lead it to its destination, so it wanders lost among the multiplicity of turnings until its appointed daimon finally drags it away by force. "The soul in a state of desire for the body, as I said earlier, flutters around it for a long time, and around the region of the seen, and after much resistance and many sufferings it goes along, brought by force and against its will by the appointed spirit."[95] The souls that, due to lack of burial, untimely death, violent execution, or some other reason, have failed to sufficiently separate themselves from the body and the mortal realm resist the guidance of their appointed daimons and fail to find their way among the many paths. Only when forced finally to separate from the mortal world are they dragged to the place of judgement.

The description of the soul wandering lost among the many paths until dragged away by its daimon evokes the traditional motifs of crossroads,

[93] Euripides' chorus of Trojan women laments the fate of their husbands, left unburied after the sack of Troy; while in Euripides' *Hekabe*, the prologue is spoken by the ghost of Polydoros, whose body floats unburied on the sea waves. ὦ φίλος ὦ πόσι μοι, σὺ μὲν φθίμενος ἀλαίνεις ἄθαπτος ἄνυδρος, ἐμὲ δὲ πόντιον σκάφος ἄισσον πτεροῖσι πορεύσει ἱππόβοτον Ἄργος (1084ff.) "Dearest husband, dear lost ghost, Seas and worlds divide our ways; You, unwashed, unburied, Roam the shadowy spaces, I to Argos wing the sea with restless oars." Lattimore translation. cp. *Hekabe*, ll. 1–40.

[94] cp. Euripides, *Helen* 570; Hippocrates, *On the Sacred Disease*, vi, 362L; Trag. Incert. fr. 375 – εἴτ᾽ ἔνυπνον φάντασμα φοβῇ χθονίας θ᾽ Ἑκάτης κῶμον ἐδέξω. See Rohde 1925, pp. 593–595. cp. Lattimore 1962, p. 113, regarding Rohde's citation of Epig. Gr. p. 149. Johnston has argued that Homer's reference (*Od.* xx. 77–78) to the Pandareids wandering with the Erinyes after their untimely death before marriage means that "the Pandareids familiar to Homer's audience must have been imagined to belong to a vast army of other dead, miserable women who 'Devoured' and 'Frightened' the living." (Johnston 1994, p. 149.)

[95] ἡ δ᾽ ἐπιθυμητικῶς τοῦ σώματος ἔχουσα, ὅπερ ἐν τῷ ἔμπροσθεν εἶπον, περὶ ἐκεῖνο πολὺν χρόνον ἐπτοημένη καὶ περὶ τὸν ὁρατὸν τόπον, πολλὰ ἀντιτείνασα καὶ πολλὰ παθοῦσα, βίᾳ καὶ μόγις ὑπὸ τοῦ προστεταγμένου δαίμονος οἴχεται ἀγομένη (108a7–b3).

soul guides, and the restless dead, but it also provides a vivid illustration of the fate of the unphilosophic person bewildered by the multiplicity of the phenomenal world. The unphilosophic person becomes the liminal figure of the restless shade, who presents a threat to the community through his disruption of the normal categories, while the philosopher follows the guide of his more divine part past the perplexities that the phenomenal world presents.

The multiplicity of the phenomenal world that appears to the senses of the body bewilders the soul. "Whenever the soul sets about examining anything in company of the body, it is completely taken in by it."[96] Since the objects perceived by the bodily senses are multiple and inconstant, the soul is stunned by the variety of things it perceives: "It wanders and is confused and dizzy, as if drunk."[97] Plato uses the same word for confusion (ταράττειν) when Socrates describes the effect of explanations that do not rely on a simple hypothesis. Socrates claims that he is confused (ταράττομαι) by explanations that something is beautiful because of brightness or color or shape, or anything but Beauty (100d). Plato brings up this contrast between the confusion caused by multiple phenomena and the simple path to understanding when, in response to Simmias's admission that many things confuse him (πολλά με ταράττει), Socrates replies that, nevertheless, they agree simply (ἁπλῶς) that opposites can never become their opposites.[98] The simple, single, and uncomposite nature of the soul is thrown into confusion when confronted with the compound and complex phenomena of the world of the body. "Since by sharing opinions and pleasures with the body, it is, I believe, forced to become of like character and nurture to it, and to be incapable of entering Hades in purity; but it must always exit contaminated by the body."[99] This contamination of the

---

[96] ὅταν μὲν γάρ μετὰ τοῦ σώματος ἐπιχειρῇ τι σκοπεῖν, δῆλον ὅτι τότε ἐξαπατᾶται ὑπ'αὐτοῦ (65b9–11).

[97] αὐτὴ πλανᾶται καὶ ταράττεται καὶ εἰλιγγιᾷ ὥσπερ μεθύουσα. (79c6–8, cp. 66a5 ὡς ταράττοντος καὶ οὐκ ἐῶντος τὴν ψυχὴν κτήσασθαι ἀλήθειάν τε καὶ φρόνησιν ὅταν κοινωνῇ; 66d5 ἐν ταῖς ζητήσεσιν αὖ πανταχοῦ παραπῖπτον θόρυβον παρέχει καὶ ταραχὴν καὶ ἐκπλήττει, ὥστε μὴ δύνασθαι ὑπ'αὐτοῦ καθορᾶν τἀληθές.) cp. Johnston 1999, p. 145, n. 65 on the use of this verb in describing the madness brought on by angry ghosts.

[98] cp. also Socrates' assertion that the prohibition of suicide in the mysteries is the only thing that applies simply, without exception, to every mortal. τοῦτο μόνον τῶν ἄλλων ἁπάντων ἁπλοῦν ἐστιν (62a2–3).

[99] ἐκ γὰρ τοῦ ὁμοδοξεῖν τῷ σώματι καὶ τοῖς αὐτοῖς χαίρειν ἀναγκάζεται οἶμαι ὁμότροπός τε καὶ ὁμότροφος γίγνεσθαι καὶ οἷα μηδέποτε εἰς Ἅιδου καθαρῶς ἀφικέσθαι, ἀλλὰ ἀεὶ τοῦ σώματος ἀναπλέα ἐξιέναι (83d6–10).

soul by the body is expressed by the term, ἀναπλέα, compounded – not simple. Again, the soul that has become too mixed into the living world is not simple but compounded, a thing of multiplicity, because it tries to pursue the multiple paths presented by senses. Perplexed, it wanders through the world, following first one impulse and then another, until it suddenly is forced reluctantly into the unseen world by death.

The philosopher, by contrast, has engaged in the proper preparation for death (μελέτη θανάτου). Prepared by a life of philosophy, the philosopher is accustomed to perceiving the unseen world and to obeying his more divine part. "Now the wise and well-ordered soul follows along, and is not unfamiliar with what befalls it."[100] In life, his body is guided by his soul (cp. 80a1–4; 94c8–de4); after death, his soul is guided by the semi-divine daimon and accompanied in his journey by other divine beings. "The soul that has passed through life with purity and moderation finds gods for traveling companions and guides."[101] Whereas the impure soul resists the guidance of its daimon and wanders blindly amid the many paths, the pure soul obeys its daimon and is led straightway to the proper place.

Plato's myth of the fate of the souls of the impure and the pure after death corresponds perfectly to his description of the souls of the un-philosophic and the philosophic during life and makes clever use of the oppositions of visible/invisible and multiple/simple that have shaped the dialectic argument. In addition to making use of the word play of ἀιδές to play off the idea of the unseen spirit becoming visible as a ghost in the first narrative crux, Plato toys with the derivation from εἰδέναι in this narrative crux to bring in the traditional idea of the daimonic guide. Just as the soul of the unphilosophic in life is bewildered by the multiplicity perceived through the senses and wanders lost and in torment, paying no heed to the more divine part of itself that should be its guide, so too the impure soul after death wanders lost amid the multiple paths, unheeding of its guide. Finally, just as the unphilosophic person is wrenched from the world of the living by the physical fact of death, so too the impure soul is finally dragged by force to the realm of the dead, where judgement awaits. The philosopher, on the other hand, who sought the simple and single world of the invisible and was guided by his soul's reasoning, follows his guide after death down the proper path.

---

[100] ἡ μὲν οὖν κοσμία τε καὶ φρόνιμος ψυχὴ ἕπεταί τε καὶ οὐκ ἀγνοεῖ τὰ παρόντα· (108a6–7).
[101] ἡ δὲ καθαρῶς τε καὶ μετρίως τὸν βίον διεξελθοῦσα. καὶ συνεμπόρων καὶ ἡγεμόνων θεῶν τυχοῦσα (108c3–5).

Plato manipulates the traditional mythic idea of finding one's way in the underworld to illustrate his argument for the philosophic life. He tweaks the description of the traditional obstacle and result to fit with his descriptions of the experiences of the unphilosophic in the dialectic, while he substitutes another traditional motif, the guiding daimon, as the solution to the obstacle of the choice of paths. He evokes the traditional category of the restless dead who cannot make their way to Hades, but transforms their miserable wanderings into the bewildered wanderings of the unphilosphic confused by the multiplicity of the phenomenal world. The daimon who shapes an individual's destiny becomes the guiding principle of reason for the soul, the divine connection between the mortal person and the divine realm of the unseen true reality.[102] Plato uses this narrative crux of the soul finding its way to Hades to reinforce and illustrate the arguments about how the philosopher should live by means of the familiar and authoritative mythic elements.

## CONFRONTATION WITH THE POWERS OF THE UNDERWORLD

The final obstacle that the deceased faces in the myth of the journey to the underworld in the *Phaedo* is the judgement of the dead, which determines whether the deceased receives a favorable or unpleasant afterlife. This idea of a judgement of the dead as an obstacle for the deceased departing from the land of the living is found in the Greek mythic tradition, both explicitly and implicitly through the idea of differentiated lots in the afterlife. Plato borrows this idea of a process of judgement which the

---

[102] The Neoplatonic commentators, who spent a great deal of time and energy exploring the concept of daimons, disagreed vigorously on how to interpret this daimon. Plotinus saw the daimon as a part of the soul, which served as the guiding principle after death and was always one metaphysical level higher than the dominant principle during life. Thus, the philosopher ruled by his reason would have a divine guide after death, while someone guided by his appetites would find a rational guide after death. Proclus protested that making the daimon part of the soul "is excessively to admire the life of men" and neglects the superiority of these daimons to the parts and faculties of the soul. He also opposed the Stoic view that daimon is simply the individual intellect. "The guardian spirit alone moves, controls and orders all our affairs, since it perfects the reason, moderates the emotions, infuses nature, maintains the body, supplies accidentals, fulfils the decree of fate and bestows the gifts of providence; and this one being is ruler of all that lies in us and concerns us, steering our whole life." (Proclus on *Alcibiades* I, 78.) The later Platonic discussions of the daimon can be found in Plotinus III.4; Damascius on *Phaedo* I 477–86, II 94–101; Proclus 67.19–83.16 and Olympiodorus 15.5–2014 on *Alcibiades* I (103a5–6).

deceased must undergo, but he assimilates philosophic activity to the traditional solutions for receiving a favorable judgement – heroic activity, virtuous living, and special service to the gods through sacrifices and initiations. Plato employs as solutions to this obstacle the same activities of the philosophic life that he uses as solutions to the obstacles of the soul separating from the body and finding its way to Hades. Plato also transforms the names and descriptions of the possible afterlives familiar from the tradition in his own complex myth. The myth describes a hierarchically organized series of worlds, ranging from most impure to most pure and from lowest to highest, and it includes a system of punishment and reward in the afterlife that corresponds to the activities of the unphilosophic and philosophic in life.

### Obstacle: The Judgement of the Soul

Very little evidence survives from before Plato of the traditional idea of the judgement of the dead, yet there are sufficient indicators that the idea was neither simply a fringe religious idea nor an invention of Plato's. The concept of differentiated lots for the dead does appear as early as Homer, in the famous punishments of Tantalus, Tityus, Sisyphus in *Odyssey* xi (576ff.). In the *Iliad*, oathbreakers are tormented by the Furies underground after death (III.278; XIX.259), but this punishment seems to be the result of a specific curse rather than of a general judgement on a person's whole life. Plato attests to a well-known idea of punishment for misdeeds in the afterlife when his Cephalus describes how an old man near the point of death begins to wonder if there is any truth in the old "tales that are told of the world below and how the men who have done wrong here must pay the penalty there."[103] Some sort of judgement is implied in the concept of different lots in the afterlife for different types of dead, since some authority must decide the fate of each deceased. However, elaborate descriptions of the judgement process itself imply a deeper concern with the exact nature of divine justice and its relation to justice, or the lack thereof, in human life. The first references to an actual process of judgement come

---

[103] οἵ τε γὰρ λεγόμενοι μῦθοι περὶ τῶν ἐν ῞Αιδου, ὡς τὸν ἐνθάδε ἀδικήσαντα δεῖ ἐκεῖ διδόναι δίκην (*Rep.* 330d). Democritus (199, 297) alludes to this same kind of fear, and such an idea is mentioned in a speech attributed to Demosthenes ([Dem] 25.52). Polygnotus' painting, described in Pausanias, provides the earliest picture of an afterlife that includes specific punishments for more than the few exceptional transgressors, but the actual judgement is not depicted there. (Pausanias, X.28.2.)

in Pindar's *Second Olympian*, where the "wicked souls straightway pay the penalty and some judge beneath the earth judges the crimes committed in this realm of Zeus, having delivered the strict account in accord with the harsh order of things."[104] A judgement after death appears in the tradition before Plato as something the departing soul must fear, an obstacle on his path to a happy existence in the afterlife. Dodds argues that the notion of a judgement may have been part of the Eleusinian Mysteries, which would have made it a familiar idea in Athenian tradition of Plato's time, even if it was not as well-known elsewhere.[105] Whether or not it was Eleusinian doctrine, the idea of a judgement in the afterlife was part of the mythic tradition familiar to Plato and his audience, with which Plato could work to create his own picture of the soul's journey to the realm of the dead.

In contrast to his eschatological myths in the *Gorgias* and the *Republic*, Plato does not elaborate on the process of judgement in the myth of the *Phaedo*. The place of judgement is not described; it is simply "the place to which the daimon has conducted him."[106] While the references to the τριόδοι among which the soul wanders (108a4) recall the descriptions of the place of judgement in the *Gorgias* and the *Republic*, this motif of a fork in the road is not employed to describe the place of judgement itself, but this traditional idea is instead used to elaborate on the fate of the impure soul after death as it tries to depart from the world of the living. The lack

---

[104] αὐτίκ᾽ ἀπάλαμνοι φρένες ποινὰς ἔτεισαν, τὰ δ᾽ ἐν τᾷδε Διὸς ἀρχᾷ ἀλιτρὰ κατὰ γᾶς δικάζει τις ἐχθρᾷ λόγον φράσαις ἀνάγκᾳ. Pindar, O. II. 57–60. Long discusses the problems with the interpretation of this passage that scholars have disputed since antiquity, involving when and where the soul pays the penalty. (Long 1948, pp. 30–37.) Although the judge is unspecified in Pindar, Aeschylus makes Hades the judge of mortals when they come to his realm. μέγας γὰρ ῞Αιδης ἐστὶν εὔθυνος βροτῶν ἔνερθε χθονός. "Hades calls men to reckoning there under the ground." (*Eumenides* 273–4) In the *Suppliants*, this judge is referred to as κἀκεῖ δικάζει τἀμπλακήμαθ᾽, ὡς λόγος, Ζεὺς ἄλλος ἐν καμοῦσιν ὑστάτας δίκας. "Another Zeus among the dead [who] works out their final punishment." (*Suppliants* 230–231, Lattimore translation.)

[105] Dodds suggests that the fact that Plato has Socrates name Triptolemus as one of the judges in the afterlife (*Apology*, 41a) points to an Eleusinian connection, as does the fact that Plato refers to this idea of judgement in the *Laws* as part of the πάτριος νόμος (*Laws* 959b4). Plato also refers to the idea of a judgement as a παλαιός τε καὶ ἱερὸς λόγος at *Seventh Letter* 335a3. cp. Dodds 1959, p. 374. Diodorus Siculus attributes the idea to Orpheus (I.92.3), which may also refer back to Eleusis, since the rites there were sometimes attributed to Orpheus or his son. cp. Graf 1974, pp. 22–39. In any case, the doctrine of a differentiated afterlife is mentioned in the *Homeric Hymn to Demeter* 480–482, although the process of judgement is not specified.

[106] τὸν τόπον οἷ ὁ δαίμων ἕκαστον κομίζει (113d2).

of description of the place of judgement stands in stark contrast to the abundance of description of the various realms to which the soul goes as a result of its judgement.

Since the focus is on the location of the soul after judgement rather than on the process, the judges are likewise anonymous.[107] To elaborate on their identity and nature in this myth as he does in the *Gorgias* would be to draw focus away from the central idea: the ways in which the philosophic mode of life creates a blissful existence in contrast to the wretched life of the unphilosophic. Whereas the *Gorgias* myth's depiction of the process of elenchos and conversion to philosophy suits the anti-philosophic interlocutors like Callicles, the myth in the *Phaedo* is addressed to Socrates' friends who need to be reassured of the value of the philosophic life. The process of judgement, the obstacle facing the soul, is less important for Plato's purpose here than the solutions to this obstacle that the soul must employ – the practices of the philosophic life.

### Solutions: Heroic Deeds, Virtue, Relations with the Gods, and Philosophy

The mythic tradition supplied a variety of solutions to the problem of obtaining a favorable afterlife. Traditional solutions that might bring about a positive judgement include performing heroic deeds, refraining from injustice, and forming a special relation, by sacrifice, initiation, or other special connection, with certain gods who might intervene on behalf of the deceased. The earliest example comes from the *Odyssey*, in which Menelaus is promised a blissful existence in Elysium (iv. 563–4). The reason for the preferential treatment is one of the oldest and most fundamental in any social system, personal connections. Menelaus, in Homer's tale, receives a better lot than even Achilles, simply because he made the right marriage and joined the family of the gods.[108] In later

---

[107] cp. Olympiodorus's comment that, of the three *nekyiai*, the one in the *Phaedo* is about the places, the one in the *Gorgias* about those judging, and the one in the *Republic* about those being judged. τριῶν δὲ οὐσῶν νεκυιῶν . . . ἥδε μὲν περὶ τῶν τόπων μᾶλλον ποιεῖται τὸν λόγον, ἡ δὲ ἐν Γοργίᾳ περὶ τῶν δικαζόντων, ἡ δὲ ἐν Πολιτείᾳ περὶ τῶν δικαζομένων (Norvin 228, 25f). The process in the *Phaedo* is described in the passive as something the souls undergo, without a mention of who is doing the judging. cp. διαδικασαμένους (107d8) and διεδικάσαντο (113d3). Only once are the anonymous judges referred to, αὕτη γὰρ ἡ δίκη ὑπὸ τῶν δικαστῶν αὐτοῖς ἐτάχθη (114b5–6).

[108] "This, because Helen is yours and you are son-in-law therefore to Zeus." οὕνεκ' ἔχεις Ἑλένην καί σφιν γαμβρὸς Διός ἐσσι (iv. 570).

versions, Achilles is among the first to be moved from Homer's bleak Hades on the strength of his own divine connections. His mother, Thetis, brings him to the Isles of the Blessed, just as the divine Eos brings her son, Memnon.[109] The power of the claim to divine connections emerges again in the gold tablets, where the deceased's boast, "I claim to be of your blessed race," serves as her passport into the favor of Persephone.[110] In death, as in life, a family connection with the authorities was often the best solution for securing a favorable judgement.

However, it was not the fact that Achilles' claim to divine lineage was as good as Menelaus's that inspired the poets of the tradition to place him in the Blessed Isle, but rather a sense that he should receive some reward for his heroic valor. The heroes of Hesiod's semi-divine fourth race go to the Isles of the Blessed as a result of their valiant deeds in the battles of epic.[111] While Hesiod speaks in general terms, later authors named specific heroes worthy of an afterlife on the Blessed Isles. Not surprisingly, the two greatest Greek heroes of the *Iliad*, Achilles and Diomedes, are the earliest to be named.[112] But heroic deeds worthy of a favorable afterlife need not be deeds of epic; a sixth century drinking song places Harmodios in the company of Diomedes and Achilles on the Blessed Isles, "Dear Harmodios, surely you have not perished. No, they say, you live in the blessed islands where Achilles the swift of foot, and Tydeus' son, Diomedes, are said to have gone."[113] The assassination of Hipparchus ranked, at least for some, with the epic heroism of Diomedes and Achilles, and such heroic deeds sufficed for admission to a better place after the mortal life was over.

Heroic deeds of valor, however, were not the only means by which one could win a better afterlife. For some, the deeds that induced the gods to

---

[109] Apparently recounted in the *Aithiopis*, according to Proclus's summary, p. 69 PEG. Aeschylus wrote a trilogy of plays concerning the deaths of Memnon and Achilles, which apparently involved interventions by the divine mothers, but the plays are lost. cp. Gantz 1993, pp. 37, 623–624.

[110] A1. In the B series of tablets, the claim, "I am the child of Earth and starry Heaven," provides the same kind of link to the divine family. See above, ch. 2, pp. 75–82.

[111] *W&D* 167ff.

[112] cp. Ibycus 291 = Simonides 558, where the scholiast records that, in Ibycus and Simonides, Achilles goes to Elysium and is paired with Medea (of all people!). cp. Pindar *Nem.* 10.7, who mentions Diomedes, and Hellanikos (4F19) who puts the otherwise unknown Lykos, son of Poseidon, on the Blessed Isles.

[113] φίλταθ' Ἁρμόδι', οὔ τί που τέθνηκας, νήσοις δ' ἐν μακάρων σέ φασιν εἶναι, ἵνα περ ποδώκης Ἀχιλεὺς Τυδείδην τέ φασιν Διομήδεα. Carm. Conv. 894 = Diehl 10 = Lattimore 1 (Lattimore trans.).

grant a favorable life after death were not necessarily those of epic battle, but simply refraining from deeds of great injustice. Pindar describes the favorable afterlife granted to the good (ἐσλοί), those who have refrained from breaking oaths. If, for three cycles of reincarnation, they can keep their souls from any injustice (ἀπὸ πάμπαν ἀδίκων ἔχειν ψυχάν), they are sent along the road of Zeus to the tower of Kronos on the Isles of the Blessed.[114] Rather than any sort of positive good or just deed, it is the absence of unjust deeds that provides the key to a favorable afterlife in Pindar.

If the individual lacked heroic deeds or doubted his ability to win a favorable judgement simply because he had refrained from the more spectacular forms of injustice, the Greek religious tradition provided another solution for obtaining a happy afterlife. One who made special sacrifices to the gods or who dedicated himself to the gods in an initiation created a special connection with the god that not only entitled him to special treatment in life, but also could win him a favorable afterlife.[115] The *Hymn to Demeter* proclaims, "Blessed is he among men on earth who has seen these mysteries; but he who is uninitiate and who has no part in them, never has lot of like good things once he is dead, down in the darkness and gloom."[116] The crucial qualification for a good afterlife, in this idea, is the initiation. Any injustice or wrongdoing is purged away by the initiation, while no amount of other good deeds could make up for the lack of it. The initiation, with its rituals of purification and special sacrifices, establishes a relation between the mortal and the deity that entitles the mortal to special treatment. "Tell Persephone that Bacchios himself has released you," say the Pelinna tablets.[117] Dionysos intervenes on behalf of his special servants, just as Persephone is willing to grant favorable treatment to those who have become initiated in the Mysteries

---

[114] ἑκατέρωθι μείναντες ἀπὸ πάμπαν ἀδίκων ἔχειν ψυχάν, ἔτειλαν Διὸς ὁδὸν παρὰ Κρόνου τύρσιν· ἔνθα μακάρων νᾶσον ὠκεανίδες αὖραι περιπνέοισιν· ἄνθεμα δὲ χρυσοῦ φλέγει, τὰ μὲν χερσόθεν ἀπ᾽ ἀγλαῶν δενδρέων, ὕδωρ δ᾽ ἄλλα φέρβει, ὅρμοισι τῶν χέρας ἀναπλέκοντι καὶ στεφάνους βουλαῖς ἐν ὀρθαῖσι Ῥαδαμάνθυος, ὃν πατὴρ ἔχει μέγας ἑτοῖμον αὐτῷ πάρεδρον, πόσις ὁ πάντων Ῥέας. Pindar *Olympian* II, 63–73. The Hesiodic Isles of the Blessed are also ruled by Kronos, cp. *W&D* 173.

[115] cp. the standard *do ut des* formula in prayers; the mortal creates a relationship with the god that predisposes the god to help and protect him. cp. Burkert 1987, pp. 13–15, on the relation between benefits for the mortal world and benefits expected in the afterlife.

[116] ὄλβιος ὃς τάδ᾽ ὄπωπεν ἐπιχθονίων ἀνθρώπων· ὃς δ᾽ ἀτελὴς ἱερῶν, ὅς τ᾽ ἄμμορος, οὔ ποθ᾽ ὁμοίων αἶσαν ἔχει φθίμενός περ ὑπὸ ζόφῳ εὐρώεντι. *Homeric Hymn to Demeter*, 480–482. cp. Pindar fr. 137 and Sophocles fr. 837.

[117] εἰπεῖν Φερσεφόναι σ᾽ ὅτι Β⟨άκ⟩χιος αὐτὸς ἔλυσε. P1.2.

dedicated to her at Eleusis.[118] Establishing such a relation with the deity, be it Dionysos, Persephone, or even Apollo, is a matter of piety, of good behavior; to neglect which is impious.[119]

The uninitiate are depicted as suffering in the afterlife as early as Polygnotus's painting, where women trying to carry water in sieves are labeled 'the uninitiate.'[120] The same punishment, according to Adeimantus in the *Republic*, is reserved for the impious in the afterlife by Musaeus and his son.[121] However, Adeimantus complains that the traditional idea, found in Homer, that the gods can be moved by sacrifice, has been perverted to mean that the gods can be persuaded to treat favorably even one who has committed great crimes, if the criminal makes large enough sacrifices or goes through the right sort of rituals.[122] Rather than the initiation being a sign of piety and a good character, it becomes a replacement for it. While Plato is undoubtedly stretching the argument to an extreme in his critique of the traditional ideas of justice, the idea of winning a favorable afterlife through sacrifices and rituals of initiation was undoubtedly present in the tradition, showing up not just in the countercultural Orphic rituals Adeimantus treats so harshly, but even in the respectable and mainstream Eleusinian Mysteries.

Plato adapts a number of these ideas from the tradition in creating his own solution for obtaining a favorable afterlife, the practice of philosophy. "It seems likely to me that a man who has truly spent his life in philosophy feels confident when about to die, and is hopeful that, when he has died, he will win very great benefits in the other world."[123] Philosophy is depicted not as the useless pursuit of strange old men who corrupt the youth of

---

[118] As Aidoneus tells Persephone, "And while you are here, you shall rule all that lives and moves and shall have the greatest rights among the deathless gods: those who defraud you and do not appease your power with offerings, reverently performing rites and paying fit gifts, shall be punished for evermore." ἔνθα δ᾽ ἐοῦσα δεσπόσσεις πάντων ὁπόσα ζώει τε καὶ ἕρπει, τιμὰς δὲ σχήσησθα μετ᾽ ἀθανάτοισι μεγίστας, τῶν δ᾽ ἀδικησάντων τίσις ἔσσεται ἤματα πάντα οἵ κεν μὴ θυσίαισι τεὸν μένος ἱλάσκωνται εὐαγέως ἔρδοντες ἐναίσιμα δῶρα τελοῦντες. *Homeric Hymn to Demeter*, 364–369.

[119] Aristophanes jokingly notes the importance of initiation in the *Peace*, "For I must be initiated before I die." δεῖ γὰρ μυηθῆναί με πρὶν τεθνηκέναι (*Peace*, 371).

[120] Pausanias X.31.9–11. cp. *Gorgias* 493bc.

[121] *Republic*, 363d. At 533c dialectic draws the soul out of the mire. cp., Aristophanes, *Frogs* 145.

[122] *Republic* 363c–366b, citing Homer *Iliad* IX.497ff. and referring to the books and rituals of Orpheus, Musaeus, and his son.

[123] μοι φαίνεται εἰκότως ἀνὴρ τῷ ὄντι ἐν φιλοσοφίᾳ διατρίψας τὸν βίον θαρρεῖν μέλλων ἀποθανεῖσθαι καὶ εὔελπις εἶναι ἐκεῖ μέγιστα οἴσεσθαι ἀγαθὰ ἐπειδὰν τελευτήσῃ (63e9–64a2).

Athens, but as a heroic action and the truest kind of virtuous behavior. Moreover, Plato portrays philosophy as a kind of initiation ritual that purifies and establishes a special relation between the philosopher and the gods. Plato assimilates philosophy to all of the familiar solutions found in the tradition, replacing the need for heroic deeds, traditional justice, and initiations with his own solution to the obstacle of a post-mortem judgement.

Through Plato's use of the mythic images, the philosophic debate becomes an epic battle, and the philosophers become the heroes performing valiant exploits. Socrates explicitly likens the interlocutors to Homeric heroes in battle when he says, "It is our task to come to close quarters in the Homeric fashion and test the validity of your contention."[124] Plato assimilates philosophic activity to the deeds of the heroes with his reference to the labors of Herakles in the *Phaedo*. When Simmias and Cebes both raise objections to Socrates' argument, Socrates and Phaedo liken themselves to Herakles and his companion Iolaus, battling the multiple heads of the Hydra.[125] The great deeds of philosophy, like the feats of the epic heroes, may be the key to an afterlife better than that granted to the undistinguished.

While Plato has Socrates explicitly liken himself and the interlocutors to Herakles and the Homeric heroes, he also sets the dialogue in such a way as to assimilate his philosophic hero, Socrates, with two other traditional mythic heroes, Theseus and Odysseus. The story of Theseus's journey to Crete, his slaying of the Minotaur, and his saving of the Athenian youths who are his companions is brought up at the beginning of the

---

[124] ἡμεῖς δὲ Ὁμηρικῶς ἐγγὺς ἰόντες πειρώμεθα εἰ ἄρα τι λέγεις (95b7–8).

[125] "If I were you and the argument got away from me, I should swear an oath, like the Argives, not to grow my hair again till I'd fought back and defeated the argument of Simmias and Cebes in a return battle. But, I said, even Herakles is said to have been no match for two. Then summon me as your Iolaus, he said, while there's still light." καὶ ἔγωγ' ἄν, εἰ σὺ εἴην καί με διαφεύγοι ὁ λόγος, ἔνορκον ἂν ποιησαίμην ὥσπερ Ἀργεῖοι, μὴ πρότερον κομήσειν, πρὶν ἂν νικήσω ἀναμαχόμενος τὸν Σιμμίου τε καὶ Κέβητος λόγον. Ἀλλ', ἦν δ' ἐγώ, πρὸς δύο λέγεται οὐδ' ὁ Ἡρακλῆς οἷός τε εἶναι. Ἀλλὰ καὶ ἐμέ, ἔφη, τὸν Ἰόλεων παρακάλει, ἕως ἔτι φῶς ἐστιν. The reference is to Herakles' battle with the Lernaean Hydra, which was complicated by the appearance of a giant crab, sent by Hera to distract him. Plato elaborates on the reference in the *Euthydemus* 297c, where the monstrous opponents are likened to visiting sophists. τοῦ Ἡρακλέους, ὃς οὐχ οἷός τε ἦν τῇ τε ὕδρᾳ διαμάχεσθαι... καὶ καρκίνῳ τινὶ... ἐκ θαλάττης ἀφιγμένῳ... ὃς ἐπειδὴ αὐτὸν ἐλύπει οὕτως ἐκ τοῦ ἐπ' ἀριστερὰ .. δάκνων, τὸν Ἰόλεων τὸν ἀδελφιδοῦν βοηθὸν ἐπεκαλέσατο. ὁ δὲ αὐτῷ ἱκανῶς ἐβοήθησεν. The story of the Argives is related in Hdt. I, 82.

dialogue, for it is in celebration of this heroic deed that the Athenians send a ship to Delos each year. While the ship is on its sacred mission, no executions may take place in the city, a ritual observance which causes the delay in Socrates' execution and permits the dialogue to take place. By alluding to this myth as the background for the dialogue, Plato brings up the parallel of the actions of Theseus, who made his way through a bewildering labyrinth to deliver his companions from the Minotaur and the life of Socrates, who, by means of philosophy, makes his way through the bewildering world of sense perception and helps deliver his companions.[126]

While Plato develops the idea of Odysseus as a philosophic hero in the *Republic*, a few references in the *Phaedo* suggest that Odysseus serves as a model in this dialogue as well. Socrates quotes Odysseus disciplining his appetites as a model of the soul governing the body.[127] Moreover, Plato employs two images that seem to create a parallel between Odysseus's voyages and the process of philosophic inquiry. Simmias refers to the process of choosing the best hypothesis available in the absence of a certain and divinely revealed truth, "and take it as a raft on which to

---

[126] The identification between Theseus and Socrates and other correspondences between the dialogue and the myth should not be pressed too hard. While the list of fourteen (depending on how one counts) companions with Socrates in prison *may* have been intended to recall the fourteen companions of Theseus, to claim, as Burger does, that the seven native Athenians and two other native Athenians listed, plus the five non-Athenians, correspond to the seven youths and five maidens along with the two youths disguised as maidens that appear in Plutarch's version of the story is an exercise in creative ingenuity that adds nothing to the interpretation of the text. The substitution of two youths for maidens does not appear before Plutarch, who introduces it not in the context of Theseus's journey to Crete, but rather in his description of the Oschophoria ritual said to be founded by Theseus. This explanation of why the youths in the Oschophoria procession wear women's garments seems most likely to be a later explanation for the element of cross-dressing that often appears in the initiation rites of young men. Burger goes even further, identifying Phaedo as Socrates' Ariadne (instead of his Iolaus, as the passage she cites explicitly says) and linking the Minotaur with the *mormolukos* that is the fear of death. Such identifications strain the text, ignoring the context in which Plato introduces the ideas of a helper and a fearsome monster. The former clearly is part of the identification with Herakles, while the latter is part of the identification of philosophy with charms and incantations, in this case the kind of magic used by old nurses to keep the fear of monsters from children. (Burger 1984, pp. 19-20.)

[127] 94de, quoting *Odyssey* xx.17-18. In the myth in the *Republic* (620cd), Odysseus is the only one in the lottery of souls to make a prudent choice of a new life. Although he picks late, he chooses the life of an ordinary man who minds his own business, and he proclaims that such would have been his choice even if he had had first pick.

accomplish the dangerous voyage of life."[128] The allusion seems to be to the raft on which Odysseus embarked from Calypso's isle (*Od.* v. 232–281). Socrates describes his search for the truth about the universe after his disappointment with the theories of the physicists and their inability to reveal the role of the Good and the divine order in the cosmos as a δεύτερος πλοῦς, a second voyage.[129] Eustathius, in his commentary on the *Odyssey*, explains this proverb as a reference to taking to oars when the wind fails, i.e., slower and more laborious form of travel in default of the swifter and easier.[130] Philosophical dialectic is this slower and more laborious journey, employed by the philosopher in his odyssey toward the truth in lieu of some direct divine revelation.[131]

The figures of Theseus and Odysseus appear in the background of the dialogue, subtly bringing up the parallel between the heroic action of Socrates in his philosophic quest and the traditional heroic deeds of these epic heroes. It is perhaps not coincidental that both of these heroes, like Herakles to whom Socrates is explicitly compared, are among the few in the Greek mythic tradition who numbered among their exploits a journey to the realm of the dead. In comparing the philosophic activity of Socrates to the deeds of these heroes, Plato puts Socrates, about to embark on his own journey to the underworld, on a par with the great heroes of the mythic tradition.

Plato not only depicts philosophy as heroic action of the kind that traditionally brings a favorable afterlife to the heroes of epic, but he also argues that it is in the truest sense good, moral behavior - a positive virtue in contrast to the avoidance of injustice traditionally required for a favorable judgement. All other types of virtuous behavior are impure in comparison to philosophic activity, for they are centered on the body rather than the soul. These virtues are alien adornments (τοὺς κόσμους ἀλλοτρίους) in contrast to the true and proper beauties of the philosophically

---

[128] ἐπὶ τούτου ὀχούμενον ὥσπερ ἐπὶ σχεδίας κινδυνεύοντα διαπλεῦσαι τὸν βίον (85d1–2).

[129] ἐπειδὴ δὲ ταύτης ἐστερήθην καὶ οὔτ' αὐτὸς εὑρεῖν οὔτε παρ' ἄλλου μαθεῖν οἷός τε ἐγενόμην, τὸν δεύτερον πλοῦν ἐπὶ τὴν τῆς αἰτίας ζήτησιν ᾗ πεπραγμάτευμαι (99c6–d1).

[130] Eustathius 1453.20 δεύτερος πλοῦς λέγεται, ὅτε ἀποτυχών τις οὐρίου κώπαις πλέει. cp. 661.43 ὁ τῶν κωπηλατούντων πλοῦς δεύτερος λέγεται πλοῦς, ὡς πρώτου ὄντος τοῦ πλέειν πρὸς ἄνεμον.

[131] Again, the parallel should not be pushed too hard. Gilead 1994 discusses "Plato's Mental Odyssey," in the second chapter of his *The Platonic Odyssey*, bringing in parallels ranging from Sophocles and Parmenides to Freud, Joyce, and Proust. Such parallels do show the great potential that such an image of life as a voyage contains, but do little to explicate the way Plato uses it in the *Phaedo* specifically.

virtuous soul.[132] Socrates argues that what are commonly known as bravery and temperance are merely a certain kind of fear and self-indulgence, since people are brave through fear of something worse or moderate in some pleasures through desire for other pleasures. Only philosophers, he claims, are truly brave and temperate in their lifelong quest for true reality, since they alone realize that the pains and pleasures feared and desired by others are illusory in comparison with the true reality. "But, as for their being parted from wisdom and exchanged for one another, goodness of that sort may be a kind of illusory facade, and fit for slaves indeed, and may have nothing true or healthy about it; whereas, truth to tell, temperance, justice, and bravery may in fact be a kind of purification of all such things, and wisdom itself a kind of purifying rite."[133]

Plato thus likens philosophy not only to the virtuous behavior that was one traditional solution to the judgement but also to a purificatory ritual of initiation, a τελετή, that makes the philosopher worthy of a favorable afterlife.

So it really looks as if those who established our initiations are no mean people, but have in fact long been saying in riddles that whoever arrives in Hades unadmitted to the rites, and uninitiated, shall lie in the slough, while he who arrives there purified and initiated shall dwell with the gods. For truly there are, so say those concerned with the initiations, "many who bear the wand, but few who are *bacchoi*." Now these latter, in my view, are none other than those who have practised philosophy aright.[134]

---

[132] ἀλλὰ τούτων δὴ ἕνεκα θαρρεῖν χρὴ περὶ τῇ ἑαυτοῦ ψυχῇ ἄνδρα ὅστις ἐν τῷ βίῳ τὰς μὲν ἄλλας ἡδονὰς τὰς περὶ τὸ σῶμα καὶ τοὺς κόσμους εἴασε χαίρειν, ὡς ἀλλοτρίους τε ὄντας, καὶ πλέον θάτερον ἡγησάμενος ἀπεργάζεσθαι, τὰς δὲ περὶ τὸ μανθάνειν ἐσπούδασέ τε καὶ κοσμήσας τὴν ψυχὴν οὐκ ἀλλοτρίῳ ἀλλὰ τῷ αὐτῆς κόσμῳ, σωφροσύνῃ τε καὶ δικαιοσύνῃ· καὶ ἀνδρείᾳ καὶ ἐλευθερίᾳ καὶ ἀληθείᾳ, οὕτω περιμένει τὴν εἰς Ἅιδου πορείαν ὡς πορευσόμενος ὅταν ἡ εἱμαρμένη καλῇ (114d8–115a3).

[133] χωριζόμενα δὲ φρονήσεως [καὶ] ἀλλαττόμενα ἀντὶ ἀλλήλων μὴ σκιαγραφία τις ᾖ ἡ τοιαύτη ἀρετὴ καὶ τῷ ὄντι ἀνδραποδώδης τε καὶ οὐδὲν ὑγιὲς οὐδ' ἀληθὲς ἔχῃ, τὸ δ' ἀληθὲς τῷ ὄντι κάθαρσίς τις τῶν τοιούτων πάντων καὶ ἡ σωφροσύνη καὶ ἡ δικαιοσύνη καὶ ἀνδρεία, καὶ αὐτὴ ἡ φρόνησις μὴ καθαρμός τις ᾖ (69b5–c3).

[134] καὶ κινδυνεύουσι καὶ οἱ τὰς τελετὰς ἡμῖν οὗτοι καταστήσαντες οὐ φαῦλοί τινες εἶναι, ἀλλὰ τῷ ὄντι πάλαι αἰνίττεσθαι ὅτι ὃς ἂν ἀμύητος καὶ ἀτέλεστος εἰς Ἅιδου ἀφίκηται ἐν βορβόρῳ κείσεται, ὁ δὲ κεκαθαρμένος τε καὶ τετελεσμένος ἐκεῖσε ἀφικόμενος μετὰ θεῶν οἰκήσει. εἰσὶν γὰρ δή, [ὡς] φασιν οἱ περὶ τὰς τελετάς. "ναρθηκοφόροι μὲν πολλοί, βάκχοι δέ τε παῦροι" οὗτοι δ' εἰσὶν κατὰ τὴν ἐμὴν δόξαν οὐκ ἄλλοι ἢ οἱ πεφιλοσοφηκότες ὀρθῶς (69c3–d2). I have substituted the transliteration 'bacchoi' for the 'devotees' in Gallop's translation.

Plato takes the traditional idea of an initiation that qualifies the deceased for a favorable afterlife and transforms it into a way of referring to philosophy. Even the slogan from the Dionysiac mysteries that Olympiodorus attributes to Orpheus, "Many bear the wand, but few are *bacchoi*," is allegorically interpreted to mean that true philosophers are few, despite the number who pretend to philosophic virtue.[135] Since philosophy is also defined as a preparation for dying (81a), Plato can make use of the similarity between τελετή and τελευτᾶν, initiation and dying. Both initiation and death bring normal life to an end (τέλος), and the goal of philosophy is likewise to end the life devoted to the body in favor of a life devoted to the soul. Plato appropriates the traditional privileges of the initiate for the philosopher.

The philosopher, like the initiate in mysteries, dedicates special service to a deity, establishing a bond between mortal and immortal that benefits the mortal after death. Socrates speaks of himself as dedicated to Apollo, like the servants of Apollo (θεράποντες τοῦ Ἀπόλλωνος), the swans who sing at the approach of death in the joy of rejoining their master. "Now I hold that I myself am a fellow-servant of the swans, consecrated to the same god."[136] Socrates' life is spared for the period in which Apollo is being honored for his deliverance of Theseus and the Athenians (58bc), and he has spent this extra time composing hymns to Apollo (60d) in addition to the practice of his usual kind of music, philosophy.

This idea of being in the special service of the god is echoed in the discussions of the soul in mortal life being under the care of some god, θεόν τε εἶναι τὸν ἐπιμελούμενον ἡμῶν (62d2–3). Cebes protests that if this is the case, why should one not protest at leaving the service (θεραπεία) of such a good master at death?[137] In building his argument that the philosopher will serve other good and wise gods after death (cp. 63c), Socrates draws the contrast with those who are in the service of the body

---

[135] cp. Olympiodorus 7.10, who gives this as an example of how Plato borrows from Orpheus everywhere.

[136] ἐγὼ δὲ καὶ αὐτὸς ἡγοῦμαι ὁμόδουλός τε εἶναι τῶν κύκνων καὶ ἱερὸς τοῦ αὐτοῦ θεοῦ (85b4–5). In the *Apology*, Socrates regards himself as specially dedicated to Apollo because of the Delphic Oracle that proclaimed him the wisest of men. He recounts how his service to the god has reduced him to poverty and stirred up people's anger against him. (*Apology* 21a, 23b.)

[137] τὸ γὰρ μὴ ἀγανακτεῖν τοὺς φρονιμωτάτους ἐκ ταύτης τῆς θεραπείας ἀπιόντας, ἐν ᾗ ἐπιστατοῦσιν αὐτῶν οἵπερ ἄριστοί εἰσιν τῶν ὄντων ἐπιστάται, θεοί, οὐκ ἔχει λόγον· (62d3–6).

(τῷ σώματι θεραπεύουσα), who must cater to its appetites and passions.[138] Unlike these people, for whom the φρουρά of the body is indeed a prison, the philosopher's soul serves out its garrison duty in the body under the guidance of the god in life and, after death, it departs into the presence of a god, "And as is said of the initiated, does it not pass the rest of time in very truth with the gods?"[139] In Socrates' argument in the *Phaedo*, the philosopher, in return for his special service to the god, is rewarded after death, just as, in the tradition, the initiate is rewarded for his dedication to the god.

Plato thus takes the solutions familiar from the mythic tradition and appropriates them for philosophy, depicting philosophy as heroic action, virtuous behavior, and a kind of initiation that puts the philosopher in special service to the god. Plato appropriates not only the efficacy of the solutions but also the authority and prestige that these solutions have within the tradition. Not only is philosophy as effective as, for example, heroic action in gaining a favorable judgement after death, but the philosopher should be regarded as positively as one of the great heroes of old. By subsuming the traditional solutions under the rubric of philosophy, Plato redefines the position of philosophers in society so that they are no longer marginal figures like the Orpheotelests or even the Pythagoreans, but are akin to heroes like Theseus, Herakles, and Odysseus who stand at the center of the Greek heroic tradition.

## Result: The Places of Punishment and Reward

The Greek mythic tradition offered a number of possibilities for someone describing the results of a soul's journey to the land of the dead. The soul could end up in a variety of locations and experience a wide range of conditions in the afterlife, from the torments of Tartarus to the joys of the Isles of the Blessed. Plato incorporates the whole range of locations into a unified picture of the cosmos in which different souls are assigned to appropriate places as a result of their judgements, and the nature of the destination allotted for the philosophic and unphilosophic in the myth corresponds to their respective experiences in life.

---

[138] τῷ σώματι ἀεὶ συνοῦσα καὶ τοῦτο θεραπεύουσα καὶ ἐρῶσα καὶ γοητευομένη ὑπ' αὐτοῦ ὑπό τε τῶν ἐπιθυμιῶν καὶ ἡδονῶν (81b2-4), cp. 64d8, 66d2.

[139] ὥσπερ δὲ λέγεται κατὰ τῶν μεμυημένων, ὡς ἀληθῶς τὸν λοιπὸν χρόνον μετὰ θεῶν διάγουσα (81a8-9).

The most common name for the realm of the dead in the mythic tradition is simply "(the realm) of Hades" ("Aιδου), the lord of the dead. In Homer, this realm, which lies beyond the great river of Ocean, is characterized by shadows and gloom. Circe describes the entrance to Hades to Odysseus, "There Pyriphlegethon and Kokytos, which is an off-break from the water of the Styx, flow into Acheron. There is a rock there, and the junction of two thunderous rivers."[140] The souls dwelling in this realm beyond the rivers are the "senseless dead . . . mere imitations of perished mortals."[141] They are not subject to punishment, but neither are they happy.[142] Some of the dead continue in activities they pursued in life. Contentious even in death, the souls of the Greek tradition continue to bring lawsuits against one another even in death, and Minos continues to judge them, while Orion hunts the same beasts he chased in life. Some early vases depict the dead in Hades, playing board games or pursuing other activities of daily life.[143] Except for the perpetual gloom, life seems to continue pretty much the same for most of the dead in the Homeric realm of Hades.

Three notable exceptions to this rule are Tantalos, Tityos, and Sisyphos, whom Odysseus sees in torment during his journey to the underworld. Each suffers endless torture for crimes against the gods. Homer mentions the crime of Tityos, his attempted rape of Leto; but later tradition is left to supply the crimes of Tantalos and Sisyphos. In each case, their crimes are not the sort of injustice that any mortal might commit, but specific crimes against gods.[144] Later tradition includes more souls among those

---

[140] ἔνθα μὲν εἰς Ἀχέροντα Πυριφλεγέθων τε ῥέουσι Κώκυτός θ', ὅς δὴ Στυγὸς ὕδατός ἐστιν ἀπορρώξ, πέτρη τε ξύνεσίς τε δύω ποταμῶν ἐριδούπων· Od. x.513–515. The unnamed rock is perhaps the same as the Leukas Rock, which Homer mentions in the descent of the suitors' shades in Odyssey xxiv, along with the gates of Helios, and the land of dreams. (Od. xxiv 11–13.) While the Styx is mentioned as a boundary river in the Iliad reference to the descent of Herakles (VIII.369), the rivers at the boundary of Hades are not always the same in later tradition. Alcaeus is the first after Homer to mention Acheron, although the name then shows up repeatedly as a river or lake of the underworld, and the Cocytus appears in Aeschylus. (Acheron – Alcaeus 38a LP; cp. Sappho 95 LP; Aeschylus, Seven 854–860. Cocytus – Aeschylus Seven 690, Agamemnon 1558.)

[141] νεκροὶ ἀφραδέες . . . βροτῶν εἴδωλα καμόντων. Odyssey, xi.476.

[142] The famous words of Achilles reveal the Homeric attitude to the afterlife, "I would rather follow the plow as thrall to another man, one with no land allotted him and not much to live on, than be a king over the perished dead." ibid. 489–491.

[143] Odyssey, xi. 568–575. cp. Garland 1985, pp. 68–72. However, "The principle activities of the Homeric dead appear to be gossip, sententious moralising and self-indulgent regret" (p. 68).

[144] Tantalos tried to steal the ambrosia of the gods, according to Pindar, who denies the other crime, that he fed his son, Pelops, to the gods, thus making them cannibals. cp.

being punished in Hades. Polygnotus's painting of the underworld, dating from around the mid-fifth century, depicts not only the uninitiate being punished but also a son who injured his father being choked by him, a temple robber being forced to take poison, and Oknos, personification of sloth or hesitation, eternally plaiting a rope, which is endlessly consumed by his donkey.[145] Their crimes are the injustices of ordinary mortals, and their punishments have a certain symbolic value. In the strand of the tradition represented by Polygnotus, the realm of Hades becomes a place of punishment as well as the locale where the souls of the many unpunished dead linger.

Beneath Hades lies a deep pit known to both Homer and Hesiod as Tartarus. Homer refers to the Titans as imprisoned in Tartarus.[146] Hesiod describes it as an enormous pit, bordered with gates of bronze to keep the Titans in. "It is a great gulf, and if once a man were within the gates, he would not reach the floor until a whole year had reached its end, but cruel blast upon blast would carry him this way and that."[147] Tartarus is the prison and punishment of gods; mortals do not seem to be imprisoned in Tartarus, although Tartarus seems occasionally to have been used as another name for Hades in general.[148]

The Greek mythic locales for the afterlife were not only gloomy realms of punishment; the Blessed Isles provide a blissful existence for the select few. Even in Homer, the Elysian Field presents another possibility for an afterlife.[149] The Elysian Field does not appear again in the tradition until well after Plato (in the *Argonautica* of Apollonius Rhodius), but the

---

*Olympian* I. Sisyphos's crime seems to have been his evasion of death and his trickery of Hades, but the story is not told clearly in the early tradition. Theognis (699–718) provides the earliest version of his escape from Hades, but makes no mention of it as a crime against the god that merited eternal punishment.

[145] Pausanias X.28.

[146] *Iliad* XIV 274–9; VIII. 478–91. At VIII.10–16, Zeus threatens to send down to Tartarus any god who opposes him.

[147] χάσμα μέγ', οὐδέ κε πάντα τελεσφόρον εἰς ἐνιαυτὸν οὖδας ἵκοιτ', εἰ πρῶτα πυλέων ἔντοσθε γένοιτο. ἀλλά κεν ἔνθα καὶ ἔνθα φέροι πρὸ θύελλα θυέλλης ἀργαλέη· Hesiod, *Theog.* 739–742. cp. Pherekydes 7B5, in which the Harpuiai and Thyellai, both types of wind demons, guard Tartarus.

[148] cp. Gantz' 1993 discussion, pp. 129–131, with citations of archaic fragments.

[149] Proteus describes the Elysian Field to Menelaus. "There is life made easiest for mortals, for there is no snow, nor much winter there, nor is there ever rain, but always the stream of Ocean sends up breezes of the West Wind blowing briskly for the refreshment of mortals." τῇ περ ῥηῗστη βιοτὴ πέλει ἀνθρώποισιν· οὐ νιφετός, οὔτ' ἄρ χειμὼν πολὺς οὔτε ποτ' ὄμβρος, ἀλλ' αἰεὶ ζεφύροιο λιγύ πνείοντος ἀήτας Ὠκεανὸς ἀνίησιν ἀναψύχειν ἀνθρώπους. *Od.* iv.565–8.

equivalent blessed locale is the Isles of the Blessed described by Hesiod as the residence of his race of heroes.[150] Life on Hesiod's Isles of the Blessed bears a strong resemblance to the life he describes for the golden race, a proverbially golden age existence, "without sorrow of heart, remote and free from toil and grief... the fruitful earth unforced bare them fruit abundantly and without stint."[151] Both the golden race and the heroes of the Blessed Isles are ruled over by Kronos, a feature of the Blessed Isles as described by Pindar as well.[152] In a fragment of a dirge, Pindar describes the blissful afterlife of those in the Isles, including their recreations. "And some with horses and exercise, some with draughts-games, some with lyres take their pleasure, and a whole life of bliss breaks into flower upon them."[153] This blissful existence, filled with aristocratic leisure activities, was often thought to include the supreme leisure activity, the symposium. In the *Republic*, Adeimantus refers to this symposium of the blessed, συμπόσιον τῶν ὁσίων, as the promise of eternal drunkenness held out by Musaeus and his son, "where, reclined on couches and crowned with wreaths, they entertain the time henceforth with wine, as if the fairest meed of virtue were an everlasting drunk."[154] While only a few pre-Platonic traces of this traditional motif exist in literature, the image of the deceased in a symposium setting is well known in funeral

---

[150] "And they live untouched by sorrow in the islands of the blessed along the shore of deep swirling Ocean, happy heroes for whom the grain-giving earth bears honey-sweet fruit flourishing thrice a year." καὶ τοὶ μὲν ναίουσιν ἀκηδέα θυμὸν ἔχοντες ἐν μακάρων νήσοισι παρ' Ὠκεανὸν βαθυδίνην, ὄλβιοι ἥρωες, τοῖσιν μελιηδέα καρπὸν τρὶς ἔτεος θάλλοντα φέρει ζείδωρος ἄρουρα (Hesiod, *W&D* 170–173).

[151] ἔζωον ἀκηδέα θυμὸν ἔχοντες νόσφιν ἄτερ τε πόνων καὶ ὀιζύος.... ἐσθλὰ δὲ πάντα τοῖσιν ἔην· καρπὸν δ' ἔφερε ζείδωρος ἄρουρα αὐτομάτη πολλόν τε καὶ ἄφθονον· (Hesiod, *W&D*. 112–113, 117–118).

[152] ἔνθα μακάρων νᾶσον ὠκεανίδες αὖραι περιπνέοισιν· ἄνθεμα δὲ χρυσοῦ φλέγει, τὰ μὲν χερσόθεν ἀπ' ἀγλαῶν δενδρέων, ὕδωρ δ' ἄλλα φέρβει, ὅρμοισι τῶν χέρας ἀναπλέκοντι καὶ στεφάνους βουλαῖς ἐν ὀρθαῖσι Ῥαδαμάνθυος, ὃν πατὴρ ἔχει μέγας ἑτοῖμον αὐτῷ πάρεδρον, πόσις ὁ πάντων Ῥέας. "The ocean-breezes blow around the Islands of the Blest, and flowers of gold are blazing, some on shore from radiant trees, while others the water fostereth; and with chaplets thereof they entwine their hands, and with crowns according to the righteous councils of Rhadamanthys, who shareth for evermore the judgement-seat of the mighty Father, even the lord of Rhea." (Sandys' Loeb translation) Pindar *Olympian* II. 71–77.

[153] καὶ τοὶ μὲν ἵπποις γυμνασίοις ⟨τε⟩, τοὶ δὲ πεσσοῖς, τοὶ δὲ φορμίγγεσσι τέρπονται, παρὰ δέ σφισιν εὐανθὴς ἅπας τέθαλεν ὄλβος (Pindar fr. 130. Lattimore translation).

[154] εἰς Ἅιδου γὰρ ἀγαγόντες τῷ λόγῳ καὶ κατακλίναντες καὶ συμπόσιον τῶν ὁσίων κατασκευάσαντες ἐστεφανωμένους ποιοῦσιν τὸν ἅπαντα χρόνον ἤδη διάγειν μεθύοντας, ἡγησάμενοι κάλλιστον ἀρετῆς μισθὸν μέθην αἰώνιον (Plato, *Rep.* 363c4–d2).

iconography.[155] The symposium of the blessed, despite Adeimantus' sneers, seems to be part of the traditional picture of the afterlife on the Isles of the Blessed, a golden age existence of pleasure and leisure pursuits.

Another, very different idea of the afterlife existence of souls appears in the tradition: the concept of the soul floating up to the aither, while the body sinks into the earth. This idea is undoubtedly connected with speculations on the nature of the soul as the life breath returning to the air.[156] Although the idea is certainly wrapped up in the so-called pre-Socratic philosophers' cosmological speculations, the return of the soul to the aither was not an esoteric doctrine confined to a few avant-garde thinkers, but part of the mainstream tradition. The fifth century epigram for the dead at Potidaea attests to this belief, "Aither has taken their souls, and earth their bodies."[157] The soul of the deceased, coming out with the dying breath, just as in Homer, naturally rises to the level of the aither, which is also sometimes thought of as the abode of the gods themselves.[158]

Plato makes use of all of these traditional motifs in his complex myth about the regions to which the souls of the deceased journey as a result of their judgement. Plato constructs from these mythic elements a vision of the whole world, hierarchically arranged from the lowest pits of Tartarus to the Isles of the Blessed in the upper regions of the cosmos. Each region has conditions appropriate to the nature of the souls sent there after judgement. Socrates' lengthy description of the hollow earth and the realms above the known world weaves traditional place names and motifs into a complex picture of life and afterlife existence that is carefully linked with Plato's descriptions of the lives of the philosophic and unphilosophic.

Plato brings together the lowest pit of Tartarus with the underground realm of Hades, bounded by its rivers, into one global hydraulic system, endlessly pulsating like the breathing of a living creature.[159] Plato takes the names of the rivers of the underworld straight from Homer, but he arranges them in balanced sets of opposing forces, with Ocean flowing

---

[155] cp. Graf 1974, pp. 98–103, for some of the literary evidence; for the *Totenmahl* reliefs, see Garland 1985, pp. 70ff.

[156] cp. Lattimore 1962, pp. 31–32; Bremmer 1983, pp. 70–76.

[157] αἰθὴρ μὲμ ψυχὰς ὑπεδέξατο, σώ[ματα δὲ χθων. cp. other early epitaphs with similar themes in Lattimore 1962, pp. 31–33. cp. also similar ideas in Euripides, *Suppl.* 1140, 531–536; fr. 971.

[158] Especially Zeus. cp. Eur. fr. 487 αἰθὴρ οἴκησις Διός.

[159] cp. Aristotle's literalist critique of the impossibility of the system, *Meteor.* 356a12–33.

in the opposite direction from Acheron and the blazing Pyriphlegethon coiling in the opposite direction to the cold blue Cocytus.[160] All of these rivers and, indeed, all the rivers of the world flow eventually into Tartarus and flow out again at different places on the other side of the world.[161] The connections between these rivers and Tartarus provide the geographical setting for Plato's system of purification and punishment in the afterlife, the destination of those who do not receive a favorable judgement.

The majority of souls who go to the realm of the unseen, Hades, are sent by their judges to the lake of Acheron, since they are neither so bad as to deserve punishment nor sufficiently purified to ascend to higher realms. "And those who have lived indifferently journey to Acheron, embark upon certain vessels provided for them, and on these they reach the lake; there they dwell and are purified, paying the penalty for their wrongdoings, and are absolved, if any has committed any wrong, and they secure reward for their good deeds, each according to his desert."[162] These souls receive recompense for every good and evil deed in a process of purification. Those who have committed great crimes must suffer punishment in Tartarus, where the flow of waters buffets them about for at least a full year. In Plato's Tartarus, the more solid element of water replaces the great winds that buffet the one who falls into Tartarus in Hesiod, although the period of time remains the same, a year.[163] While the lighter element of air is reserved for the upper realms, the constant motion in Tartarus is reminiscent of the fluidity and variability ascribed to the phenomenal world,

---

[160] cp. *Od.* x.513–515. *Phaedo* 112e–113c. The Neoplatonic commentator, Damascius, attributes special significance to each of these opposing rivers. "The power of delimitation is symbolized by the Oceanus, that of purification by the Acheron, that of chastisement by heat by the Pyriphlegethon, that of chastisement through cold by the Cocytus." (Dam. II 145 Westerink.)

[161] 111e–112e. The shape of Plato's entire world, whether it is spherical, disc-shaped, or otherwise formed, has been much debated, but the description of Tartarus piercing through the whole earth with various rivers flowing into and out of it seems to fit best with a spherical conception of the earth, which is also preferable in light of Socrates' references to the earth staying in place because of the equal pressure of the heavens around it (109a). On the debate, see, e.g. Sedley 1989–1990; Morrison 1959; Baensch 1903.

[162] καὶ οἳ μὲν ἂν δόξωσι μέσως βεβιωκέναι, πορευθέντες ἐπὶ τὸν Ἀχέροντα, ἀναβάντες ἃ δὴ αὐτοῖς ὀχήματά ἐστιν, ἐπὶ τούτων ἀφικνοῦνται εἰς τὴν λίμνην, καὶ ἐκεῖ οἰκοῦσί τε καὶ καθαιρόμενοι τῶν τε ἀδικημάτων διδόντες δίκας ἀπολύονται, εἴ τίς τι ἠδίκηκεν, τῶν τε εὐεργεσιῶν τιμὰς φέρονται κατὰ τὴν ἀξίαν ἕκαστος· (113d4–e1). The fact that the majority go to Acheron recalls the argument from opposites and the idea that the majority of things always fall between the two extremes (90ab).

[163] 114a, cp. *Theog.* 739–742.

as opposite elements of hot and cold, fire and mud, air and water, all swirl into the pit of Tartarus so that conditions are never the same.[164] The fate of the punished soul in Tartarus is thus like the lot of an unphilosophic person who distrusts all arguments and relies only on his senses. Socrates describes the misologist as being tossed up and down by the flow of the Euripus, a narrow channel with proverbially rapid and dramatic tides, just as the punished soul is tossed about in the ever-changing waters of Tartarus.[165] The experience of the soul in Tartarus is thus equivalent to the mortal who lives entirely through his senses, perceiving only the endless variation of the material world and mistrusting the reasonings of the mind which alone can lead it to the truth.

Only those few who have committed crimes so great as to be incurable are condemned to dwell forever in the chaos of Tartarus, however. Those who have committed crimes but may yet be reformed are cast out of Tartarus after a year's cycle and into one of the rivers that flows past the Acherusian Lake, into Pyriphlegethon or Cocytus. Socrates gives some examples of such criminals, those who in a momentary fit of passion have killed someone or injured a parent, and he assigns the killers to Cocytus and the parent-beaters to Pyriphlegethon. Plato is undoubtedly borrowing this detail of symbolic punishment from a traditional source now lost to us, but the precise symbolism of the punishments is difficult to ascertain.[166] Nevertheless, Plato makes use of the idea of punishment of

---

[164] 111d–112b. On the variability of the sensible, cp. 79c and the discussion above.

[165] ἐν Εὐρίπῳ ἄνω κάτω στρέφεται 90c5. cp. the description of the waters of Tartarus: κυμαίνει ἄνω καὶ κάτω 112b3.

[166] Why, after all, should those who kill in anger be frozen, while those who beat their parents be immersed in burning lava? Even though he does not answer this question, Kingsley sees in this detail the remnant of a complex set of allegorical punishments left over from a Pythagorean myth that Plato plagiarized without understanding. "The *Phaedo* myth in its entirety, even down to the smallest details, derives from a Pythagorean source." (Kingsley 1995, p. 192.) Kingsley accuses Plato of destroying the rich meanings of the earlier myths that he used as sources. "This is not to deny that Plato introduced changes of his own into the myth as he tells it. On the contrary, he very probably jumbled some of the details and blurred the edges of some originally fine distinctions – either through lack of interest or even through misunderstanding. However, there is no evidence whatever that he contributed to the creation – or even the arrangement – of the mythical material in any significant way" (p. 109). Kingsley does not take into account the careful construction of Plato's myths in relation to the themes of their surrounding dialogues. Plato is certainly altering the meanings that the traditional mythic details had in earlier tellings, but, as any storyteller must who retells a traditional tale, he is giving them new significance in the new context in which he is deploying them. Plato's skill at this mythic manipulation, along with the vagaries of preservation, resulted in

the unjust in the mud of the afterlife by having these wrongdoers carried through the mud and lava of the underground rivers.[167] These criminals remain in a cycle of punishment, floating along the river system back into Tartarus and then back out again the next year, until they can convince their victims to forgive them, at which point they are admitted into the Acherusian Lake, presumably to undertake the same kind of purification allotted to those without such outstanding criminal records.[168]

A few fortunate souls do not need a sojourn of purification on the Acherusian Lake, but the result of their judgement is an ascent to the higher realms. Plato here manages to combine the traditional features of the Isles of the Blessed with the idea that souls ascend to rejoin the aither. Only souls made pure by philosophy, that is, only those that have entirely freed themselves from the weightiness of materiality and the body, are able to rise to the heights as though released from prison.[169] Plato thus brings in the motifs of philosophy as a release from prison and as a separation from the body in the description of the results of a good judgement of the soul. These souls live on the surface of the true earth, where the air serves as water and aither as air. "Some dwelling inland, some living by the

his versions being preserved over the millennia while earlier versions, including the Pythagorean texts Kingsley hypothesizes, have been lost.

[167] cp. πολὺ μὲν ὕδωρ ῥεῖν ἐξ ἀλλήλων εἰς ἀλλήλους ὥσπερ εἰς κρατῆρας, καὶ ἀενάων ποταμῶν ἀμήχανα μεγέθη ὑπὸ τὴν γῆν καὶ θερμῶν ὑδάτων καὶ ψυχρῶν, πολὺ δὲ πῦρ καὶ πυρὸς μεγάλους ποταμούς, πολλοὺς δὲ ὑγροῦ πηλοῦ καὶ καθαρωτέρου καὶ βορβορωδεστέρου, ὥσπερ ἐν Σικελίᾳ οἱ πρὸ τοῦ ῥύακος πηλοῦ ῥέοντες ποταμοὶ καὶ αὐτὸς ὁ ῥύαξ· (111d4–e2).

[168] The idea of remission of punishment through the forgiveness of the victim seems unprecedented in the mythic tradition. A possible parallel may, however, be found in Attic law, where the killer may be exempt from prosecution (and the relatives freed from the obligation of prosecution), if the killer is forgiven by the victim before he expires (Demosthenes 37.59). Nevertheless, Plato here introduces an element into the traditional idea of post-mortem punishment that increases the focus on the reformative and purificatory character of the punishment. The fact, however, that some souls are regarded as incurable and thus condemned to eternal punishment in Tartarus would seem to work against this reformative notion of punishment, since the incurables are not explicitly held up as deterrents, as they are in the *Gorgias*. Still, they may function as deterrents in the *Phaedo* as well, since the myth itself is intended as a warning to practice philosophy, and the description of the fate of the incurables, especially with its parallel to the description of the prisoner of the senses, serves as a warning to engage in the purifications of philosophy. Quibbles about the plight of a murderer whose victim is in Tartarus or up in the higher realms and thus unable to be reached for forgiveness miss the point with an overly literal interpretation. On the penal system of the *Phaedo* myth as predominantly reformative rather than retributive, cp. Saunders 1991, e.g., pp. 162, 198; *contra* White 1989, p. 263.

[169] 114b7–c2.

air, as we live by the sea, and some on islands surrounded by the air and lying close to the mainland."[170] Plato's islands in the air are his version of the traditional Blessed Isles, and they share many of the same features found in the tradition. Like the men of Hesiod's golden race, they enjoy a beneficial climate and blissful existence that includes contact with the gods.[171] By relocating the Blessed Isles to the aither, Plato reconciles two different strands of the tradition and works them into his picture of a cosmos set in order with the heaviest and most mixed things at the center bottom and the lightest and most pure at the highest edges. Just as aither is purer than water, so too the realms above contain things proportionately more pure than the familiar objects in the ordinary world below. Such things are not subject to the corruption and decay of the lower worlds, the ceaseless process of change that creates the impurities of the lower realms. The souls purified by the philosophical pursuit of the unchanging and ideal forms in this life go to an afterlife in a realm less subject to change.

Some few of the souls headed for realms above go beyond the surface of the earth into indescribable realms of purity and dwell there entirely freed from bodies.[172] This realm, like the realm above the heavens in the *Phaedrus*, is so far beyond mortal experience that "of that place beyond the heavens none of our earthly poets has sung, and none shall sing worthily."[173] This hint of indescribable realms above accessible through philosophic purification should not be taken to put philosophy or philosophers on a higher level than the gods, as White would seem to suggest. Just because mortals can meet the gods on the true surface of the earth does not mean

---

[170] τοὺς μὲν ἐν μεσογαίᾳ οἰκοῦντας, τοὺς δὲ περὶ τὸν ἀέρα ὥσπερ ἡμεῖς περὶ τὴν θάλατταν, τοὺς δ' ἐν νήσοις ἃς περιρρεῖν τὸν ἀέρα πρὸς τῇ ἠπείρῳ οὔσας· (111a4–7).

[171] "Their climate is such that they are free from sickness and live a far longer time than people here . . . Moreover, they have groves and temples of gods, in which gods are truly dwellers, and utterances and prophecies, and direct awareness of the gods; and communion of that kind they experience face to face." τὰς δὲ ὥρας αὐτοῖς κρᾶσιν ἔχειν τοιαύτην ὥστε ἐκείνους ἀνόσους εἶναι καὶ χρόνον τε ζῆν πολὺ πλείω τῶν ἐνθάδε . . . καὶ δὴ καὶ θεῶν ἄλση τε καὶ ἱερὰ αὐτοῖς εἶναι, ἐν οἷς τῷ ὄντι οἰκητὰς θεοὺς εἶναι, καὶ φήμας τε καὶ μαντείας καὶ αἰσθήσεις τῶν θεῶν καὶ τοιαύτας συνουσίας γίγνεσθαι αὐτοῖς πρὸς αὐτούς· (111b1–c1).

[172] τούτων δὲ αὐτῶν οἱ φιλοσοφίᾳ ἱκανῶς καθηράμενοι ἄνευ τε σωμάτων ζῶσι τὸ παράπαν εἰς τὸν ἔπειτα χρόνον, καὶ εἰς οἰκήσεις ἔτι τούτων καλλίους ἀφικνοῦνται, ἃς οὔτε ῥᾴδιον δηλῶσαι οὔτε ὁ χρόνος ἱκανὸς ἐν τῷ παρόντι (114c2–6).

[173] τὸν δὲ ὑπερουράνιον τόπον οὔτε τις ὕμνησέ πω τῶν τῇδε ποιητὴς οὔτε ποτὲ ὑμνήσει κατ' ἀξίαν. *Phaedrus* 247c2–3.

that the gods cannot ascend to the higher realms.[174] Plato's myth works within the tradition to place philosophy at the highest level of human activity, equating it to the most revered purifications and initiations and assimilating its rewards to the most blissful afterlife reserved for the greatest and most worthy of the heroes of myth. Rather than trying to replace the traditional ideas, Plato co-opts them, transforming them to suit his own purposes.

The final chapter in the myth of the afterlife in the *Phaedo* is the rebirth of the soul into another life, completing the cycle – since the process of dying must be followed by the process of coming to birth again.[175] Socrates refers to the idea of reincarnation as an old legend (παλαιὸς λόγος), and the notion does appear in the Greek tradition before Plato, in poems of Pindar and Empedokles as well as in tales about Pythagoras.[176] Plato incorporates this idea into his myth of the soul's journey to the realm of the dead. In his discussion of the effects of the mixture of body and soul, Socrates relates that one of the effects of the failure to separate is rebirth into the forms of animals appropriate to the ruling passions of the former life. The gluttonous become donkeys and the violent become carnivorous beasts, while those who practiced unphilosophic virtue are reincarnated as ants or bees or even as humans again (81e–82b). This process of the soul falling straightaway back into another body (ταχὺ πάλιν πίπτειν εἰς ἄλλο σῶμα – 81d10–e1) contrasts with the lengthier process described in the final eschatological myth, where reincarnation becomes the fate of

---

[174] *Contra* White 1989, p. 249. "But if the gods are in residence in the surface of the true earth, and if there is a degree of reality higher than that represented by this surface, then the gods cannot exemplify the highest reality. In general then, any appeal to the gods or to the divine as a sanctioning authority will be incomplete if the gods are superseded by a higher degree of reality." On the contrary, being more pure and divine, the gods are more likely than mortals to be able to ascend to higher realms. cp. the *Phaedrus* (247d–248b), in which the chariots of the gods make without difficulty the ascent to the realm above the heavens that mortals can only make with risk and trouble. Nor can philosophic endeavor be divorced from service to the gods, as White would argue. "Such salvation [disembodiment] is achieved only by appropriate philosophical purification – not by divine intervention. If Socrates achieves this highest purification and is saved, it is not by Asclepius or any other deity but by his own philosophical efforts." (White 1989, p. 277.) The philosophical purification is, like the traditional rituals of purification performed in Greek religion, in some sense a contact with the god, who becomes the agent of purification. This principle of dual actors, god and mortal, is a familiar one throughout Greek religious thought, from the battlefields of Homer to Socrates' service to Apollo in the Athenian courtroom.

[175] The conclusion of the cyclical argument at 72a.

[176] cp. the study of this tradition by Long 1948.

those in Acheron after they have finished their process of purification. "The souls of most of the dead arrive there, and, after they have stayed for certain appointed periods, some longer, some shorter, they are sent forth again into the generation of living things."[177] To some extent, of course, incarnation in animal form is an extension of the punishment, a more vivid illustration of the life of the unphilosophic, who not only suffer the torments of Tartarus but fail to make any more use of their human reason than a brute beast. Within the myth, moreover, such a *talionic* punishment is not retributive; it serves instead as a powerful deterrent within a system of births and rebirths, both for the punished and for those who know of their fate.[178] Thus, for Plato, the ancient tale that men can be reborn as animals serves as a warning to use the mental faculties and not live life like beasts without human reason.[179]

[177] αἱ τῶν τετελευτηκότων ψυχαὶ τῶν πολλῶν ἀφικνοῦνται καί τινας εἱμαρμένους χρόνους μείνασαι, αἱ μὲν μακροτέρους, αἱ δὲ βραχυτέρους, πάλιν ἐκπέμπονται εἰς τὰς τῶν ζῴων γενέσεις (113a2-5). Indeed, if the details are pressed, this process would be longer for those most attached to the body, since they would presumably have committed crimes for which they are punished in Tartarus and adjoining rivers. Moreover, the incurables tormented forever in Tartarus would never return to incarnation. Such considerations show the dangers of an overliteral reading of the details of the myths. Reincarnation permits those who have undergone purification in Acheron to benefit from this experience. Plato's theories of punishment stress the reformative rather than retributive purpose of punishment. cp. Saunders, "Protagoras and Plato share a single central insight: that punishment should not look to the past but to the future. Both indicate the pointlessness of backward-looking punishment by citing the maxim 'what's done cannot be undone'. That is to say, punishment should not be vengeful or retributive: its purpose is not to inflict suffering on an offender in return for the suffering he has inflicted, but the reformative effect it should have on him henceforth." (Saunders 1991, p. 162.)

[178] Saunders 1991 distinguishes the *talionic* punishment from the *mirroring*. "A talionic punishment is therefore one in which the notion of 'aptness' or 'appropriateness' is expressed by pointed *identity* of offence and penalty; a mirroring punishment is one in which that notion is expressed by pointed *associative detail* reminiscent or indirectly descriptive of the offence" (p. 77).

[179] The myth does not refer to the reincarnation of souls pure enough to ascend to higher realms rather than being purified in Acheron, but neither does it refer to anything that would rule out this possibility. According to the cyclical argument, all souls that die should be subject to rebirth, but there is no reason to suppose that souls purified by philosophy would necessarily be reborn in the material realm in the hollows of the earth. The inhabitants of the upper realms live longer than those of the lower realms and without the pains of sickness, but they are only more like the immortals, not actually immortal themselves. τὰς δὲ ὥρας αὐτοῖς κρᾶσιν ἔχειν τοιαύτην ὥστε ἐκείνους ἀνόσους εἶναι καὶ χρόνον τε ζῆν πολὺ πλείω τῶν ἐνθάδε (111b1-3). When they die, they presumably face judgement and are assigned to an appropriate locale, depending on their conduct. Perhaps it is from certain of these inhabitants of the upper realms who have lived

In Socrates' myth, Plato transforms mythic elements familiar from the traditional descriptions of the judgement of the soul and the various possibilities for an afterlife. The familiar positive afterlife of the Isles of the Blessed, a fate reserved for the greatest heroes, becomes the afterlife allotted to the philosopher and corresponds to the philosopher's experience in life, coming into contact with the pure realities through his intellectual searching. The torments reserved in myth for the unjust or unworthy become, in Socrates' myth, the punishments of the unphilosophic and correspond to the experience of the unphilosophic in their bodies, unguided by reason and tormented by their desires and appetites. Plato thus maps the contrast between the afterlives in the traditional tales onto his distinction between the philosopher and non-philosopher and, in so doing, borrows the traditional evaluation of those two fates. Plato's use of the traditional elements not only illuminates the contrast between the

many lives of purification that the few who ascend even higher to a disembodied life are selected. These souls might only descend to lower realms in punishment for some crime or failing, a fate such as Empedokles, fr. 115, claimed for himself. cp. *Phaedo* 114c1–5. Olympiodorus argues that in Plato even the souls of those who ascend to the intelligible realm must descend eventually to lower realms (Olympiodorus, 10 § 14). Such speculation may be pressing the details too far, but it preserves the analogy Plato makes between the conduct in life and the conditions of afterlife, as well as his proportions between the realms of air and aither. On the other hand, from a literalist reading, the fates of those disembodied for all time to come and those condemned to an eternity in Tartarus would seem to be the only ones who will never be reborn in bodies. But the notion of a total escape from the cycle of rebirths, familiar to the modern scholar as the ultimate goal from the Nirvana of Indian religion, does not appear in any other of Plato's eschatological myths. Although it has been read into the myths since the early Neoplatonists, such an idea would be particularly inappropriate in the *Phaedo*, given the importance of the cyclical argument in the proof of immortality. Some inconsistency must be noted here, however, for either the extremes are not subject to rebirth or all things must pass from one state into another, meaning that even the disembodied eventually pass back into other forms and that even the incurable return to the body. The contradiction was noted as early as the Neoplatonic interpreters, who used all manner of special pleading to argue that the tormented in Tartarus would not remain there forever, but would be freed after a really long time, e.g., a complete cosmic revolution or Great Year, or that the threat of eternal punishment is a falsehood for the good of the community, to deter people from irremediable crimes. (cp. Damascius I. § 547, II. § 147; Olympiodorus 10 § 14.) The best interpretation seems to be that the idea of reincarnation and the idea of endless disembodiment in torment or bliss are meant to be considered separately rather than as parts of a coherent system. Both the idea of the cycle of reincarnations and the images of torment or bliss without end have their significance within the myth. The endlessness of the bliss or torment serves as the ultimate magnification of the reward or punishment for the philosophic or unphilosophic life, while the cycle of reincarnations serves to reinforce the cyclical nature of the cosmos.

philosopher and non-philosopher but also sanctions the value of philosophy with the authority of tradition.

## CONCLUSION

The life of the philosopher, according to Plato, should be spent in search of the true realities of life, the principles underlying the sensible world that are only accessible to the mind. Only such principles provide a stable and trustworthy guide for governing the behavior of an individual or a community, and only a life lived in accordance with these principles is truly happy or worthwhile. In the *Phaedo*, Plato uses the traditional tale of the journey to the underworld to expand upon the arguments his interlocutors expound dialectically. The complexes of obstacle, solution, and result that provide the dramatic action of Socrates' telling of this traditional tale not only contrast the fate of the philosophic and unphilosophic souls after death but also illustrate their fates during life. The unphilosophic person is imprisoned in the body by chains of pain and pleasure; he wanders astray in the bewildering multiplicity of the phenomenal world; and, ultimately, he suffers the torments of Tartarus as he is buffeted this way and that by the ever-shifting currents of pain and pleasure. The philosopher, however, freed from the constraints of his body, follows the guide of his mind through the labyrinth of sensible existence and, purified by his endeavors, experiences the delights of the true reality. The myth provides vivid images of these alternatives, couched in the familiar patterns and elements of tradition. As White notes, "The mythic details provide what might be called discursive possibilities derived from the arguments preceding it. The inherent persuasiveness embodied in the strictly rational phase of the inquiry will be extended by this form of development. The arguments will then more likely be persuasive as a result of this mythic chant than if they remained unadorned in their original prosaic setting."[180] This persuasiveness, however, stems not only from the imagery itself, but also from the traditional authority attendant upon these images. Plato employs the myth not just because of the potential of the narrative form of the tale but because it is a traditional tale. Socrates' myth of the soul's journey after death reinforces his claims about the nature of the philosopher, extending his listener's understanding of his

[180] White 1989, p. 238.

ideas and supporting his reasoning with the authority of the familiar elements of the traditional myths.

Socrates' tale should not be interpreted simply as an allegory in which the fate of the soul after death is actually the fate of the soul before death. The myth does more than encode the fate of the living in a traditional format; it also presents a view of the afterlife which both incorporates traditional ideas and remains consistent with Plato's philosophic ideas. Moreover, by depicting Socrates telling such a myth at the end of his life, as his final philosophic effort, Plato assimilates philosophy to the traditional authoritative discourse of myth, illustrating that for the ideal philosopher, telling a good myth is merely another way of practicing philosophy. Although the myth should not be read as mere allegory, it also should not be taken as a simple statement of Plato's 'religious' viewpoint about life after death. Plato's own personal beliefs about the afterlife are, of course, impossible for us to know, but the view he provides in the myth in the *Phaedo* presents a vivid picture consistent with his ontological and epistemological assumptions. As Socrates cautions, "Now to insist that these things are just as I've related them would not be fitting for a man of intelligence, but that either this or something like it is true about our souls and their dwellings, given that the soul evidently is immortal, this, I think, *is* fitting and worth risking, for one who believes that it is so – for a noble risk it is."[181]

---

[181] τὸ μὲν οὖν ταῦτα διισχυρίσασθαι οὕτως ἔχειν ὡς ἐγὼ διελήλυθα, οὐ πρέπει νοῦν ἔχοντι ἀνδρί· ὅτι μέντοι ἢ ταῦτ'ἐστὶν ἢ τοιαῦτ'ἄττα περὶ τὰς ψυχὰς ἡμῶν καὶ τὰς οἰκήσεις, ἐπείπερ ἀθάνατόν γε ἡ ψυχὴ φαίνεται οὖσα, τοῦτο καὶ πρέπειν μοι δοκεῖ καὶ ἄξιον κινδυνεῦσαι οἰομένῳ οὕτως ἔχειν καλὸς γὰρ ὁ κίνδυνος (114d1–6).

# 5 | Conclusions: The End of the Road

Having reached the end of the road, it is perhaps worthwhile to look back at the route we have taken. The starting point is a group of texts: the Orphic gold tablets, Aristophanes' *Frogs*, and the myth in Plato's *Phaedo*, all of which share a common pattern of action: the journey to the underworld. To analyze these texts more neatly, I divided the narratives into complexes of obstacle, solution, and result. Despite the similarity of the obstacles for the traveler described in these myths of the journey to the underworld, the limited types of solutions employed to bypass these obstacles, and the same basic descriptions of the possible positive and negative results, these elements all have profoundly different significance within the individual narratives.

This variation, I argue, calls into question the attribution of any single meaning to the story of the journey to the underworld as well as any simple explanation of the myths as the products of Orphic doctrines about the afterlife. The definitions of 'Orphism' as a sect with an exclusive set of eschatological ideas, definitions rooted in Christian models of what a religion ought to be, must be replaced by a definition that takes into account the ways in which the 'Orphic' sources make use of the common stock of traditional material. Redefining Orphism in such a way permits a better understanding of the variety of eschatological ideas in Greek religion, including the much-debated relation of the Eleusinian Mysteries to the various countercultural Bacchic and Orphic movements.[1]

Rather than being a statement of the cycle of rebirth after an (initiatory) experience of death, the significance of each of the tellings of the underworld journey differs with the model of the world that the teller of

---

[1] cp. my discussion of the labels 'Orphic' and 'magic' in "Pure from the Pure and the Sheep from the Goats" (unpublished paper presented at APA 133rd Annual Meeting, 2002)

the myth is communicating through the tale. The creators of the tablets tell their myths to mark the *déviance* of the deceased from the mainstream society, illustrating how her special, marginal status in this world provides privilege in the next. Aristophanes, by contrast, uses his comic telling to provide a distorted image of Athens that reflects his ideas of what Athens needs to be saved. Plato repositions the philosopher within the order of the city and the world by co-opting the authority of the tradition for his philosophic project.

Each of these myths is designed to appeal to its intended audience to accept its model of the world and models for behavior within it. The myths must compete for acceptance and influence against rival versions of the traditional tale as well as other myths that incorporate different models. The way the myth is told differs with the stakes in this competition for authority, with the varying audiences at which the myth is aimed, and with the agenda of the teller. The tablets are aimed at a much smaller audience than Aristophanes' *Frogs*, and their influence has been significantly smaller. Plato, on the other hand, has a more ambitious program than either the tablets or the *Frogs*, and although he did not succeed in all his goals, the influence of the Platonic myths on Western tradition has been very great indeed. The examination of Plato's attempt to co-opt the authority of the mythic tradition for his philosophic program, moreover, illuminates the way other tellers of myth, less self-conscious in their myth-crafting, shaped their stories to suit their audiences. Although the way in which the process is performed varies in each set of texts examined here, the creation of the individual myth occurs in each case through a process of *bricolage*, as the tellers work in useful chunks of traditional material to communicate their ideas and win authority for them from their audiences.

## RETRACING THE PATHS

Although the myths I have examined communicate different perspectives on the realities and idealities of their world through their reflection of the world in the narrative of the journey to the other world, these myths use a limited number of traditional motifs to convey their ideas. These motifs, however, have no fixed meaning in and of themselves; rather, their meaning derives from the way in which they are employed within the individual narrative. A brief review of the obstacles, solutions, and results found in these texts will demonstrate this variety of meanings.

The first obstacle that the traveler could possibly face on the journey from the land of the living to the realm of the dead is a difficulty in departing from the world of the living. In the gold tablets, however, the deceased immediately finds herself already in the realm of the dead. In the A and P tablets, she is already in the presence of Persephone, but even in the B tablets, she has already reached the halls of Hades. In the tablets, no further ties bind the deceased to the world of the living and the society to which she has set herself in opposition.

In the *Frogs*, on the other hand, Aristophanes makes a joke of the traditional separation of the realms of the living and dead. Dionysos consults Herakles as though he were embarking on an ordinary journey, asking for advice on the best inns, brothels, and eating places. Herakles, by contrast, gives him a number of possible ways to commit suicide, all of which Dionysos rejects because of the discomforts of the route.[2] Despite all this wrangling, however, Dionysos needs to do nothing but arrive at the lake of Acheron to depart from the world of the living. This traditional water barrier presents a test of the traveler's qualifications, for Dionysos must be a citizen and able to row to the music of the frogs to cross the lake. Although his comic blurring of the lines between the realms of the living and the dead helps create the carnivalesque atmosphere of the *Frogs*, Aristophanes uses the rowing test on Acheron to renegotiate the boundaries between citizen and slave in Athens, as well as between aristocrat and democrat.

Plato makes a very different use of this kind of obstacle, playing off the traditional idea that some dead fail to separate themselves from the world of the living and remain haunting this world as restless ghosts. In the *Phaedo* he describes the unphilosophic as imprisoned in their materiality, unable to move beyond the phenomenal world like ghosts who haunt graveyards because they are unable to make their way to Hades. The practices of philosophy permit the philosopher to make the normal transition, whereas the unphilosophic is left stranded at the threshold of the two worlds. Plato uses the motif of the restless dead unable to cross

---

[2] Thus, the way of hanging is stifling (πνιγηρὰν), taking hemlock – ground by mortar and pestle – is a well-beaten shortcut (ἀτραπὸς ξύντομος τετριμμένη), but too cold and numbing (ψυχρὰν γε καὶ δυσχείμερον), while jumping off a building is a short, quick, downhill path (ταχεῖαν καὶ κατάντη). All these suggested routes are rejected by Dionysos, who wants a path neither too warm nor too cold (μήτε θερμὴν μήτ᾽ ἄγαν ψυχρὰν), but the traditional way that Herakles took.

to the land of the dead to emphasize the misery of the unphilosophic life and the importance of living philosophically.

In the *Phaedo*, Plato makes use of another traditional mythic obstacle for the deceased, the difficulty of finding the right path in the underworld, to illustrate his contrast between the material, phenomenal world and the unseen world of true reality. The unphilosophic person, bewildered by the multiplicity of the phenomenal world and unaccustomed to following the guidance of his reason, cannot easily make his way to the place of judgement, whereas the philosopher follows the daimonic guide on a single and simple path to an even clearer vision of the truth.

The B tablets also use the motif of the two paths to separate the privileged from the unprivileged, but the distinction comes not between the philosophic and unphilosophic, but between those who want to quench their thirst at the first spring and those who know to press on to the spring flowing from the lake of Memory.[3] The traditional fork in the path serves in the B tablets to separate the deceased from the masses who have gone astray.

In the *Frogs*, the chorus of Eleusinian initiates has the special knowledge that can guide the travelers wandering lost in the murky underworld. Dionysos and Xanthias, terrified by their encounters with the denizens of the underworld, join in the celebrations of the initiates to ask them the way to the house of Hades. Like the special deceased of the tablets, the Eleusinian initiates know how to find the way in the underworld, and they share this knowledge with those whom they do not exclude from their company. Aristophanes uses his own variant of the Eleusinian *prorrhesis* to redefine the barbarian and the impure as the corrupt politicians and others whom he feels are detrimental to the unity of Athens.

Once the traveler has found his way to the halls of Hades, he must encounter the powers of the underworld. In each text, however, the teller's choice of the entity encountered and of the context of the confrontation sets up the differing solutions. In the *Frogs*, the ferocious guardian is a doorkeeper slave and the halls of Hades is a typical domestic setting on a street just like those of Athens in the world above, reinforcing Aristophanes' comic blending of the two realms. In Plato, the deceased comes before the court of the underworld for judgement. Plato transforms the

---

[3] While this second spring may be located either on the left or right, the instructions in A4 seem to privilege the right-hand way, in keeping with the traditional correctness of the right way and the sinister associations of the left.

confrontation with the powers of the underworld into an examination of the deceased before the underworld court to advocate living not only a just life but also the examined life of philosophy. In the B tablets, the guardians serve merely to demand the identity of the deceased, but in the A and P tablets the encounter is less a check with the guards at the gate than an audience with the ruler of the underworld, Persephone. In all the tablets, however the encounter with the underworld powers is described, the obstacle is constructed so that the deceased must proclaim her identity to pass, making the tablets a statement of religious self-definition.

While all three sets of texts employ the motif of a declaration of identity as a solution to the obstacles facing the deceased, its significance is different in every text. In the A and B tablets, the deceased lays claim to divine lineage, linking herself with the ideal world of primordial unity between gods and men instead of the ties to family, clan, or city that place the individual in the ordinary world. The claims in various tablets to purity or freedom from penalty reinforce the extraordinary nature of the deceased, her difference from the mainstream. The modes of self-identification that the tablets prescribe for the deceased highlight her separation from normal society, placing her beyond the ordinary in divine connection, lineage, or purity.

Purity is also essential in the *Phaedo*, but Plato describes this purity as the dissolving of the prison of the material world by philosophical concentration on the unseen realm. He manipulates the language of ritual purity from the countercultural initiation cults into a description of the philosophic way of living that strips away the chains that bind a prisoner or a slave and produces a free citizen. The impure become the unphilosophic, who keep themselves in fetters like criminals or slaves. Plato reduces the unphilosophic to the marginal status of slaves through his transformation of the traditional solution of revealing one's identity to the powers of the underworld. In the *Phaedo*, moreover, the purifications of philosophy are depicted not only as the only kind of truly virtuous behavior, but as heroic deeds like those of Theseus and Herakles. Plato assimilates philosophy to the kind of initiations and purifications that the tablets portray as the solution to the encounter with the powers of the underworld.

Aristophanes, on the other hand, plays with the traditional motif of the declaration of identity by having Dionysos disguise himself as Herakles and switch roles with Xanthias whenever the identity of the hero and archetypal initiate threatens to bring trouble. Instead of setting up the specific qualifications needed to pass the encounter, Aristophanes toys with the categories of mortal and god, slave and noble, hero and coward, blurring the definition of the worthy person and then ultimately undermining the whole test of identity by having the doorkeeper refer the question to Persephone.

While Aristophanes does not make a sojourn in the underworld the result of Dionysos's journey, he nonetheless plays off the traditional positive and negative lots in the afterlife, using the same options as the other texts. The chorus of initiates, the ideal group of Athenians, live a blissful life of endless revelry, a permanent festival time from which the unworthy are excluded. The traditional lot of the unhappy dead, wretched wallowing in filth and mire, is reserved for the real group of Athenians, the audience whom Xanthias cheerfully points out to Dionysos as parricides and other types of criminals.

The lot of the initiates in the *Frogs* resembles the afterlife promised to the deceased on many of the tablets (A2, A3, P1, P2, B1, B10, and possibly B11), the company of other blessed dead, perhaps in celebration of rituals, as in P1. The tablets offer little description of the fate of the ordinary dead, who cannot make the same identity claims as the special deceased who is buried with a gold tablet. The ordinary dead are simply excluded from the company of the blessed, marginalized in the afterlife. Two of the Thurii tablets, however, promise an even more exceptional fate for the deceased – transformation into divine state: "Fortunate and blessed one, a god you shall be instead of a mortal."[4] This reward transcends even a permanent holiday, the greatest of joys for a mortal in Greek culture.

Even the *Phaedo's* description of the rewards of the most pure philosophers does not go so far, although the ineffable bliss of the disembodied state seems to approach it. The reward of the philosopher in Plato resembles that of the tablets and the *Frogs*, but the company of the blessed is delightful in Plato because of the purity and clarity of the upper world. Moreover, Plato ascribes this traditionally postmortem reward to the philosopher during his life, if he can sufficiently free himself from the undue consideration of the phenomenal world. In the same way, the unphilosophic person suffers the torments of Tartarus not only in the

---

[4] ὄλβιε καὶ μακαριστέ, θεὸς δ' ἔσηι ἀντὶ βροτοῖο. A1.9, cp. A4.4.

underworld but in his present life, buffeted about in the ever-changing flux of the phenomenal world. By weaving together the details of his myths with the ideas in the dialogues' arguments, Plato extends the traditional mythic rewards and punishments to life before death as well as life after death.

## ORPHISM AS ORIGIN OR ORIENTATION?

The range of ways in which the limited set of traditional motifs are combined shows that these myths are the products of *bricolage*, carefully constructed to express the teller's model of the world. Moreover, the widely varying applications to which these myths are put argues against any simple or single 'meaning' for the traditional pattern. Certainly, these texts are not all describing the experience of initiatory rebirth after an ecstatic ritual experience. Even the Pelinna tablets, which do explicitly describe the deceased as having been born again on the same day she died, use the traditional pattern to position the deceased in a network of relations with Persephone and Dionysos that identifies her in ways beyond the normal polis system of identification. Aristophanes' *Frogs*, Plato's myths, and even the other tablets are using the traditional pattern in more complicated ways. That the pattern of action for the journey to the underworld derives ultimately from initiatory or even shamanic practices of pre-Greek peoples may very well be true, but such an unprovable supposition tells the reader little about any of these texts. Worse still, the assumption of such an origin may (and often has) obscured the interesting ways in which the mythic tradition is used in the texts and the ideas that the creators of these myths are communicating.

These texts have often been seen as a group related by the fact that they all contain a similar set of traditional motifs or that they are among the few literary texts that focus upon life after death. The common thread that produces this concern has been identified as the strange current in Greek religion known as 'Orphism' and the motifs that the texts share have thus been labelled 'Orphic'. The myths of Plato are then seen as products of some kind of Orphic influence, while the question of Orphic influence on the Eleusinian Mysteries and on Aristophanes' underworld in the *Frogs* is argued on the basis of the pitifully few bits of evidence for both the Mysteries and Orphism. Such a definition of Orphism is a relic of the turn of the century debates about primitive religion and no longer remains satisfactory in the wake of the scholarship of Burkert, Graf, Detienne, Sabbattucci, and others. Either the term 'Orphism', taken in its old sense, must be abandoned, or it must be redefined so that the term helpfully describes a religious phenomenon in ancient Greece.

What do the materials that have been labelled 'Orphic' have in common? The evidence for Orphic texts goes far beyond merely eschatological doctrines; it includes a range of cosmological speculation and practical magic that can be linked to the eschatology only with a great deal of effort.[5] West sums it up best: "It is a fallacy to suppose that all 'Orphic' poems and rituals are related to each other or that they are to be interpreted as different manifestations of a single religious movement.... There was no doctrinal criterion for ascription to Orpheus, and no copyright restriction. It was a device for conferring antiquity and authority upon a text that stood in need of them."[6] What all 'Orphic' materials do share, it seems, is the appeal to an authority outside the mainstream; they represent, in Detienne's terms, a *chemin de déviance*. While, strictly speaking, an 'Orphic' text should be one that specifically grounds its claims on the authority of Orpheus, the definition might be extended to materials that, even if they do not explicitly claim the authority of Orpheus, nevertheless appeal to a source of authority that contradicts the mainstream tradition.[7] Whether Orphism is taken as a general term for such countercultural religious movements or is limited to a specific type that is grounded in what Plato calls the βίος Ὀρφικός is less important than that Orphism is defined by the way it handles the mythic tradition rather than by the particular elements of that tradition it employs.

## MYTHIC REFLECTIONS OF THE WORLD

Again, J. Z. Smith's terminology of 'locative' and 'utopian' may be helpful in distinguishing the models put forth in these texts. Whereas a locative worldview sets forth the cosmos as an order in which everything has its proper place and hierarchical relation to the other parts of the system, the utopian worldview focuses on escape from the oppressive order of the

---

[5] The Zagreus anthropogony myth is an important example of such a fabricated link between the cosmologies and the eschatology. cp. Edmonds 1999.

[6] West 1983, p. 3.

[7] Linforth's extreme definition of Orphism as only those materials sealed with the name of Orpheus unduly limits the scope, given that so much evidence for the mythic tradition comes without such specific attribution.

present world, a relocation from the fixed place within a locative order to 'no-place', a space or time beyond the ordinary world. Such spatial metaphors help clarify the different agendas of the myths.

Although he takes advantage of the Dionysian festival of the comic competition to present a comically distorted vision of the city, Aristophanes presents a locative view of Athens, reinforcing the unity and stability of the city's order even as he satirizes it. Comedy is a temporary disruption, a carnivalesque festival, in which the performance depicts a topsy-turvy Athens to itself. The use of myth in this forum nevertheless remains within the bounds of locative religious expression, for Aristophanes is not altering the fundamental structure of Athenian society, merely making use of the liminal space to create alterations within the hierarchies. Aristophanes reproduces the basic model of Athens with the 'best' citizens at the center of power, followed by the common citizens, then metics, with slaves on the periphery, and barbarians excluded. In this locative model, everyone has his place and should be treated accordingly.

Aristophanes does, however, shift the boundaries between the groups, moving some people from one fixed category to another. Slaves may become citizens and kinsmen, while leading politicians may be treated as barbarians, because, in the disruption of the war, they are behaving as those groups behave, they are locating themselves in those spaces. Likewise, Aristophanes pleads that the oligarchs who were exiled, removed from the center to beyond the bounds, should be restored to their central place. In the moment of flux provided by the Dionysiac festival of the comic competitions, Aristophanes engages in shuffling the categories of society, in rearranging the borders. The categories themselves remain basically the same, but who is in and who is out can be shifted in Aristophanes' depiction of Athens in the *Frogs*.

The tablets, rather than simply relocating people within the categories of the society, reinforce the marginal status of the deceased, the factors that separate her from the mainstream of the society. Rather than trying to relocate herself within the societal structure, the deceased positions herself beyond the structure, not only by the appeal to the afterlife, but through the markers of status to which she appeals. The normal markers of status within the community, the locators of family lineage and place associations, are replaced by claims that link the deceased directly to the gods and differentiate her from the mainstream by her ritually pure status or special knowledge. The variations in the tablets provide testimony to the different *chemins de déviance* taken by people who registered a protest to the normal order, but all the tablets present a utopian worldview, in contrast to Aristophanes' locative, albeit carnivalesque, one.

Plato, like the tablets, marks the philosopher apart from the mainstream through special knowledge and direct connection with the divine. However, the philosopher also is relocated to the center of the political community – Socrates is the only true politician and only a philosopher king can organize a truly just society. The very skills that mark the philosopher off from the ordinary throng qualify him or her for leadership. Mainstream society is in trouble precisely because it fails to realize its need for the philosopher, who is, in present reality, marginalized instead of put at the center. Plato uses myth, which encodes the traditional models of the order of society, to move the philosopher from the margins to the center. All of the features that the myth legitimizes and puts value on – the role of the hero, the pious initiate, the properly buried dead man, etc. – are all made to pertain, in the appropriate context set up by the dialogue, to the philosopher. Instead of locating the philosopher only with the extraordinary and marginal, as the tablets' tales do, Plato's myths make use of the familiar elements to identify the philosopher with the most authoritative and central features of the Greek tradition.

Both the tablets and the Platonic myths, then, privilege a marginal group in society by appealing to standards beyond the normal order to justify the special privilege. But whereas the tablets reinforce the marginal status of the deceased by emphasizing the different basis for her claims, Plato manipulates the mythic tradition to assimilate the philosophic life to the most privileged positions within the locative order. This renegotiation of the positions within the locative order resembles more Aristophanes' manipulations in the *Frogs*. While Aristophanes uses the other world to provide a distorted reflection of Athens, the basic structure of society remains remarkably the same – for who knows if life is death and death life? The three sets of texts make use of the journey to the underworld and the traditional motifs not just in different ways to present their various models of the world, but with fundamentally different approaches to the relation of their telling with the tradition of mythic discourse in which their tales are created.

The eschatological ideas of the gold tablets and the famous σῶμα-σῆμα slogan could thus be considered 'Orphic' because the models of the world that they imply devalue mortal existence in favor of the afterlife, rejecting the importance of the social structures of this world. The Eleusinian Mysteries, by contrast, while they promise good things to initiates in the afterlife, nevertheless remain within the locative structure of mainstream polis religion. Aristophanes, indeed, uses the familiar elements of the Mysteries to reinforce the unity of the Athenian polis, renegotiating some of the boundaries within the system but preserving the basic hierarchies that govern polis order. Plato's use of myth is more 'Orphic' than the *Frogs* in this sense because, like the tablets, he privileges a marginal group by appealing to a structure beyond the locative order of the polis. On the other hand, Plato relocates the philosophers within the polis order, placing them at the very center and buttressing their position with all the traditional authority that he can contrive in his myths. The 'Orphic influence' on Plato or Aristophanes, therefore, can be seen in the similarity or differences in their outlook on mainstream society. The speculative reconstructions of direct transmission of Orphic ideas from Thracian shamans to the southern Italian Orphics to the Pythagoreans to Socrates from Pythagorean exiles or to Plato in his journeys to Sicily are unnecessary for understanding why Plato's myths resemble the gold tablets and why both differ from the *Frogs*, despite the common pattern of action and traditional mythic elements.

Instead of attempting to compete within the tradition for mainstream acceptance and authority, Orphic texts appeal to the margins of society, setting themselves in opposition to the general model of the world set forth in the various authoritative tellings in the tradition. If Orphism is understood in such a way, not only can more sense be made of the similarities and differences among the tablets, the *Frogs*, and the Platonic myths, but other texts which have, under other definitions, been classified as Orphic can be reexamined for the models of the world they present. An exploration of the theogonies attributed to Orpheus might produce a particularly interesting analysis of the ways in which these myths reorder the world order by rejecting or transforming traditional patterns and motifs in other cosmogonies in the tradition. Such a definition of Orphism, moreover, would apply not only to the countercultural religious groups of the classical period but also to the later traditions that appealed to the ancient wisdom of Orpheus to validate their ideas.

## THE POWER OF MYTH

If a myth, as I defined it in the Introduction, is the telling of a traditional tale, each of these myths makes use of different aspects of the nature of mythic discourse, its narrative structure and its traditional authority.

In the tablets, the use of mythic narrative serves to express cosmological ideas, the models of and for the universe that are important to the creators of the tablets. The narrative structure of the journey to the underworld helps articulate an underlying model of the cosmos and the deceased's place within it, marking her as special and privileged. The vivid images of, e.g., the white cypress and the water of Memory, make evocative and memorable the ideas in the text. Regardless of how literally and sincerely the deceased may have believed in the vision of the afterlife depicted on the tablets, the myth is an expressive and memorable way to articulate vital ideas.

While the expressive power of mythic imagery is not neglected by Aristophanes, it is the familiarity of the mythic images that is central to Aristophanes' manipulations of myth. The comedy of the *Frogs* depends on the audience's recognizing the familiar motifs and being amused at the way they are twisted. This gap between the familiar versions and the alterations is central not just to Aristophanes' humor but to the expression of his serious ideas as well, since Aristophanes uses the comic framework to dissolve and recreate the boundaries of society.

Plato is making use of both the expressive and familiar aspects of mythic narrative, of myth both as traditional and as a tale. The vivid imagery of the myths and the narrative structure of the tale allows Plato to communicate ideas in a form that is both memorable and intense. The torments of Tartarus capture the problems of an unphilosophic life that is dependent on sense impressions and crystallize them into an unforgettable image. On the other hand, the traditional nature of the elements he uses lends authority to the often radical ideas he is putting forth. Everyone in his audience is familiar with the stories of Tartarus, of the restless dead, of Herakles, Theseus, and Odysseus. Unlike Aristophanes, however, Plato is not extracting humor from the gap between the familiar versions and his own. Rather, Plato uses the familiarity of the tradition to disguise his own innovations, to make them seem in line with traditional authorities.

## THE AGON FOR AUTHORITY

Understanding the ways in which texts deploy traditional material clarifies the relation of the texts not only to each other but also to the tradition as a whole. The significant relations between tellings of a traditional tale cannot be reduced to a stemma tracking the similarities and differences between mythic tellings like the variations in a manuscript tradition; they lie instead in the way the elements are shaped to convey the teller's ideas and to appeal to the audience. This approach to the relations between the texts brings out some important implications for the understanding of the way myths compete to influence audiences.

All the myths I have examined are designed to communicate their models of the world to their audience, but they differ in their effectiveness and the audience at which they aim. Each text situates itself as part of the agonistic discourse of myth, in implicit or explicit competition against other narratives that present alternative (albeit not usually radically different) ways of understanding the world. Every myth seeks to win the acceptance of its audience and thus incorporation into the tradition as an authoritative model of the world and for behavior within it. In the three sets of texts examined here, the form in which the myth is presented, including the orality or written form of the text, is shaped by the teller's understanding of the audience and ambitions to authoritative status for the myth.

Any speaker derives his influence or authority from the reception of his discourse by his audience. Poets and other makers of myths were often described within the Greek society as deriving their authority from their connection to the gods by the process of inspiration. Thus, the poet invokes the Muse at the beginning of an epic, signaling the connection of his discourse with the divine realm. Viewed from within the community, the audience acknowledges the authority of the poet's discourse because the audience has judged that the discourse stems from the ultimate source of authority, the gods and the divine realm. The audience also acknowledges that the poet is within the tradition of discourse that is recognized as authoritative. Viewed from an outside perspective, however, the audience bestows this authority upon the poet, who has persuaded them of the value of his discourse, and thus it places the poet within the authoritative tradition.

Mark Griffith argues that the judgement in a poetic contest was made on the basis of an assessment of the poets' *sophia*, which he divides into three categories: factual, moral, and aesthetic.

(a) *Knowledge and factual accuracy* (the *sophos*-poet knows how things were and are, tells them 'truly', gets names, pedigrees, and events right, and is therefore valuable to the community as a repository of information); (b) *moral and educational integrity* (the *sophos* presents advice or instruction, or unambiguous examples of good and bad conduct, by which the community is supposed to be collectively and individually improved); (c) *technical skill and aesthetic/emotional impact* (the *sophos*' uncanny verbal, musical and histrionic powers can excite the ear and eye as well as the mind, dazzle and delight an audience, and arouse in it irresistible feelings of wonder, sympathetic engagement, and emotional release...).[8]

These three types of criteria for judgement were the basis on which the story was evaluated, the basis on which the telling was preserved and repeated in the community, the basis on which it was cited as example in rhetorical or philosophical argument. The mythmaker who best demonstrated these qualities was the most persuasive to his audience and, as a result, was granted the most authority as a voice for determining the rules of the cultural order. The poets were, of course, constantly competing for this influence on their audience, constantly trying to undermine the claims of previous poets and replace them with their own, to win for themselves a place within the tradition.[9]

In different types of poetic and nonpoetic speech contests, the relative importance of these three criteria for judging the speech would vary, just as the authority within the community that was at stake in the judgement varied. A poem might be selected for a prize, remembered by the audience members, or passed down from one generation to another because it contained important genealogical or historical information, illustrated the proper behavior of the rulers of the society, or simply was beautiful. But what was most important in determining the authoritative status, the overall influence of a poem within the society? What determined whether a poem would be considered "true" and not replaced by another poem that claimed "οὐκ ἔστ᾽ ἔτυμος λόγος οὗτος"?

### AUDIENCE AND INFLUENCE

To win wide influence and authority, a myth must present a useful and appealing model of the world to its audience. Although sheer technical skill, of which Plato and Aristophanes undoubtedly had more than

---

[8] Griffith 1990, pp. 188–189.

[9] Pindar's First Olympian and Stesichorus's Palinode are some of the more explicit examples of these poetic attempts to supplant the authority of previous poets and their versions of a story. "That story is not true," οὐκ ἔστ᾽ ἔτυμος λόγος οὗτος, claims Stesichorus, referring to Homer's famous story of the adultery of Helen. The poets attack the truth value of another poem, but it is often uncertain which of the three criteria is under attack in any given case, factual, moral, or aesthetic. As Griffith puts it, "Ancient critics, and even the poets themselves, often blur the distinctions and slide heedlessly - or opportunistically - from one to another, as if poets should be held accountable at every moment for all three." (Griffith 1990, p. 189.)

most of their competitors, plays a major role in crafting a convincing tale, the scope of the audience to which the tale appeals is an important criterion for judging the influence and authority a myth can win. The tablets are designed for a very small audience, the individual deceased and perhaps a small group on the margins of the society who already share her countercultural outlook. As a result, the influence of the tablets on other Greek literature seems very small; even their possible influence on Plato's myths must remain speculative. The gold tablets were, in effect, lost in the garbage heap of history until they were uncovered by modern archaeologists. Despite their use of the common tradition, the tablets' formulation of the mythic elements appealed only to a very small audience, which was unable or unwilling to incorporate it into the mainstream tradition.

Aristophanes, on the other hand, proved very successful at appealing to not only his initial audience in the Athenian theatre but also audiences for millennia beyond the original performance. The *Frogs* won the prize in the comedy competition in 405, proving that Aristophanes' telling of his tale was more appealing to his audience than the productions of his rivals. Moreover, the *Frogs* received an unprecedented revival the next year because, in their new situation after their defeat by Sparta, the ideas Aristophanes put forth in his play appealed to the Athenians (or at least those in power at the time). The relation of the *Frogs'* parabasis to the decree of Patrokleides that recalled the exiled oligarchs and the subsequent coup that established the Thirty Tyrants should be as much a reminder of the potential authority of a myth as a model for behavior as the debate between the tragedians in the *Frogs*. This contest between Euripides and Aeschylus influenced the later literary criticism of these two tragedians, not to mention the genre of tragedy itself, and Aristophanes' humorous way of telling of the journey to the land of the dead seems also to have appealed to Lucian and later satirists. That the *Frogs* survived in manuscript through the millennia until the present day is due to many vagaries of fate, but the excellence of his storytelling cannot be disregarded as a factor.

Plato's myths have been even more influential on later generations due to the prestige that Plato and the Academic tradition acquired. While he may not have succeeded in entirely replacing the discourse of myth with philosophy as the primary form of authoritative discourse in his society, the extent to which he did succeed in establishing the legitimacy of his project is astonishing. Plato's myths themselves have been re-used and reinterpreted through the millennia and put to many different uses, despite Plato's attempts to limit the interpretation of the mythic narrative by enclosing it within his philosophic dialogue. The vivid images of the underworld – the rivers of burning mud and the souls crying out for pardon to those whom they have wronged – have been picked up by later writers and re-used for purposes other than inducing the audience to practice Platonic philosophy. While Plato probably did not invent this motif, his formulation of it helped lend it the authority within the tradition that permitted it to be told and retold to many audiences over the generations. Plato's artistry, his ability to manipulate the traditional material to appeal to his audience, ensured a place in that tradition for his myths.

Despite his inability to entirely subvert the entire mythic tradition to his philosophic projects, Plato's critique of the traditional material and of the discourse of myth provided a framework for the re-evaluation of traditional material and artistic compositions ever since. The very distinction between μῦθος and λόγος that hampers the modern scholar's attempts to uncover the workings of Plato's myths springs from Plato's critique of traditional tales and their ungoverned authority in the hands of poets. The age-old quarrel to which Plato refers in the *Republic* between poetry and philosophy may continue even today, but the debate has been shaped by Plato's formulation of the problems and issues.

## MANIPULATIONS OF MYTH

While Plato's attempts to settle the age-old quarrel bring a new dimension to the competition for authority in the mythic tradition, the ways that Aristophanes and the makers of the gold tablets craft their myths also reveal some of the mechanics of the Greek mythic tradition. The myths in the gold tablets make fairly straightforward use of the traditional mythic elements to communicate their models of the world. Stemming from an apparently oral tradition, the tellings on the tablets reflect minute shifts of perspective from tablet to tablet, crystallized in the process of transformation from a remembered oral tale to a written text. Perhaps even written down by the deceased herself before her death, the myth presents its narrative elliptically, recording only the elements essential to the deceased's understanding of herself and her relation to the world. Nevertheless, the tablets communicate their ideas by evoking the resonances associated with the traditional elements familiar to the audience, shaping their meaning through the narrative structure of the journey to the underworld.

Aristophanes, on the other hand, plays with the mythic elements at the same time he is making use of them. Not only does he play off the familiarity of the traditional elements to tell his story, but he deliberately subverts the expectations of his audience to create humor in his play. The *Frogs* is a written text, carefully crafted to make this sophisticated use of the mythic tradition to compete with Aristophanes' rivals in oral performance in the theatrical competition. As befits a comedy at the Lenaean festival, Aristophanes crafts the mythic narrative in the *Frogs* "to say many silly things as well as many serious, and, having played around and jested worthily for this festive occasion, to wear the ribbons as the victor."[10]

Plato takes this conscious use of myth one step further, not only manipulating the mythic tradition, but subverting and co-opting it at the same time. Plato employs myths within his dialogues because they are an effective means of communicating his ideas to his readers immersed in the Greek mythic tradition. He tailors the myths to fit the ideas discussed in the dialogue, deftly weaving in complicated allusions and correlations between different parts of the dialogue and bringing them together in narrative form.

At the same time, however, Plato uses the myths to supplant the traditional sources of authority, the poets and their mythic descriptions of the world and the gods, with his own model of the world. By manipulating the mythic tradition to produce a myth that relates the ideas he expresses in the philosophic discussions, Plato employs the authority of mythic discourse in service of philosophy. Plato enters the contest in which rival tellers compete for cultural authority for their models of the world expressed in myth and tries to discredit his rivals and establish the authority of his own philosophic ideas with his audience.

Although Plato is engaged in the most complex use of myth, his manipulations of mythic discourse are at the same time more visible because his myths are to a greater extent literary productions rather than oral performances. Oral performance permits fluid variations between tellings, subtle changes of nuance and emphasis that reflect the personal interaction between teller and audience. The previous oral tellings cannot be

---

[10] 389-393 – Καὶ πολλὰ μὲν γέλοιά μ' εἰπεῖν, πολλὰ δὲ σπουδαῖα, καὶ τῆς σῆς ἑορτῆς ἀξίως παίσαντα καὶ σκώψαντα νικήσαντα ταινιοῦσθαι.

easily compared with the new one; only if the differences are shocking will they be contested. With written texts, on the other hand, every alteration and manipulation of the traditional elements can be checked against other versions; the competition becomes more explicit as every innovation must be justified. Nevertheless, the process of manipulation of traditional elements remains essentially the same, be it in written forms of oral performances like the gold tablets and Homeric epic or in literary productions like Plato's myths and the sophisticated dramas of Attic tragedy and comedy.[11] The intended audiences and specific strategies for appealing to those audiences may vary, but the teller always selects and alters the traditional material to appeal to the intended audience, crafting the tale from familiar elements to convey his or her ideas efficiently and effectively.

All of these texts, then, perform *bricolage* with a limited set of traditional elements, but the range of ways they can deploy these elements is large, allowing them to communicate widely varying ideas in their narratives. The discourse of myth, even in myths about the afterlife, is not restricted to the transmission of religious doctrines, rigid formulations of dogma that serve as shibboleths to distinguish groups of believers, whether Orphics or any other sect. Nor is myth in the fifth and fourth centuries BCE merely a relic, scoffed at by the intelligent and mature as fit only for children and the feebleminded. On the contrary, myth is an effective and authoritative mode of communicating ideas within the society, relying on the familiarity of the materials transmitted through the generations to convey, in an efficient and compact manner, complex models of the world and for behavior within it.

This mode of discourse is obviously most effective for those most familiar with the mythic tradition from which all the elements are drawn. While the tellers of these myths could rely on their original audiences' familiarity with the tradition to permit them to unpack the subtleties and

---

[11] The idea of primary or pristine myth simply told and simply accepted by ignorant savages too deep in Urdummheit to distinguish between myth and reality is itself a modern 'myth', a fabrication based in notions of the primitive that contrast with our modern society. J. Z. Smith stresses that all myths are 'applications' and compares the interactions of myth-teller and audience to the interactions of diviner and client in ritual divination. (Smith 1978, p. 206.) cp. Detienne 2003, p. xiii–xiv, "There is no reason to imagine any deep cleavage between, on the one hand, 'real' myths that are bound to rituals deeply anchored in beliefs and, on the other, stories that have become literary and seem no longer to have anything to do with the mythological tradition."

ramifications of their tellings, the modern reader approaches these texts at a disadvantage. So much of the traditional material is forever lost that any reconstruction of the pool of elements on which myth-tellers were drawing must remain incomplete. Moreover, the assumptions about and associations with the traditional elements built up over the intervening millennia create more obstacles for understanding the ideas these authors were trying to convey. Nevertheless, careful analysis of the texts with attention to the manipulations of the mythic elements can uncover many of the complexities obscured in previous interpretations. The traditional tale of the journey to the underworld in Greek mythology is indeed neither simple nor single, but each telling reveals a perspective on the cosmos, a reflection of the order of this world through the image of the other.

# Bibliography

Adam, Jean-Michel, *Le Récit*, Presses Universitaires de France: Paris, 1984.

Adkins, Arthur, *Merit and Responsibility: A Study in Greek Values*, Clarendon Press: Oxford, 1960.

Adkins, Arthur, "ΕΥΧΟΜΑΙ, ΕΥΧΟΛΗ, and ΕΥΧΟΣ in Homer," *Classical Quarterly* 19 (1969), pp. 20-33.

Alderink, Larry J. *Creation and Salvation in Ancient Orphism*, American Classical Studies, Vol. 8, Scholars Press: Atlanta, GA, 1981.

Allison, Richard, "Amphibian Ambiguities: Aristophanes and his Frogs," *Greece & Rome 30*.1 (1983), pp. 8-20.

Alt, Karin, "Diesseits und Jenseits in Platons Mythen von der Seele (Teil I)," *Hermes* 110 (1982), pp. 278-299.

Annas, Julia, "Plato's Myths of Judgement," *Phronesis* 27 (1982), pp. 119-143.

Arnott, W. Geoffrey, "A Lesson from the *Frogs*," *Greece & Rome* 38.1 (1991), pp. 18-23.

Babut, Daniel, "ΟΥΤΟΣΙ ΑΝΗΡ ΟΥ ΠΑΥΣΕΤΑΙ ΦΛΥΑΡΩΝ: Les Procédés Dialectiques dans le *Gorgias* et le Dessin du Dialogue," *Revue des Études Grecs* 105 (1992/1), pp. 59-110.

Baensch, Otto, "Die Schilderung der Unterwelt in Platons Phaidon," *Archiv für Geschichte der Philosophie* 16.2 (1903), pp. 189-203.

Barry and Schlegel, "Adolescent Initiation Ceremonies: A Cross-Cultural Code," *Ethnology* 18 (1979), pp. 199-210.

Barthes, Roland, "Myth Today," in *Mythologies*, trans. Annette Lavers, The Noonday Press: New York, 1972, pp. 109-159.

Belfiore, Elizabeth, "*Elenchus, Epode*, and Magic: Socrates as Silenus," *Phoenix* 34 (1980), pp. 128-137.

Bérard, Claude, *Anodoi: Essai dur l'Imagerie des Passages Chthoniens*, Institut Suisse de Rome, 1974.

Bergman, Jan, "Zum Zwei-Wege-Motiv: Religionsgeschichtliche und Exegetische Bemerkungen," *Svensk Exegetisk Årsbok* 41-42 (1976-1977), pp. 27-56.

Bernabé, Alberto, and Ana Isabel Jiménez San Cristobal, *Instrucciones para el Más Allá: Las Laminillas Órficas de Oro*, Ediciones Clásicas, S.A.: Madrid, 2001.

Bernabé, Alberto, *Poetae Epici Graeci II: Orphicorum Graecorum testimonia et fragmenta*, Munich, (forthcoming).

241

Betz, Hans Dieter, "'Der Erde Kind bin ich und des gestirnten Himmels': Zur Lehre vom Menschen in den orphischen Goldplättchen," in *Ansichten griechischer Rituale: Geburtstags-Symposium für Walter Burkert*, ed. Fritz Graf, B.G. Teubner: Stuttgart und Leipzig, 1998, pp. 399–419.

Bianchi, Ugo, "Péché Originel et Péché 'Antécédent'," *Revue de l'Histoire des Religions* 170 (1966), pp. 117–126 (reprinted on pp. 177–187 of Bianchi 1978).

Bianchi, Ugo, *Selected Essays on Gnosticism, Dualism and Mysteriosophy*, E.J. Brill: Leiden, 1978.

Blank, David, "The Fate of the Ignorant in Plato's *Gorgias*," *Hermes* 119 (1991), pp. 22–36.

Bloch, Enid, "Hemlock Poisoning and the Death of Socrates: Did Plato Tell the Truth?" in *The Trial and Execution of Socrates: Sources and Controversies*, eds. Thomas C. Brickhouse and Nicholas D. Smith, Oxford University Press: New York, 2002.

Boardman, John, "Herakles, Peisistratos and Eleusis," *Journal of Hellenic Studies* 95 (1975), pp. 1–12.

Borthwick, E. K., "Seeing Weasels: The Superstitious Background of the Empusa Scene in the *Frogs*," *Classical Quarterly* 18 (1968), pp. 200–206.

Bostock, David, *Plato's Phaedo*, Clarendon Press: Oxford, 1986.

Bottini, Angelo, *Archeologia della Salvezza: L'Escatologia Greca nelle Testimonianze Archeologiche*, Longanesi: Milano, 1992.

Bowie, A. M., *Aristophanes: Myth, Ritual and Comedy*, Cambridge University Press: Cambridge, 1993.

Bowie, A. M., "Greek Sacrifice: Forms and Functions," in *The Greek World*, ed. A. Powell, Routledge: London, 1995, pp. 463–482.

Boyancé, Pierre, "Sur l'Orphisme: A propos d'un Livre Récent," *Revue des Études Anciennes* (1938), pp. 163–172.

Boyancé, Pierre, "Remarques sur le Salut selon l'Orphisme," *Revue des Études Anciennes* 43 (1941), pp. 166–171.

Boyancé, Pierre, "Le Disque de Brindisi et l'Apothéose de Sémélé," *Revue des Études Anciennes* 44 (1942), pp. 191–216.

Boyancé, Pierre, "Xénocrate et les Orphiques," *Revue des Études Anciennes* (1948), pp. 218–231.

Boyancé, Pierre, "Note sur la ΦΡΟΥΡΑ Platonicienne," *Revue de Philologie* 37 (1963), pp. 7–11.

Boyancé, Pierre, *Le Culte des Muses Chez les Philosophes Grecs: Études d'Histoire et de Psychologie Religieuses*, Éditions E. de Boccard: Paris, 1972.

Bremmer, Jan, *The Early Greek Concept of the Soul*, Princeton University Press: Princeton, NJ, 1983.

Bremmer, Jan, "Orpheus: Guru to Gay," in *Orphisme et Orphée: En l'honneur de Jean Rudhardt*, ed. Bourgeaud, Recherches et Rencontres 3: Geneva, 1991, pp. 13–30.

Bremmer, J., and E. W. Handley, eds., *Aristophane: Entretiens sur l'Antiquité Classique Tome XXXVIII*, Fondation Hardt: Genève, 1993.

Bremmer, Jan, "Rationalization and Disenchantment in Ancient Greece: Max Weber among the Pythagoreans and Orphics?" in *From Myth to Reason?: Studies in the Development of Greek Thought*, ed. Richard Buxton, Oxford University Press: Oxford, 1999, pp. 71–83.

Brickhouse, Thomas C., and Nicholas D. Smith, "The Problem of Punishment in Socratic Philosophy," in *Wisdom, Ignorance and Virtue: New Essays in Socratic Studies*, ed. Mark L. McPherran, Academic Printing & Publishing: Edmonton, 1997, pp. 95–108.

Brisson, Luc, "Le Mythe de Protagoras, Essai d'Analyse Structurale," *Quaderni Urbinati di Cultura Classica* 20 (1975), pp. 7–37.

Brisson, Luc, *Platon: Les Mots et les Mythes*, Librairie François Maspero: Paris, 1982.

Brisson, Luc, "Mythes, Écriture, Philosophie," in *La Naissance de Raison en Grèce*, ed. Jean-François Mattéi, Presses Universitaires de France: Paris, 1990, pp. 49–58.

Brisson, Luc, "Le Corps 'Dionysiaque' l'Anthropogonie Décrite dans le *Commentaire sur le Phédon de Platon* (1, par. 3–6) Attribué à Olympiodore est-elle Orphique?" in *ΣΟΦΙΗΣ ΜΑΙΗΤΟΡΕΣ Chercheurs de Sagesse: Hommage à Jean Pepin*, Institut d'Études Augustiniennes, 1992, pp. 483–499.

Brisson, Luc, *Orphée et l'Orphisme dan l'Antiquité Gréco-Romaine*, Variorum Collected Studies Series, Ashgate Publishing: Burlington VT, 1995.

Brochard, V., "Les Mythes dans la Philosophie de Platon," *L'Année Philosophique* 11 (1900), pp. 1–13.

Brown, Christopher G., "Empousa, Dionysus and the Mysteries: Aristophanes, *Frogs* 285ff," *Classical Quarterly* 41 (1991), pp. 41–50.

Brunet, Christian, "Mythes et Croyances," *Revue de Metaphysique et de Morale* 69 (1964), pp. 276–288.

Burger, Ronna, *The Phaedo: A Platonic Labyrinth*, Yale University Press: New Haven, CT, 1984.

Burkert, Walter, "Elysion," *Glotta* 39 (1961) pp. 208–213.

Burkert, Walter, "ΓΟΗΣ. Zum griechischen 'Schamanismus'," *Rheinische Museum für Philologie* 105 (1962), pp. 36–55.

Burkert, Walter, "Das Proömium de Parmenides und die Katabasis de Pythagoras," *Phronesis* 14 (1969), pp. 1–30.

Burkert, Walter, *Lore and Science in Ancient Pythagoreanism*, trans. Edwin L. Minar, Jr., Harvard University Press: Cambridge, MA, 1972.

Burkert, Walter, "Le Laminette Auree: Da Orfeo a Lampone," in *Orfismo in Magna Grecia: Atti del quattordicesimo Convegno di Studi sulla Magna Grecia*, Arte Tipografica: Napoli, 1975, pp. 81–104.

Burkert, Walter, "Orphism and Bacchic Mysteries: New Evidence and Old Problems of Interpretation," in *Protocol for the Center for Hermeneutical Studies in Hellenistic and Modern Culture: Colloquy* 28, 1977, pp. 1–10.

Burkert, Walter, *Structure and History in Greek Mythology and Ritual*, University of California Press: Berkley, 1979.

Burkert, Walter, "Craft Versus Sect: The Problem of Orphics and Pythagoreans," in *Jewish and Christian Self-Definition: Volume Three – Self-Definition in the Greco-Roman World*, ed. Ben Meyer and E. P. Sanders, Fortress Press: Philadelphia, 1982, pp. 1–22.

Burkert, Walter, *Homo Necans: The Anthropology of Ancient Greek Sacrificial Ritual and Myth*, trans. Peter Bing, University of California Press: Berkeley, 1983.

Burkert, Walter, *Ancient Mystery Cults*, Harvard University Press: Cambridge, 1987.

Burkert, Walter, *Creation of the Sacred: Tracks of Biology in Early Religions*, Harvard University Press: Cambridge, 1996.

Burnet, John, *Plato's Phaedo*, Clarendon Press: Oxford, 1911.

Calame, Claude, *Thésée et l'Imaginaire Athénien: Légende et Culte en Grèce Antique*, Editions Payot: Lausanne, 1990.

Calame, Claude, "Invocations et Commentaires 'Orphiques': Transpositions Funéraires de Discours Religieux," in *Discours Religieux dans l'Antiquité*, ed. Marie-Madeleine Mactoux and Evelyne Geny, *Annales Littéraires de l'Université de Besançon*, # 578, Les Belles Lettres: Paris, 1995, pp. 11–30.

Calame, Claude, *Mythe et Histoire dans l'Antiquité Grecque: La Création Symbolique d'une Colonie*, Editions Payot: Lausanne, 1996.

Calame, Claude, "The Rhetoric of *Muthos* and *Logos*: Forms of Figurative Discourse," in *From Myth to Reason?: Studies in the Development of Greek Thought*, ed. Richard Buxton, Oxford University Press: Oxford, 1999, pp. 119–144.

Calame, Claude, *Poétique des Mythes dans la Grèce Antique*, Hachette Superieur: Paris, 2000.

Camassa, G., "Passione e Rigenerazione. Dioniso e Persefone nelle Lamine 'Orfiche'," in *Forme di Religiosità e Tradizioni Sapienzali in Magna Grecia*, eds. A. C. Cassio and P. Poccetti, *Annali dell'Istituto Universitario Orientale di Napoli* XVI, Istituti Editioriali Poligrafici Internazionali: Pisa, Roma, 1994, pp. 171–182.

Campbell, D. A., "The Frogs in the *Frogs*," *Journal of Hellenic Studies* civ (1984), pp. 163–165.

Campbell, Joseph, *Hero with a Thousand Faces*, Princeton, 2th ed., Princeton University Press: Princeton, 1968.

Cantarella, Raffaele, "Dioniso, fra *Bacchannti* e *Rane*," in *Serta Turyniana: Studies in Greek Literature and Palaeography in Honor of Alexander Turyn*, ed. John Heller, University of Illinois Press: Urbana, 1974, pp. 291–310.

Carriere, Jean Claude, *Le Carnaval et la Politique: Une Introduction à la Comédie Grecque Suivie d'un Choix de Fragments*, Annales Litteraires de l'Université de Besançon, 212, Les Belles Lettres: Paris, 1979.

Casadio, Giovanni, "Adversaria Orphica et Orientalia," *Studi e Materiali di Storia delle Religioni* 52 (1986), pp. 291–322.

Casadio, Giovanni, "Adversaria Orphica. A Proposito de in Libro Recente sull' Orfismo," *Orpheus* 1987, pp. 381–395.

Casadio, Giovanni, "La Metempsicosi tra Orfeo e Pitagora," in *Orphisme et Orphée: En l'Honneur de Jean Rudhardt*, ed. Bourgeaud, Recherches et Rencontres 3: Geneva, 1991, pp. 119–155.

Casadio, Giovanni, *Il Vino dell' Anima: Storia del Culto di Dioniso a Corinto, Sicione, Trezene*, Il Calano: Roma, 1999.

Cassio, A. C., "Πιέναι e il modello ionico della laminetta di Hipponion," in *Forme di Religiosità e Tradizioni Sapienzali in Magna Grecia*, eds. A. C. Cassio and

P. Poccetti, *Annali dell'Istituto Universitario Orientale di Napoli* XVI, Istituti Editioriali Poligrafici Internazionali: Pisa, Roma, 1994, pp. 183–205.

Chamay, J., "Des Défunts Portant Bandages," *Bulletin Antieke Beschaving* 52–53 (1977–1978), pp. 247–251.

Clark, Raymond J., *Catabasis: Vergil and the Wisdom-Tradition*, B.R. Grüner: Amsterdam, 1979.

Clay, Diskin, "The Art of Glaukos (Plato *Phaedo* 108D4–9)," *American Journal of Philology* 106 (1985), pp. 230–236.

Clay, Jenny Strauss, "Rowing for Athens," in *Vertis in Usum: Studies in Honor of Edward Courtney*, eds. John F. Miller, Cynthia Damon, and K. Sara Myers, K.G. Saur München: Leipzig, 2002, pp. 271–276.

Clinton, Kevin, *Myth and Cult: The Iconography of the Eleusinian Mysteries*, Skrifter Utgivna av Skvenska Institutet i Athen, 8, 11: Stockholm, 1992.

Clinton, Kevin, "The Eleusinian Mysteries and Panhellenism in Democratic Athens," in *The Archaeology of Athens and Attica under the Democracy*, eds. Coulson, Palagaia, Shear, Shapiro, and Frost, Oxbow Monograph 37: Oxford, 1994, pp. 161–172.

Cobb-Stevens, V., "Mythos and Logos in Plato's *Phaedo*," *Analecta Husserliana* 12 (1982) pp. 391–405.

Cole, Susan, "New Evidence for the Mysteries of Dionysos," *Greek, Roman, and Byzantine Studies* (1980), pp. 223–238.

Cole, S. G., "Voices from Beyond the Grave: Dionysos and the Dead," in *Masks of Dionysos*, eds. Faraone and Carpenter, Cornell University Press: Ithaca, 1993, pp. 276–296.

Colli, Giorgio, *La Sapienza Greca*, Vol. I, Delphi Edizioni: Milano, 1977.

Comparetti, D., in Cavallari, Francesco Saverio, *Notizie degli Scavi* (1879), p. 156ff.; (1880) p. 152ff.

Comparetti, D., "The Petelia Gold Tablet," *Journal of Hellenic Studies* 3 (1882), pp. 111–118.

Comparetti, Domenico, "Laminetta Orfica di Cecilia Secundina," *Atene e Roma* VI 54–55 (1903), pp. 161–170.

Comparetti, Domenico, *Laminette Orfiche*, Tipografia Galletti e Cocci: Firenze, 1910.

Cook, Erwin, "Ferrymen of Elysium and the Homeric Phaeacians," *The Journal of Indo–European Studies* 20 (1992), pp. 239–267.

Cornford, F. M., *Principium Sapientiae: The Origins of Greek Philosophical Thought*, ed. W. K. C. Guthrie, Cambridge University Press: Cambridge, 1952.

Cornford, Francis M., *The Origin of Attic Comedy*, Doubleday & Co., Inc.: New York, 1961.

Cosi, D. M., "L'Orfico Fulminato," *Museum Patavinum*, Vol. 2 (1987), pp. 217–231.

Cougny, E., *Epigrammatum Anthologiae Palatina, etc.*, Vol. 3, #102, Paris, 1890, pp. 483–484, 542.

Couliano, Ioan P., *Expérience de l'Extase: Extase, Ascension et Récit Visionnaire de l'Hellénisme au Moyen Âge*, Payot: Paris, 1984.

Couloubaritsis, Lambros, "De la Généalogie à la Geneséologie," in *La Naissance de Raison en Grèce*, ed. Jean-François Mattéi, Presses Universitaires de France: Paris, 1990, pp. 83–98.

Culianu, Ioan Petru, *Psychanodia I: A Survey of the Evidence Concerning the Ascensions of the Soul and Its Relevance*, E.J. Brill: Leiden, 1983.

de Polignac, François, *Cults, Territory, and the Origins of the Greek City-State* (1984), trans. Janet Lloyd, University of Chicago Press: Chicago, 1995.

Defradas, Jean, "Le Chant des Grenouilles: Aristophane Critique Musicale," *Revue des Études Anciennes* 71 (1969), pp. 23–37.

Demand, Nancy, "The Identity of the Frogs," *Classical Philology* 65 (1970), pp. 83–87.

Deonna, W., "Croyance Funéraires: La Soif des Morts – Le Mort Musicien," *Revue de l'Histoire des Religions* 109 (1939), pp. 53ff.

Depew, Mary, "Reading Greek Prayers," *Classical Antiquity* 16 (1997), pp. 229–258.

Detienne, Marcel, *De la Pensée Religieuse à la Pensée Philosophique: La Notion de Daïmôn dans le Pythagorisme Ancien*, Société d'Édition "Les Belles Lettres": Paris, 1963.

Detienne, Marcel, "Les Chemins de la Déviance: Orphisme, Dionysisme et Pythagorisme," in *Orfismo in Magna Grecia: Atti del Quattordicesimo Convegno di Studi sulla Magna Grecia*, Arte Tipografica: Napoli, 1975, pp. 49–79.

Detienne, Marcel, *Dionysos Slain*, trans. Mireille and Leonard Muellner, Johns Hopkins University Press: Baltimore, MD, 1979.

Detienne, Marcel, *The Creation of Mythology*, trans. Margaret Cook, University of Chicago Press: Chicago, 1986.

Detienne, Marcel, *The Writing of Orpheus: Greek Myth in Cultural Context*, trans. Janet Lloyd, Johns Hopkins Unviersity Press: Baltimore, MD, 2003.

Detienne, Marcel, and Jean-Pierre Vernant, *The Cuisine of Sacrifice Among the Greeks*, trans. Paula Wissing, University of Chicago Press: Chicago, 1989.

Dickie, Matthew, "The Dionysiac Mysteries in Pella," *Zeitschrift für Papyrologie und Epigraphik* 109 (1995), pp. 80–86.

Diels, H., *Die Fragmente der Vorsokratiker*, 2 Aufl., Weidmannsche Buchhandlung: Berlin, 1907, II, pp. 480–482.

Dieterich, Albrechtus, *De Hymnis Orphicis: Capitula Quinque*, Impensis Elwerti Bibliopolae Academici: Marpurgi Cattorum, 1891.

Dieterich, Albrecht, *Nekyia: Beiträge zur Erklärung der Neuentdeckten Petrusapokalypse*, B.G. Teubner: Leipzig, 1893.

Dijk, Geert-Jan van, *ΑΙΝΟΙ, ΛΟΓΟΙ, ΜΥΘΟΙ: Fables in Archaic, Classical, and Hellenistic Literature*, Mnemosyne Suppl. 166, Brill: Leiden, 1997.

Dodds, E. R., *The Greeks and the Irrational*, University of California Press: Berkeley, 1951.

Dodds, E. R., *Plato: Gorgias*, Clarendon Press: Oxford, 1959.

Dover, K. J., "Excursus: The Herms and the Mysteries," in *A Historical Commentary on Thucydides*, by A. W. Gomme, A. Andrewes, and K. J. Dover, Vol. 4, Clarendon Press: Oxford, 1970, pp. 264–288.

Dover, K. J., *Aristophanic Comedy*, University of California Press: Berkeley and Los Angeles, 1972.

Dover, Kenneth, *Greek Homosexuality*, Harvard University Press: Cambridge, MA, 1978.

Dover, Kenneth, *Aristophanes: Frogs*, Clarendon Press: Oxford, 1993.

Duchemin, Jacqueline, "Recherche sur un Thème Aristophanien et ses Sources Religieuses: Les Voyages dans l'Autre Monde," *Les Études Classiques* 25, 3 (1957), pp. 273–295.

Edelstein, Ludwig, "The Function of Myth in Plato's Philosophy," *Journal of the History of Ideas* 10, 4 (1949), pp. 463–481.

Edmonds, Radcliffe, "Tearing Apart the Zagreus Myth: A Few Disparaging Remarks on Orphism and Original Sin," *Classical Antiquity* 18.1 (1999), pp. 35–73.

Edmonds, Radcliffe, "Who in Hell is Heracles? Dionysos' Disastrous Disguise in Aristophanes' *Frogs*," in *Initiation in Ancient Greek Rituals and Narratives: New Critical Perspectives*, eds. Dodds & Faraone, Routledge 2003, pp. 181–200.

Edmunds, Lowell, "Introduction: The Practice of Greek Mythology," in *Approaches to Greek Myth*, ed. Edmunds, The Johns Hopkins University Press: Baltimore, MD, 1990, pp. 1–22.

Elderkin, George, *Mystic Allusions in the Frogs of Aristophanes*, The Princeton University Store: Princeton, NJ, 1955.

Eliade, Mircea, *Rites and Symbols of Initiation: The Mysteries of Birth and Rebirth*, trans. Willard Trask, Harper & Row: New York, 1958.

Eliade, Mircea, *Shamanism: Archaic Techniques of Ecstasy*, trans. Willard Trask, Princeton University Press: Princeton, NJ, 1964.

Eliade, Mircea, *Zalmoxis The Vanishing God: Comparative Studies in the Religions and Folklore of Dacia and Eastern Europe*, trans. Willard Trask, University of Chicago Press: Chicago, 1972.

Elias, Julius A., *Plato's Defence of Poetry*, State University of New York Press: Albany, 1984.

Epp, Ronald, "Some Observations on the Platonic Concept of *Katharsis* in the *Phaedo*," *Kinesis* 1, 2 (1969), pp. 82–91.

Epstein, Paul, "Dionysus' Journey of Self-Discovery in *The Frogs* of Aristophanes," *Dionysius* 9 (1985), pp. 19–36.

Farnell, L. R., "The Value and the Methods of Mythologic Study," *Proceedings of the British Academy* (1919), pp. 37–51.

Farnell, L. R., *Greek Hero Cults and Ideas of Immortality*, Oxford University Press: Oxford, 1921.

Festugière, A. J., "Les Mystères de Dionysos," *Revue Biblique* (1935), pp. 192–211, 366–396.

Festugière, A. J., "Comptes Rendus Bibliographiques: Guthrie (W. K. C.) Orpheus and Greek Religion," *Revue des Études Grecques* (1936), pp. 306–310.

Feyerabend, Barbara, "Zur Wegmetaphorik beim Goldblättchen aus Hipponion und dem Proömium des Parmenides," *Rheinische Museum für Philologie* 127.1 (1984), pp. 1–22.

Findlay, J. N., "The Myths of Plato," *Dionysius* 2 (1978), pp. 19–34.

Fontinoy, C., "Le Sacrifice Nuptial de Polyxène," *L'Antiquité Classique*, 19 (1950), pp. 383–396.

Foti, J., and G. Pugliese Carratelli, "Un Sepulcro di Hipponion e un Nuovo Testo Orfico," *La Parola del Passato* 29 (1974), pp. 91–126.

Foucault, Michel, *The Use of Pleasure*, trans. Robert Hurley, Random House: New York, 1985.

Franz, G., "Epigrafe Greca Sopra Lamina d'Oro Spettante al sig. Millingen," *Bullettino dell'Instituto di Corrispondenza Archeologica* (1836), pp. 149–50.

Franz, G., *Corpus Inscriptiones Graecae*, Vol. 3 (1857).

Frel, Jiri, "Una Nuova Laminella 'Orfica'," *Eirene* 30 (1994), pp. 183–184.

Friedländer, Paul, *Plato: An Introduction*, trans. Hans Meyerhoff, 2nd Ed., Bollingen Foundation LIX, Princeton University Press: Princeton, 1969.

Frutiger, Perceval, *Les Mythes de Platon*, Librairie Félix Alcan: Paris, 1930.

Funghi, Maria Serena, "Il Mito Escatologico del *Fedone* e la Forza Vitale dell'*Aiora*, *La Parola del Passato* 35 (1980), pp. 176–201.

Gadamer, Hans-Georg, "The Proofs of Immortality in Plato's *Phaedo*," in *Dialogue and Dialectic: Eight Hermeneutical Studies on Plato*, trans. P. Christopher Smith, Yale University Press: New Haven, CT, 1980, pp. 21–38.

Gaffney, S. K., "Dialectic, the Myths of Plato, Metaphor, and the Transcendent in the World," *Proceedings of the American Catholic Philosophical Society* 45 (1971), pp. 77–85.

Gallop, David, *Plato: Phaedo*, Clarendon Press: Oxford, 1975.

Gantz, Timothy, *Early Greek Myth: A Guide to the Literary and Artistic Sources*, Johns Hopkins University Press: Baltimore, MD, 1993.

Garland, Robert, *The Greek Way of Death*, Cornell University Press: New York, 1985.

Geertz, Clifford, "Religion as a Cultural System," in *The Interpretation of Cultures*, Harper Collins: New York, 1973.

Gelinne, Michel, "Les Champs-Élysées et les Îles des Bienheureux," *Les Études Classiques* 56 (1988), pp. 225–240.

Giangrande, G., "La Lamina Orfica di Hipponion," in *Orfeo e l'Orfismo: Atti del Seminario Nazionale*, ed. Agostino Masaracchia, Gruppo Editoriale Internazionale: Roma, 1993, pp. 235–248.

Gigante, M., "Per l'Esegesi del Testo Orfico Vibonese," *Parola del Passato* 30 (1975), pp. 223–225.

Gigante, M., "Una Nuova Lamella Orfica e Eraclito," *Zeitschrift für Papyrologie und Epigraphik* 80 (1990), pp. 17–18.

Gilead, Amihud, *The Platonic Odyssey: A Philosophical-Literary Inquiry into the Phaedo*, Value Inquiry Book Series, Vol. 17, Rodopi: Amsterdam and Atlanta, 1994.

Gill, Christopher, "The Death of Socrates," *Classical Quarterly* 23 (1973), pp. 225–228.

Ginouvès, René, *Balaneutiké: Recherches sur le Bain dans l'Antiquité Grecque*, Bibliothèque des Écoles Françaises d'Athènes et de Rome, Vol. 120, Éditions E. de Boccard: Paris, 1962.

Goettling, Carl, *Narratio de Oraculo Trophonii*, Typis Schreiberi: Ienae, 1843.

Goldhill, Simon, *The Poet's Voice: Essays on Poetics and Greek Literature*, Cambridge University Press: Cambridge, 1991.

Graf, Fritz, *Eleusis und die orphische Dichtung Athens in Hellenistischer Zeit*, RVV 33, de Gruyter: Berlin, 1974.

Graf, Fritz, "Culti e Credenze Religiose della Magnia Grecia," in *Megale Hellas – Nome e Immagine: Atti del Ventunesimo Convegno di Studi sulla Magna Grecia*, Instituto per la Storia e l'Archeologia della Magna Grecia: Taranto, 1982, pp. 155–185.

Graf, Fritz, "Orpheus: A Poet Among Men," in *Interpretations of Greek Mythology*, ed. Jan Bremmer, Barnes & Noble Books: Totowa, NJ, 1986, pp. 80–106.

Graf, Fritz, "Textes Orphiques et Ritual Baccchique. A Propos des Lamelles de Pélinna," in *Orphisme et Orphée: En l'honneur de Jean Rudhardt*, ed. Bourgeaud, Recherches et Rencontres 3: Geneva, 1991, pp. 87–102.

Graf, Fritz, "Dionysian and Orphic Eschatology: New Texts and Old Questions," in *Masks of Dionysos*, ed. Faraone and Carpenter, Cornell University Press: Ithaca, 1993a, pp. 239–258.

Graf, Fritz, *Greek Mythology: An Introduction*, trans. Thomas Marier, The Johns Hopkins University Press: Baltimore, 1993b.

Gregory, M. J., "Myth and Transcendence in Plato," *Thought* 43 (1968), pp. 273–296.

Greimas, A. J., *Semantique Structurale: Recherche de Méthode*, Presses Universitaires de France: Paris, 1986.

Griffith, Mark, "Contest and Contradiction in Early Greek Poetry," in *Cabinet of the Muses: Essays on Classical and Comparative Literature in Honor of Thomas G. Rosenmeyer*, ed. Mark Griffith and Donald Mastronarde, 1990, pp. 188–189.

Guarducci, Margherita, *Inscriptiones Creticae*, 2, Rome, 1939, pp. 168–171, 314.

Guarducci, Margherita, "Laminette auree Orfiche: Alcuni Problemi," *Epigraphica* 36 (1974), pp. 7–32.

Guarducci, Margherita, "Qualche Osservazione sulla Laminetta Orfica di Hipponion," *Epigraphica* 37 (1975), pp. 19–24.

Guarducci, Margherita, "Aristofane e la Topografia Ateniese," in *Studi in Onore di Aristide Colonna*, Instituto di Filologia Classica: Università degli Studi di Perugia, 1982, pp. 167–172.

Guarducci, Margherita, "Nuove Riflessioni sulla Laminetta 'Orfica' di Hipponion," *Rivista di Filologia Classica* 113 (1985), pp. 385–397.

Guarducci, Margherita, *Epigrafia Greca dalle Origini al Tardo Impero*, Istituto Poligrafico e Zecca dello Stato: Roma, 1987, pp. 320–325.

Guthrie, W. K. C., *The Greeks and Their Gods*, Beacon Press: Boston, 1950.

Guthrie, W. K. C., *Orpheus and Greek Religion*, 2nd Ed., Methuen: London, 1952.

Guthrie, W. K. C., *A History of Greek Philosophy, Vol. 4, Plato: The Man and his Dialogues – Earlier Period*, Cambridge University Press: Cambridge, 1975.

Haavio, Matti, "A Running Stream They Dare na Cross," *Studia Fennica* 8 (1959), pp. 125–142.

Hadzisteliou-Price, Theodora, "'To the Groves of Phersephoneia...' A Group of 'Medma' Figurines," *Antike Kunst* 12 (1969), pp. 51–55, pls. 29, 30.

Hansen, Mogens Herman, *Apagoge, endeixis and ephegesis against kakourgoi, atimoi and pheugontes: a study in the Athenian administration of justice in the fourth century B.C.*, [Odense]: Odense University Press, 1976.

Harrison, G., and D. Obbink, "Vergil, Georgics I 36–39 and the Barcelona *Alcestis* (*P. Barc. Inv. No. 158–161*) 62–65: Demeter in the Underworld," *Zeitschrift für Papyrologie und Epigraphik* 63 (1986), pp. 75–81.

Harrison, Jane Ellen, *Themis: A Study of the Social Origins of Greek Religion*, Cambridge, 1912.

Harrison, Jane Ellen, *Prolegomena to the Study of Greek Religion*, Princeton: Princeton University Press, 1991.

Hatzfeld, Jean, *Alcibiade: Étude sur l'histoire d'Athènes à la Fin du V$^e$ Siècle*, Presses Universitaires de France: Paris, 1951.

Havelock, Eric, *Preface to Plato*, Belknap Press of Harvard University Press: Cambridge, MA, 1963.

Hegel, G. W. F. *Lectures on the History of Philosophy, Vol. 2, Plato and the Platonists*, trans. E. S. Haldane and F. H. Simson, Routledge and Kegan Paul: London, 1963.

Henderson, Jeffrey, *The Maculate Muse: Obscene Language in Attic Comedy*, Yale University Press: New Haven, CT, and London, 1975.

Henderson, Jeffrey, "The *Dêmos* and the Comic Competition," in *Nothing to Do with Dionysos: Athenian Drama in Its Social Context*, eds. John J. Winkler and Froma I. Zeitlin, Princeton University Press: Princeton, NJ, 1990, pp. 271–313.

Henrichs, Albert, "Greek Maenadism from Olympias to Messalina," *Harvard Studies in Classical Philology* 82 (1978), pp. 121–160.

Henrichs, Albert, "Changing Dionysiac Identities," in *Jewish and Christian Self-Definition, Vol. 3, Self-Definition in the Greco-Roman World*, eds. Ben Meyer and E. P. Sanders, Fortress Press: Philadelphia, 1982, pp. 137–160.

Henrichs, Albert, "Three Approaches to Greek Mythography," in *Interpretations of Greek Mythology*, ed. Jan Bremmer, Barnes & Noble: Totowa, NJ, 1986, pp. 242–277.

Henrichs, Albert, "'He Has a God in Him': Human and Divine in the Modern Perceptions of Dionysos," in *Masks of Dionysos*, eds. Faraone and Carpenter, Cornell University Press: Ithaca, NY, 1993, pp. 13–43.

Higgins, W. E., "A Passage to Hades: The Frogs of Aristophanes," *Ramus* 6 (1977), pp. 60–79.

Hirsch, Walter, *Platons Weg zum Mythos*, Walter de Gruyter: Berlin and New York, 1971.

Hitchcock, David L., *The Role of Myth and Its Relation to Rational Argument in Plato's Dialogues*, dissertation Claremont Graduate School, 1974.

Hofmann, Heinz, *Mythos and Komödie: Untersuchungen zu den Vögeln des Aristophanes*, Spudasmata 33, Georg Olms Verlag Hildesheim: New York, 1976.

Hooker, G. T. W., "The Topography of the *Frogs*," *Journal of Hellenic Studies* (1960), pp. 112–117.

Hooker, J. T., "The Composition of the Frogs," *Hermes* 108 (1980), pp. 169–182.

House, Dennis K., "A Commentary on Plato's *Phaedo*," *Dionysius* 5 (1981), pp. 40–65.

Hultkrantz, Åke, *The North American Indian Orpheus Tradition: A Contribution to Comparative Religion*, The Ethnographical Museum of Sweden Monograph Series, No. 2, Caslon Press: Stockholm, 1957.

Jaeger, Werner, *Paideia: The Ideals of Greek Culture*, Vol. 1, trans. Gilbert Highet from 2nd German Ed., Oxford University Press: New York, 1945.

Janko, R., "Forgetfulness in the Golden Tablets of Memory," *Classical Quarterly* 34 (1984), pp. 89–100.

Johnston, Sarah Iles, "Penelope and the Erinyes: *Odyssey* 20.61–82," *Helios* 21.2 (1994), pp. 137–159.

Johnston, Sarah Iles, "Defining the Dreadful: Remarks on the Greek Child-Killing Demon," in *Ancient Magic and Ritual Power*, eds., Marvin Meyer and Paul Mirecki, *Religions in the Graeco-Roman World*, Vol. 129, E.J. Brill: Leiden, 1995, pp. 361–390.

Johnston, Sarah Iles, *The Restless Dead: Encounters Between the Living and the Dead in Ancient Greece*, University of California Press: Berkeley and Los Angeles, 1999.

Johnston, Sarah Iles, and Timothy J. McNiven, "Dionysos and the Underworld in Toledo," *Museum Helveticum* 53 (1996), pp. 25–34.

Joly, R., "L' Exhortation au Courage (θαρρεῖν) dans les Mystères," *Revue des Études Grecques* 68 (1955), pp. 164–170.

Jourdain-Annequin, Colette, *Héraclès aux Portes du Soir: Mythe et Histoire*, Annales Littéraires de l' Université de Besançon, No. 402: Paris, 1989.

Kahn, Charles H., *Plato and the Socratic Dialogue: The Philosophical Use of a Literary Form*, Cambridge University Press: Cambridge, 1996.

Kaibel, G., *Epigrammata Graeca ex Lapidibus Collecta*, Berolini, 1878, pp. 453–454.

Kern, Otto, *Orphicorum Fragmenta*, Weidmann: Berlin, 1922.

Keuls, Eva, *The Water Carriers in Hades: A Study of Catharsis through Toil in Classical Antiquity*, Adolf M. Hakkert: Amsterdam, 1974.

Kingsley, Peter, *Ancient Philosophy, Mystery, and Magic: Empedocles and Pythagorean Tradition*, Clarendon Press: Oxford, 1995.

Knight, W. F. Jackson, *Elysion: on Ancient Greek and Roman beliefs concerning a life after death*, Rider: London, 1970.

Kobusch, Theo, "Die Wiederkehr des Mythos. Zur Funktion des Mythos in Platons Denken und in der Philosophie der Gegenwart," *Mythos: Erzählende Weltdeutung im Spannungsfeld von Ritual und Rationalität*, eds. Gerhard Binder and Bernd Effe, Wissenschaftlicher Verlag Trier: Trier, 1990, pp. 13–32.

Konstan, David, "Poésie, Politique et Ritual dans les *Grenouilles* d'Aristophane," *Metis* 1 (1986), pp. 291–308.

Kotansky, Roy, "Incantations and Prayers on Inscribed Greek Amulets," in *Magika Hiera: Ancient Greek Magic and Religion*, eds. Christopher Faraone and Dirk Obbink, Oxford University Press: Oxford, 1991, pp. 107–137.

Kotansky, Roy, *Greek Magical Amulets*, Vol. 1, Westdeutscher Verlag: Opladen, 1994, pp. 107–112.

Kraemer, Ross, "Ecstasy and Possession: Women of Ancient Greece and the Cult of Dionysus," in *Unspoken Worlds: Women's Religious Lives in Non-Western Cultures*, eds. Nancy Auer Falk and Rita M. Gross, Harper & Row, San Francisco, 1980, pp. 53–72.

Kraut, Richard, "Comments on Gregory Vlastos, 'The Socratic Elenchus'," *Oxford Studies in Ancient Philosophy* 1 (1983), pp. 59–70.

Kurtz, Donna, and John Boardman, *Greek Burial Customs*, Cornell University Press: Ithaca, NY, 1971.

Lada-Richards, Ismene, *Initiating Dionysus: Ritual and Theatre in Aristophanes' Frogs*, Clarendon Press: Oxford, 1999.

Lapalus, Étienne, "Le Dionysos et l'Héracles des 'Grenouilles'," *Revue des Études Grecques* 47 (1934), pp. 1–20.

Lattimore, Richmond, *Themes in Greek and Latin Epitaphs*, University of Illinois Press: Urbana, 1962.

Lawson, J. C., "ΠΕΡΙ ΑΛΙΒΑΝΤΩΝ," *Classical Review* 40 (1926), pp. 52–58.

Lazzarini, M. L., and A. C. Cassio, "Sulla Laminetta di Hipponion," *Annali della Scuola Normale Superiore di Pisa: Classe di Lettere e Filosofia*, Series 3, Vol. 17, 2 (1987), pp. 329–334.

Levi, Adolfo, "I miti platonici sull' anima e sui suoi destini," *Rivista di Filosofia* 30 (1937), pp. 137–166.

Levi, Adolfo, "I miti platonici," *Rivista di Storia della Filosofia* 1 (1946), pp. 197–225.

Levi-Strauss, Claude, "The Structural Study of Myth," in *Structural Anthropology*, trans. Claire Jacobsen and Brooke Grundfest Schoepf, Basic Books: New York, 1963, pp. 206–231.

Levi-Strauss, Claude, *The Savage Mind*, The University of Chicago Press: Chicago, 1966.

Lewis, I. M., *Ecstatic Religion: An Anthropological Study of Spirit Possession and Shamanism*, Penguin Books: Harmondsworth, 1971.

Lieb, Irwin, "Philosophy as Spiritual Formation," *International Philosophical Quarterly* 3 (1963), pp. 271–285.

Lincoln, Bruce, *Death, War, and Sacrifice*, University of Chicago Press: Chicago, 1991.

Lincoln, Bruce, "Socrates' Prosecutors, Philosophy's Rivals, and the Politics of Discursive Forms," *Arethusa* 26 (1993), pp. 233–246.

Lincoln, Bruce, "Competing Discourses: Rethinking the Prehistory of *Mythos* and *Logos*," *Arethusa* 30 (1997), pp. 341–363.

Lincoln, Bruce, *Theorizing Myth: Narrative, Ideology, and Scholarship*, University of Chicago Press: Chicago, 1999.

Linforth, I., *The Arts of Orpheus*, Berkeley, University of California Press: 1941.

Linforth, I. "Telestic Madness in Plato, Phaedrus 244d-e," *University of California Publications in Classical Philology* 13 (1946), pp. 163–172.

Littlefield, David J., ed., *Twentieth Century Interpretations of The Frogs*, Prentice Hall: Englewood Cliffs, NJ, 1968.

Lloyd, Geoffrey, "Mythology: Reflections from a Chinese Perspective," in *From Myth to Reason?: Studies in the Development of Greek Thought*, ed. Richard Buxton, Oxford University Press: Oxford, 1999, pp. 145–165.

Lloyd-Jones, Hugh, "Heracles at Eleusis: P. Oxy. 2622 and PSI 1391," *Maia* 19 (1967), pp. 206–229.

Lloyd-Jones, Hugh, "On the Orphic Tablet from Hipponion," *Parola del Passato* 30 (1975), pp. 225–226.

Lobeck, Chr. Augustus, *Aglaophamus*, Fratrum Borntraeger: Regiomontii Prussorum, 1829.

Long, Herbert Strainge, *A Study of the Doctrines of Metempsychosis in Greece from Pythagoras to Plato*, J.H. Furst: Princeton, 1948.

Loraux, Nicole, "Donc Socrate est Immortel," *La Temps de la Réflexion* 3 (1982), pp. 19–46.

Loraux, Nicole, *The Invention of Athens: The Funeral Oration in the Classical City*, trans. Alan Sheridan, Harvard University Press: Cambridge, MA, 1986.

Luppe, Wolfgang, "Abermals das Goldblättchen von Hipponion," *Zeitschrift für Papyrologie und Epigraphik* 30 (1978), pp. 23–26.

Luppe, W., "Zu den zeuen Goldblättchen aus Thessalien," *Zeitschrift für Papyrologie und Epigraphik* 76 (1989), pp. 13–14.

Luria, Salomo, "Demokrit, Orphiker und Ägypten," *Eos* 51 (1961), pp. 21–38.

Macchioro, Vittorio, "La Catabasi Orfica," *Classical Philology* 23 (1928), pp. 239–249.

MacDowell, Douglas, *Aristophanes and Athens*, Oxford University Press: Oxford, 1995.

Mackenzie, M. M., *Plato on Punishment*, University of California Press: Berkeley, 1981.

Marcovich, Miroslav, "The Gold Leaf from Hipponion," *Zeitschrift für Papyrologie und Epigraphik* 23 (1976), pp. 221–224.

Martin, Richard P., *The Language of Heroes*, Cornell University Press: Ithaca, NY, 1989.

Mattei, Jean-François, "The Theater of Myth in Plato," *Platonic Writings, Platonic Readings*, ed. Charles Griswold, Routledge: New York, 1988, pp. 110–125.

Merkelbach, Reinhold, "Bakchisches Goldtäfelchen aus Hipponion," *Zeitschrift für Papyrologie und Epigraphik* 17 (1974), pp. 8–9.

Merkelbach, Reinhold, "Ein neues 'orphisches' Goldblättchen," *Zeitschrift für Papyrologie und Epigraphik* 23 (1977), p. 276.

Merkelbach, Reinhold, "Zwei neue orphisch-dionysische Totenpässe," *Zeitschrift für Papyrologie und Epigraphik* 76 (1989), pp. 15–16.

Merkelbach, Reinhold, "Die goldenen Totenpässe: ägyptisch, orphisch, bakchisch," *Zeitschrift für Papyrologie und Epigraphik* 128 (1999) 1–13.

Meuli, K., "Scythica," *Hermes*, 70 (1935), p. 137ff.

Moors, Kent F., *Platonic Myth: An Introductory Study*, University Press of America: Washington, D.C., 1982.

Moors, Kent, "Muthologia and the Limits of Opinion: Presented Myths in Plato's *Republic*," *Proceedings of the Boston Area Colloquium in Ancient Philosophy* 4 (1988a), pp. 213–247.

Moors, Kent, "Named Life Selections in Plato's Myth of Er," *Classica et Medievalia* 39 (1988b), pp. 55–61.

Moorton, Richard F., Jr., "Rites of Passage in Aristophanes' *Frogs*," *Classical Journal* 84 (1989), pp. 308–324.

Morgan, Kathryn Anne, *Myth and Method: Studies in the Manipulation of Myth from Parmenides to Plato*, dissertation University of California, Berkeley, 1991.

Morgan, Kathryn Anne, *Myth and Philosophy from the Presocratics to Plato*, Cambridge University Press: Cambridge, 2000.

Morrison, J. S., "Parmenides and Er," *Journal of Hellenic Studies* 75 (1955), pp. 59–68.

Morrison, J. S., "The Shape of the Earth in Plato's Phaedo," *Phronesis* 4 (1959), pp. 101–119.

Most, Glenn W., "From Logos to Mythos," in *From Myth to Reason?: Studies in the Development of Greek Thought*, ed. Richard Buxton, Oxford University Press: Oxford, 1999, pp. 25–47.

Moulinier, Louis, *Orphée et l'Orphisme a l'Époque Classique*, Société d'Édition 'Les Belles Lettres': Paris, 1955.

Moulton, Carroll, "Comic Myth-Making and Aristophanes' Originality," in *Oxford Readings in Aristophanes*, ed. Erich Segal, Oxford University Press: Oxford, 1996, pp. 65–97.

Muellner, Leonard Charles, *The Meaning of Homeric εὔχομαι Through Its Formulas*, Innsbrucker Beiträge zur Sprachwissenschaft 13: Innsbruck, 1976.

Mühll, Peter van der, "Zur Erfindung in der Nekyia der Odysse," *Philologus* 93 (1938), pp. 3–11.

Murray, Oswyn, "The Affair of the Mysteries: Democracy and the Drinking Group," in *Sympotica: A Symposium on the Symposium*, ed. Oswyn Murray, Clarendon Press: Oxford, 1990, pp. 149–161.

Murray, Penelope, "What is a *Muthos* for Plato?" in *From Myth to Reason?: Studies in the Development of Greek Thought*, ed. Richard Buxton, Oxford University Press: Oxford, 1999, pp. 251–262.

Musso, Olimpio, "Eufemismo e Antifrasi nella Laminetta Aurea di Hipponion," *Giorno Italiano di Filologia* n.s. 8 (1977), pp. 172–175.

Musti, Domenico, "Le Lamine Orfiche e la Religiosità d'Area Locrese," *Quaderni Urbinati di Cultura Classica* n.s. 16 (1984), pp. 61–83.

Mylonas, George, *Eleusis and the Eleusinian Mysteries*, Princeton University Press: Princeton, NJ, 1961.

Nagy, Gregory, "Mythological *Exemplum* in Homer," in *Innovations of Antiquity*, eds. Ralph Hexter and Daniel Selden, Routledge: New York, 1992, pp. 311–331.

Nilsson, Martin, "Early Orphism and Kindred Movements," *Harvard Theological Review* XXVIII (1935), pp. 181–230.

Nilsson, Martin, "Die Quellen der Lethe und der Mnemosyne," *Eranos* 41 (1943), pp. 1–7.

Norden, Eduard, *P. Vergilius Maro: Aeneis Buch VI*, reprint of 1927 3rd ed., B.G. Teubner: Stuttgart and Leipzig, 1995.

Obbink, Dirk, "Dionysus Poured Out: Ancient and Modern Theories of Sacrifice and Cultural Formation," in *Masks of Dionysos*, eds. Faraone and Carpenter, Cornell University Press: Ithaca, NY, 1993, pp. 65–86.

Ober, Josiah, *Mass and Elite in Democratic Athens: Rhetoric, Ideology, and the Power of the People*, Princeton University Press: Princeton, 1989.

Olivieri, Alexander, *Lamellae Aureae Orphicae*, A. Marcus und E. Weber's Verlag: Bonn, 1915.

Osborne, Robin, *Demos: The Discovery of Classical Attika*, Cambridge University Press: Cambridge, 1985.

Padilla, Mark, "The Heraclean Dionysus: Theatrical and Social Renewal in Aristophanes' *Frogs*," *Arethusa* 25 (1992), pp. 359–84.

Paisse, Jean-Marie, "Réminiscence et Mythes Platoniciens," *Les Études Classiques* 39 (1969), pp. 19–43.

Parker, Robert, *Miasma: Pollution and Purity in Early Greek Religion*, Clarendon Press: Oxford, 1983.

Parker, Robert, "Early Orphism", in *The Greek World*, ed. A. Powell, Routledge: London, 1995, pp. 483–510.

Parker, Robert, *Athenian Religion: A History*, Clarendon Press: Oxford, 1996.

Parry, Richard D., *Plato's Craft of Justice*, State University of New York Press: Albany, 1996.

Petre, Zoe, "Le Haut, le Bas et la Cité Comique. La Katabase des *Grenouilles*," *Pallas* 38 (1992), pp. 277–285.

Picard, Charles, "Éleusinisme ou Orphisme? Les Nouvelles Lamelles d'Or Inscrites d'Éleutherna," *Revue de l'Histoire des Religions* 159 (1961), pp. 127–130.

Pickard-Cambridge, Sir Arthur, *The Dramatic Festivals of Athens*, 2nd Ed., Clarendon Press: Oxford, 1968.

Popper, K. R., *The Open Society and Its Enemies, Vol. I: The Spell of Plato*, Routledge: London, 1945.

Pretagostini, Roberto, "L'Episodio di Caronte (Aristoph. *Ran.* 180–270)," *Atene e Roma* 21 (1976), pp. 60–67.

Price, Theodora Hadzisteliou, *Kourotrophos: Cults and Representations of the Greek Nursing Deities*, Brill: Leiden, 1978.

Prontera, Francesco, "Sulla Laminetta di Hipponion," *Parola del Passato* 33 (1978), pp. 48–58.

Propp, Vladimir, *Theory and History of Folklore*, trans. Ariadna Y. Martin and Richard P. Martin, ed. Anatoly Liberman, University of Minnesota Press: Minneapolis, 1984.

Propp, Vladimir, *Morphology of the Folktale*, 2nd. Ed., trans. Laurence Scott, University of Texas Press: Austin, 1990.

Pugliese Carratelli, Giovanni, "ΟΡΦΙΚΑ," *Parola del Passato* 29 (1974), pp. 135–144.

Pugliese Carratelli, Giovanni, "Sulla Laminetta di Hipponion," *Parola del Passato* 30 (1975), pp. 226–231.

Pugliese Carratelli, Giovanni, "Ancora sulla Lamina Orfica di Hipponion," *Parola del Passato* 31 (1976), pp. 458–466.

Pugliese Carratelli, Giovanni, "Mnemosyne e l'immortalità," *Archivio di Filosofia* (1983), pp. 71–79.

Pugliese Carratelli, Giovanni, *Lamine d'Oro 'Orfiche'*, Libri Scheiwiller: Milano, 1993.

Pugliese Carratelli, Giovanni, *Lamine d'Oro Orfiche: Istruzioni per il Viaggio Oltremondano degli Iniziati Greci*, Adelphi Edizioni: Milano, 2001.

Puhvel, Jaan, "'Meadow of the Otherworld' in Indo-European tradition," *Zeitschrift für vergleichende Sprachforschung* 83 (1969), pp. 64–69.

Radermacher, Ludwig, *Aristophanes' 'Frösche': Einleitung, Text und Kommentar*, 2nd Ed., Österreichische Akademie der Wissenschaften 198.4: Wien, 1954.

Reckford, Kenneth J., *Aristophanes' Old-and-New Comedy Vol. 1: Six Essays in Perspective*, University of North Carolina Press: Chapel Hill, 1987.

Redfield, James, "The Economic Man," in *Approaches to Homer*, eds. Carl Rubino and Cynthia Shelmerdine, University of Texas Press: Austin, 1983, pp. 218–247.

Redfield, James, "Sex into Politics: The Rites of Artemis Triklaria and Dionysos Aisymnetes at Patras," in *Before Sexuality: The Construction of Erotic Experience in the Ancient Greek World*, eds. David Halperin, John Winkler, and Froma Zeitlin, Princeton University Press: Princeton, NJ, 1990, pp. 115–134.

Redfield, James, "The Politics of Immortality," in *Orphisme et Orphée: En l'honneur de Jean Rudhardt*, ed. Bourgeaud, Recherches et Rencontres 3: Geneva, 1991, pp. 103–117.

Redfield, James, *Nature and Culture in the Iliad: The Tragedy of Hector*, expanded edition, Duke University Press: Durham and London, 1994.

Reinach, Salomon, "ΛΥΣΙΣ ΠΡΟΓΟΝΩΝ ΑΘΕΜΙΣΤΩΝ," *Revue de Philologie* 23 (1899), pp. 228–231.

Reinach, Salomon, "ΑΩΡΟΙ ΒΙΑΙΟΘΑΝΑΤΟΙ," *Archiv für Religionswissenschaft* 9 (1906), pp. 312–322.

Renard, M., "Hérclé allaité par Junon," *Hommages à Jean Bayet, Latomus* LXX (1964), pp. 611–618.

Rhodes, P. J., *A Commentary on the Aristotelian Athenaion Politeia*, Clarendon Press: Oxford, 1981.

Riedweg, Christoph, "Initiation – Tod – Unterwelt: Beobachtungen zur Kommunikationssituation und narrativen Technik der orphisch-bakchischen Goldblättchen," in *Ansichten griechischer Rituale: Geburtstags-Symposium für Walter Burkert*, ed. Fritz Graf, B.G. Teubner: Stuttgart and Leipzig, 1998, pp. 359–398.

Riedweg, Christoph, "Poésie orphique et rituel initiatique. Éléments d'un 'Discours sacré' dans les lamelles d'or," *Revue de l'histoire des religions* 219.4 (2002), pp. 459–481.

Riu, Xavier, *Dionysism and Comedy*, Rowman and Littlefield: Lanham, MD, 1999.

Robertson, Noel, "Heracles' 'Catabasis'," *Hermes* 108 (1980), pp. 274–299.

Rogers, Benjamin Bickley, *The Comedies of Aristophanes*, Vol. 5, G. Bell and Sons, Ltd.: London, 1919.

Rohde, Erwin, *Die Religion der Griechen*, Universitäts-Buchdruckerei von J. Hörning: Heidelberg, 1895.

Rohde, Erwin, *Psyche: The Cult of Souls and Belief in Immortality among the Greeks*, trans. W. B. Hillis, Kegan Paul, Trench, Trubner & Co., Ltd.: London, 1925.

Romanelli, Pietro, ed., *Orfismo in Magna Grecia: atti del quattordicesimo Convegno di studi sulla Magna Grecia, Taranto, 6–10 ottobre 1974*, Napoli: Arte tipografica, 1975.

Rose, H. J., "The Bride of Hades," *Classical Philology* 20 (1925), pp. 238–242.

Rose, H. J., "A Study of Pindar, Fragment 133 Bergk, 127 Bowra," in *Greek Poetry and Life: Essays Presented to Gilbert Murray*, eds. C. Bailey et al., Clarendon Press: Oxford, 1936, pp. 79–96.

Rösler, Wolfgang, and Zimmerman, Bernhard, *Carnevale e Utopia nella Grecia Antica*, Levante Editori: Bari, 1991.

Rowe, Christopher, "Myth, History, and Dialectic in Plato's *Republic* and *Timaeus-Critias*," in *From Myth to Reason?: Studies in the Development of Greek Thought*, ed. Richard Buxton, Oxford University Press: Oxford, 1999, pp. 263-278.

Russo, Carlo Ferdinando, "The Revision of Aristophanes' *Frogs*," *Greece & Rome* n.s. 13 (1966), pp. 1-13.

Russo, Carlo Ferdinando, *Aristophanes: An Author for the Stage*, Routledge: London, 1994.

Russo, Cristina, "Sul v.9 della Laminetta Orfica di Hipponion," *La Parola del Passato* 47.3 (1993), pp. 181-182.

Sabbatucci, D., "Criteri per una Valutazione Scientifica del 'Mistico-Orfico' nell Magna Grecia," in *Orfismo in Magna Grecia: Atti del Quattordicesimo Convegno di Studi sulla Magna Grecia*, Arte Tipografica: Napoli, 1975, pp. 35-49.

Sabbatucci, Dario, *Saggio sul Misticismo Greco*, 2nd ed., Edizioni dell' Ateneo & Bizzarri: Rome, 1979.

Sahlins, Marshall, *Islands of History*, University of Chicago Press: Chicago, 1985.

Salviat, Jacqueline, "ΚΑΛΟΣ ΓΑΡ Ο ΚΙΝΔΥΝΟΣ Risque et Mythe dans le *Phédon*," *Revue des Études Grecques* 78 (1965), pp. 23-39.

Saunders, Trevor J., *Plato's Penal Code: Tradition, Controversy, and Reform in Greek Penology*, Clarendon Press: Oxford, 1991.

Scalera McClintock, Giuliana, "Non fermarsi alla prima fonte. Simboli della salvezza nelle lamine auree," *Filosofia e Teologia* 5.3 (1991), pp. 396-408.

Scarpi, Paolo, "Diventare dio. La Deificazione del Defunto nelle Lamine Auree dell'Antica Thurii," *Museum Patavinum* 5.2 (1987), pp. 197-216.

Schuhl, Pierre-Maxime, *La Fabulation Platonicienne*, Librairie Philosophique J. Vrin: Paris, 1968.

Seaford, Richard, "Dionysiac Drama and the Dionysiac Mysteries," *Classical Quarterly* 31 (1981), pp. 252-275.

Seaford, Richard, "Immortality, Salvation, and the Elements," *Harvard Studies in Classical Philology* 90 (1986), pp. 1-26.

Seaford, Richard, "The Tragic Wedding," *Journal of Hellenic Studies* 107 (1987), pp. 106-130.

Sedley, D., "Teleology and Myth in the *Phaedo*," *Proceedings of the Boston Area Colloquium in Ancient Philosophy* 5 (1989-1990), pp. 359-398.

Segal, C. P., "The Character of Dionysos and the Unity of the Frogs," *Harvard Studies in Classical Philology* 65 (1961), pp. 207-242.

Segal, Charles, "'The Myth Was Saved': Reflections on Homer and the Mythology of Plato's Republic," *Hermes* 106 (1978), pp. 315-335.

Segal, Charles, "Greek Myth as a Semiotic and Structural System and the Problem of Tragedy," in *Interpreting Greek Tragedy: Myth, Poetry, Text*, Cornell University Press: Ithaca, NY, 1986, pp. 48-74.

Segal, Charles, "Dionysus and the Gold Tablets from Pelinna," *Greek, Roman, and Byzantine Studies* 31 (1990), pp. 411-419.

Sifakis, G. M., "The Structure of Aristophanic Comedy," *Journal of Hellenic Studies* 112 (1992), pp. 123–142.

Smith, Janet, "Plato's Myths as 'Likely Accounts Worthy of Belief'," *Apeiron* 19 (1985), pp. 24–42.

Smith, Janet, "Plato's Use of Myth in the Education of Philosophic Man," *Phoenix* 40 (1986), pp. 20–34.

Smith, Jonathan Z., "Hellenistic Religions," in *The Encyclopedia Britannica*, 15th Ed. (1974), Vol. 8, p. 750.

Smith, Jonathan Z., *Map is not Territory: Studies in the History of Religions*, University of Chicago Press: Chicago, 1978.

Smith, Jonathan Z., *Imagining Religion*, University of Chicago Press: Chicago, 1982.

Smith, Jonathan Z., *To Take Place: Toward Theory in Ritual*, University of Chicago Press: Chicago, 1987.

Smith, Jonathan Z. *Drudgery Divine: On the Comparison of Early Christianities and the Religions of Late Antiquity*, University of Chicago Press: Chicago, 1990.

Smith, Jonathan Z., "Trading Places," in *Ancient Magic and Ritual Power*, eds. Marvin Meyer and Paul Mirecki, E.J. Brill: New York, 1995, pp. 13–27.

Sommerstein, Alan, "Kleophon and the Restaging of *Frogs*," in *Tragedy, Comedy and the Polis: Papers from the Greek Drama Conference, Nottingham, 18–20 July 1990*, eds. Sommerstein, Halliwell, Henderson, and Zimmerman, Levante Editori: Bari, 1993, pp. 461–476.

Sourvinou-Inwood, Christiane, "What is *Polis* Religion?" in *The Greek City from Homer to Alexander*, eds. O. Murray and S. Price, 1987, pp. 295–322.

Sourvinou-Inwood, Christiane, "Further Aspects of *Polis* Religion," *Annali, Istituto Orientale di Napoli: Archeologia e Storia Antica*, 10 (1988), pp. 259–274.

Sourvinou-Inwood, Christiane, '*Reading Greek Culture*': *Texts and Images, Rituals and Myths*, Clarendon Press: Oxford, 1991.

Sourvinou-Inwood, Christiane, '*Reading*' *Greek Death*, Clarendon Press: Oxford, 1995.

Sourvinou-Inwood, Christiane, "Reconstructing Change: Ideology and the Eleusinian Mysteries," in *Inventing Ancient Culture: Historicism, periodization, and the ancient world*, eds. Mark Golden and Peter Toohey, Routledge: New York, 1997, pp. 132–164.

Srebny, Stephanus, "Quaestiunculae Comicae," *Eos* 43, 1 (1948), pp. 48–52.

Stanford, W. B., *Aristophanes: Frogs*, reprint of 1963 2nd Ed., Bristol Classical Press: Bristol, 1983.

Stevens, Susan, "Charon's Obol and Other Coins in Ancient Funerary Practice," *Phoenix* 45 (1991), pp. 215–229.

Stewart, Douglas, "Socrates' Last Bath," *Journal of the History of Philosophy* 10 (1972), pp. 253–259.

Stewart, J. A., *The Myths of Plato*, (re-edited with new introduction by G. R. Levy from 1905 edition) Centaur Press Ltd.: Fontwell, Sussex, 1960.

Stewart, Robert, "The Epistemological Function of Platonic Myth," *Philosophy and Rhetoric* 22 (1989), pp. 260–280.

Stöcklein, Paul, "Über die Philosophische bedeutung von Platons Mythen," *Philologus* Supplementband 30, Heft 3 (1937), pp. 1–58.

Stormer, Gerald D., "Plato's Theory of Myth," *The Personalist* 55 (1974), pp. 216–223.

Strachan, J. C. G., "Who *Did* Forbid Suicide at *Phaedo* 62b?" *Classical Quarterly* 20 (1970), pp. 216–220.

Strauss, Leo, *Socrates and Aristophanes*, Basic Books: New York, 1966.

Sutton, Dana, *The Catharsis of Comedy*, Rowman & Littlefield: Lanham, MD, 1994.

Tambiah, Stanley, *Culture, Thought, and Social Action: An Anthropological Perspective*, Harvard University Press: Cambridge, MA, 1985.

Tannery, Paul, "Orphica, *fr. 208 Abel*," *Revue de Philologie* (1899), pp. 126–129.

Tarrant, H. A. S., "Myth as a Tool of Persuasion in Plato," *Antichthon* 24 (1990), pp. 19–31.

Tate, J., "Socrates and the Myths," *Classical Quarterly* 27 (1933), pp. 74–80, with response by A. E. Taylor and rebuttal by Tate, pp. 158–161.

Tate, J., "Plato, Socrates and the Myths," *Classical Quarterly* 30 (1936), pp. 142–145.

Tessier, Andrea, "La Struttura Metrica della Laminetta di Hipponion. Rassegna di Interpretazioni," *Museum Patavinum* 2 (1987), pp. 232–242.

Thayer, H. S., "The Myth of Er," *History of Philosophy Quarterly* 5, 4 (1988), pp. 369–384.

Thiercy, Pascal, *Aristophane: Fiction et Dramaturgie*, Les Belles Lettres: Paris, 1986.

Thomas, Hans Werner, *EΠEKEINA: Untersuchungen über das Überlieferungsgut in den Jenseitsmythen Platons*, Würzberg, 1938.

Tierney, Michael, "A New Ritual of the Orphic Mysteries," *Classical Quarterly* 16 (1922), pp. 77–87.

Tsantsanoglou, K., "The First Columns of the Derveni Papyrus and their Religious Significance," in *Studies on the Derveni Papyrus*, eds. André Laks and Glenn Most, Clarendon Press: Oxford, 1997, pp. 93–128.

Tsantsanoglou, K., and Parássoglou, G., "Two Gold Lamellae from Thessaly," *Hellenika* 38 (1987) pp. 3–17.

Turcan, R., "L'Âme-Oiseau et l'Eschatologie Orphique," *Revue de l'Histoire des Religions* 155 (1959), pp. 33–40.

Turcan, Robert, "Bacchoi ou Bacchants?" in *L'Association Dionysiaque dans les Sociétés Anciennes*, École Française de Rome: Palais Farnese, 1986, pp. 227–246.

Vaio, John, "On the Thematic Structure of Aristophanes' *Frogs*," in *Hypatia: Essays in Classics, Comparative Literature, and Philosophy Presented to Hazel E. Barnes on her Seventieth Birthday*, eds. Calder, Goldsmith, and Kenevan, Colorado Associated University Press: Boulder, 1985, pp. 91–102.

Van der Valk, M., "A Few Observations on the *Ranae* of Aristophanes," *Humanitas* 33 (1981) pp. 95–126.

Van Gennep, Arnold, *Rites of Passage*, trans. M. B. Vizedom and G. L. Caffee, University of Chicago Press: Chicago, 1960.

Velasco-Lopez, M. H., "Le Vin, la Mort, et les Bienheureux," *Kernos* 5 (1992), pp. 209–220.

Verdelis, Nikolaos, "Ορφικά ἐλάσματα ἐκ Κρήτης," *Archaiologike Ephemeris* (1953–1954), pt. 2, pp. 56–60.

Vermeule, Emily, *Aspects of Death in Early Greek Art and Poetry*, University of California Press: Berkeley, 1979.

Vernant, Jean-Pierre, *Myth and Thought Among the Greeks*, Routledge and Kegan Paul: London, 1983.

Vernant, Jean-Pierre, *Myth and Society in Ancient Greece*, trans. Janet Lloyd, Zone Books: New York, 1990.

Versnel, H. S., "Greek Myth and Ritual: The Case of Kronos," in *Interpretations of Greek Mythology*, ed. Jan Bremmer, Barnes & Noble: Totowa, NJ, 1986, pp. 121–152.

Versnel, H. S., *Inconsistencies in Greek Religion*, Vols. 1 & 2, Brill: Leiden, 1990–1993.

Veyne, Paul, *Did the Greeks Believe Their Myths? An Essay on the Constitutive Imagination*, trans. Paula Wissing, University of Chicago Press: Chicago, 1988.

Vidal-Naquet, Pierre, *The Black Hunter: Forms of Thought and Forms of Society in the Greek World*, trans. Andrew Szegedy-Maszak, Johns Hopkins University Press: Baltimore, MD, 1986.

Voegelin, Eric, *Anamnesis*, trans. & ed. Gerhart Niemeyer, University of Notre Dame Press: Notre Dame, IN, 1978.

von Wilamowitz-Moellendorff, Ulrich, *Der Glaube der Hellenen*, bd. 2, Weidmannsche Buchhanflung: Berlin, 1932.

Weinrib, Ernest J., "Law as Myth: Reflections of Plato's *Gorgias*," *Iowa Law Review* 74 (1989), pp. 787–806.

West, M. L., "Zum neuen Goldblättchen aus Hipponion," *Zeitschrift für Papyrologie und Epigraphik* 18 (1975), pp. 229–236.

West, M. L., "The Orphics of Olbia," *Zeitschrift für Papyrologie und Epigraphik* 45 (1982), pp. 17–29.

West, M. L., *The Orphic Poems*, Oxford University Press: Oxford, 1983.

Westerink, L. G., ed., *The Greek Commentators on Plato's Phaedo, I: Olympiodorus; II: Damascius*, Royal Netherlands Academy of Arts and Sciences: Amsterdam, 1976–1977.

White, D. A. *Myth and Metaphysics in Plato's Phaedo*, Associated University Presses: London, 1989.

Whitman, Cedric, *Aristophanes and the Comic Hero*, Harvard University Press: Cambridge, MA, 1971.

Wills, Garry, "Why are the Frogs in the Frogs?" *Hermes* 97 (1970), pp. 306–317.

Windelband, W., *Platon*, 7th Ed., trans. Hitchcock, Frommann: Stuttgart, 1923.

Winkler, John J., "Laying Down the Law: The Oversight of Men's Sexual Behavior in Classical Athens," *Before Sexuality: The Construction of Erotic Experience in the Ancient Greek World*, eds. Halperin, Winkler, and Zeitlin, Princeton University Press: Princeton, NJ, 1990, pp. 257–308.

Wright, Rosemary, "How Credible are Plato's Myths?" in *Arktouros: Hellenic Studies presented to Bernard M. W. Knox on the Occasion of His 65th Birthday*, ed. Bowersock, Burkert, and Putnam, Walter de Gruyter: Berlin, 1979, pp. 364–371.

Zaslavsky, R., *Platonic Myth and Platonic Writing*, University Press of America: Washington, D.C., 1981.

Zeller, Eduard, *Plato and the Older Academy*, 3rd Ed., trans. Sarah Frances Alleyne and Alfred Goodwin, Longmans, Green: London, 1888.

Zhmud, L., "Orphism and Grafitti from Olbia," *Hermes* 120 (1992), pp. 159–168.

Zuntz, Günther, *Persephone: Three Essays on Religion and Thought in Magna Graecia*, Clarendon Press: Oxford, 1971.

Zuntz, Günther, "Die Goldlamelle von Hipponion," *Wiener Studien* 10 (1978), pp. 129–151.

# Index Locorum

263

# Index

Lightning Source UK Ltd.
Milton Keynes UK
UKOW04f1809090914

238319UK00006B/239/P